Language, Self, and Society

Language, Self, and Society

A Social History of Language

Edited by
Peter Burke and Roy Porter
with an Afterword by Dell Hymes

Polity Press

Copyright © Polity Press 1991

First published 1991 by Polity Press
in association with Basil Blackwell

Editorial office:
Polity Press, 65 Bridge Street,
Cambridge CB2 1UR, UK

Marketing and production:
Basil Blackwell Ltd
108 Cowley Road, Oxford OX4 1JF, UK

3 Cambridge Center
Cambridge, MA 02142, USA

ISBN 0 7456 0765 9

The relevant CIP catalogue record for this book is available from the British Library or the Library of Congress.

Typeset in 10 on 12pt Ehrhardt
by Wearside Tradespools, Fulwell, Sunderland
Printed in Great Britain by TJ Press, Padstow

Contents

Acknowledgements

The warm reception given to *The Social History of Language*, which we edited for the Cambridge University Press in 1987, suggested a further collection of essays upon similar lines. The idea was favoured by the Press, and the editors proceeded to commission contributions to a volume to be published in the *Cambridge Studies in Oral and Literate Culture* series, under the general editorship of Peter Burke and Ruth Finnegan. In the end, however, the CUP decided that it could not agree to the arranged slate of authors and topics. At this stage, the editors approached Polity Press. Polity took up the proposed book with enthusiasm, and we are deeply grateful for their encouragement and support. It is our desire that, despite the change of publisher, this present volume will be seen as complementary to *The Social History of Language*.

The editing of this book has been rendered a pleasure by the energetic cooperation of the contributors. Thanks in particular to Patrick Joyce for graciously accepting delays in publication of a piece originally destined elsewhere, and to Dell Hymes for his willingness to write an overview, from the viewpoint of sociolinguistics, under considerable time pressure once all the other contributions had been received. Others have also given notable help. At the Wellcome Institute, Jacqui Canning has helped word-process some of the essays with redoubtable accuracy; Frieda Houser has given us her ever-efficient administrative skills, and Andy Foley has gallantly manned the xerox machine.

Peter Burke
Roy Porter

July 1990

Introduction

Roy Porter

Language is so intimate to living that it has long been overlooked by historians, rather in the way that little historical attention has been paid to such other home truths as the body, its gestures and clothing, and the everyday objects with which people surround themselves. At long last, however, thanks to the 'new social history', interest is stirring in the phenomenology of everyday life and the meaning of things.[1] This state of renewed scholarly inquiry certainly applies to language, a development which is itself surely a response to the fact that our own (Anglo-American) linguistic universe is currently in turmoil.[2]

Not all historians, of course, have been deaf: half a century ago, G.M. Young famously enjoined his colleagues to study their subjects till they could hear them speaking. And certain methodological schools have urged scholars to train their antennae onto language as the prime site of meaning. In the history of political thought, 'contextualists' like Quentin Skinner have insisted that the past is a foreign language: to avoid anachronism, it is essential to be attuned to, and to respect, the nuances of former terminologies. Within the last decade, post-structuralist and post-modernist critics have taught us to 'deconstruct' texts, developing new techniques for laying bare their mazy meanings. Now that the 'author' has been proclaimed dead, all there is left to analyse, it seems, are language's own rules of writing itself, the 'software' of the text.[3]

Semiological strictures such as these, derived from literary theory, have done signal service in requiring historians to address the polyphonic, polysemic, problematic nature of discourse, the underbelly of utterance. But in strenuously denying the existence of extra-textual life, and hence the reality of 'history' as the objective past ('back there'), post-modernist directives run the risk of reducing history to commentaries upon texts – indeed, to commentaries upon commentaries upon texts; and, in the practice of constructing these glosses, of encouraging the bizarre assumption that, on the basis of this or that random extract, former discursive universes can easily be read off by the theoretically sophisticated deconstructor. At worst, such approaches condone ignorance, and perpetuate, under the excuse of 'theory', the elitist arrogance of the superior reader, long enshrined in Leavisite 'practical criticism'.[4] Dan Rosenberg's essay below touches upon some of the dangers of this kind of premature appropriation.

That literary theory has provided valuable imputs is not to be denied; but easily the greatest stimulus in the recent past to the social-historical study of language – to analysis of the power of speech, by its presence or absence, to define, to coerce, or to empower, to victimize and scapegoat, to exercise hegemony and organize consensus, to make, unmake, and remake lived worlds – has surely been feminism. Thanks to the contributions of women's studies, we have learned that language, and the conceptual and symbolic worlds framed by it, are comprehensively gendered, both explicitly and covertly. Feminist scholarship – one thinks especially of Sandra Gilbert and Susan Gubar's *The Madwoman in the Attic: The Woman Writer and the Nineteenth Century Imagination* – has exposed the ideological underpinnings of the male arrogation of linguistic authority (the right to speak), and the traditional exclusion of women from the forum. It has revealed the operation of double standards which are no less linguistic than sexual. Women's studies have directed attention to the ceaseless, surreptitious, and grimly banal operations of linguistic discrimination, in the home and family, within marriage, in schools and employment, and in the public domain. Symbolic of all of these is the use, in earlier centuries, of 'Silence' as a female Christian name.[5]

Peter Burke's 'Introduction' to our previous volume, *The Social History of Language*, and its appended 'Bibliographical Essay', together suggested how historians might learn from ethnolinguistics, and proposed an agenda for treating language as an object, a resource, for historical inquiry in its own right, rather than as just a window onto the past, more or less translucent or opaque as the case might be. There is no need to repeat such injunctions here, though the reader is referred to the final piece in this collection, in which the sociolinguist, Dell Hymes, offers further reflections upon the interplay between historical case studies and the analytical tools and philosophical assumptions of sociolinguistics.[6]

Our earlier volume contained essays examining access to language (literacy); particular linguistic modalities (insults, proverbs, puffery, scientific jargon); and the uses of speech as an instrument of political domination. This volume contains groupings of papers which develop some of these issues.

Part I, 'Authoritative Tongues', focuses upon languages, especially written ones, which claim special power: learned and ancient tongues, and, above all, religious speech-forms. It may be worth stressing here that the need and capacity to exploit such languages of power was not exclusive to groups themselves in authority: often the reverse was true – the effect was compensatory. As Nigel Smith and Hugh Ormsby-Lennon show in their studies on the uses of Hebrew and on Quakerism, the deployment of holy tongues, especially perhaps the transcendental and numinal, offered small, weak, and marginal religious groups the only mode of authority they could realistically seek to command: the Highest.[7]

Part II, 'Language and Social Authority', looks quite explicitly at the politics of linguistic use, above all hierarchies of language, the questions of the languages of the powerful and of the excluded. If the pen is in fact mightier than the sword, historians must study access to and exclusion from free speech. Within systems of crude dominion, especially, as Victor Kiernan emphasizes, imperial rule, one language may simply supersede another through political or administrative *fiat*. Dialects and patois are often proscribed, or reduced to secondary, informal roles, while other languages are given official status. This was the prerogative, too, of the newly independent nineteenth-century nation states, neatly turning the tables on the bureaucrats who had formerly run their affairs in some imperial tongue. The nationalist fervour unleashed by the current turmoil in eastern Europe is now repeating these linguistic conflicts, with, for example, Turks in Bulgaria repudiating the Bulgarian names they had been forced to adopt.

But linguistic politics commonly operate in more subtle ways. A social group, as Bourdieu has emphasized, may prefer to utilize a certain language, dialect, vocabulary, or accent, to establish cultural difference and hegemony. In other situations, language may provide – or at least be touted as – a unifying force, binding a people against a common foe; occasionally the language of patriotism and the patriotism of language may be the only ties uniting masses otherwise divided by class, wealth, and other material interests.[8] This middle group of essays touches upon the almost Darwinian question of the triumph, survival, or extinction of different languages in competition with each other, and the different socio-cultural niches they fill within larger political and class struggles.[9]

The final part, 'Meaning and the Self', narrows the focus to vocabulary and expression. What do words mean, privately, to ourselves, and publicly, to others? These essays attempt to prise out the historical significance of specialized, changing ways of naming things and expressing feelings. Here the emphasis is upon medical language. Investigation of the ways people traditionally referred to their bodies in sickness and in health will perhaps give us heightened insight into the impact of health and sickness in the past, of relations between the sick and the medical profession, of earlier notions of suffering, salubrity, and salvation; rather as Jo Gladstone, in her essay on regional dialects, demonstrates the ways in which local variations in the terms for foodstuffs in the seventeenth and eighteenth centuries may form the most sensitive indices of real differences in kinds of diet and standards of nutrition. But earlier languages of sickness may in the end tell us more about 'inner states', about earlier notions of selfhood and the soul.

These three groupings, successively spotlighting language and culture, language and politics, and language and self, raise issues central to the social historiography of language today. The remainder of this introduction explores some of the underlying issues in greater detail.

The Word: Speech and Writing

In his recent study of the experience of deafness, *Seeing Voices*, Oliver Sacks has argued that communication by making signs ('signing') must not be regarded as no better than a crude phrase-book of pantomimic gestures (of the 'Me Tarzan, you Jane' genre), but as an authentic language in its own right.[10] As a language, it is visual rather than verbal, spatial not sequential, multi-dimensional rather than linear. This does not mean, Sacks contends, that sign language is inferior as a bearer of meanings. Indeed, in some respects, sign may be particularly pliant, inventive, and expressive: after all, critics such as Marshall McLuhan and Walter Ong long ago exposed the poverty of print, prisoner of its own frozen, sequential, linearity.[11] Moreover, linguists have now transcribed the syntax of sign, showing it to possess formal structures in much the same way as other tongues. And, finally, neurological experiments have revealed that signing is controlled by the left hemisphere of the brain, the part which routinely governs linguistic competence in those who speak, as well as other 'logical' and 'technical' functions.

These facts require reflection. They remind social historians of language that they must bear in mind more than merely an inventory of what has been *spoken* and what has been *written down*. To put it another way, Latin, English, Pidgin, and so forth are not the only communication systems which structure thought, broadcast information, and cement interpersonal contacts. Not all exchange is verbal: we have the 'language of clothes', the 'language of art', and so forth.[12] The study of language is impoverished if it addresses itself only to formal structures (phonemes, morphemes, words, sentences, texts), and ignores the analysis of such functions as communication, memory- and record-keeping, the exercise of governmental documentation, the very development of selfconsciousness.

For all such reasons, the history of language raises issues beyond those of technical linguistics. Anthropology, sociology, and, in the Foucauldian sense, 'archaeology' (exploring the prehistory of the disciplines) – all these must be central to historical sociolinguistics.[13] Not least, Sacks's revelations about sign language force us to confront the fact that many communications systems, and not only signing, leave not a rack behind in the archives. We have not the slightest permanent record of the billions of conversations conducted between signers in the past – because sign never routinely had a written correlate; maybe we know less about the *mentalités* of profoundly deaf Victorians than we do of Friulian millers in the age of the Counter-Reformation.[14]

Attention to sign thus reminds us that the history of language cannot be divorced from wider consideration of communication. It also highlights some of the aspects which, taken in the light of all the languages there have ever been, give a degree of distinctiveness to those of the Western world – and they it is that form the core of this book, as of its predecessor.[15] Above all, the tongues principally dealt with below – Hebrew, Latin, Greek, French, English, and so forth – are ones which, for many centuries, have been both spoken and written down (and, more recently, recorded by electric technologies). Obviously, had this not been so, it would be exceedingly difficult, using established scholarly assumptions and methods, to trace the distant histories of the cultures defined by such tongues: a problem constantly plaguing historians of those cultures which, till recently, have been exclusively oral (for those cultures, it is inescapably true that all history is oral history). What little we indubitably know about the distant histories of such peoples comes through an archaeology of things, not words.[16] The greatest conceptual challenge facing the historian of language thus lies in addressing the fact that simultaneous oral articulation (speaking and listening) and inscription (writing and reading) confer upon a language and its users an especially complex and contested history – or better, perhaps, a tangled skein of histories.[17]

The discrete 'technologies' of speaking and of writing create differentiations of utterance. Consider how little of the totality of what is voiced upon a stage is actually present in the original play-text; or, to go one step further back, how little of all the playwright himself or herself 'heard' or 'vocalized' in his or her head found its way into the script in the first place. Equally, imagine what a tiny percentage of all the Babel sounds brayed in the House of Commons finally end up in Hansard, how little of the mumbo-jumbo of an English law court appears in the stenographer's legal transcript.

Yet what all these instances also show is that conventions readily arise to regularize those discrepancies between what is spoken and what is written, to preclude (or stabilize) the confusion of tongues. We generally know, after all, how to decode the typed-up minutes of a committee meeting: we learn to read between the lines, to reconstruct tonalities, even (as with the dog that didn't bark) to hear silences. Most of the time, we are not troubled by the fact that we deal in spoken language, and also in written language, and that the two are not exact equivalents. So ingrained are our learnt habits of 'translation' that we do not even commonly *notice* that the two are, in fact, highly divergent, or that we conduct our lives 'bilingually' – or trilingually, or quadralingually. For it will be appreciated here that it is, in any case, a grossly oversimplifactory *façon de parler* to speak (or, one should say, *write!*)[18] as if only two, rigidly differentiated, forms of expression exist: on the contrary, it is better to think of a continuum, on which certain forms of speech approximate written language, and vice versa.

All these modes of expression are subject to pressures, some leading to convergence, and others to divergence, between speaking and writing. As Peter Burke emphasizes in his contribution below, throughout the latter Middle Ages and the early modern centuries Europe's educated elites could boast a fluent and supple grasp of classical written Latin (and, to a lesser degree, Greek), even though, all the while, spoken Latin was becoming increasingly rudimentary, ceremonial, stilted, and moribund. The same may be said of Biblical Hebrew within Europe. As Nigel Smith demonstrates, the centuries after Luther produced a goodly company of capable Hebraic textual scholars, some of them alert to the finer points of grammar and etymology, but no community of speakers.

These are perhaps extreme cases of dislocations or drift between what is spoken and what is written. More commonly we find both distinct modes of expression falling into each other's gravitational field, and undergoing mutual modification in the process. Grassroots colloquialisms and neologisms constantly force entry into 'standard English', the seal of approval of which is the printed word and, ultimately, the dictionary. At the same time, mass education, mass literacy, and the mass media – all, of course, over the last couple of hundred years, heavily print-oriented – serve to standardize the spoken word, by bringing it into line with the written.[19] It has been a widespread hypothesis that, in societies tending towards total literacy, once-dramatic chasms between spoken idioms (dialects, patois) and authorized tongues begin to close. Indeed, as Patrick Joyce notes in his essay below, precisely that has been the constantly reiterated fear of the protagonists of dialect, regional speech, and linguistic diversity. Jo Gladstone shows below that dialect-recorders have frequently been activated by the fear that such forms of speach were in the process of becoming as dead as the dodo.

Even so, most groups within such societies – from the very privileged to the underclasses, to say nothing of immigrants and minorities – have continued, and still continue, to manifest high levels of distinctiveness in speech or writing (or both), because of either a disinclination or an inability to conform.[20] As Hugh Ormsby-Lennon indicates in his essay, it became a mark of dissenting religious sects in Stuart and Georgian England to cultivate both verbal and written idiosyncrasies (such as Quaker 'theeing'). In addition, they also developed peculiarities of intonation and diction (for example, the nasal twang called 'canting'), often preserved for posterity only in the parodies of their enemies.[21]

Elite cadres in rigidly stratified social structures may strive to keep the written tongue 'pure', and uncontaminated by the spoken idiom, so often regarded as slovenly, vulgar, and cheapening. Such practices parallel the tendency in many regions of *ancien régime* Europe for lords to disdain to speak the same language (the native language, the mother tongue) as their peasantry. With the coming of mass society and mass democracy, things have surely changed. In everyday life in modern Western societies, the registers of speech and printed prose engage symbiotically, mutually modifying. The traditionally stuffy prose of *The Times* is fast disappearing in the age of television.

But this is far from saying that all utterance is becoming homogenized. There remain times and places in which, by general convention, propriety requires that high and low speech should be differentiated, and, all the more so, that speech and writing must constitute mutually 'separate spheres'. We have many extempore forms of speech that are never written down, which *cannot* perhaps be adequately written down – for instance, pentecostal speaking in tongues, or 'rapping', the essence of which lies in highly personal rhythmic patterns which the linearity of writing can neither record nor replicate.[22] In certain religious, emotional, and literary contexts, speech commonly transcends writing, intuitively seeming more 'primary', original, or bardic. Though it gratified elite tastes in Georgian times, no one today craves to hear elegantly composed sermons read out, though, in these days of autocue, we seem to have resigned ourselves to the demise of spontaneous political rhetoric. People commonly dream they are hearing voices, but much more rarely that they are reading.

Thus speech, however, ephemeral, sometimes assumes supremacy over the printed word. Nevertheless, there are features of formal written prose which customarily confer upon it superior socio-cultural authority, even for those quite unable to cipher or decipher it: visibility, permanence, and tangibility. The holy books of the world's great faiths were long used talismanically – being touched, kissed, sworn on or by ('bell, book and candle').[23] As the Salman Rushdie affair demonstrates, blasphemy is peculiarly offensive when perpetrated through the written word.[24] Or take Latin again: it was precisely once Latin ceased to be a commonly spoken language that its written form acquired its full solemnity, indelibility, and universality (for there was no living speech community around to debase it).[25]

The written word has a special authority; though this may be acquired in quite opposite ways. The terminology of the English common law is notoriously pompous, archaic, florid, and barely intelligible to outsiders. It is a trade argot, incapable of being *spoken* outside a very circumscribed professional context – the court of justice – and even then commonly with effects barely short of the ludicrous. Other written languages, however, pride themselves upon their simplicity. Since the seventeenth century, a plain style of scientific reporting has been cultivated, designed to be pellucid, unambiguous, direct, and free from all the messy subjectivity of personal reportage.[26] At its lapidary best, scientific prose is a most effective instrument of communication: it bears no relationship, however, to any form of speech that ever passed a scientist's lips. The same is all the more true for mathematics and the various artificial languages devised to program calculating machines (will computers ever develop chatty vernaculars of their own?). Finally, it is noteworthy that, a full century after technology achieved the recording of vocal speech (phonographs and beyond), the official record-keeping of our society still relies almost exclusively upon print (though in popular parlance 'record' now mainly denotes a black vinyl disc with a hole in the middle). Tapes are still barely admissible as evidence in courts of law.

In the socio-politics of language, both spoken and written forms have by turns been prized and belittled. The ceaseless dialectic between those two modes has sparked acrid and unresolved debates – amongst scholars and grammarians on the one hand, politicians and people on the other – as to wherein the Word ultimately lies, and who is its guardian. The tensions between speech and writing are equally sources of fascination, fun, and fantasy. Puns, riddles, and parapraxes rely upon the fact that a single sound (a homophone) can have a plurality of spellings on the page and a multiplicity of meanings – that is, can constitute different *words*; while there can be groupings of alphabetical letters with different pronunciations and meanings: row/row; sow/sow (both these examples also bringing out the discrepancies between English English and American English); lead/lead; reading/Reading.[27] Take away our training in simultaneously seeing and hearing language, and would we be capable of such double-takes?

Whose Language Is It, Anyway?

In most societies, practically everybody speaks, though members of a few religious orders choose not to do so for much of the time; and there are others who are silenced by disabilities that may or may not be natural: the archetypical censorship is the excising of the tongue.[28] Writing and reading have been more restricted. Getting one's writings read is a matter for particular self-congratulation.

All polities are more or less polyglot. But there is never *liberté, egalité, fraternité* of tongues, nowhere a genuinely linguistically 'leveller society'. Languages are arranged into pecking orders, which are commonly officially enforced (if just as often subverted, through the parodic modes of comedy, carnival, and the cartoon).[29] The language of a governing elite, *a fortiori* of a colonial power, as Victor Kiernan stresses below, usually takes precedence over that of its subjects; that of the rich over the poor, the educated over the illiterate, the media manipulators over the masses, the metropolitan heart-land over farflung patois. Sometimes the reverse occurs: the 'barbarian' conquerors of Rome speedily adopted Latin, to prove they were worthy of the mantle of *imperium*.

All this is obvious. More interesting, perhaps, are the ways in which linguistic hierarchies have been formed and rationalized by the adumbration of theories of language, religious, scientific, philosophical, historical, and psychological. Humanity's philosophical claims to dominion over the animals has traditionally rested upon the difference between possession and absence of speech or language (hence the crucial nature of modern experiments seeking to teach chimpanzees to 'speak').[30]

Notions of the divine origins of the gift of speech, of original linguistic purity and unity, the construction of mythic genealogies, etymologies, and philological evolutionary descents: all these ratify ranking orders of linguistic primacy. In particular, while nineteenth-century anthropologists were work-ing out their pedigrees for nations and races, their philologist colleagues were plotting those of the postlapsarian languages, those arising after the fall of the Tower of Babel. On the basis of traits such as glottal stops and vowel shifts, the highly prestigious discipline of comparative philology dedicated itself to tracing linguistic affinities and erecting boundaries, demonstrating the demarcations between the more advanced, the more highly evolved forms of utterance, and the lower and cruder.[31]

Certain assumptions shaped notions of the intrinsic scale of linguistic superiority, linguistic perfection. The philologists' just-so stories assumed a semiotic progression from rudeness to refinement. Rudimentary utterance, like the conversation of children, supposedly abounded in nouns (the 'pointing' theory of the origins of speech: referring us back to the popular stereotype of sign language); perhaps also in verbs (our myths of human development have it that primitive language is concrete and body-fixated). Certain tongues – those spoken by 'backward' peoples – never got beyond such primitive modes; others grew in complexity, range, expressiveness, in the power of abstraction, in suppleness of syntax, grammar, and vocabulary. Nineteenth-century theorists were thus confident that the laws of progress, ensuring the survival of the fittest, guaranteed that the lords of human kind were not just superior in physique and techniques, but lords of language and literature. 'Show me the Shakespeares of the dark continent' was the stock riposte of the Victorian social Darwinist; 'When a Zulu writes a great novel, I'll read it', echoes Saul Bellow today.[32]

Yet it was always easier to pontificate about top tongues than to prove to the world that a particular language – one's own – was semantically, grammatically, expressively superior. French was supposedly etymologically pure and economical in its vocabulary. Did this make it a good language, or was it impoverished and fossilizing? Did the apparently promiscuous parentage of English strengthen its stock and enrich its expressiveness, or render it merely a mongrel mishmash? Paladins of the Celtic, the Gallic, and the Latin linguistic heritages battled in post-Revolutionary France, just as, nearer home, champions of 'Anglo-Saxon' qualities clashed with upholders of the 'Celtic' legacy as to the nature of the truly 'native', and hence authentic, voice of Britain.[33]

By the nineteenth century, the task of proving to the world that one's own language was the nearest approximation to Adam's, or even Cicero's, was increasingly left to the cranks.[34] But as mere primevality or antiquity lost their cachet, Romanticism increasingly validated native tongues as the authentic voice of the *Volk*, and developed the claim, stemming partly from Herder, that language was a kind of collective cultural identity and history.

To take an instance: as has been argued by Gwyn Williams, what might be called Welsh nationalism was part of the more general European Romantic movement in the nineteenth century. The Welsh cause was not, prima facie, the easiest to promote. Unlike Scotland or Ireland, Wales had all too long a history of supine submission to the English yoke, and there was rather little upon which to ground an emancipated and independent identity.[35] Hence Welsh ideologues looked to culture to fill the gap left by politics and arms. The trump card was language. Welsh (argued its advocates) was especially suited to artistic glories (poetry, song, hymns, the triumphs of the bardic past). This euphonious, musical, emotive tongue captured the unique temper of the Welsh people: their superior spirituality. It was thus upon *cultural* supremacy that the Welsh staked their claim to nationhood, to a real place in the sun.

In this forging of the myth of Welsh nation, united by a common tongue, we may see a process repeated in many parts of nineteenth-century Europe.[36] Emancipatory in some ways, it could also prove mystifying in others, for it served to deny internal differences, of birth, wealth, class, and status. In larger, more complex polities, such as England, it was harder to mask social conflict behind the rhetoric of a common language, though many of course tried. In England, class struggles over ownership of property, over political rights, over the means of production, became overtly associated (through 'Norman yoke' theories) with questions of the ownership of language, the title to speak. From the Civil War, debate raged as to who the 'nation' truly was – all freeborn Englishmen, or their king or representatives, or their 'natural leaders' in the aristocracy or clerisy? Who were the nation's spokesmen? And whose language was it that was being spoken?

As John Lucas has emphasized, from Milton, Dryden, and Pope through to Wordsworth and Tennyson, great poets developed a strong claim to 'speak for England', and increasingly so in the 'language of common men'. This was itself a profoundly problematic concept; since what speaking for England meant for the very patrician (and Hellenistic) Matthew Arnold was naturally radically different from the East Midlands vernacular expressions of the peasant poet, John Clare.[37]

And, on a larger scale, as Patrick Joyce contends below, the 'language question' became central to localized class and popular politics in indus-trializing England. Spokesmen of the people represented the King's English as a language of oppression, imposed by conquerors, from Caesar to the man Tom Paine called 'William the Bastard'; it was, moreover, a language of show, sycophancy, and mystification, masking truths, promoting fictions, legitimating frauds. Common men, common sense, common speech – all were to go together.

But 'common speech' was, in its own turn, ambiguous. As the language the people spoke, it might well be dialect, local and highly individual. Yet the formulation of 'commonness' was a claim not to sectional virtues, but to common interests, to universality. Hence, there was a powerful attempt to equate the language of the commons with that of patriotism itself. As, in the age of the 'march of mind', radicalism associated itself with the politics of 'moral force', possessing a language of legitimacy grew ever more important. In nineteenth-century struggles for identity, emancipation, and mastery, language ceased to be merely a medium of clear communication, and became the key to the collective soul. Even so, complexities remained. As Joyce argues, dialect verse and fiction produced by, or at least for, working-class communities in the north of England helped to forge common identities, but sometimes at the cost of a certain self-apologetic, self-deprecatory ambience. The aggressive/defensive role of Yiddish might serve as a parallel.[38]

Language and the Self

Language could help fashion collective identity. But it could also function as the midwife of individual identity, the bearer of autobiography. In recent explorations of the growth of self-awareness, one of the thorniest problems facing historians lies in explaining the emergence of modern conceptions of the 'self': Renaissance individualism, Puritan introspection, the Cartesian ego, Enlightenment sensibility, Romantic individualism – all have been touted, and have undoubtedly played their part.[39] But none of these explanations will suffice without consideration of the role played by language, by the rise in literacy.[40] Such habits as private reading and diary-keeping were surely crucial in representing and outlining the objectified self, which could thereby be composed (or discomposed), contemplated, and immortalized. In so far as our selfconsciousness depends upon possessing the appropriate language, the words to say 'I', we should think of the emergence of modern subjectivity not just as the creation of an intensely private realm, but as rendered possible by certain sorts of public discourse.[41]

Yet there are fundamental problems in expressing a self in words. Things out in the world are (pragmatically speaking) real; we attach labels to them. Things go with words, the signified with the signifiers. It is much more disputable whether our 'inner states' – feelings, moods, intentions, motives, personality – are 'things' in the same way as apples and tables; and powerful positivist and scientistic movements within psychology – above all, behaviourism, of course – have argued that such supposed entities ought to be regarded as nothing other than reifications, semantic solecisms, and, as a consequence, should be dismissed from discourse.

Be that as it may, what can hardly be doubted is that our talk about inner states is systematically borrowed from the language used to depict the real, tangible, material things around us: we may think of our mind/body systems as operating like riders on horseback, like clocks or textile machinery, like computers, or even (as in *Tristram Shandy*) like smoke-jacks. The changing language of such 'physiomorphism' is a superb index of changing models of the embodied self.[42]

Even so, when faced with strange physical and mental reactions it is extremely difficult to find the 'words to say it'. Feelings *are* impalpable, ineffable. It is hard to translate body states adequately into words, difficult above all to find the right terms for pains and sickness, longings, anxieties, stress, and distress.[43] But we must. We want to tell, to confess, to share, to seek solace. Not least, we need medical help, and so have to voice our 'complaint' to the doctor.

The rise of diagnostic technologies over the last couple of hundred years has increasingly enabled the doctor to bypass the patient's story. Go back, however, to the seventeenth or eighteenth centuries, as Porter suggests below, and the very enterprise of medicine hinges upon the art of shrewd linguistic management: the wrong words (consider curses, spells, and hypochondria) make people sick; words shape diagnoses, and talking *cures*, whether it is initiated by the patient or by the physician ('a disease named, is a disease half cured', runs the proverb).[44]

Above all, perhaps, medicine itself is constantly having to shape and reshape its vocabulary,[45] forming concepts that serve multiple functions: they articulate 'complaints'; they also represent professional, scientific objectivity; and, finally, they create publicly intelligible sign-systems in the general culture (not infrequently, as Susan Sontag notes, of a victim-blaming nature).[46] Prominent amongst the new medical terminology of the eighteenth century was the language of 'nerves', borrowed from the emergent discipline of neurology. It created, as G.S. Rousseau shows below, a certain prestigious frisson in the sufferer, while at the same time carving out wider social expectations for the sick role.[47] The language of nerves forged an effective negotiating point between patient and doctor, sufferer and society. Not least, it helped to fabricate new senses of the 'tremulous, private self'.[48]

As this volume of essays suggests, there can be no single social history of language. Language remains enigmatic. Its ambiguities have never, perhaps, been more provokingly, more teasingly, embraced than in that strange work, Horne Tooke's *The Diversions of Purley*, which, as Dan Rosenberg shows below, is a classic 'self-consuming artefact',[49] a work utterly vulnerable to its own critical apparatus. As Rosenberg's study indicates, Tooke created, two hundred years ago, the kind of agenda for a socio-cultural history of language pursued in this book, by posing the historical question of the relations between language, truth, and meaning. Study language if you want to find truth, Tooke suggests, while at the same time showing the difficulty of pursuing the very notion of truth beyond the words themselves.

Tooke may or may not be the first of the post-modernists, but, as Rosenberg's discussion of his relations to Derrida and others demonstrates, Tooke raises many of the problems which still confront historians. They will be interested in the totality of meaning-codes within one coherent system; they will explore the uses individuals and groups make of the language available to them; they will be concerned with the myths and ideologies surrounding language in general (*homo loquens*, man or woman as the speaking animal) and particular individual languages. They will be alert to the relations between languages and imagined worlds. When (Boswell unaccountably failed to record this Johnsonism) a man is tired of language, he is tired of life.

NOTES

1   For analyses of the everyday world of meanings, see Roland Barthes, *Mythologies*, trans. Annette Lavers (London: Cape, 1972); Barthes, *The Fashion System*,

trans. Matthew Ward and Richard Howard (New York: Hill and Wang, 1983); Mihaly Csikszentmihalyi and Eugene Rochberg-Halton, *The Meaning of Things: Domestic Symbols and the Self* (New York: Cambridge University Press, 1981). For the body, see Piero Camporesi, *Bread of Dreams: Food and Fantasy in Early Modern Europe* (Cambridge: Polity Press, 1989); Camporesi, *The Incorruptible Flesh: Bodily Mutation and Mortification in Religion and Folklore* (Cambridge: Cambridge University Press, 1988); Camporesi, *The Body in the Cosmos: Natural Symbols in Medieval and Early Modern Italy* (Cambridge: Polity Press, 1992); M. Feher (ed.), *Fragments for a History of the Human Body*, 3 vols (New York: Zone, 1989). For gesture, see Peter Burke, *The Historical Anthropology of Early Modern Italy: Essays on Perception and Communication* (Cambridge: Cambridge University Press, 1987); for clothes see Anne Hollander, *Seeing Through Clothes* (New York: Avon, 1980). For things, see W. Rybczynski, *Home: A Short History of an Idea* (London: Heinemann, 1988); D. Miller, *Material Culture and Mass Consumption* (Oxford: Basil Blackwell, 1987); Asa Briggs, *Victorian Things* (London: Batsford, 1988); John Brewer and Roy Porter (eds), *Consumption and the World of Goods* (London: Routledge, 1992). For the claim that historians are rather blind to visual evidence, see Roy Porter, 'Seeing the Past', *Past and Present*, 118 (February 1988), 186–205.

Some evidence of the continuing neglect by historians of the social history of language is the omission of language, and communications more generally, from a huge new collective social history venture. See F.M.L. Thompson (ed.), *The Cambridge Social History of Britain, 1750–1950*, vol. 1, *Regions and Communities*; vol. 2, *People and their Environment*; vol. 3, *Social Agencies and Institutions* (Cambridge: Cambridge University Press, 1990).

2   See Christopher Ricks and Leonard Michaels, *The State of the Language: 1990 Edition* (London: Faber and Faber, 1990). Many of the contributors to that volume reflect upon changes in English usage since the publication of the initial *State of the Language* volume a decade earlier. The greatest transformation seems to have been the huge and rapid rise of non-standard English, spoken by assorted ethnic minorities. See the essay by Sidney Greenbaum, 'Whose English?' (15–23).

3   See J. Culler, *On Deconstruction* (London: Routledge and Kegan Paul, 1983); Q.R.D. Skinner, 'Meaning and Understanding in the History of Ideas', *History and Theory*, vii (1969), 3–53.

4   For one such text, see Francis Barker, *The Tremulous Private Body: Essays on Subjection* (London: Methuen, 1984). For criticisms of such approaches, see J.R.R. Christie, 'Bad News for the Body', *Art History*, ix (1986), 263–70. For a more historically sensitive deployment of such text-based approaches, see Stephen Greenblatt, *Shakespearian Negotiations: The Circulation of Social Energy in Renaissance England* (Oxford: Clarendon Press, 1988).

5   On these topics today's literature is vast. See in particular R.T. Lakoff, *Language and Women's Place* (New York: Harper and Row, 1975); Dale Spender, *Man Made Language* (London: Routledge and Kegan Paul, 1980); J.B. Elsthain, *Public Man, Private Woman: Women in Social and Political Thought* (Oxford: Martin Robertson, 1981); Sandra Gilbert and Susan Gubar, *The Madwoman in the Attic: The Woman Writer and the Nineteenth Century Imagination*

(New Haven, Conn.: Yale University Press, 1979); Gilbert and Gibson, *No Man's Land: The Place of the Woman Writer in the Twentieth Century* (New Haven, Conn.: Yale University Press, 1988); Anna Clark, *Women's Silence, Men's Violence: Sexual Assault in England, 1770–1845* (London: Pandora, 1987); L.J. Jordanova, *Sexual Visions* (Hemel Hempstead: Harvester, 1989); Dorinda Outram, '*Le Langage Male de la Vertu*: Women and the Discourse of the French Revolution', in Peter Burke and Roy Porter (eds), *The Social History of Language* (Cambridge: Cambridge University Press, 1987), 120–35; Marina Warner, 'Fighting Talk', in Ricks and Michaels, *The State of the Language: 1990*, 100–9; Hermione Lee, '*Power*: Women and the Word', in ibid., 110–17; Sandra M. Gilbert, 'Reflections on a (Feminist) Discourse of Discourse, or Look, Ma, I'm Talking', in ibid., 130–7.

6 See also Dell Hymes, 'Towards Ethnographies of Communication', in P.P. Giglioli (ed.), *Language and Social Context* (Harmondsworth: Penguin, 1972), 21–44. For useful anthologies on the subject, see J.B. Pride and J. Holmes (eds), *Sociolinguistics* (Harmondsworth: Penguin, 1972); J.J. Gumperz and D. Hymes (eds), *Directions in Sociolinguistics* (New York: Holt, Rinehart and Winston, 1972); R. Bauman and J. Sherzer (eds), *Explorations in the Ethnography of Speaking* (Cambridge: Cambridge University Press, 1974).

7 A classic instance of the special use of language by a powerless group is the speech of the mad. See, for instance, Roy Porter, *A Social History of Madness* (London: Weidenfeld and Nicolson, 1987).

8 See M. Szegedy-Maszak, 'Romanticism in Hungary', and D. Pirie, 'The Agony in the Garden: Polish Romanticism', in Roy Porter and Mikulas Teich (eds), *Romanticism in National Context* (Cambridge: Cambridge University Press, 1988), 217–39, 317–44. All these issues are brilliantly discussed in Eric Hobsbawm, *Nations and Nationalism since 1780* (Cambridge: Cambridge University Press, 1990). On distinction and difference, see Pierre Bourdieu, *Distinction: A Social Critique of the Judgement of Taste*, trans. Richard Nice (Cambridge, Mass.: Harvard University Press, 1984).

9 Jonathan Steinberg, 'The Historian and the *Questione della Lingua*', in Burke and Porter, *The Social History of Language*, 198–209.

10 Oliver Sacks, *Seeing Voices: A Journey into the World of the Deaf* (London: Picador, 1989). Concern with communication is central to Sacks's earlier works. See Sacks, *Awakenings* (Harmondsworth: Penguin, 1976); Sacks, *A Leg to Stand On* (London: Duckworth, 1984); Sacks, *The Man Who Mistook His Wife for a Hat* (London: Duckworth, 1985).

11 Marshall McLuhan, *Understanding Media: The Extension of Man* (London: ARK, 1987); Walter J. Ong, *Orality and Literacy: The Technologizing of the Word* (London: Methuen, 1982); Jack Goody, *The Domestication of the Savage Mind* (Cambridge: Cambridge University Press, 1977).

12 See Alison Lurie, *The Language of Clothes* (New York: Random House, 1981); Ludmilla J. Jordanova (ed.), *Languages of Nature: Critical Essays on Science and Literature* (London: Free Association Books, 1986); Norman Bryson, *Word and Image: French Painting of the Ancien Régime* (Cambridge: Cambridge University Press, 1983).

13 For Michel Foucault, see *The Order of Things: An Archaeology of the Human*

Sciences (London: Tavistock, 1970); Foucault, *The Archaeology of Knowledge* (London: Tavistock, 1972); Foucault, *The Birth of the Clinic: An Archaeology of Medical Perception* (London: Tavistock, 1973); Foucault, *Discipline and Punish: The Birth of the Prison* (Harmondsworth: Penguin, 1976). For archaeologies of material things see Thomas J. Schlereth, 'Material Culture Studies in America, 1876–1976', in Thomas J. Schlereth (ed.), *Material Culture Studies in America* (Nashville, Tenn.: The American Association for State and Local History, 1982), 1–75; Schlereth, 'Material Culture Studies and Social History Research', *Journal of Social History*, xvi (1983), 111–43; Schlereth, 'Contemporary Collecting for Future Recollecting', *Museum Studies Journal*, ii (1984), 23–30; Schlereth, 'The Material Culture of Childhood: Problems and Potential in Historical Explanation', *Material History Bulletin*, xxi (1985), 1–14.

14   This is not the place to debate the accessibility of earlier *mentalités*, upon which see, for instance, Peter Burke, 'Popular Culture between History and Ethnology', *Ethnologi Europaea*, xiv (1984), 5–13; Burke, 'Revolution in Popular Culture', in Roy Porter and M. Teich (eds), *Revolution in History* (Cambridge: Cambridge University Press, 1986), 206–25; Burke, *The Historical Anthropology of Early Modern Italy: Essays on Perception and Communication* (Cambridge: Cambridge University Press, 1987); Robert Darnton, *The Great Cat Massacre and Other Episodes in French Cultural History* (New York: Basic Books, 1984); Carlo Ginzburg, *The Cheese and the Worms: The Cosmos of the Sixteenth Century* (London: Routledge and Kegan Paul, 1980).

15   Burke and Porter, *The Social History of Language*; see especially the introduction by Peter Burke, 1–20.

16   See, for instance, Arjun Appadurai (ed.), *The Social Life of Things: Commodities in Cultural Perespective* (Cambridge: Cambridge University Press, 1986).

17   Note that the distinction being made here is somewhat different from, though of course related to, the traditional literacy v. orality debate, for which see Ong, *Orality and Literacy: The Technologizing of the Word.*

18   We never, of course, say (or rather, write) 'properly *writing*'.

19   For a broad analysis of these processes of cultural standardization see E. Weber, *Peasants into Frenchman* (London: Chatto and Windus, 1979).

20   See Bourdieu, *Distinction: A Social Critique of the Judgement of Taste*; Bourdieu, *Questions of Culture* (Cambridge: Polity Press, 1989). For empirical examples, see K.C. Phillipps, *Language and Class in Victorian England* (Oxford: Basil Blackwell, 1984); G. Stedman Jones, *Languages of Class* (Cambridge: Cambridge University Press, 1983); D. Vincent, *Literacy and Popular Culture, England 1750–1914* (Cambridge: Cambridge University Press, 1989); R. Fowler (ed.), *Language and Control* (London: Routledge, 1979).

21   For the Quakers, see also Richard Bauman, *Let Your Words be Few: Symbolism of Speaking and Silence among Seventeenth-Century Quakers* (Cambridge: Cambridge University Press, 1983); R. Vann, *The Social Development of English Quakerism 1655–1750* (Cambridge, Mass.: Harvard University Press, 1969).

22   A parallel, though more complex, instance would be cultural forms in which the *visual* assumes priority over the printed word. See David Kunzle, *The Early Comic Strip: Picture Stories and Narrative Strips in the European Broadsheet ca. 1450–1826* (Berkeley, Cal.: University of California Press, 1973); Kunzle, *The*

History of the Comic Strip: The Nineteenth Century (Berkeley, Cal.: University of California Press, 1989); Margaret Spufford, *Small Books and Pleasant Histories: Popular Fiction and its Readership in Seventeenth-Century England* (Athens, Ga.: University of Georgia Press, 1981); R.L.W. Collison, *The Story of Street Literature: The Forerunner of the Popular Press* (London: Dent, 1973). The conventions of musical notation are worth consideration in this light.

23 David Cressy, 'Books as Totems in Seventeenth-Century England and New England', *Journal of Library History*, xxi (1986), 92–106. Generally, on the powers of the written and printed word, see the important survey by Henri-Jean Martin, *Histoire et pouvoirs de l'écrit* (Paris: Perrin, 1989).

24 Malise Ruthven, *A Satanic Affair: Salman Rushdie and the Rage of Islam* (London: Chatto, 1990).

25 As this metaphor shows, language systems and money systems have long been viewed as parallels. See Foucault, *The Order of Things: An Archaeology of the Human Sciences*, chs 1 and 2; C.G. Caffentzis, *Clipped Coins, Abused Words and Civil Government* (New York: Autonomedia, 1989); J.-C. Agnew, *Worlds Apart: The Market and the Theater in Anglo-American Thought, 1550–1750* (Cambridge: Cambridge University Press, 1986).

26 Discussion of the history of the ideal of an objective, pellucid, scientific prose may be found in Hans Aarsleff, *From Locke to Saussure: Essays on the Study of Language and Intellectual History* (Minneapolis, Minn.: University of Minnesota Press, 1982); Aarsleff, *The Study of Language in England, 1780–1860* (Minneapolis, Minn.: University of Minnesota Press, 1983); Douglas Bush, *Science and English Poetry: A Historical Sketch, 1590–1950* (New York: Oxford University Press, 1950) Donald Davie, *The Language of Science and the Language of Literature, 1700–1740* (London: Sheed and Ward, 1963); M.H. Abrams, *The Mirror and the Lamp: Romantic Theory and the Critical Tradition* (New York: Norton, 1958).

27 Note Hilaire Belloc's self-composed epitaph: 'His sins were scarlet, but his books were read.'

28 Peter Barnes's play, *Sunsets and Glories*, contains a servant, Jacapone, who has had his tongue removed. Ironically, his power depends upon his impaired speech. When proper speech is miraculously restored to him, his hold over people vanishes.

29 Mikhail M. Bakhtin, *Rabelais and his World*, trans. H. Iswolsky (Cambridge, Mass.: MIT Press, 1968); Bakhtin, *The Dialogic Imagination: Four Essays by Mikhail M. Bakhtin*, ed. Michael Holquist, trans. Caryl Emerson and Michael Holquist (Austin, Tex.: University of Texas Press, 1981); P. Stallybrass and A. White, *The Politics and Poetics of Transgression* (Ithaca, NY: Cornell University Press, 1986).

30 Keith Thomas, *Man and the Natural World: Changing Attitudes in England, 1500–1800* (London: Allen Lane, 1983); Donna Haraway, *Primate Visions* (Berkeley, Cal.: University of California Press, 1989).

31 See John Burrow, *Evolution and Society* (Cambridge: Cambridge University Press, 1966); Burrow, *A Liberal Descent: Victorian Historians and the English Past* (Cambridge: Cambridge University Press, 1981); George Stocking, *The Shaping of American Anthropology, 1883–1911* (New York: Basic Books, 1974);

H. MacDougall, *Racial Myth in English History: Trojans, Teutons and Anglo-Saxons* (Montreal: Harvest House, 1982). For the myth of the civilizing power of language, see David Spadafora, *The Idea of Progress in Eighteenth Century Britain* (New Haven, Conn.: Yale University Press, 1990).

32   Aarsleff, *From Locke to Saussure: Essays on the Study of Language and Intellectual History*; Aarsleff, *The Study of Language in England, 1780–1860*. For such assumptions today, see the discussion in David Dabydeen, 'On Not Being Milton: Nigger Talk in Modern England', in Ricks and Michaels, *The State of the Language: 1990*, 3–14. The Bellow quotation is taken from an interview in the *Independent* (10 February 1990). Thanks to Dr Christine Stevenson for pointing it out to us.

33   Philippa Levine, *The Amateur and the Professional. Antiquarians, Historian and Archaeologists in Victorian England, 1838–1886* (Cambridge: Cambridge University Press, 1986).

34   On primitive languages, Vico is obviously crucial. See Peter Burke, *Vico* (Oxford: Oxford University Press, 1985); and, for the wider Vichian sense of human and natural history, P. Rossi, *The Dark Abyss of Time: The History of the Earth and the History of Nations from Hooke to Vico* (Chicago: University of Chicago Press, 1984).

35   The kinds of fictions involved herein are well explored in Eric Hobsbawm and Terence Ranger (eds), *The Invention of Tradition* (Cambridge: Cambridge University Press, 1983). For Wales, see Gwyn Williams, 'Romanticism in Wales', in Porter and Teich, *Romanticism in National Context*, 9–36.

36   See Porter and Teich, *Romanticism in National Context*.

37   John Lucas, *England and Englishness. Ideas of Nationhood in English Poetry 1688–1900* (London: Hogarth Press, 1990). For the role of language within the creation of a sense of community, see further Marilyn Butler, 'Romanticism in England', in Porter and Teich, *Romanticism in National Context*, 37–67; Porter and Teich, *Romantics, Rebels and Reactionaries: English Literature and its Background 1760–1830* (Oxford: Oxford University Press, 1981); Gerald Newman, *The Rise of English Nationalism: A Cultural History, 1740–1830* (New York: St Martin's Press; London: Weidenfeld and Nicolson, 1987); Raymond Williams, *Culture and Society, 1780–1950* (London: Chatto and Windus, 1958).

38   For the political contestation of the English language, especially in context of patriotism and national feeling, see Linda Colley, 'The Apotheosis of George III: Loyalty, Royalty and the English Nation', *Past and Present*, cii (1984), 94–129; Colley, 'Whose Nation? Class and National Consciousness in England, 1750–1830', *Past and Present*, cxiii (1986), 96–117; H. Cunningham, 'The Language of Patriotism, 1750–1914', *History Workshop Journal*, xii (1981), 8–33; Iain McCalman, *Radical Underworld: Prophets, Revolutionaries and Pornographers in London, 1795–1840* (Cambridge: Cambridge University Press, 1988); James T. Boulton, *The Language of Politics in the Age of Wilkes and Burke* (London: Routledge and Kegan Paul, 1963); Olivia Smith, *The Politics of Language* (Oxford: Clarendon Press, 1984); Raphael Samuel (ed.), *Patriotism, The Making and Unmaking of British National Identity*, 3 vols (London: Routledge, 1989). On a wider canvas, see O. Macdonagh, *States of Mind: A Study of Anglo-Irish Conflict, 1780–1880* (London: Allen and Unwin, 1983). For

Yiddish, see Sander Gilman, *Jewish Self-Hatred. Anti-Semitism and the Hidden Language of the Jews* (Baltimore: Johns Hopkins University Press, 1986).

39 See A.O.J. Cockshutt, *The Art of Autobiography in Nineteenth and Twentieth Century England* (New Haven, Conn.: Yale University Press, 1984); P. Delany, *British Autobiography in the Seventeenth Century* (London: Routledge and Kegan Paul, 1969); J.O. Lyons, *The Invention of the Self* (Carbondale, Ill.: Southern Illinois University Press; London: Feffer and Simons, 1978); P.M. Spacks, *Imagining a Self* (Cambridge: Mass.: Harvard University Press, 1976); and, most recently and sensitively, Felicity A. Nussbaum, *The Autobiographical Subject: Gender and Ideology in Eighteenth-Century England* (Baltimore: Johns Hopkins University Press, 1989).

40 For the role of post-Gutenberg technology in creating the self, see Roger Chartier (ed.), *A History of Private Life*, vol. 3 (Cambridge, Mass.: The Belknap Press, 1989); more generally, Lewis Mumford, *Technics and Civilization* (London: Routledge and Kegan Paul, 1934); Mumford, *The Condition of Man* (London: Warburg Institute, 1944).

41 See the valuable discussion, drawing upon Foucault, in Nikolas Rose, *Governing the Soul. The Shaping of the Private Self* (London: Routledge, 1990). For Foucault see, in particular, *The History of Sexuality*, vol. 1, *Introduction* (London: Allen Lane, 1979); Foucault, *Discipline and Punish: The Birth of the Prison*; Foucault, *Power/Knowledge: Selected Interviews and Other Writings 1972–1977* (Brighton: Harvester Wheatsheaf, 1977). For discussion, see John Forrester, *The Seductions of Psychoanalysis* (Cambridge: Cambridge University Press, 1990), 'Michel Foucault and the History of Psychoanalysis', 286–315.

42 These ideas are explored in Graham Richards, *On Psychological Language and the Physiomorphic Basis of Human Nature* (London: Routledge, 1990). See also Mark Johnson, *The Body in the Mind: The Bodily Basis of Meaning, Imagination and Reason* (Chicago: University of Chicago Press, 1987); P. Henry, 'On Language and the Body', in C. McCabe (ed.), *The Talking Cure: Essays in Psychoanalysis and Language* (London: Macmillan, 1981), 70–4. Also suggestive for the complex triangle of relations between the body, the outside world, and linguistic metaphor, is O. Mayr, *Authority, Liberty and Automatic Machines in Early Modern Europe* (Baltimore: Johns Hopkins University Press, 1986).

43 On pain, and its implications for the self, see David Bakan, *Disease, Pain and Sacrifice: Towards a Psychology of Suffering* (Chicago: University of Chicago Press, 1968); Andrew Wear, 'Puritan Perceptions of Illness in Seventeenth Century England', in Roy Porter (ed.), *Patients and Practitioners* (Cambridge: Cambridge University Press, 1985), 55–99; Wear, 'Interfaces: Perceptions of Health and Illness in Early Modern England', in Roy Porter and Andrew Wear (eds), *Problems and Methods in the History of Medicine, 1750–1850* (London: Croom Helm, 1987), 230–55. Literary workings-out of these dilemmas are analysed in Carol Houlihan Flynn, 'Running out of Matter: The Body Exercised in Eighteenth Century Fiction', in G.S. Rousseau (ed.), *Languages of the Psyche* (Los Angeles: University of California Press, 1990); Elaine Scarry, *The Body in Pain: The Making and Unmaking of the World* (Oxford: Oxford University Press, 1985); Scarry (ed.), *Literature and the Body: Essays on Populations and Persons* (Baltimore: Johns Hopkins University Press, 1988);

Julia L. Epstein, 'Writing the Unspeakable: Fanny Burney's Mastectomy and the Fictive Body', *Representations* (1986), 131–66.

44   For the point where 'inner feelings' turn into medical expression, see H. Brody, *Stories of Sickness* (New Haven, Conn.: Yale University Press, 1987); Arthur Kleinman, *Illness Narratives: Suffering, Healing, and the Human Condition* (New York: Basic Books, 1988); S.J. Reiser, *Medicine and the Reign of Technology* (Cambridge: Cambridge University Press, 1978); W.F. Bynum and Roy Porter (eds), *Medicine and the Five Senses* (Cambridge: Cambridge University Press, 1992); Johanna Geyer-Kordesch, 'Cultural Habits of Illness: The Enlightened and the Pious in Eighteenth Century Germany', in Porter, *Patients and Practitioners*, 177–204; G. Groddeck, *The Meaning of Illness: Selected Psychoanalytical Writings* (London: Hogarth Press, 1977); Roy Porter, 'Laymen, Doctors and Medical Knowledge in the Eighteenth Century: The Evidence of *The Gentleman's Magazine*', in Porter, *Patients and Practitioners*, 283–314; Porter, 'The Patient's View: Doing Medical History from Below', *Theory and Society*, xiv (1985), 175–98.

45   J.H. Dirckx, *The Language of Medicine: Its Evolution, Structure, and Dynamics* (New York: Praeger, 1983); for wider views of the interfaces of technical and general vocabulary, see S. Tucker, *Protean Shape* (London: Athlone Press, 1967); Raymond Williams, *Keywords* (London: Croom Helm, 1976).

46   Susan Sontag, *Illness as Metaphor* (London: Allen Lane, 1979); Sontag, *AIDS as Metaphor* (London: Allen Lane, 1989).

47   For nerves and nervousness, see G.S. Rousseau, 'Nerves, Spirits and Fibres: Towards Defining the Origins of Sensibility; with a Postscript', *The Blue Guitar*, ii (1976), 125–53; Rousseau, 'Psychology', in G.S. Rousseau and Roy Porter (eds), *The Ferment of Knowledge* (Cambridge: Cambridge University Press, 1980), 143–210; Rousseau (ed.), *The Languages of Psyche: Mind and Body in Enlightenment Thought* (Berkeley and Los Angeles: University of California Press, 1990); Rousseau, 'Science', in P. Rogers (ed.), *The Context of English Literature: The Eighteenth Century* (London: Methuen, 1978); Rousseau, 'Literature and Medicine: The State of the Field', *Isis*, lxxii (1981), 406–24.

48   Barker, *The Tremulous Private Body: Essays on Subjection*; B. Anderson, *Imagined Communities: Reflections on the Origin and Spread of Nationalism* (London: Verso Editions and New Left Books, 1983).

49   S. Fish, *Self-Consuming Artifacts* (Berkeley, Cal.: University of California Press, 1972).

Note: An important recent addition to the literature on many of these issues is Penelope J. Corfield (ed.), *Language, History and Class* (Oxford: Blackwell Publishers, 1991).

Part I

Authoritative Tongues

1

Heu domine, adsunt Turcae: A Sketch for a Social History of Post-medieval Latin[1]

PETER BURKE

The importance of Latin in the learned culture of medieval Europe is well known. After 1500, however, the story becomes complicated. Did the Renaissance lead to the rise of Latin or the rise of the vernacular? Did Latin decline in the sixteenth century, the seventeenth, the eighteenth, the nineteenth, or only in the twentieth? Posed in this simple form, the questions are impossible to answer. They need rephrasing in the language of the sociolinguists, some of whom are currently preoccupied with language spread, language maintenance, language shift, and language recession.[2]

The advantage of drawing on sociolinguistic theory is that it helps us to discriminate not only between different parts of Europe and different kinds of Latin (classical and non-classical, spoken and written), but also between different kinds of user (clerical and lay, male and female, and so on), and between different topics or, to use the technical term, linguistic 'domains'.[3] The 'diglossia' or linguistic division of labour between Latin and the vernacular in early modern Europe was not so different from that between classical and vernacular forms of Arabic as analysed by contemporary sociolinguists.[4]

If these discriminations are made, it should become clear that Latin remained a living language in a number of areas as late as the nineteenth century. Such is the argument of the essay which follows, which is divided into three main sections, corresponding to the three main linguistic domains in which Latin was employed; the ecclesiastical, the academic, and the pragmatic.

If it were only possible, this study of 'post-medieval' Latin would take the Middle Ages as a base-line from which to measure change. However, as students of modern 'secularization' or 'dechristianization' have already discovered, it is exceedingly problematic to work with a base-line of about a thousand years. As an Italian scholar recently remarked, 'Medieval Latin is one, but it is not monolithic.'[5] For example, Latin was used much more widely in thirteenth-century lay society in Italy than it was (say) in England.[6] Unfortunately, there is no general history of the uses of Latin in the Middle Ages. The most that can be done here is to invoke the later Middle Ages from time to time in specific contexts.[7]

Still less work has been done on the post-medieval period, in any of the three domains to be studied below. All this essay can hope to do is to offer examples which conflict with the conventional picture of the triumph of the vernacular in the seventeenth century (if not the sixteenth), and to draw a few provisional conclusions, which might be summed up in the form of three paradoxes, as follows.

1 The Protestants who were committed to the rejection of Latin in the Church were often better Latinists than the Catholics who were committed to maintaining it.
2 The decline of Latin was mainly due not to the opponents of classical antiquity but to its supporters, the humanists, whose insistence on classical standards turned it from a living to a 'dead' language.
3 Although declared 'dead', Latin would not lie down. It remained useful, indeed vigorous, in particular domains and in particular parts of Europe throughout the eighteenth and nineteenth centuries.

Ecclesiastical Latin[8]

Latin has been the official language of the Roman Catholic Church for most of its history, not only for the liturgy (replacing Greek in the fourth century AD), but as the language of papal government, ecclesiastical courts, episcopal visitations, provincial synods, general councils, and other church business. The encyclical letters from the popes to the faithful were and are written in Latin, as their titles remind us (*Rerum Novarum, Quadragesimo Anno*, etc). The proceedings of Vatican II were published in Latin only a few years ago.[9]

Social historians must of course be attentive to the distance between the official and the unofficial. It may have been the case that the clergy who attended provincial synods employed the vernacular for their discussions, although the decrees which emerged were recorded in Latin. After all, many fifteenth- and sixteenth-century sermons by so-called popular preachers such as Gabriele Barletta and Olivier Maillard were published in Latin, when they must have been delivered in the vernacular.[10] On the other hand, it is unlikely that masses were said in languages other than some kind of Latin, or that the bishops from different parts of Europe assembled at general councils could have communicated in any other way.

More than one explanation can be offered for the persistence of Latin in this domain. In the first place, an international language was a valuable resource for an international organization (which in turn helped establish and maintain Latin as an international language). In the second place, the use of a non-vernacular language acted as a marker, underlining the special nature of texts such as the Bible and rituals such as the Mass.[11] The controversy following the introduction of a vernacular liturgy after the second Vatican Council revealed the strength of the attachment to Latin, at least in some parts of Catholic Europe.[12] Catholics are not of course the only religious group to use a 'dead' language as their language of spiritual power; the Hindus, Buddhists, Jews, and Muslims, for example, employ Sanskrit, Pali, classical Hebrew, and classical Arabic in a similar manner.[13]

Equally obvious, however (at least to us), are the disadvantages of attempting to communicate with the whole population of Christendom in a language understood only by a relatively small minority of that population. Some of the laity believed that the use of Latin was a clerical trick to keep the faith secret, 'then sell it back to us retail' (*le vendono a poco a poco, come si dice a minuto*).[14] It should be emphasized, however, that the minority which understood Latin excluded many of the medieval clergy. It is not surprising to learn that many of the parish clergy were ignorant of Latin, given the lack of facilities for training them, but even in the case of the monks, according to a well-known medievalist, 'we find the authorities assuming a great deal of Latin ignorance, and making special translations for the use of ignorant brethren.'[15]

Criticisms of the preponderance of Latin in the Church were in fact made from time to time in the later Middle Ages, notably by the Waldensians and the Wyclifites, who insisted on having vernacular versions of the scriptures. These criticisms were made still more vigorously in the early sixteenth century. Erasmus, for example, appealed for the translation of the Bible into the vernacular:

> I would that even the lowliest women read the Gospels and the Pauline
> Epistles. And I would that they were translated into all languages so
> that they could be read and understood not only by Scots and Irish but

also by Turks and Saracens . . . Would that, as a result, the farmer sing some portion of them at the plough, the weaver hum some parts of them to the movement of his shuttle, the traveller lighten the weariness of the journey with stories of this kind.[16]

The irony of the situation is that Erasmus made this appeal in Latin, and had to do so in order to be heard. Heard he was, but not heeded; the Council of Trent outlawed the vernacular bibles which had been circulating in the Catholic world from the late Middle Ages, but were now associated with heresy.

As for the liturgy, in 1513 the Venetian hermits Paolo Giustiniani and Vincenzo Quirini wrote to the pope in favour of the vernacular, and this proposal was discussed at the Council of Trent and supported by the cardinal of Lorraine and the French bishops.[17] Since liturgies had been devised in Greek, Coptic, and Church Slavonic earlier in the history of the Church, this suggestion did not breach any principle. All the same, and despite the felt need to win back recent converts to Protestantism, the proposal was unsuccessful so far as Europe was concerned. After a long debate in which some leading clerics argued in favour of the vernacular, the Council of Trent finally declared in 1562 that 'if anyone should say . . . that Mass should be celebrated in the vernacular . . . let him be anathema.'[18] In the later sixteenth century, the *Scuole della dottrina cristiana*, organized to give the children of the poor an elementary knowledge of theology and literacy, taught the Ave Maria, the Credo, the Pater Noster, and the Salve Regina in Latin, not Italian.[19]

In practice, concessions were made. Following the Council of Brest-Litovsk, at which the Orthodox Church in the kingdom of Poland-Lithuania agreed to accept papal supremacy if it could retain its own customs, Catholic services in Old Church Slavonic could be heard. In East-Central Europe, the bishops showed some sympathy for local vernaculars. In the diocese of Esztergom, for example, Hungarian German and Slovak as well as Latin could be used for baptisms and marriage services.[20] In the mission field outside Europe, concessions were also made on occasion. The Council of Lima, for example, decreed in 1582 that the Indians (unlike the Italian pupils of the *Scuole della dottrina cristiana*) should not be forced to learn prayers or the catechism in Latin.[21] In 1615 the Chinese and in 1631 the Persians were granted the privilege of a liturgy in a language other than Latin (in Mandarin in one case, in classical Arabic in the other).

Sermons to the laity were generally in the vernacular. When San Carlo Borromeo criticized his episcopal colleague Gabriele Paleotti for preaching in Latin, Paleotti explained that his sermon had been addressed to the magistrates and doctors sitting near the high altar, while the rest of the people in the body of the church would have been unable to hear him.[22] In the case of French episcopal visitations, a shift from Latin to French took place in the course of the sixteenth and seventeenth centuries.[23] In these cases, the introduction of the vernacular did not carry the dangerous implication that Protestants had been right all the time.

In any case, the simple contrast associating Catholicism with Latin and Protestantism with the vernacular is in need of qualification from the Protestant as well as the Catholic side. In the early years of Protestantism, the reformed liturgy was a Latin one. Even Luther's German Mass, issued in 1526, was intended for Sundays only, with a Latin liturgy continuing to be used on weekdays. Luther, Melanchthon, and Zwingli wrote in Latin as well as in German, Calvin in Latin as well as in French. Indeed, of Calvin's 130 works, 79 were written in Latin.[24]

Like Erasmus, these reformers were caught in a dilemma. To write in Latin was to cut themselves off from ordinary people, but to write in a vernacular was to cut themselves off from the rest of Europe. Since the mother tongue of Erasmus was spoken by relatively few people, it is scarcely surprising to find that he opted for Latin, in his three thousand private letters as well as in his voluminous works, and is recorded to have spoken his native language only on his deathbed.[25]

The Protestant reformers, on the other hand, tended to prefer a bilingual compromise, switching from the vernacular to Latin according to the topic and the audience.[26] This compromise worked all the better because – another irony – the sixteenth-century Protestant clergy, many of whom had attended university, were probably more competent in Latin than their Catholic colleagues. So far as the liturgy is concerned, the difference between the Protestant and the Catholic positions has been summed up as 'an evolution in opposite directions', as the reformers came to see the problems in abandoning Latin, and the Catholics those entailed by retaining it.[27]

Academic Latin

The importance of Latin literature in the sixteenth and seventeenth centuries – and even later – has been emphasized in recent studies, so there is little need to discuss it at length in this place.[28] Some humanists were hostile to the use of the vernacular in literature – Giovanni del Virgilio, for example, who advised Dante to write his *Divine Comedy* in Latin.[29] A number of leading sixteenth-century humanists wrote treatises in defence of Latin.[30]

Latin was employed in lyric and epic, poetry and prose, fiction and non-fiction. In the fifteenth century the leading Latin poets included Mantuanus, Pontano, and Sannazzaro, all active in Italy; in the sixteenth century, the German humanist Conrad Celtis, the Pole Clemens Janicius (Janicki), and the Netherlander Johannes Secundas, famous for his *Kisses* (*Basia*) first published in 1541; and in the seventeenth century, Milton and two Jesuits, the Italian Famiano Strada and the 'Polish Horace', Maceij Kazimierz Sarbiewski. In France too, Latin poetry continued to flourish in the early part of the reign of Louis XIV.[31] In the eighteenth century, no fewer than nine poems on Newton's system of the universe were published in Latin, one of them by the leading Jesuit astronomer Boscovitch.[32] As late as the nineteenth century first-rate poetry was being written in Latin, notably by Giovanni Pascoli (who died in 1912). Pope Leo XIII was also an accomplished Latin poet.[33]

In the case of prose, it is perhaps worth stressing the survival of imaginative literature in Latin into the seventeenth and eighteenth centuries. Obvious examples are John Barclay's political *roman à clef*, the *Argenis* (1621), and Ludvig Holberg's satirical novel on the adventures of Niels Klimt underground, *N. Klimii Iter Subterraneum* (1741). As for the drama, its association with the teaching of Latin ensured a steady flow of plays throughout the sixteenth and seventeenth centuries, in particular in Jesuit colleges.[34]

However, the importance of Latin in post-medieval European culture is illustrated still more vividly by the large number of translations into that language made in the fifteenth, sixteenth, and even seventeenth centuries, translations which have not yet been studied as they deserve. Among the late medieval vernacular texts which were Latinized were Boccaccio's *Decameron*, Froissart's *Chronicles* and Marco Polo's travels.[35] A number of the famous vernacular texts of Renaissance Italy were also 'popularized' in this way, including Aretino's *Letters*, Machiavelli's *The Prince*, Guicciardini's *History of Italy*, Giovanni Della Casa's *Galateo*, and two of Ariosto's plays, while no fewer than three Latin versions of Castiglione's *The Courtier* (or part of it) appeared in the course of the century.[36] Translations from Spanish into Latin included versions of Guevara's *Dial of Princes*, Alemán's novel *Guzmán de Alfarache* and Huarte's treatise on psychology, *Examen des ingénios*. Translations from French included the political writers Commynes, Seyssel, and Bodin; translations from German, Brant's *Ship of Fools* and the travels of Heinrich von Staden; and translations from English, Chaucer's *Troilus and Cressida* and Spenser's *Shepherd's Calendar*.[37]

Translations of this kind continued to be made in the seventeenth century, when they included works by Arnauld (the *Logic* of Port-Royal), Bacon (the *Essays*), Boileau (the *Lutrin* and the ode on the capture of Namur), Corneille, Descartes, Galileo (the *Letter to the Grand Duchess*), Hobbes, Locke, Malebranche, Pascal (the *Lettres provinciales*), the *History of the Council of Trent* by Paolo Sarpi, and even the *History of the Reformation* by Gilbert Burnet, first published in 1679.[38] The fact that we still call the Chinese philosopher K'ung Fu Tzu 'Confucius' is a reminder that knowledge of his writings were spread in Europe from the late seventeenth century onwards in a Latin translation by a group of Jesuits.[39]

Until the late seventeenth century, if not the early eighteenth, it was more common for works of learning to be published in Latin than in any vernacular, even French. Descartes's *Discours de la méthode* has won him a distinguished place in the history of the 'rise' or 'emancipation' of French, so it is worth emphasizing the fact that he produced some of his books, such as his *Meditations*, in Latin. So did Francis Bacon, Thomas Hobbes (*De cive*, for example), John Locke, and Isaac Newton. Although Galileo chose the vernacular from 1612 onwards because he wanted 'everyone' to be able to read about his discoveries and opinions, his *Starry Messenger* and other works had been written in Latin.[40] Spon felt the need to apologize for writing a scholarly work, on medals, in French. Even the vindications of their native tongues produced in the seventeenth century by the German poet Martin Opitz and the Czech Jesuit Bohuslav Balbín were themselves written in Latin, whether to reach an international public or because the dignity of the subject required it.[41]

It has been argued that the middle of the seventeenth century was the turning point from Latin to the vernacular in France, the early eighteenth century in Germany. In the case of France, the evidence comes from the contents of libraries; in the case of Germany, from the books displayed for sale at the annual Frankfurt and Leipzig book fairs. At Leipzig in 1701, 55 per cent of the works displayed were in Latin; by 1740 the proportion had shrunk to 27 per cent.[42] The foundation of the *Journal des Savants*, the *Nouvelles de la République des Lettres*, and other learned journals of the later seventeenth century did a good deal to establish French as the new language of the Commonwealth of learning.

A good deal, but not quite enough. One of the most important international scholarly journals was the *Acta Eruditorum* of Leipzig, which began to appear in 1682 and utilized Latin, even when reviewing books in the vernacular such as Bayle on comets, or Bossuet on universal history. Its Swedish imitation in the 1720s followed the same policy, doubtless to acquire an international readership.[43] When the Academy of St Petersburg began to publish its proceedings in 1720s, it utilized Latin.[44] As late as the mid-eighteenth century scholars can still be found who read little that was not in Latin – Vico, for example. Although he decided to write his *New Science* in Italian, his earlier works had been in Latin. Vico's lament over the fall in the price of Latin books in Naples as a result of declining demand is well known.[45]

By the eighteenth century such attitudes were old-fashioned, and the victory of the vernaculars was unquestionable. The French journalist Jacques Vincent Delacroix was cruelly correct when he wrote in the 1770s comparing Latin to a house '*richement meublée, spacieuse et abandonée*'.[46] Yet the defeat of Latin was not complete, and it may be worth emphasizing how late learned works continued to be written in that language. The Swiss mathematician Jakob Bernoulli I published his *Ars conjectandi* in 1713. Later in the eighteenth century, his compatriot Leonhard Euler published his *Mechanica* (1736) and his *Introductio in analysin infinitorum* (1748), although he also wrote in French and German. As late as the middle of the nineteenth century, the German mathematician Carl Friedrich Gauss was publishing his work in Latin.

Mathematicians were not alone in this respect. Some academic traditions positively required Latin publications. In nineteenth-century France, the supplementary thesis for the doctorate of letters had to be written in Latin, whether the subject was the poetry of Keats, the criminal jurisdiction of the Paris Châtelet, the fiscal policies of Louis XVI, or the development of sociological method, despite the need for neologisms such as *scientiae 'sociologicae'*. The authors of such published theses included Bergson, Renan, Seignebos, and Durkheim.[47] It would be interesting to know whether these Latin theses were entirely the work of their authors, or whether there was some kind of unofficial translation service available.[48]

Academic Latin was not only a written but also a spoken language. It is well known that university lectures and disputations took place in that language, while many schools not only taught Latin but taught in Latin, and insisted that pupils speak Latin even in the playground. What is difficult is to distinguish between theory and practice, to chart regional and other variations in that practice, and to date changes, all on the basis of written sources. The examples which follow are not claimed to be typical; they are offered simply in order to show the difficulty of generalization, and to encourage more systematic research in this area.

In the case of schools, there is little doubt that proficiency in spoken Latin was frequently required from the pupils, understandably so given Latin's practical value (to be discussed in the following section of this essay). Hence the importance of printed dialogues for use in schools, notably those of Erasmus and Cordier; the study of the plays of Plautus and Terence (despite suspicion of their immorality); the rise of the so-called 'school drama', in other words the regular performance of Latin plays by schoolboys; and the institution of the *lupus*, the 'wolf' or spy who was supposed to tell the teacher if he heard his comrades speak in the vernacular during playtime. Montaigne was exceptional in being taught Latin as his first language, but this exception should be seen as an extreme case of a general insistence that upper-class children come early to Latin.

It may still come as something of a shock to pick up one of the most famous Latin grammars of the Renaissance, Lorenzo Valla's *Elegantiae linguae latinae*, and to discover that it is written throughout in Latin, so that it cannot be understood without a knowledge of the language it claims to impart. The prevalence of Latin grammars in Latin has led one historian of education to comment on the importance of the 'direct method' in Renaissance education.[49] He may be right.

However, we should not jump to conclusions about teaching methods in the Renaissance. We do not know whether this book was a manual for the student or only for the teacher, or whether many teachers mixed explanation in the vernacular with their insistence on spoken Latin. In any case, there is evidence of increasing dissatisfaction with the monopoly of Latin in the classroom, at least from the seventeenth century onwards, from Jan Amos Comenius to Jean-Baptiste de la Salle.[50] All the same, teaching children to read in Latin remained normal practice in France until the 1870s and survived until the twentieth century in some places.[51]

In the case of universities, there is a little more information available about variations and changes in practice. Spoken Latin was the norm in early modern Europe, as far east as the Theological Academy of Kiev in the early seventeenth century, where Peter Mogila, who opposed the union with Rome, wanted his students to understand the enemy.[52] All the same, some teachers employed the vernacular themselves or allowed their students to do so. Antonio Genovesi, in 1765, claimed to be the first professor to teach philosophy in Italian at the university of Naples (what would Vico have thought?), but this was not the first time Italian had been heard in lectures elsewhere in the peninsula.[53] In the law faculty of the University of Rome in the sixteenth century, Latin was the language most commonly used for the disputations, but provision was made for the use of Italian in case of difficulties.[54] In Paris at about the same time, Louis Le Roy, who taught politics, gave some of his lectures in French.[55] An English student of medicine, Edward Browne (son of the famous Sir Thomas) went to Paris in 1664 and attended the lectures of Guy Patin, 'but I was much disappointed in my expectation of understanding all hee said by reason hee used the French tongue so much'.[56] At Montpellier a few years later, John Locke attended a disputation in the Faculty of Medicine; his laconic comment was 'hard Latin' and 'Much French'.[57] At the Collège Royal in Paris, lectures in French law in French were given by Professor Delaunay in 1680.[58]

Exceptions to the Latin rule can also be found in the German-speaking world. As early as 1501, the humanist Heverlingh lectured on Juvenal in German at the university of Rostock. Paracelsus delivered his notorious lectures in Basel in 1526–7 in German, before he was asked to leave, and one wonders whether the untraditional medium was not found as offensive as the unorthodox message. However, it was Christian Thomasius who seems at least 'to have been the first person to announce a course of lectures in German', a course on the ethics of the Spanish writer Baltasar Gracián, delivered at the university of Halle in 1687.[59] He was followed by A.H. Francke at Leipzig.

In Britain too we can find exceptions to the rule of Latin. In the early seventeenth century, English was used as well as Latin in the lectures at Gresham College, Latin for the sake of foreign listeners and English because 'the greatest part of the auditory is like to be of such citizens and others as have small knowledge, or none at all, in the Latin tongue.'[60] John Webster's criticism of the universities of Oxford and Cambridge for teaching in Latin seems to have been little heeded in his own time; indeed, a few years later, the president and fellows of Queens' College Cambridge enjoined the undergraduates to speak Latin in hall at dinner and supper.[61] In Harvard College in the seventeenth century, the use of English was prohibited within the college precincts.[62] Speaking Latin was the sign of a student, which was apparently enough to lead to brawling in the streets and even to homicide, at least in northern France in the sixteenth and seventeenth centuries.[63]

In the early eighteenth century, on the other hand, a Danish student at Oxford (later to become a famous man of letters) reported that although he spoke Latin 'with difficulty and hesitation', he found that 'the English admired the readiness and fluency with which I expressed myself in that language. The truth is, that this exercise is so neglected in England that I met with no one, except Dr Smalridge, who could speak Latin tolerably.'[64] In Scotland, it seems that the eighteenth century was the turning point from Latin to the vernacular. The philosopher Francis Hutcheson is said to have been the first professor at Glasgow to lecture in English, though even he gave his inaugural in Latin in 1730.[65]

In some parts of Europe, however, Latin persisted into the nineteenth century as the language of teaching. The advocate George Bergmann (1805–92), who studied at Leiden and Ghent, recalled oral examinations in Latin. Gauss was still lecturing in Latin at Göttingen in the middle of the nineteenth century, while Jean Charles Naber is supposed to have lectured on Roman law in Latin at the university of Utrecht as late as 1911.[66]

On special occasions Latin lasted even longer, perhaps to give these occasions added solemnity, to show that they were in some sense sacred. Inaugural lectures, for example, continued to be given in Latin in the nineteenth century. Ranke gave his inaugural lecture at Berlin in 1836 on history and politics, *'De historiae et politicae cognitione atque discrimine'*, complaining while he was preparing it that 'Unfortunately a Latin dissertation and lecture are still required, which I have little desire to do.'[67] At the university of Leiden in 1850, a distinguished Arabist, Dozy, gave offence (to the curators, at least) by lecturing in Dutch at his inauguration instead of in Latin. In Cambridge, Latin remained the language of the Harveian orations until the late nineteenth century, leading to at least one acutely embarrassing occasion remembered as 'that dreadful day in October, 1864, when Robert Lee began the Harveian Oration in Latin, and had perforce to finish it in his own tongue'.[68] Latin remains to this day the language of the panegyrics on honorary doctorands delivered by the public orator on degree days in Oxford and Cambridge.

In any case, until the early twentieth century it was possible to assume that educated Europeans had at least an elementary knowledge of Latin, while other people did not. Hence the employment of Latin as a cipher by middle-class whites in Africa in one of the novels of John Buchan.[69]

Pragmatic Latin

I have coined the phrase 'pragmatic Latin' to refer to a variety of practical uses for that language, usually in international contexts such as diplomacy and travel, but also in that of the law, and even of business on occasion. As late as the 1870s some Oxford colleges, such as Lincoln and Merton, were keeping their accounts in Latin.[70]

To a greater or lesser extent Latin was used as the language of the law all over Europe. As terms like *habeas corpus* remind us, it was even employed in regions such as England where the influence of Roman law was relatively slight. Early in the English civil war the Commission of Array, calling out the militia to fight for the king, was in Latin, with the result that in Somerset the king's opponents 'translated it into what English they pleased'.[71] In some parts of early modern Europe there was a revolt against lawyer's Latin. In 1534, for example, the Polish gentry criticized its use at the 'Dietine' or local assembly held at Sroda, while in 1539, in the famous ordinance of Villers-Cottêrets, François I ordered French to be used in legal documents.[72] Similar demands were made by radicals during the English Revolution.[73]

The criticism of legal Latin was probably strongest in Italy, despite or because of the fact that the law was even more involved with Latin there than elsewhere. In 1444, for example, the people of Curzola complained that the 'gentlemen' were exploiting their knowledge of Latin to the disadvantage of ordinary people (the *popolari*).[74] Carlo Ginzburg's Menocchio was not alone in denouncing the use of Latin in court as 'treason to the poor' (*un tradimento de'poveri*).[75] The parallel with Gelli's critique of Church Latin (discussed above) is an obvius one, and it is interesting to find that Paolo Giustinian and Vincenzo Quirini advocated the use of Italian in notarial documents as well as in the Mass. However, legal Latin survived in the States of the Church until the revolution of 1831.[76]

Latin was on occasion the language of domestic politics. There is at least one example of a chief minister speaking Latin to his sovereign: Sir Robert

Walpole to George I. His son Horace recalled that 'Sir Robert governed George 1st in Latin, the King not speaking English, & his Minister no German, nor even French. It was much talked of, that Sir Robert detecting one of the Hanoverian Ministers in some trick or falsehood before the King's face, had the firmness to say to the German, *Mentiris impudentissime!*[77]

The best-known case of the domestic use of Latin, however, is that of the Hungarian Diet. Its *Acta* were recorded in Latin and it is likely that that language was used for most of the speeches, since speakers of Hungarian, Croat, and Slovak would not otherwise have been able to communicate with one another. Latin was also used for many official communications in the Holy Roman Empire, whether for practical or symbolic reasons. The Austrian monarchy also used Latin for convenience to communicate with Hungary and Slovakia (which were outside the Empire). The financial officials of the Hofkammer in Vienna, for example, corresponded in Latin with their counterparts in Bratislava (Pressburg, Pozsony). Emperor Joseph II decided that German should be the language of administration, telling the Hungarians in 1784, in true enlightened-despotic style, that a dead language could not reasonably be used for official purposes. The nobility disliked the change, associating Latin with liberty, and in the 1790s Leopold brought it back. Latin remained the official language of the kingdom of Hungary until 1844.[78]

It was, however, in international relations that Latin, spoken and written, really came into its own, remaining important all over Europe throughout the sixteenth and seventeenth centuries and surviving considerably longer in some areas. No wonder there was a demand for Latin secretaries to princes, not only in the Renaissance, when Budé served François I and Ammonio served Henry VIII, but well into the seventeenth century. The English Commonwealth, for example, employed Georg Weckherlin, John Milton, and Andrew Marvell in this capacity.[79] George I is far from the only ruler recorded to have spoken Latin. The Emperor Maximilian prided himself on his knowledge of that language (and of a number of others).[80] Queen Elizabeth lost her temper in Latin on a famous occasion in 1597, when she considered herself insulted by the Polish ambassador.[81] On a more friendly occasion, in Copenhagen in 1634, Christian IV spoke Latin to the French ambassador d'Avaux, who had addressed him in Italian.[82] D'Avaux also spoke Latin to the eight-year-old Queen Christina of Sweden, or more exactly spoke over her head to Salvius, who replied in the same language.[83] It should not be assumed that early modern diplomats were fluent in Latin, but only that they were expected to manage somehow. George Downing was unusually frank but may not have been otherwise exceptional when he confessed that he had spoken 'as well as I could in Latin' during a two-hour interview with Cardinal Mazarin.[84]

Latin was not the sole language of diplomacy in the seventeenth century, but it certainly had its advantages. Treaties were commonly drafted in Latin in the sixteenth and seventeenth centuries; the Peace of Westphalia of 1648, for example.[85] And how else could, say, a Portuguese have communicated with a Swede? When Francisco de Sousa Coutinho was ambassador to Stockholm in the seventeenth century, the communications of both sides were translated into Latin.[86]

The advantages of Latin were symbolic as well as pragmatic, as the Swedish chancellor, Axel Oxenstierna, explained to the English ambassador, Bulstrode Whitelocke, in 1653:

> He spake Latin, plain and fluent and significant; and though he could, yet would not speak French, saying he knew no reason why that nation should be so much honoured more than others as to have their language used by strangers; but he thought the Latin more honourable and more copious, and fitter to be used, because the Romans had been masters of so great a part of the world, and yet at present that language was not peculiar to any people.[87]

Whichever reasons were paramount, in some quarters Latin was able to resist the rise of French as the language of diplomacy in the reign of Louis XIV. Contrary to legend, both oral and written Latin were employed in the negotiations at Nijmegen leading to the peace treaty of 1679 between France and its enemies (the Empire, Spain, and the United Provinces).[88] At Frankfurt in 1682, the Empire insisted on Latin, and France on French.[89] Treaties continued to be made in Latin much later, including those between England and Sweden in 1720 and between the Empire and Sweden in 1757. At the end of the nineteenth century, the Habsburg emperor was still writing to the king of Sweden in Latin.[90]

In the reign of Louis XIV, a considerable effort was made by Colbert to project a favourable image of the king and his achievements, abroad as well as at home. To this end medals were struck to commemorate the major events of the reign, statues were erected, and engravings of these statues were circulated. Voices were raised in favour of French as the language of the inscriptions, but in practice Latin was almost always used, despite the fact that the famous dispute between ancients and moderns was taking place at this time. Latin was still the only sure way to reach an international public.[91]

Private individuals also found Latin useful or even, on occasion indispensable. As late as the mid-eighteenth century, Voltaire was conducting a small part of his international correspondence in Latin (though less than Italian or even English).[92] English travellers abroad in the early modern period were more likely (like Sir Robert Walpole) to be fluent in Latin than in French,

Italian, Spanish, or German. Among those who recorded having spoken Latin in France and Italy are Thomas Coryat, Sir George Courthop (who conversed with a Jesuit in the famous convent of possessed nuns in Loudun), Peter Heylyn (who got lost in Paris and asked some priests the way), and John Locke (who failed to communicate in Lyons).[93] Samuel Johnson was also, according to Boswell, 'very resolute in speaking Latin' in France.[94] Seventeenth-century French visitors to England found Latin equally useful, as two examples mentioned by John Evelyn suggest. When he introduced 'a young French Sorbonnist' to Jeremy Taylor, the two men began to argue in Latin about the problem of original sin. Similarly, the refugee Huguenot minister Pierre Allix found Latin the best means to communicate with the archbishop of Canterbury.[95] Dr Johnson was perhaps a little old-fashioned in keeping up the Latin habit in the late eighteenth century. It is understandable that he should have spoken Latin with the Jesuit astronomer Boscovitch (a Croat who taught in Italy), but a little more surprising that when he was introduced to a distinguished Frenchman at the Royal Academy, 'he would not deign to speak French, but talked Latin, though his Excellency did not understand it, owing, perhaps, to Johnson's English pronunciation.'[96] Yet Johnson was not the last Englishman to have recourse to Latin when confronted by foreigners. In our own century Hilaire Belloc, with a kind of Johnsonian perversity, insisted on speaking Latin in Italy, beginning a conversation with a priest in the village of Sillano, 'Pater, habeo linguam latinam, sed non habeo linguam italicam.'[97]

In an age when the Dutch were less proficient in English than they are now, it was only to be expected that Englishmen would speak Latin in the Netherlands, and Sir Philip Sidney, for example, spoke Latin on his deathbed at Zutphen.[98] Again, Queen Elizabeth's extempore speech to the Polish ambassador in 1597 has its parallel in her conversation with a Spanish captain, Pedro Sarmiento de Gamboa, in 1586: 'He conversed with her in Latin for more than two hours and a half.' Sarmiento also conversed in Latin with Sir Walter Raleigh.[99] Examples of this kind could easily be multiplied.

It was above all in East-Central Europe that Latin came into its own as an indispensable *lingua franca*, as the example of the Hungarian Diet has already suggested. When Henri, Duc d'Anjou, went to Poland after his election as king of that country in 1573, the Frenchmen in his suite were surprised (and doubtless relieved) to discover that almost all the gentry and 'all sorts of people, even the innkeepers' spoke Latin.[100] They obviously noticed a genuine difference between Poland and France, even if they exaggerated it. A Polish gentleman of the mid-seventeenth century, Jan Pasek, on campaign in Denmark, tells us that he was posted to Jutland 'chiefly owing to my Latin', as if his comrades were unskilled in the language. He goes on to explain that 'the peasants there can speak Latin', probably another exaggeration, to judge from the lack of communication when he arrived.[101] Another witness to the Polish nobility's familiarity with Latin of some kind is the Duc de St-Simon, who noted that when the Poles entertained the prince de Conti, '*ils parlaient tous Latin, et fort mauvais Latin*.'[102] The evidence of Polish family letters points in the same direction.[103]

The relative importance of Latin in eighteenth-century Finland might also be explained in practical terms as a lingua franca for a nation which could not reasonably expect foreigners to learn its language.[104] A similar point might be made about Iceland. A visitor to Reykjavik in 1856 discovered that 'Many of the inhabitants speak English, and one or two French, but in default of either of these, your only chance is Latin.' He also records going to a banquet where the speeches were in Latin.[105] In Hungary the situation was much the same. It is not at all uncommon to find Hungarians corresponding in Latin – some sort of Latin – in the sixteenth and seventeenth centuries.[106] They also spoke the language in everyday life. The physician Edward Browne (whom we have already encountered as a student in Paris) noted that 'The Latin-Tongue is very serviceable in Hungaria and Transylvania', where 'very great numbers' spoke it, 'especially the Gentry and Souldiers', while even 'Coachmen, Watermen and mean Persons ... could make themselves understood thereby.'[107] That Browne was right, particularly about the soldiers, is suggested by an incident involving the future Maréchal de Bassompierre, who was on campaign against the Turks near Esztergom in 1603. Scouts were sent out to look for the enemy, and one of them, riding back at full speed, shouted to the foreigner, '*Heu domine, adsunt Turcae*', 'Look out, sir, the Turks are here!' In this case knowledge of Latin might be described as necessary for survival.[108]

Conclusions

This brief survey of the uses of Latin in different linguistic domains raises a number of questions about the kind of Latin which was written and spoken in postmedieval Europe, and about the geography, sociology, and chronology of its use. In the present state of knowledge it is impossible to do more than hint at the answers to these questions, but at this point it may be useful to define more precisely the major problems for future research.

It would, for example, be interesting to know more about the division of labour between Latin and vernacular, and the conscious and unconscious rules for switching codes. The exceptional case of Montaigne helps reveal the norm. Montaigne tells us that he was taught in Latin as his first or 'natural' language, with the result that forty years later he would find himself reverting to it in the case of '*extremes et soudaines esmotions*'.[109] Normally, however, even the most fluent Latin speaker and writer (Erasmus, for example, as his last words suggest), used Latin as a second language, while most users probably thought in the vernacular. It is likely that Coulton's comment on medieval Latinists remained true in the early modern period: 'In the inmost thoughts even of the most learned men, the mother-tongue seems always, or nearly always, to have remained uppermost.'[110] Even the encyclicals of the accomplished Latinist Leo XIII were drafted in Italian and translated into Latin by the Secretary of Latin Letters (although the pope might extemporize alterations).[111] It has been plausibly argued that neo-Latin poets faced a serious problem when it came to expressing and communicating emotions, because they were writing in a language which for writer and reader alike was devoid of the associations of early childhood.[112]

Yet the second language was in some respects richer than the first. The 'dead' language Latin was employed, ironically, to express new ideas, because of the lack of abstract terms in most European vernaculars. The gradual rise of the vernacular in the sixteenth and seventeenth centuries as the language of scientific treatises was, paradoxically enough, associated with its Latinization; new words had to be coined, and they were normally derived from Latin.[113]

The varieties of Latin employed in this period deserve emphasis. One might start from the fact that different pronunciations of Latin sometimes made international communication problematic. The English pronunciation of Latin was (and perhaps still is) notoriously difficult for other Latinists to understand. Samuel Sorbière complained about this when he visited England in the middle of the seventeenth century.[114] So did the Biblical scholar Samuel Bochart.[115] John Evelyn confirmed the justice of the complaint when he commented on the 'odd pronouncing of Latine' by his fellow-countrymen, 'so that out of England no nation were able to under-stand or endure it'.[116]

The humanists of the Renaissance revived classical and especially Cicero-nian Latin, and employed it not only for their literary works but also in the chanceries where some of them spent a good deal of their time. Some of them, Leonardo Bruni for example, obtained important posts in government on the basis of their proficiency in Latin.[117]

However, medieval Latin survived, in the Church and in the offices of many lawyers and notaries. In the case of the Church, medieval and Renaissance Latin coexisted. For a sixteenth-century example of the clash between the two varieties we may turn to the text of the *Spiritual Exercises* of St Ignatius Loyola, which was 'translated' from Ignatius's own Latin into a more classical form. A more recent and highly controversial example is that of the new translation of the Psalter into classical (or at any rate classicizing) Latin commissioned by Pope Pius XII and completed in 1944, much criticized for its break with a long Christian tradition.[118]

Traditional ecclesiastical Latin included not only post-classical terms but also constructions modelled on the vernacular. For example, the fifteenth-century Italian chronicler Stefano Infessura uses phrases which need to be translated back into Italian to become intelligible. His phrase for 'cheap' is *pro bono fora* (in Italian, *a buon mercato*), and for 'he stood up' *erexit se in pedes* (in other words, *si levò in piedi*).[119] It is this kind of 'coarse Latin' (*Latinus grossus*) which was parodied by the humanist monk Teofilo Folengo in poems such as the *Liber Macaronices* (1517), so called because it was written in 'macaronic Latin', as coarse as macaroni.[120] Other humanists wrote macaronic prose, producing at least two masterpieces, the *Epistolae obscurorum virorum* and the *Passavant*, a piece of anti-papal propaganda written in a truly Rabelaisian style; for example, it describes Pope Julius III taking the work of an anti-Protestant propagandist to read in the lavatory, '*et ibi cum voluisset semel suas nates abstergere cum illo, reperit vestrum stilum tam durum, quod sibi decorticavit totam Sedem Apostolicam*'.[121] Macaronic Latin was at once an object of satire, a symbol of the ignorance of the traditional clergy, and a medium of satire, close to the direct, colloquial, earthy vernacular.[122] These different types of vernacularized Latin are the inverse of the Latinized vernacular which was employed in certain circles in late medieval and early modern Europe.

Along with this interaction and interpenetration of Latin and vernacular, it is hardly surprising to find examples of switching from one to the other. Latin documents such as contracts or interrogations may suddenly slip into the vernacular when some untranslatable technical term is needed. In the case of the contract between Domenico Ghirlandaio and Giovanni Torna-buoni, for example, for paintings in the church of Santa Maria Novella in Florence, it was laid down that the paintings were to be 'as they say in the vernacular, frescoed' (*ut vulgariter dicitur, posti in frescho*).[123] Italian diocesan synods frequently slip into the vernacular to identify the popular practices which they were trying to reform; '*vulgo cicale*', '*vulgato nomine Nizzarda*', etc.[124]

The reverse process was also a common one. In both speech and writing there was a tendency to slip into Latin at certain points. Luther did this in his *Table-Talk*, and the records of the Swedish Riksdag of the seventeenth century, or indeed the English House of Commons, are also full of Latin phrases, like the following: 'As in *corruptissima republica* there may be *plurimae leges*, so it is true, as the Bishop of Winchester said today in his sermon, *ex malis moribus bonae leges oriuntur*.'[125] Interrogations by inquisitors and other ecclesiastics were generally recorded in Latin, but the answers might be recorded in the vernacular. In fifteenth-century Italy, for example, or seventeenth-century Germany, letters in the vernacular might begin or end with Latin phrases, perhaps to give the text more dignity.[126] In a similar manner, Machiavelli employed Latin for the titles of the chapters in his *The Prince*.[127] Again, the diarist Marino Sanudo regularly switched from his

Venetian vernacular to Latin terms such as *licet, etiam, tamen, tunc, succincte, in sacris*, etc., and back again.[128]

This kind of switching may have been easier for Italians than for most Europeans, but it was certainly not confined to them. Another famous diarist who has already appeared in these pages, the seventeenth-century nobleman Jan Pasek, included many Latin phrases in his vernacular text, probably because equivalents were lacking in his native Polish (we cannot be sure of the explanation until the contexts in which Latin phrases were used have received more careful and systematic study).[129]

The final question to be addressed in this essay is the one which social historians are likely to consider the most important. Who employed Latin in the ways described above? The conventional response to the question is 'the educated class', in the sense of adult male clerics, nobles, and professional men, especially in the sixteenth and seventeenth centuries. According to this conventional view, early modern Europe was divided into two cultures, an international learned culture based on Latin and a popular culture based on the local vernaculars. For a dramatic illustration of this binary opposition, we may turn to the city of Metz in January 1502, when the bishop had a comedy of Terence performed in the original Latin, and a riot ensued because the ordinary people in the audience could not understand what was going on.[130]

Even a brief essay is long enough to suggest that this conventional wisdom is inadequate.

In the first place, it is not too difficult to find examples of people without the Latin conventionally expected of them – priests, for example, as the bishops of the Counter-Reformation discovered when they visited their dioceses. Rulers did not always know Latin, thus creating complications for foreign diplomats. The Burgundian chronicler Georges Chastellain tells a story about Philip the Good failing to understand a speech made to him in Latin.[131] That some Renaissance noblemen were in the same situation is suggested by treatises such as the conduct book by Saba de Castiglione, knight of Malta, written expressly for young *cavalieri* without a knowledge of Latin.[132] Some scholars appear to have found it difficult to speak Latin. Holberg's comments on eighteenth-century Oxford have already been discussed. Even in Renaissance Italy, some famous scholars seem to have had little facility in speaking Latin. When the emperor Frederick III visited Florence in 1453, the humanist Carlo Marsuppini was unable to make the Latin oration expected of him, while a scholar of the calibre of Carlo Sigonio appears to have failed to communicate in Latin with a French visitor.[133]

The people who lacked the knowledge they should have possessed are perhaps less interesting and less surprising than the examples of people who possessed the knowledge they should (according to the conventional wisdom) have lacked. If the accounts of Oxford and Cambridge colleges were kept in Latin, this suggests that the clerks as well as the fellows understood that language. Again, European women seem to have known more Latin than they have generally been given credit for. Queen Elizabeth's skill in Latin has already been made obvious enough, and she was far from the only Renaissance lady to handle that language with competence. The Renaissance princess Isabella d'Este spoke Latin. Other ladies, such as Isotta Nogarola, wrote it with an ease and elegance which entitles them to be called 'humanists'.[134] As late as the eighteenth century a princess without scholarly pretensions, Sophia, mother of George I, spoke Latin.[135] Even low-status women might understand something. The famous Estienne family of printers spoke Latin at table in their house in Paris 'so that the very maidservants came to understand what was said and even to speak it a little'.[136] The situation in the Montaigne household must have been a similar one if the young Michel was able to grow up speaking Latin as his first language. A still more unusual case was that of the blind girl George Borrow met at Manzanares, who told him in Latin that she had been taught the language by a Jesuit.[137]

Still more surprising are cases of lower-class males who knew Latin without these upper-class contacts. A sixteenth-century Venetian shoemaker, for example, explaining his theological views to the inquisition, switched to Latin to say that 'God wants everyone to be saved' [*Deus vult omnes homines salvos fieri*].[138] Of course this case may have been exceptional. But we should remember the evidence of travellers that in East-Central Europe at least, some innkeepers and coachmen spoke Latin, or at least enough of it to communicate with Englishmen and Frenchmen. There is a geography of Latin as well as a sociology. This is the place to record a few examples of non-Europeans with Latin, from the anonymous Turk who spoke Latin to Coryate in France, to Rustam Khan who spoke Latin to François Bernier in India.[139]

There is also a chronology of Latin, and here too the conventional wisdom needs correction. Latin did not suddenly disappear at the end of the seventeenth or even the end of the eighteenth century. It was still being spoken and written in some places and in some domains in the nineteenth century and even the twentieth. Its empire may have contracted in the later seventeenth century, and if this turns out to be the case, it gives the universal language schemes of the period an added significance, an added urgency.[140] Ironically enough, however, John Wilkins's treatise *Towards a Real Character and a Philosophical Language* was itself one of the works of the period which was translated into Latin.

In any case, these universal language schemes bore little practical fruit until the late nineteenth century. Ludovic Zamenhof, for example, published the first book in Esperanto, *Internacia Linguo*, in 1887. As these two words suggest, Esperanto is virtually a simplified form of Latin, despite or because of the fact that it was devised in eastern Europe.

The conventional view of the history of Latin is that it declined because it was not adapted to the modern world, because it could not change with the times and incorporate new words for new or newly discovered phenomena.[141] I have tried to suggest that on the contrary, it is the practical uses of Latin, on which I have placed particular emphasis in this paper, which help explain why its use was so widespread and why it survived so long. It was indeed convenient for students to understand lectures in universities all over Europe, and when Latin declined, so did the custom of the 'academic tour', *peregrinatio academica*, no less important than the better-known Grand Tour. It was convenient for diplomats, travellers, and traders to have a lingua franca. Of course, these conveniences had their price. For example, the use of Latin made the gap between elite culture and popular culture wider than it might otherwise have been. It also excluded women from much of high culture. The decline of Latin in the eighteenth century is surely associated with the rise of a female reading public at much the same time and in much the same places. The sociolinguists are certainly right to stress the cumulative element in 'language shift', the extent to which particular languages spread because they are perceived to spread (since parents come to think that it would be useful for their children to learn them) and, conversely, decline because they are perceived to decline.

It would be wrong, however, to explain the rise and fall of Latin in purely practical terms. 'Latin to survive' was important, as Bassompierre's memoirs brought home to us, but there was also 'Latin to impress', a sign of distinction. Its significance in this respect is revealed, for example, in the language of quackery, especially in the advertisements for remedies such as the *Elixir Vitae*, *Aqua Celestis*, or *Pillulae Radiis Solis Extractae*.[142] One late seventeenth-century quack bill even advertised the fact that its hero, among other skills, 'speaks Latin' to 'strangers that cannot speak English'.[143] It is stretching the meaning of a technical term too far to describe the study of Latin as a 'Renaissance puberty rite', but the suggestion that it was studied in part because it both conferred and symbolized status has much to be said for it.[144]

An attraction for some, to others Latin was like a red rag to a bull. To groups like the Quakers it was 'the language of the Beast', a clear reference to the Church of Rome and a possible reference to the monopolies of the learned which Latin helped defend.[145] To educational reformers such as Christian Thomasius, Latin symbolized scholastic philosophy, or more generally 'the weight of past habits of thought'.[146] Latin was loved and hated not only for what it facilitated or made more difficult, but also for its associations, for what it symbolized.

NOTES

1   My thanks to Derek Beales, Roy Porter, Nigel Spivey, and Joe Trapp for their comments on an earlier draft of this essay.

2   J.A. Fishman, 'Language Maintenance and Language Shift', reprinted in his *Language in Sociocultural Change* (Stanford, Cal., 1972), 76–134; R.L. Cooper (ed.), *Language Spread* (New York, 1982); R. Wardhaugh, *Languages in Competition* (Oxford, 1987).

3   J.A. Fishman, 'Who Speaks What Language to Whom and When' (1965), reprinted in *Sociolinguistics*, eds J.B. Pride and J. Holmes (Harmondsworth, 1972), ch. 1.

4   C.A. Ferguson, 'Diglossia' (1959), reprinted in *Language in Social Context*, ed. P.P. Giglioli (Harmondsworth, 1972), 232–51. The relevance of the concept 'diglossia' to studies of the relation between Latin and the vernacular was pointed out by M. Tavoni, 'Sulla difesa del Latino nel '500', in *Renaissance Studies in Honor of C.H. Smyth*, ed. A. Morragh (Florence, 1985), 493–505, especially 484.

5   M. Feo, 'Tradizione latina', in *Letteratura italiana 5*, ed. A. Asor Rosa (Turin, 1986), 311–78, especially 349.

6   G. Holmes, *Florence, Rome and the Origins of the Renaissance* (Oxford, 1986), 72–3.

7   A. Meillet, *Esquisse d'une histoire de la langue latin* (Paris, 1928), is the work of a great linguist but ends long before the period discussed in this essay. M. Manitius, *Geschichte der lateinischen Literatur des Mittelalters* (3 vols, Munich, 1911–31), is a magisterial work, but concerned only with literature. There is an important cluster of studies of early medieval Latin, including F. Lot, 'A quelle époque a-t-on cessé de parler Latin?', *Bulletin Du Cange*, 6 (1931), 97–159; K. Jackson, 'On the Vulgar Latin of Roman Britain', in *Medieval Studies in Honour of J.D.M. Ford*, eds U.T. Holmes and A.J. Denomy (Cambridge, Mass., 1948), 83–106; A.S. Gratwick, 'Latinitas Britannica', in *Latin and the Vernacular Languages in Early Medieval Britain*, ed. N. Brooks (Leicester, 1982), pp. 1–79; M. Richter, 'A quelle époque a-t-on cessé de parler latin en Gaule?', *Annales ESC*, 38 (1983), 439–48.

    More general contributions include P. Lehmann, 'Vom Leben des Lateinischen im Mittelalter' (1929), in his *Erforschung des Mittelalters* (5 vols, Leipzig, 1941, vol. 1, 62–81); G. Coulton, *Europe's Apprenticeship* (London, 1940); D. Norberg, 'Latin scolaire et latin vivant', *Bulletin Du Cange*, 40 (1975–6), 51–64, discusses the relation between spoken and written Latin; D. Sheerin, 'In media latinitate', *Helios*, 14 (1987), 51–67, offers a brief general survey.

8   The only general survey of this area known to me is M. Richter, 'A Socio-linguistic Approach to the Latin Middle Ages', in *Materials, Sources and Methods of Ecclesiastical History*, ed. D. Baker (Oxford, 1975), 69–82. However, early Christian Latin has been studied from a sociolinguistic point of view by J. Schrijnen, *Charakteristik des Altchristlichen Latein* (Nijmegen, 1932), and by

his pupil C. Mohrmann, *Etudes sur le Latin des chrétiens* (2 vols, Rome, 1958–61).

9 Leo XIII, *Rerum Novarum*, ed. G. Antoniazzi (Rome, 1957); *Acta Synodalia Concilii Oecumenici Vaticani II* (28 vols, Vatican City, 1970–80).

10 G. Barletta, *Sermones* (Brescia, 1497); O. Maillard, *Sermones* (Lyons, 1498).

11 C. Mohrmann, *Liturgical Latin* (London, 1959), 12, 26.

12 More exactly, the constitution *De sacra liturgica* (1963) allowed the use of a vernacular liturgy in each diocese at the discretion of the bishop.

13 S.J. Tambiah, 'The Magical Power of Words' (1968), reprinted in his *Culture, Thought and Social Action* (Cambridge, Mass., 1985), 17–59, especially 23ff. The statements about Latin are not altogether accurate, but the comparative analysis is enlightening.

14 G.B. Gelli, *Capricci del Bottaio* (Florence, 1546), the fifth dialogue: 'Anima' is speaking; *Dialoghi*, ed. R. Tissoni (Bari, 1967), 69. On this critique, A.L. de Gaetano, *G.B. Gelli and the Florentine Academy: The Rebellion against Latin* (Florence, 1976).

15 Coulton, *Europe's Apprenticeship*, 27.

16 Erasmus, 'Paraclesis' (1516), translated in *Christian Humanism and the Reformation*, ed. J.C. Olin (New York, 1965), 92–106, especially 97.

17 V. Querini and P. Giustiniani, 'Libellus', in G.B. Mittarelli, ed., *Annales Camaldulenses* (9 vols, Venice, 1755–73), vol. 9, 681ff. Cf. E. Travi, 'Il volgare nella liturgia', in his *Lingua e vita nel primo '500* (Milan, 1984), 47–62, especially 52ff.

18 'Si quis dixerit ... lingua tantum vulgari missum celebrari debere ... anathema sit', quoted in Feo, 'Tradizione latina', 369. On the debates, L. Lentner, *Volksprache und Sakralsprache: Geschichte einer Lebensfrage bis zum Ende des Konzil von Trient* (Vienna, 1964), ch. 5, and V. Coletti, 'Il volgare al Concilio di Trento', reprinted in his *Parole dal pulpito: chiesa e movimenti religiosi tra latino e volgare* (Casale, 1983), 189–211.

19 The evidence comes from the printed *Summario* distributed to the children. On the movement, P. Grendler, 'The Schools of Christian Doctrine in Sixteenth-Century Italy', *Church History*, 53 (1984), 319–31.

20 J. Béranger, 'Latin et langues vernaculaires dans la Hongrie du 17e siècle', *Revue Historique*, 242 (1969), 5–28, esp. 14, citing the *Rituale Strigoniense* (1625).

21 *Collectio Maxima Conciliorum Omnium Hispaniae*, ed. J. Saenz (Rome, 1755), vol. 4, 235. The decree itself was in Latin. On the use of Quechua by the Church in Peru, S.B. Heath and R. Laprade, 'Castilian Colonization and Indigenous Languages', in R.L. Cooper (ed.), *Language Spread* (Bloomington, 1982), 118–43.

22 Coletti, 'Il volgare al Concilio di Trento', 218.

23 M. Venard, 'Le visite pastorali francesi dal xvi al xviii secolo', in *Le visite pastorali*, eds U. Mazzone and A. Turchini (Bologna, 1985), 13–55, especially 52.

24 J. Calvin, *Opera*, eds G. Baum, E. Cunitz and C. Reuss (Berlin and Brunswick, 1863–1900). Like others in the series 'Corpus Reformatorum', this collection was edited in Latin.

25 'Lieve God' (Dear God). Before this he had been groaning in Latin, 'O Jesu, misericordia' etc. J. Huizinga, *Erasmus of Rotterdam* (English trans. London, 1952), 187.

26 Some of Luther's vernacular works were translated into Latin, including the famous pamphlets *The Freedom of a Christian* and *The Babylonish Captivity of the Church*. For details, see M. Luther, *Werke* (63 vols, Weimar, 1883–1987), vol. 61, 101–5.

27 H. Schmidt, *Liturgie et langue vulgaire* (Rome, 1950), esp. 170.

28 For a survey with a full bibliography, see J. IJsewijn, *Companion to Neolatin Studies* (Amsterdam, 1977), 93–108. Cf. IJsewijn, 'Neolatin: a Historical Survey', *Helios*, 14 (1987).

29 Feo, 'Tradizione latina', 311–12. H.W. Klein, *Latein und volgare in Italien* (Munich, 1957), surveys attitudes to the two languages from Dante to Manzoni.

30 R. Amaseo, *De latinae linguae uso retinendi* (1529); C. Sigonio, *De latinae linguae uso retinendi* (1566); U. Foglietta, *De linguae latinae praestantia* (1574), all discussed by Tavoni, 'Sulla difesa del latino nel '500', 493–505.

31 Vissac, *De la poésie latine en France au siècle de Louis XIV* (Paris, 1862).

32 J.R. Naiden, 'Newton demands the Latin Muse', *Symposium* (1952), 111–20.

33 A. Traina, *Il latino del Pascoli* (Florence, 1971); Leo XIII, *Carmina*, ed. J. Bach (Cologne, 1903).

34 J.M. Valentin, *La théâtre des Jésuites dans les pays de langue allemande* (Bern, 1978).

35 Boccaccio trans. O. Morata (n.p., 1580); Froissart trans. J. Sleidan (Paris, 1537); Marco Polo trans. F. Pipinus (Antwerp, *c.*1485). It was this Latin version of Marco Polo which Columbus owned.

36 N. Machiavelli, *Princeps* (Basel, 1560); F. Guicciardini, *Historia sui temporis*, trans. C.S. Curione (Basel, 1566); B. Castiglione, *Aulicus* trans. J. Turler (Wittenberg, 1561), trans. B. Clerke (London, 1571), and book 1 only, trans. J. Ricius (Strasbourg, 1577).

37 A. de Guevara, *Horologium Principum*, trans. J. Wanckel (1611); M. Alemán, *Vitae humanae proscenium*, trans. G. Ens (Danzig, 1652); J. Huarte, *Scrutinium Ingeniorum*, trans. A. Major (Leipzig, 1622); P. de Commynes, *De rebus gestis Lodovici*, trans. J. Sleidan (Strasbourg, 1545); C. de Seyssel, *De republica Galliae*, trans, J. Sleidan (Strasbourg, 1562); J. Bodin, *De republica libri sex*, trans. by the author (Paris, 1586); S. Brant, *Stultifera navis*, trans. J. Locher (Basel, 1497); H. von Staden, *America* (Frankfurt, 1592); Chaucer, *Troilus and Cressida*, trans. F. Kynaston (Oxford, 1635); E. Spenser, *Calendarium pastorale*, trans. J. Dove (London, 1653).

38 A. Arnauld, *Logica* (1674); F. Bacon, *Sermones fideles* (Leiden, 1641); N. Boileau, *Namurcum expugnatum*, trans. P. de Lenglet (Paris, 1692); P. Corneille, *De victoriis Ludovici XIV*, trans. C. de la Rue (Paris, 1667); R. Descartes, *Dissertatio de methodo*, trans. E. de Courcelles (Amsterdam, 1644); G. Galilei, *Nov-antiqua doctrina*, trans. A. Diodati (Augsburg, 1636); T. Hobbes, *Leviathan* (Amsterdam, 1670); J. Locke, *De intellectu humano*, trans. E. Burridge (London, 1701); N. Malebranche, *De inquirenda veritate*, trans. by the author (Geneva, 1685); [B. Pascal], *Litterae provinciales*, trans. P. Nicole

(n.p., 1658); P. Sarpi, *Historia concilii tridentini*, trans. A. Newton (Augsburg, 1620); G. Burnet, *Historia reformationis*, trans. Mittelhorzerus (Geneva, 1689).

39   *Confucius Sinarum Philosophus*, trans. P. Couplet *et al.* (Paris, 1687).

40   Galileo explained to Paolo Gualdo on 16 June 1612 that he had written on sunspots in Italian *'perché ho bisogno che ogni persona la possi leggere'*. As a result, foreign acquaintances like Mark Welser were unable to read it. I. Del Lungo and A. Favaro, eds *Galileo Galilei dal carteggio e dai documenti*, (reprinted Florence, 1968), 133, 139–40. Cf. B. Migliorini, *Storia della lingua italiana* (Milan, 1960), 432ff.

41   M. Opitz, *Aristarchus sive de contemptu linguae teutonicae* (1617); B. Balbín, *Dissertatio apologetica* (posthumously published, Prague, 1775). To these examples could be added one still more famous, Dante's *De vulgari eloquentia*, but in this case the use of Latin had the advantage of not prejudging the issue of which kind of Italian to use.

42   H.-J. Martin, *Livre pouvoirs et société à Paris* (The Hague, 1969), 598; J. Goldfriedrich, *Geschichte des deutschen Buchhandels* (Leipzig, 1908), 69.

43   *Acta Literaria Sueciae*, 1720–39.

44   *Commentarii Academiae Scientiarum Imperialis Petropolitanae.*

45   Letter to E. de Vitry, 1726, in *Autobiographia e carteggio*, ed. B Croce and F. Nicolini (Bari, 1929), 207.

46   J.V. Delacroix, 'Lettre d'un grand amateur de la langue latine', *Spectateur Français*, 11e discours (Paris, 1770–1). I owe this reference to Dr M.-L. Pallares.

47   A.-J. Angellier, *De Joh. Keatsii vita et carminibus* (Paris, 1892); L.-J. Battifol, *De castelleto parisiensi circa 1400 annum et qua ratione criminales judicaverit* (Paris, 1896); P. Signac, *Quomodo jura dominii aucta fuerint regnante Ludovico Sexto Decimo* (Paris, 1898); C. Bouglé, *Quid e Cournoti disciplina ad scientias 'sociologicas' promovendas sumere liceat* (Paris, 1899); H. Bergson, *Quid Aristotles de loco senserit* (Paris, 1889); E.J. Renan, *De philosophia peripatetica* (Paris, 1852); C. Seignobos, *De indole plebis romanae apud Titum Livium* (Paris, 1882); and perhaps the most famous of all, E. Durkheim, *Quid Secundatus politicae scientiae instituendae contulerit* (Bordeaux, 1892).

48   Specialists in the writing of Latin dissertations could be found in some universities in the Netherlands in the nineteenth century, according to G. Bergmann, *Gedenkschriften* (Antwerp, 1988), 96ff.

49   W.J. Ong, *Ramus: Method and the Decay of Dialogue* (Cambridge, Mass., 1958), 11.

50   J.A. Comenius, *Janua linguarum* (1631): ironically enough, yet again, a critique of Latin in Latin.

51   '*Il n'y a guère que quarante ans que cette pratique est interdite dans les écoles publiques. Elle continue dans certaines écoles catholiques.*' F. Brunot, *Histoire de la langue française* (14 vols, Paris, 1917), vol. 5, 39n.

52   N. Zernov, *Eastern Christendom* (London, 1961), 148.

53   '*Saro dunque il primo … a dare un corso compito delle cose Filosofiche … in italiano.*' A. Genovesi, *Lettere familiari* (2 vols, Venice, 1775), vol. 2, 51–2.

54   E. Conte, *Accademie studentesche a Roma nel '500* (Rome, 1985), 81.

55   Ong, *Ramus: Method and the Decay of Dialogue*, 13.

56   E. Browne, *Journal*, ed. G. Keynes (Cambridge, 1923), 3–4.

57   J. Locke, *Travels in France*, ed. J. Lough (Cambridge, 1953), 50.

58   Brunot, *Histoire de la langue française*, vol. 5, 59. As his published defence shows, Delaunay was criticized for speaking in French.

59   E. Blackall, *The Emergence of German as a Literary Language* (Cambridge, 1959), 12.

60   Will of Sir Thomas Gresham (died 1579), cited in C. Hill, *Intellectual Origins of the English Revolution* (Oxford, 1965), 34–5.

61   J. Webster, *Academiarum Examen* (London, 1654). Despite the title this work is not in Latin.

62   S.E. Morison, *Harvard College in the Seventeenth Century* (Cambridge, Mass., 1936), 84.

63   Lille, Archives Departementales du Nord, B 1751, f.39, B 1766 f.188, B 1801, f.143. I owe all these references to the kindness of Robert Muchembled.

64   L. Holberg, *Memoirs* (English trans., Leiden, 1970), 43. Holberg was at Oxford 1706–8.

65   F. Hutcheson, *De naturali hominum socialitate oratio inauguralis* (Glasgow, 1730),

66   Bergmann, *Gedenk schriften*, 96–101; P. Gerbenzon, 'Gaf J.C. Naber werkelijk tot 1911 college in het Latjin?', *Legal History Review*, 55 (1987), 387–91. On the basis of student notes Gerbenzon concludes that Naber was lecturing in Dutch in 1888–9, but he did use Latin on other occasions. I owe these two references – and xerox copies of the texts – to the kindness of Rudolf Dekker.

67   Quoted in R. Wines's introduction to L. von Ranke, *The Secret of World History* (New York, 1981), 106.

68   Lord Moran in *The Lancet* (1954) 167, quoted in C. Newman, *The Evolution of Medical Education in the Nineteenth Century* (London, 1957), 50–1; I should like to thank Roy Porter for this reference.

69   J. Buchan, *Prester John* (London, 1910), ch. 12.

70   V.H.H. Green, *The Commonwealth of Lincoln College* (Oxford, 1979), 492.

71   Lord Clarendon, *History*, ed. W.D. Macray (6 vols, Oxford, 1888), vol. 2, 296.

72   F.-A. Isambert, *Recueil général des anciennes lois françaises* (29 vols, Paris, 1827–33), vol. 12, 592ff.

73   E.g. by John Jones in 1650, quoted by Hill, *Intellectual Origins of the English Revolution*, 261.

74   G. Cozzi, ed., *Stato, società e giustizia nella repubblica veneta* (Rome, 1980), 74ff.

75   C. Ginzburg, *Il formaggio e i vermi* (Turin, 1976), 12. Curiously enough, Alessandro Manzoni makes his hero, the peasant Renzo, utter similar sentiments in his novel *I promessi sposi*, ch. 2.

76   Feo, 'Tradizione latina', 372.

77   H. Walpole, *Reminiscences*, ed. P. Toynbee (Oxford, 1924), 14–15. R. Hatton, *George I* (London, 1978), 129ff, claims that the king did know some English.

78   Béranger, 'Latin et langues vernaculaires dans la Hongrie du 17e siècle', 5–28.

79   Princes were not alone in their need for Latin secretaries. Archbishop Parker

of Canterbury employed J. Joscelyn in this capacity from 1558 onwards (see *Dictionary of National Biography*, under 'Joscelyn').

80   G.E. Waas, *The Legendary Character of the Emperor Maximilian* (New York, 1941), 34.

81   J. Stow, *The Annales of England* (London, 1601), 1299ff, gives a tactful account of the incident.

82   *'Legatus illum sermone italico aggressus est ... Rex haec verba Latino sermone excepit, atque inde Latiné perpetuo collocuti sunt.'* C. Ogier, *Ephemerides* (posthumously published, Paris, 1656), 52.

83   Ibid., 148, 150.

84   G. Downing to secretary Thurloe, 1655, in *Thurloe Papers*, ed. J. Birch (7 vols, London, 1742), vol. 3, 734.

85   *Tractatus Pacis inter Hispaniam et Unitum Belgium Monasterii* (Leiden, 1651). To see how long Britain continued to use Latin for international treaties, one has only to look at T. Rymer's *Foedera* (20 vols, London, 1704–32).

86   N. Ahnlund, 'Diplomatiens språk i Sverige', in his *Svenskt och Nordiskt* (Stockholm, 1943), 114–22, especially 116.

87   B. Whitelocke, *A Journal of the Swedish Embassy* (2 vols, London, 1855), vol. 1, 300.

88   Brunot, *Histoire de la langue française*, 402ff.

89   Ibid., 411ff.

90   T. Westrin, 'Några iakttagelser angående franskan såsom diplomatiens språk', *Historisk Tidskrift*, 20 (1900), 329–40, especially 336, 338–9.

91   L. Le Laboureur, *Avantages de la langue française sur la langue Latine* (Paris, 1667); F. Charpentier, *Défense de la langue française* (Paris, 1676); cf. Brunot, *Histoire de la langue française*, 16–23; B. Magne, *Crise de la littérature française* (2 vols, Paris, 1976), 404ff, 483ff; and B. Beugnot, 'Débats autour du Latin dans la France classique', in *Acta Conventus Neo-Latini Amstelodamensis*, eds P. Tuynman, G.C. Kuiper and E. Kessler (Munich, 1979), 93–106.

92   See, for example, Voltaire, *Correspondance*, ed. T. Besterman, vols 9–10 (Geneva, 1970), nos 2874, 3423 (both addressed to Germans).

93   J. Lough, *France Observed in the Seventeenth Century* (Stocksfield, 1984), 11, 12, 165, 198; G. Courthop, *Memoirs*, ed. S.C. Lomas (London, 1907), 107; Locke, *Travels in France*, 6.

94   J. Boswell, *Life of Johnson*, ed. G.B. Hill (revised edn, 6 vols, Oxford, 1934), vol. 2, 404.

95   J. Evelyn, *Diary*, ed. E.S. De Beer (6 vols, Oxford, 1955), vol. 3, 171, 288.

96   Boswell, *Life of Johnson*, vol. 2, 125, 404, 406.

97   H. Belloc, *The Path to Rome* (London, 1902), 372. My thanks to my Emmanuel colleague Nigel Spivey for this reference.

98   P. Sidney, *Miscellaneous Prose* (Oxford, 1973), 171.

99   C. Markham, ed., *Narratives* (London, 1895), 341–2.

100   L. Cimber and F. Danjou, eds, *Archives curieuses*, 1re série (15 vols, Paris, 1834–40), vol. 5, 142.

101   J. Pasek, *Pamietniki* (Cracow, 1929).

102   Louis de Rouvroy, duc de St-Simon, *Mémoires*, ed. Y. Coirault (Paris, 1983), vol. 1, 406.

103   *Archivum Domus Sapiehanae*, ed. A. Prochaska (Lwów, 1892),

104   I. Kajanto, 'The Position of Latin in Eighteenth-Century Finland', in *Acta Conventus Neo-Latini Amstelodamensis*, eds Tuynman *et al.*, 93–106.

105   The Marquis of Dufferin, *Letters from High Latitudes* (11th edn, London, 1903), 22, 39; a reference I owe to Joe Trapp.

106   Examples in E. Veres, ed., *Báthory István Levelezése* (2 vols, Kolozsvár, 1944). On the deficiencies of the Hungarian nobleman Adám Batthyány's Latin letters to the Kriegshofrat in Vienna, see R.J.W. Evans, *The Making of the Habsburg Monarchy* (Oxford, 1979), 259.

107   E. Browne, *A Brief Account of Some Travels* (London, 1673; reprinted Munich, 1975), 13–14.

108   F. de Bassompierre, *Mémoires* (Cologne, 1665), 88.

109   Montaigne, *Essais*, 1.26, 3.2.

110   Coulton, *Europe's Apprenticeship*, 15.

111   Details on the drafting in Leo XIII, *Rerum Novarum*, ed. Antoniazzi, introduction.

112   L. Spitzer, 'The Problem of Latin Renaissance Poetry', reprinted in his *Romanische Literaturstudien* (Tübingen, 1959), 923–44.

113   On the lack of abstractions in Polish, C. Backvis, *Quelques remarques sur la bilinguisme Latino-polonais dans la Pologne du 16e siècle*, (Brussels, 1958); on French, L. Febvre, *Le problème de l'incroyance* (Paris, 1942), 384ff. On the Latinization of the vernacular, F.R. Johnson, 'Latin versus English: The Sixteenth-Century Debate over scientific Terminology', *Studies in Philology*, 41 (1944), 109–35.

114   Quoted in Brunot, *Histoire de la langue française*, 390n.

115   S. Bochart, *Opera* (Leiden, 1692), 3.

116   Evelyn, *Diary*, vol. 3, 288; cf. Lauder, quoted in Lough, *France Observed in the Seventeenth Century*, 12.

117   S. Rizzo, 'Il latino nell'umanesimo', *Letteratura italiana 5*, ed. Rosa, 379.

118   The translation of Ignatius was the work of the humanist-trained Jesuit André des Freux. See I. de Loyola, *Obras Completas*, ed. I. Iparraguirre (Madrid, 1963), 186. On the Psalter, C. Mohrmann, 'The New Latin Psalter', in her *Etudes sur le latin des chrétiens* (2 vols, Rome, 1956), vol. 2, 109–31.

119   I take these examples from the introduction to S. Infessura, *Diario*, ed. O. Tommasini (Rome, 1890), xvii.

120   U.E. Paoli, *Il latino maccheronico* (Florence, 1959).

121   T. Beza, *Epistola Magistri Benedicti Passavant* (1554; ed. I. Lisieux, Paris, 1875), vol. ii, 37.

122   A good discussion of the ambiguities of '*Zweisprachigkeit*' in this context in G. Hess, *Deutsch-Lateinisch Narrenzunft* (Munich, 1971).

123   G. Milanesi, ed., *Nuovi documenti per la storia dell'arte toscana* (Florence, 1901), 134ff.

124   C. Corrain and P.L. Zampini, *Documenti etnografici e folkloristici nei sinodi diocesani italiani* (Bologna, 1970), 43n, 235, etc.

125   B. Stolt, *Die Sprachmischung in Luthers Tischreden* (Stockholm, 1964), compares Luther's practice with the Riksdag's; *Commons Debates 1621*, ed. W. Notestein (7 vols, New Haven, Conn., 1935), vol. 2, 5–6.

126   Migliorini, *Storia della lingua italiana*, 246; A. Wallenstein, *Briefe*, ed. H. Hall-wich (Vienna, 1912).
127   F. Chiappelli, *Nuovi studi sul linguaggio del Machiavelli* (Florence, 1969), 24ff.
128   All these examples from the first page of M. Sanudo, *Diarii* (58 vols, Venice, 1879–1903).
129   Pasek, *Pamietniki*. On the first page alone there are six Latin phrases, *ex commiseratione, ab antiquo, innatum odium, in vicinitate, oppressit, per amorem gentis nostrae*. On this practice, see Backvis, 'Quelques remarques sur la bilinguisme Latino-polonais dans la Pologne du 16e siècle.'
130   P. de Vigneulles, *Chronique*, ed. C. Bruneau (4 vols, Metz, 1927–33), vol. 4, 15.
131   G. Chastellain, *Chronique*, ed. L. de Lettenhove (Brussels, 1863), 66.
132   Saba da Castiglione, *Ricordi* (Venice, 1554).
133   On Marsuppini, see Vespasiano da Bisticci, *Vite*, ed. A Greco (2 vols, Florence, 1970–6), vol. 1, 519; on Sigonio, see J.A. Thou, *Mémoires* (Paris, 1838), 280.
134   A. Grafton and L. Jardine, *From Humanism to the Humanities* (London, 1986), ch. 2.
135   Walpole, *Reminiscences*, 121.
136   According to Henri Estienne, quoted in E. Armstrong, *Robert Estienne, Royal Printer* (Cambridge, 1954), 15–16.
137   G. Borrow, *The Bible in Spain* (1843), ch. 45; ed. U.R. Burke (2 vols, London, 1896), vol. 2, 216. I am grateful to Nigel Spivey for this reference.
138   R. Mackenney, *Tradesmen and Traders* (London, 1987), 184.
139   T. Morison, 'Un français à la cour du grand Mogol', *Revue historique*, 156 (1927), 88.
140   On these schemes see J. Knowlson, *Universal Language Schemes in England and France 1600–1800* (Toronto, 1975); M.M. Slaughter, *Universal Languages and Scientific Taxonomy in the Seventeenth Century* (Cambridge, 1982).
141   For an example of this type of criticism, see M.M. Slaughter, *Universal Languages and Scientific Taxonomy in the Seventeenth Century* (Cambridge, 1982), 73–4.
142   R. Porter, 'The Language of Quackery in England', in *The Social History of Language*, eds P. Burke and R. Porter (Cambridge, 1987), 73–103, especially 89.
143   The address 'At the Sign of the Moon and Stars in Leopard's Court in Baldwins Garden near Holborn'. My thanks to Roy Porter for this reference.
144   W.J. Ong, 'Latin Language Study as a Renaissance Puberty Rite', *Studies in Philology*, 56 (1959), 103–24.
145   R.F. Jones, *The Triumph of the English Language* (Oxford, 1953), 314.
146   Blackall, *The Emergence of German as a Literary Language*, 13.

2

The Uses of Hebrew in the English Revolution

NIGEL SMITH

The dissemination of Hebrew in England and Europe is an early modern phenomenon. Renaissance scholars revived the study of ancient Hebrew texts, immersing themselves also in the commentaries of medieval rabbis, and the theology of the Reformation encouraged the study of scripture in its original languages, Greek and Hebrew. While reformed religion was transmitted largely in Latin and the vernaculars, the imperative to return to the original scriptural languages would always mean that those originals at least left their traces in the vernaculars. The great tradition of sixteenth-century psalm translation is one example of a body of Hebrew literature finding its way, usually via Latin, into the devotional language of English people.

The history of attitudes towards the Jews and Judaism in early modern England has received a good deal of attention recently, but the history of Hebrew in England, especially as it affected the English language, is very largely unwritten. In this essay, I would like to open up this field of inquiry for further research by exploring a specific context – the uses of Hebrew and the Hebraic in the religious culture and politics of Interregnum England. To do this, one needs more than a single approach. It is necessary first of all to be able to identify a Hebraic linguistic or literary form inhabiting English speech or writing. Such patterns have been detected in the sermons of learned divines, like the Jacobean bishop Lancelot Andrewes. But during the course of the seventeenth century, the learning of Hebrew ceased to be the preserve of academics and the clergy. In the 1640s and the 1650s, there was a popularizing of the study of Hebrew, encouraged by the expectation that the Jews might return to England, as a prelude to the second coming of Christ. In these circumstances, the study of Hebrew, and the incorporation of the Hebrew language into speech and writing, became a political issue, in which different and competing or opposed groups and individuals struggled over the interpretation of divine truths, as they were manifested in Hebrew, and as they could be spoken or printed in the public exchange of discourse as Hebraicized English. The violent confrontation between the Fifth Monarch-ists and the Protectorate government was informed by differing interpreta-tions of Old Trestament prophecies. From the interpretations came entirely different imaginative visions of the nature of society and history, and correspondingly different kinds of discourse. As we shall see, a use of Hebrew did not necessarily have to be correct – correctness simply became another issue of debate in the language politics of the millennium. What we can see is a dynamic process in which the 'downwards' dissemination of an ancient language caused new versions and applications of the vernacular to occur. At a time when accepted forms of religious and political authority had been destabilized, and in some cases removed, the assimilation of Hebrew by lay people was a means of locating themselves with certainty in God's scheme. For the more conservative, such kinds of 'Judaizing' were danger-ous and irrational forms of religious and political behaviour, to be expunged.

A significant starting place would be to recall the recommendation of the founding General Baptist, John Smyth, that preaching and prayer in services of worship should, where appropriate, be in the original scriptural languages, Hebrew and Greek, and from memory.[1] Hebrew had been taught, of course, in the universities since the early sixteenth century, and its significance for the recovery of knowledge, the *prisca theologia* even, had been stressed by humanists from Ficino to Erasmus and Reuchlin.[2] We tend to forget the prevalence of the learning of Hebrew: the younger Samuel Jeake, born into a godly household in the mid-seventeenth century, began to learn Hebrew when he was only thirteen years old.[3] The ministers of the early separatist or Nonconformist churches were often very learned, and, as in Smyth's case, compelled by their own knowledge of the original scriptural languages to separate from the worldly and redesign ecclesiology. But many, if not most, early sectarians were not learned. If the records left by the Broadmead Baptist church in Bristol are evidence, the members were artisanal or small merchants, and shopkeepers.[4] They may well have been literate, but on the whole they were not learned. Even here, however, one should never underestimate popular autodidacticism. Samuel Hartlib noted with interest that 'Jackson the Grocer hath learn't to write Arabick and hath an excellent dexterity in it. His Brother is a Stationer, and they intend to cause all the

Alcoran to bee graven and so printed which will exceed all that hath ever beene done.'[5]

One factor which made the early Nonconformist churches so exciting for their members and finally so resilient was that very meeting of trained and learned clergy with this largely urban 'middling sort'. But we know little about the consequences upon these groups of their own scriptural fundamentalism. We do not know how fully it was possible to carry out Smyth's original recommendation, and to what extent the speaking of Hebrew in meetings of the church which followed his lead took place. We might justifiably suspect little speaking of the Hebrew in this way, evidenced by the rise of 'mechanick preachers' like Samuel How, whose influential *The Sufficiencie of the Spirits Teaching* (1st edn, 1640) maintained that the possibility of immediate personal access to the Holy Spirit made a trained and institutionalized ministry superfluous, and any language a fit medium for the spirit's teaching.[6] Greek rather than Hebrew was the original language discussed in Peter Chamberlen's Baptist church in Lothbury Square.[7] Even then, 'the letter killeth, but the spirit giveth life', said the Fifth Monarchist sympathizer William Aspinwall in 1654, replicating St Paul's words at 2 Cor. 3:6.[8]

Yet at the same time, and notably after 1640, there was a considerable rise in the possibility and popularity of learning Hebrew, both for personal and collective (or congregational) reasons. While some publications continued the earlier European tradition of using Hebraic and Arabic literature to produce a better understanding of the scripture itself, the study of Hebrew also became an ideological issue, since a greater dissemination of such knowledge would, it was hoped, further the possibilities for final reformation, once the Bishops had been removed, and perhaps also hasten the conditions favourable for the second coming of Christ.[9] In 1647, Parliament directed funds towards the purchase of a collection of Hebraic literature from Italy, the buying to be done by the bookseller George Thomason under the direction of the eminent lawyer, Parliamentarian and Hebraist John Selden.[10] By the late 1640s, the German academic and increasingly celebrated Hebraist, Christian Raue or Ravius, whose family had previously converted to Christianity from Judaism, was in London, giving public lectures on the benefits of learning Hebrew, going under the title of 'professor' of Hebrew, and talking enthusiastically to the Hartlib circle about his plans to set up a Hebrew academy.[11] In the 1650s, the Scottish academic William Robertson was resident in London, and busy publishing Hebrew dictionaries, grammars, and commentaries on popular Hebrew texts, like the Psalms and the Lamentations of Jeremiah.[12]

The fashion was soon the object of satire. A jesting pamphlet which featured Prince Rupert's dog Boy as its subject claimed that the dog spoke

Hebrew, or a mixture of Hebrew and High-Dutch, 'most probably the language of the Beasts before the curse'.[13] Here, the views of the Flemish linguistician, Goropius, that Dutch was descended from Hebrew, were being ridiculed, but there are also overtones of Dutch religious (that is, Puritan) fervour. In explicitly Royalist literature, Hebrew is a sign of Puritan prejudice, irrationality and ignorance, instanced in this mock triumphal entry of the Earl of Pembroke and Puritan ministers into a recently defeated Royalist Oxford:

Next came a Tribe of *Hebrews* on full speed,
As if they'd make this place *Sion* indeed;
Zachary, Joel, Eleazar, Ben,
Obadiah, Daniel, all *Guifted* men:
And 'twas disputed deeply as they came
If *Philip* too were not an *Hebrew* Name?
At which my Lord being mov'd began to belch,
And swore (by God) 'twas better, for't was *Welch*
But *Michael Holdsworth* reconcil'd their Tales,
And said the *Hebrew* Tongue came all from *Wales*.[14]

While this stereotype is of course an exaggeration, radical Puritan ministers made use of the work of Hebraists like Raue and Robertson. The Particular Baptist Hanserd Knollys wrote a brief Hebrew grammar, derived from Raue's works, and in English, specifically for those who knew no Latin.[15] John Rogers, Independent and Fifth Monarchist, seems to have used Robertson's commentaries on Psalms and Lamentations while imprisoned on the Isle of Wight.

Knollys made the specific point that he was attempting to aid those co-religionists who did not have the skills in languages to be able to learn the original Hebrew. In other words, to be able to learn Hebrew, one usually had to know Latin first; but the publication of the first vernacular Hebrew grammars changed this. It made available to those who were autodidactically inclined the material for teaching themselves Hebrew.[16] Moreover, the Jacobean separatist Henry Ainsworth produced a series of English commentaries on Old Testament texts which were respected by scholars from various denominations. Similar commentaries were written and published during the 1640s and 1650s. John Robotham's *An Exposition of the whole book of Solomons Song* (1651) is a popular example, and typical in its dedication to a prominent Commonwealth figure, Colonel Downes, Deputy Lieutenant of Sussex and member of Parliament. Any reader sees immediately the significance of knowing Hebrew:

The Pronoun (*Ani*) which signifieth in our tongue *I*, is common both to man or woman; as I man, or I woman, so it cannot be decided by the forme of Speech, whether Christ or his Church uttered these words: hence it is thought by some to be the speech of Christ: Of others, to be spoken by the Church. (254)

Ainsworth himself used rabbinic commentaries and the work of humanist scholars on Hebrew, and his example was specifically followed by the Fifth Monarchist sympathiser William Aspinwall when encouraging a popular insurrection against the Cromwellian Protectorate.[17]

Under the widespread assumption that Hebrew did indeed contain higher truths, it was possible for individuals to gain access to them through their own self-taught knowledge of Hebrew. Once this lay control of Hebrew knowledge had been established, there were two further consequences. First, while unlearned men or women could teach themselves Hebrew correctly, they could also educate themselves incorrectly or partially, and then use that incorrect or incomplete knowledge in their own practice, written or otherwise. Second, where a knowledge of the Hebrew was not being used directly to interpret the Old Testament, or rabbinic commentaries, or even the kabbalah, it could be put to other uses, in which case it did not matter whether it was correct or not.

As I have already said, these uses should be classified as ideological: Hebrew or the Hebraic became a means of imagining a converted or perfected self, or a reformed society, in which the traces of the chosen Ancient Israelites were reborn in the New Men (or 'late converted Jews') of Interregnum England. Moreover, the ideological was seen to reside as much in the nature of the language itself, as in that which was the 'content' of the words. For instance, Alexander Ross recounted how the letters which spelt the word for Eve, חוה, stood for three respective things: 'the first letter stands for *Challah*, [חלה] that is, a Cake; the second for *Teses*, that is, in the Rabbin's Dialect, *the menstrual issues of women*; and third for *Hadlacha*, that is, *the lighting of the candles*.[18] The first and third significations were required activities by women in religious services: not to honour them would, like not honouring the requirement for menstruation, be regarded as a sin. So English men and women had a clearer access to that sexual ideology in the Old Testament which was so domestically precise.

The Interregnum Hebraists certainly did not intend Hebrew simply to be limited to the study of the Bible, even if this was to be its primary usage. Raue, for instance, recommends Hebrew as a useful language when trading.[19] Did he have in mind English merchants who had dealings with Jewish communities in Holland or Italy, or further afield in the Middle East?[20] For Raue also, the word formation system of Hebrew had much to recommend it for utilitarian reasons:

all the compound significations of any simple word in these languages
must also be comprised in that simple *Ebrew* root . . . all the compound
words . . . have still this simple word as that *unum tertium*, a naturall
needing in that word, whereby all the compound words being joyned as
in the body, so in the essence and substance of signification with some
small alteration, addition or detraction, of and arte that simple and first
substance.[21]

Such a movement towards simplicity also exemplified the notion of Hebrew
as the least corrupt language, which holds the promise of attaining
something like Edenic perfection. Throughout his tract, Raue praises
reason, and regards it as the unifying faculty behind all languages. His
perceptions were to be the stuff of what might be called sectarian linguistic
utopianism: Hebrew 'makes us (when by the *Greec* and *Latine* we were
become beasts, by α' υζὸς ἒϕα *so tels me my Master Adam*) to become *Adam*
our selves; to be no more under the law but under the sweet yoke of
reason'.[22]

All the oriental languages become one common language for Raue –
Hebrew, Chaldean, Syrian, Ethiopian and Arabic.[23] Raue's use of body
analogy makes use of a cognate metaphor prevalent in Puritan ways of
imagining church government:

This signification having the nature of the soule of the body, which
consists of the matter and forme, cannot be but only one, because the
body being one, cannot have more soules to dwell within it, and one
soule cannot dwel in two bodies; yea that one soule is able and active
enough to doe and performe many thousand actions by and in this
body; so this signification is able to be active and extending it selfe into
many matters and occasions, and shewes its vertues still the same, and
tending to the same effects, only proportionable, according to the
matter, and with a consent.[24]

Whatever the theoretical intentions, in practice the acquisition of Hebrew
was a means of enhancing the visionary nature of religious life in the sects.
To step into a language approximating to the original language of Adam was
to enter a new and higher, or more divine, state of being. As much as
anything else, the different graphical appearance of the language, and the
unfamiliar but awesome sounds, held a fascination for early modern English
people. Hebrew already had its place in the language of spells and magic.[25]
In a sense, it did not matter how much was understood. What did matter to
the gifted enthusiast or self-proclaimed prophet was the need to increase
personal inspired authority by enunciating strange sounds.

Independents and Baptists seem to have used Hebrew originals and translations from them in order to control their own interpretation of the text, and to enter into a literal understanding of Hebraic identity and meaning, as represented in the language. There is nothing unusual about the use of originals in Reformed scholarship and preaching, but the radical usage constituted new departures in some cases.[26] Hanserd Knollys's *An Exposition of the First Chapter of the Song of Solomon* (1656) is an example of the less extreme tendency:

> *Sitteth at his table* [עד שהמלך במסבו], *While the King was in his Round*, This manner of speaking alludeth unto the *Jewish* Form of sitting at the Table, the *Hebrews* were wont to sit round about the Table at their Feasts, in a Circumference or Circle, 1 Sam. [16:11] [כי לא נסב עד באו פה] For as well not Round [the Table] till he come hither. 56)

The King James Bible (1611; AV) signifies in its margin at 1 Sam. 16:11 that 'downe' is standing for Hebrew 'round', but Knollys has in fact gone further and made his own translation. Such an attitude could also result in an evocation of the original (often transliterated) in order to stress super-rational qualities. In the following instance, John Rogers, Independent minister and Fifth Monarchist activist, raises the sense of absolute and violent divine justice in Haggai's prophecy. He keeps that sense, although he transliterates with many errors:[27]

> Seeing all these **Shakings** [?and] *Concussions* are to that end, *Hag.* 2:6. (Veani Mar ע ish) *I making them to TREMBLE*, Ver. 7 (Ve hir ע ashsheth) *and I will make them TREMBLE* (with commotions and troubles) which (Cheneddat Col Hoggojin) the *Desire*, the Delight, *the* **Beauty** *of all nations come.*[28]

While an opponent like James Harrington used the Fifth Monarchist's shaky Hebrew as ammunition against the group, how many other readers were so observant?

Rogers's publications customarily had Hebrew titles. For instance, his long work of 1653, setting out in enormous detail a Congregational church discipline, was entitled [אהל] *Ohel or Beth-shemesh. A Tabernacle for the Sun.* While this church discipline depends upon the Greek of the New Testament for its elaboration, Hebrew titles and words are used to frame interpretation and to invoke the Hebraic 'reality', as a kind of typological shadow to the New Testament reality. However, Rogers's Hebraisms seem to make the gap so necessary to typological interpretation disappear. The presence of Hebrew words predominates over the presence of Christian symbols. *Ohel* means 'tabernacle', from which derives the verb *ahal*: 'he fixed his tent, he dwelt and did inhabit', while *beth-shemesh* means 'house of the sun'. Who is the sun here? God, Christ, or the Spirit? In the Hebrew, there is a reference here back to the character of the author and minister of the Dublin church around whom the volume emerged, John Rogers, even though the ostensible reference is to an aspect of the divine. This is significant because of the tendency among Rogers's congregation to identify him subliminally as saviour.[29] Rogers's source text is Psalm 19:4 (falsely represented as Psalm 45:1 – another compositorial error or a characteristic transposition by Rogers), quoted in Hebrew to mean 'in them a tabernacle of the sun' on the title page and adumbrated 'To the Sun in altissmo gradu'. The volume by its Hebrew significations is seeking to elevate, almost to make luminous, the members of the Dublin church: 'to *ratifie the Churches* in their *Segregation* and *Aggregation*, so to raise them up *higher* from *Tents* to *Tabernacles*'.[30]

In effect, the use of the transposition from the verb to the noun ensures that process of imagistic glorification in naming. The function of the Hebraic imagery is to present the glorified church in symbolic form, to find an elevated language in which to describe the elect community of saints. To this end Knollys connects the Pauline phrase for the church with the last verse of the first chapter of the Song of Solomon: 'those particular Assemblies of believers, gathered in the Order of the Gospel, called the Churches of Saints, 1 Cor. 14.33. The text is [קרותבתינו] *The Beams of our Houses*, that is to say, the Churches of God', a figure which returns successively in John Rogers's own dream account of his conversion.[31] The effect is very much the same as that of the Neoplatonic imagery used by some of the other Puritans, usually radicals, at least Independents. But this is not just a question of imagery. It is important to remember that the language functions as a means of magnifying individuals, of attributing to them forms of agency. The role and efficacy of the saints are identified by their Hebrew naming. Thus a prefatory poem to *Ohel*, by 'H.W.' (probably Henry Walker) makes Rogers himself a taper. The incandescent language confirms Rogers's charismatic status:

הַשֶּׁמֶשׁ צְרֵקָה לְךָ בֶנָּה בְּהִירָה

כִּיד זְרְיחָלְחַב בְּמֵּךְ לָחַם אוֹרַח

וּפְאֶהֲלוֹ יְנֵי רְגְרֵם אַתָּה דוּוֹלֵשׁ

גֵרֶךְ לְקְרוֹשִׁים בַּאֲשֶׁר הוּא גוֹרְלֶךְ נֶמֶשׁ

חִנְדִי וּןאַלְקַר

The *Sun* of *Righteousness* on thee hath *shined bright*;
The *sparkles* of that *flame* in thee, have *kindled light*:
And in his *Tabernacle*, *John Rogers*, thou do'st waste
Thy *Tapor* for the *Saints*, where he thy lot hath plac'd.[32]

When *Ohel, or Beth-shemesh* was published, Rogers was not yet openly associated with the Fifth Monarchist movement, that loose association of Independents and Baptists whose demands for social and legal reforms were directly connected to the expectation of the Second Coming. They were influential in the Barebones Parliament and the committees of the pre-Protectorate Republican government. It was the emergence of Cromwell as Protector which fuelled their ire, and which provoked their intimidation and suppression by the government, including the arrest of the leaders. Their social vision and attitudes towards government were in some cases based upon an entirely autonomous translation of the Old Testament, in a manner which is consistent with the habits of Knollys and Rogers.

In *An Explication and Application Of the Seventh Chapter of Daniel* (1654), for instance, William Aspinwall is aware of the special semantics of Hebrew, that it is often untranslatable (so that one has to 'intuit' its meaning), and that single words often have various interpretations, a factor which is directly connected to prophecy: 'whence it comes to pass, that a perfect, and full application cannot well be made of such Predictions, untill the Prophecies be accomplished' (A2v).[33] Aspinwall proceeds to disagree with Geneva and AV, and produces a translation of Dan. 7 which defines the experience of inspiration through divinely implanted vision (Old Testament and contemporary prophecy were crucial to Fifth Monarchist politics) as a rational, well-ordered and contemplative activity, as opposed to frenzied enthusiasm, and, perhaps more significantly, outlines a vision of absolutist political power, both the tyranny of the Stuart monarchs, and the absolute perfection of Christ's coming kingdom in which the elite of saints rule. Substantial quantities of syntax are reordered to produce a very different 'English' Bible, more faithful to the Hebrew sense, in Aspinwall's opinion:

> This little horn is called another, not in number, but in form, because it is differenced from the former Vers. 24. And whereas he saith, three were plucked up by the roots מִן־קְדָמַהּ, I render the words by his prioritie. Indeed our translators do invert the order of the words, and read them thus, *Before whom three of the first Horns were plucked up by the root*; and had the words been so placed and pointed in the Original, the word קְדָמַהּ might have been so rendred well enough: But considering the order of the words in the Original, and the distinguishing accents preceding, and the propriety of the word קְדָמַהּ (which may as well be rendered *a priori ejus, vel a prioritate ejus*, as *a conspectu ejus*) I thinke it safer to translate it, as I have done, then to follow the Translation of the Bible, which doth not only invert the order of the word, but obscure the sense.[34]

'Priority' is the absolute right of Charles I (the fourth monarch), just as the fourth monarchy is in Dan. 7:26 deprived not of its 'dominion' (AV) but of its 'Sultan-like power, שְׁטַנְהוֹן their Absolute Sovereignty'.[35] When the translation becomes too difficult, Aspinwall falls back upon the most appropriate contemporary English context to construct a meaning:

> Which concise forme of speech is peculiar only to the Pen-men of Scripture, and cannot be expressed in any other languages, save those Easterne Tongues. And the word importeth as much, as if you should say, three of the former Horns were plucked up by his Prerogative, but one above the rest. Now what are the roots of a Nation? I answer, the Roots of a Nation are chiefly these two, Religion, and the Peoples Liberties and Civil Rights.[36]

Aspinwall is positing himself as a serious Hebraist, something which most Fifth Monarchists could not have done, and indeed the latter half of *An Explication* moves away from the question of Hebrew translation in order to accommodate his version to the immediate political context. Even so, Fifth Monarchist radicalism is here involved with a different translation of the Old Testament, which is spoken forth and published as a newly discovered political vision of millennial England.

The extent to which Rogers and Aspinwall knew Hebrew is another matter. Knollys seems to have known it, but while Rogers certainly knew Greek and Latin, and was very widely read, there are hints elsewhere in his writing that he was not as self-sufficient or expert as might at first appear to be the case. For instance, *Jegar-Sahadvtha: An Oyled Pillar* (1657), written against all forms of persecution and institutional corruption in the state, when Rogers was imprisoned at Carisbrooke Castle, reveals a reliance upon Robertson's published commentaries on the Psalms and Lamentations.[37] To all intents and purposes, Rogers establishes his own English translation of Lam. 4:3, his own authentic language of prophetic denunciation, so to speak, though his definitions can be found largely in Robertson's *A Key to the Hebrew Bible* (1656): 'The very Sea-Monster (or תַּנִּין Tannin the Old Serpent) drawn out the Breast they suckle their young ones (or Protected ones from the root גוּר gur, he sojourned with or dwelt under) the daughter of my people to a cruell one, as the Ostrich in the Wildernesse.'[38] The definitions here, for instance, will be found in Robertson's *A Key to the Hebrew Bible* (1656), 111. But Rogers's quotation on the same page of Gen. 31:36–7 seems to follow the AV. Could he not translate what was not in the vernacular grammars and lexicons of the Hebraists, or did he simply not bother to translate himself from the original when he did not disagree with AV, or when the material involved was not relevant?

For Rogers such utterances have the status of authentic prophecy, his *'Prison-Threnodies'*, and they often involve a significant gap between the

Hebrew meaning which obviously interests Rogers, and the English render-
ings he gives.[39] *Sagrir. Or Doomes-day drawing nigh. With Thunder and
Lightening to Lawyers* (1653) has a Hebrew word for the first word of the title,
and a transliteration of it for the second. In fact, the Hebrew (Prov. 27:15)
should translate as 'persistent rain', which is meant to stand as an imagistic
evocation, in Hebraic terms, of doomsday itself, although the reference in
Proverbs ('A continual dropping in a very rainy day and a contentious woman
are alike') contains no reference to doomsday itself. *Jegar-Sahadvtha* (1657)
was written from prison. Either Rogers had a Hebrew Bible with him, or he
had an astonishingly good memory.

In most cases, when he quotes Hebrew, he does so in order to provide a
different English translation from AV (and the Geneva version), and also
often provides the Greek Septuagint version of the Old Testament too:

Therefore *Isa.* 59.4. אֵי זֹ־קְרָא בְצֶדֶק וְאֵין נִשְׁפָּט בֶּאֱמוּנָה׳ There
is *none that passeth his word for righteousness*; nor is there any judgement
for the *Truth*: O sad! oΓρ.αψψεντθΓρ.αψψεντεῖς λαλεῖ δίλαια
what, not one?[40]

Geneva: No man calleth for justice: no man contendeth for truth.

AV: None calleth for justice, nor any pleadeth for truth.

The Hebrew itself is a parallelism, and Rogers's English represents the first
half in italic and the second half in roman type to emphasize this, so that its
rhetorical structure becomes directly transferred to the English. But the
picture is complicated by other instances. On p. 38 of *Jegar-Sahadvtha*
Rogers discusses the power of dream interpretation, including his own. One
part of the discourse focuses upon Dan. 5:12, 'to dissolve all doubts'. Rogers
claims that the Hebrew really means 'To *loose knots* ... פְּשַׁר וּל פְּש or
open *aenigmatical* Scriptures and Cases'. However, no Hebrew original exists
for this part of Daniel – the original is in Aramaic. Moreover, the Aramaic
does not mean 'to loose knots', but to 'dissolve', as given in the AV. Was
Rogers working from memory, and making a mistake? One reason why the
phrase might have stuck in his memory is that the Aramaic is in the form of a
cognate accusative, or rhetorically speaking a *polyptoton*.

Another curious slip comes in the second part of *Jegar-Sahadvtha*, entitled
'A Heart-appeal to Heaven and Earth', paginated separately. Rogers picks
up on a fairly well-known crux in Psalm 45:12, *'ubat tzōr be miuchah* the
daughter of (*tzōr*) Straits and Afflictions'. To render *tzōr* as 'straits' suits
Rogers's purposes of underlining persecution and struggle, and it is
following the original Hebrew. But Rogers has transliterated what should be

tzăr as *tzōr*. *Tzōr* is the correct transliteration of the AV reading (which follows the Septuagint) of 'Tyre' (daughter of Tyre). In this case, did the compositor make an error, or was Rogers himself responsible for this curious half-mistake?

Other Hebraicisms appear to us as more dubious, rather than problematic, today. During the late 1640s, the Independent minister and pamphleteer Henry Walker edited a newsbook, entitled *Perfect Occurrences*, which celebrated the Parliamentary victories of the Second Civil War. Walker makes Hebrew do the work of providing divine assurance by taking English names, spelling them in Hebrew characters, and then translating the 'meaning' of the Hebrew words thereby created back into English. Walker has to bend his spelling considerably, but short words, relating to simple roots, yield the prophetic meanings: '*Scot*, is in Hebrew written שׁוֹט *A Scourge*.'[41] Others are more difficult to understand. Colonel Robert Hammond, Governor of the Isle of Wight, is 'in Hebrew written thus, /רות־ארע חפ י ן/ which is in English thus, *He makes the Region of Tumultuous Assemblies to tremble*'; the victory at Newport is a sanctification, since Newport, נות ארצ, means the 'perfuming of the land'.[42] הֲמוֹי ן represents 'Hammon(d)', and in Hebrew means 'sound', 'roar', 'crowd', 'multitude', while אֶרֶצ represents 'Robert' and means 'land' or 'make to tremble'. By a series of near and punning but not absolutely grammatically correct links, one can see what Walker was doing. Newport is a literal fit as דוּף means 'to perfume' (Prov. 7:17). The names of generals promise an end to the military campaign: מרלשׁה הפסילו ב ול בלל' Middlesex, Hopsley, Bucksley … *They caused the measure of the Tabernacle to be drawn out: October will consummate the work*.'[43]

Walker creates an aesthetic of anti-cavalierism from these Hebrew word-games. Given his extended career as a pamphleteer, and his intricate knowledge of the subtle codes of traduction, his very strategically direct introduction of Hebrew deliberately shatters the cavalier conventions of chivalry:

> Souldiers shoote at fine *Cloakes*, as their chief markes. *A George* and *Blue Ribbon* makes no man shot-free. Nor can the best Horses shelter any hand of them all from the *Bullets* in *Warre*.
> Sir *Miles Livesay* hath done gallant Service in subduing the new risen *hoards*, and their great *Chivalry*, Looke upon his name in *Hebrew*
> פהל ללי ׁ שׂה Michael Lucey
>   Which is in the *English* thus
> *He causeth the spirits of the Horse to be smitten.*[44]

Accordingly, and with an effect not unlike Milton's reference to London as a

Hebraic 'City of Refuge' in *Areopagitica*, the capital is transliterated as
לוּן - דוּן, and translated back as *'Waite for deliverance.'*[45] Again, the apocalyptic promise hangs over those who will not listen: just after this Walker tells of
a godly soldier in London denounced by Royalist ballad singers as 'one of
King TOM'S men who killed the Lord Francis [Villiers], and would wash
his hands in the King's blood'.

More significantly still, Walker uses Hebrew to display a prophetic future
for the future Charles II. The language is in exactly the same terms as
Royalist epigrams and other verse which lamented the unfortunate fate of
the unfathered prince. Perhaps Walker was attempting to seize the mode of
signification from the Royalists and put it in authoritative Parliamentary and
Puritan hands: 'The Common Councel of *London* met about the Parliaments
desire for the originalls of Prince *Charles* his papers. *Carolus princeps.* Prince
Charles is in *Hebrew* written חרה-ליש̇א which (also) signifies in *English*
thus. *He was in flames to disperse a Cloud.'*[46] It is none the less very difficult to
agree with Walker when he says 'it is very plain, how punctually things have
come to passe, of men, and places, according to what their names in Hebrew
have foretold. /Sir Peter Killigrew לגרדו קיל ספר / *He is the opening of a
voice of comfort to a jangling* People.'[47] In Walker's journalism, the (largely
Royalist) fashion for the half-hidden, half-revealed cryptogram (anagram or
chronogram) met the sense of pure divine power which Puritans felt in
Hebrew words.

The movement into Hebrew was also a movement towards the rediscovery
of the liturgical and ritualistic framework of the experience of the ancient
Israelites. Independents, Baptists, and Fifth Monarchists thought that Judaic
ceremony was no longer necessary, while Mosaic law might usefully be
reintroduced. But more extreme radicals went beyond this, some Antinomians finding a liberated spiritual identity in the Hebraic, in direct
contradiction to the claims of the Law. Abiezer Coppe's *Some Sweet Sips, of
some Spirituall Wine* (1649), published in the year before he became a
Ranter, and the product of the 'Seeker' milieu in the Thames Valley of
Richard Coppin, is pseudo-Hebraic in its employment of Hebrew song
forms. Coppe signs the tract with the original characters of his Hebrew
Christian name, אביעזן, which means 'my father is help'. Coppe also
describes himself as a *'late Converted JEW'*, thereby enforcing the millennial
element. The New Testament sense of taking on a new name to signify
regeneration was literalized by radicals in Hebraic fashion: George Foster,
whose visionary writings are perhaps closest to Coppe's in nature, renamed
himself 'Jacob Israel'.

The general organization is into epistles, on the Pauline model, but these
incorporate *'A Prayer of* אביעזן *upon Sigonoth* [Shigionoth]', the kind of
psalm referred to in Hab. 3:1.[48] Coppe has a current reputation as a plebeian
'tub-preacher', no doubt started by Baxter's initial depiction of him as a

Baptist preacher in the New Model Army. However, his tutelage under the Presbyterian schoolmaster William Dugard in Warwick, and his time in Oxford, left him with an acute sense of the role and power of literary forms. Indeed, Dugard reports that Coppe read in his company Homer and Crashaw's Latin epigrams.[49] In *Some Sweet Sips*, Coppe does not follow Habakkuk's prophecy, but uses the expectation of prophetic prayer to express the idea of spiritual union in a marriage feast, broadly referring to the Song of Solomon:

> Oh day of the Lord! come upon them unawares, while they are *eating* and *drinking*, and giving in *marriage*, divorce them from all strange *flesh*; give a bill of divorce to all carnall, fleshly fellowships, betroath them to thy self, (O God,) and to one another in the *Spirit*, marry them to the Spirit, to thine own Son, to thine own Self, O our *Maker*, our *Husband*.[50]

'Selah', the Hebrew word indicating a pause or rest, or 'Up!' in musical or liturgical literature (see Hab. 3:3, 9, 13), and frequently used in the Psalter, takes on a new status: 'Who is the *King of glory*? The *Lord of hosts*, he is the *King of glory. Selah.* O! Open ye doors, Hearts open; let the *King of glory* come *in*. Open dear hearts.'[51]

The same word is used by Rogers, so that his vision of the Hebraicized military republic is delivered as a song. Its delivery should be imagined as incanted, with the clear intention of moving into Hebrew, the lingua franca of the millennium.[52] The consequent reversal of the direction in which words are read carries the sense of reordering, or revolution: '*Generals, Officers, Army*, and *all* in Christ, yea, into Christ, that Christ may *swallow* up all; *Selah*; and in *order* to this (Gods *Designe*) his most speciall *Acts of Providence*, like *Hebrew letters* are to be *read rightest backward*, and this will be our *orientall tongue* indeed, ere long.'[53]

Coppe also quotes a little Hebrew directly (Ps. 89:26) later in *Some Sweet Sips*, and the general impression is one of using Hebraic sound patterns in an intricate way to effect a spiritual millennium of incantatory delicacy and power. This element disappears in Coppe's writing after 1649. The interest in sound patterns as part of prophetic discourse remains in *A Fiery Flying Roll* but other, more popular and non-Biblical, verse forms are explored. The reason for this must have been in part Coppe's adoption of the Leveller cause; the rarified Hebraicisms of the earlier writings become less useful in a more public milieu. Whatever Coppe's opinions regarding original languages in these years, other Ranters, like Laurence Clarkson and Jacob Bauthumley, specifically denied that they knew any language other than English.[54]

But other radicals moved further into what they thought was the Hebraic, and into solipsism, despite their apparent assertion of populist claims. Thomas Tany (or 'Theauraujohn'), the self-proclaimed king of the Jews and most of the thrones of Europe, is now becoming rightly recognized as the unusual and important writer that he is. He claimed that over a period of time God had given him the original language and the other languages spoken in the early history of the world. This gave him the knowledge to make the claims to power that he did, and to call the Jews back to Jerusalem, though his representations of this original language are often incomprehensible. The letter *thau* is fixed upon as the first letter of Tany's new names 'Theauraujohn' and 'Thau Ram Tanjah Rex Israel & Anglise', though it is the last letter in the Hebrew alphabet, imitating the circularity of God's name in Greek (Alpha and Omega). Like Henry Walker, and many other radicals, Tany would have agreed on the importance of language as hieroglyph. As Walker says:

> We expresse what is in our mindes by writing, as well by words; and so the Egyptians did the like by *Hereglifixes*: And men by their lives and conversation thus speake what it is in their hearts and mindes: And therefore saith the Prophet *David*, Psal. 94.4 כֹּל פֹּעֲלֵי אָוֶן תָאַמְרוּ (jithammeru col pongale aven) which our English translation renders thus. *All the members of iniquity boast themselves*, speak themselves, their hearts speak by their works.[55]

Tany had a remarkably extreme Neoplatonic cosmology. Action was what counted: all objects and all names (or words) are simply shadows of a divine reality which is continually outpouring from the divine essence or 'one'. So all actions and words 'speak', but their true meaning is available only to Tany and his true perception of the divine language. Thus, Isa. 8:10 is articulated 'from the original root in Caldean tongue, *Ousono oon a sabat olemus mem devata abbat abbat alus beneal sabat allu phene solamo as inter apti sagat men.*'[56] And no one is any the wiser.

However, it would be a mistake to follow David Katz in affirming that Tany had no knowledge of Hebrew.[57] What he seems to have done is to have apprehended bits and pieces of knowledge of Hebrew and other oriental languages and to have put them together in his own way, which he claims is divinely instilled in him. He stops short of developing a formal and usable grammar for his languages, but remains comprehensible on the level of etymology. Originally, says Tany, Hebrew was written in a purely hieroglyphic and 'virgin' state, but was given 'roots' by Moses. Three 'radaxes' form any word in creation, so enhancing the implicit connection between words and things. This is, of course, a mythologized version of the very nature of Hebrew word formation (see above). If divorced from the divine, naming is negative, and misconstrues the world. Hieroglyphs, however, always signify essential truths:

> Now ק Sambah [properly *samekh*; Paradise for Tany] stands on her soul intire, as ש doth, but she is closed and barred upward, I speak as they are Hebraically wrote in their first Apparition: *Let there be light, and it was so.*[58]

Tany's Hebrew is always changing, carrying its significance into other languages, and sound is the means by which this is often achieved. ש [*shin* or *sin*] signifies to Tany the English 'sin'. His original language is a reflection of the impacted and unitary 'one' – as in Hebrew words, there are no vowels, and it is necessary (a rare gesture of Tany in the direction of the reader) to 'open up' the meaning first by transliteration, and then by the insertion of Latin or English words.

One of Tany's repeated political complaints, one which he regards as an infringement of Magna Carta, is the appropriation of money in taxes and excise, be the appropriator king or Parliament. 'Self-lessening', a state of denial or self-negation, is preferred, which is represented by the Hebrew כ, '*kof in morphe*'.[59] The Parliament (and presumably the Council of State, since the date is 1650) have strayed away from the true understanding of signification:

> now though for the present your monies would not make much of it above 4 shil. a pound, it would be inquired into how the cause came that procured the effect of your fail of your due earned debt; was it weakness in your radax, that it was not[e] able to state a strong essence, that must be denyed; for their power and your power would have fetched in you dues, being the whole kingdome was under your commands.[60]

Tany, however, is in touch with the true meaning of the words. He can 'make the last letter take the whole state, when I write in Mo[r]phes, that is in the Medish method then I write k for cosse which strong now from a radax.'[61] The true nature of the language's interpretation enables Tany to justify unfair appropriation. The constellation of the Parliament's 'signature' inevitably means exploitation: 'the souldier is necessitated through you, he is forced to sell, you must be paymasters your derivacies draws up into essencie; ... is it fair or foule let the world judge.'[62] And Tany's own mangled syntax and grammar force one back to concentrate on his own manifestation of prophetic otherness, whether intended or not.

English names do not, for Tany, require transliteration into Hebrew characters, as they do for Walker, to achieve Hebraic interpretation. It is clear to Tany that Abergavenny ('Abbar Gauveni') is where Cromwell's 'holdment unto his true Line', is located, except that 'the LORD hath cut him off and his issue', so that, with pathos, 'onely in *Clapool* is something found.'[63]

Elsewhere Tany launches into Hebraically inspired repetitions: 'the Temple shall be new built in that stately high glory that al glory before is not worth the naming, which holy pattern I have in its living intrinsecality, and provide every one a Tent, a Tent, Tent, Tent, Tent, Tent, Tent, for thus saith your *Iah*.'[64] The Hebraic repetition patterns which were represented in the English translations were deeply attractive to sectarian rhetoric, notably the often repeated revolutionary cry of 'overturn, overturn, overturn' (Ezek. 21:27). But prophets like Tany and Joshua Garment took Hebrew as well as English words, and broke down the syllables in acts of dissective repetition, which move the name of the subject further back towards identification with the primal syllable which created the world: '*So I, Josherbah, tanquam, tanquan, pistauvah, Jah, pashtauvah, Jah, achor, ab, sha, she bah, Jah*'.[65] Garment himself was seen attending the pseudo-prophet John Robins, attempting to match his glossolalia to the text of a Hebrew Bible.[66]

A final piece of Hebraic riddling in the prophetic domain takes us to the very limits of believability. In April 1654, a broadsheet entitled *A True Alarm, in Weakness, Unto Babel, from God* appeared under the name of John Cole-venman. The author claims that words are falsely spelt, and that correct spelling reveals divine immanence: 'spirit' becomes 'spi-right' – 'spi' is the perceptive faculty from God, the 'single eye' which facilitates the comprehension of the distinction between light and darkness.[67] 'Cole' itself, deliberately separated from the rest of the name, sounds like Hebrew כֹּת 'kol', 'voice' or 'sound', as in the favourite of the Cambridge Platonists and the enthusiasts, קֹול בַּת *Bath kol*, 'soul-whisperings'.[68] So 'Cole-venman' could be decoded as 'voice of venman', and the finger of suspicion would point at the Welsh prophet Arise Evans as 'venman'. The case becomes more convincing when we consider that absolutely nothing is known about any John Cole-venman, and that *A True Alarm* is not only concerned with a mysterious, hidden meaning, but literally attempts to become one: the author instructs the readers to hang the sheet up in a public place or in houses, so that it becomes the writing on the wall of Dan. 5:5. The prophet has changed his name and in doing so has turned himself into an Hebraic enigma.

How socially powerful, or destabilizing, was the language of sectarian Hebrew? Where Fifth Monarchists used their interpretations in debate with others, including the Protectorate government, they were disputed and refuted. The use of Hebrew was neither so prominent nor so effective that it motivated popular support beyond that which could be contained by sheer physical repression. But it was a significant component in the raising of consciousnesses, in enlarging definitions of subjectivity (even to a prophetic degree), and thereby multiplying the possibilities of action. As I have tried to show, the dissemination of Hebrew was at the heart of the ideals of Interregnum England, although its effects, in the way of inducing mystifying or incendiary writing or behaviour, were upsetting to more staid people, even if they were Commonwealthsmen. Possibly the most important long-term effect of the 1640s and 1650s was the very possibility of plebeian Hebrew study, another version of the Bible reading habits central to the hold of Puritanism. While sectarian Hebrew habits no doubt helped in the sustaining of prejudice against dissent after 1660, private, lay Hebrew reading and speaking must have continued in a different context: the prayer meeting among New Model Army troops and in churches in Civil War London gave way in the following century to prophecy in the bourgeois parlour. In this way, perhaps raw Hebrew became even more private: while Robert Lowth was accommodating Biblical poetry to eighteenth-century aesthetics, a Hebraic solipsism close to Thomas Tany's was generated by Christopher Smart's *Jubilate Agno*, a mad poem written in a madhouse.

Clearly, the history of the Hebraic (as distinct from the Jews) in mid-seventeenth-century and early modern England needs to be explored more carefully and extensively: this essay is an argument for a beginning. Some of the examples drawn upon above have been seen previously as neglectable nonsense, others as unimportant in the realm of historical change. But when added together, they form a significant and interesting body of material which provides a series of novel insights into the dynamics of Interregnum religion and politics, and the process of education within this context. Moreover, the attempts to make Hebrew, as it was 'properly' to be translated, exist inside English, thereby reforming and purifying the vernacular, provides a new dimension to the history of language and literature. If the sectarian Hebraicizing of English was in some senses a genuine recourse to the original languages, as John Smyth had prescribed, we can now see that when Swift ridiculed enthusiasts by arguing that Hebrew was derived from English, we know that he was not entirely joking.

NOTES

1   John Smyth, *A Paterne of True Prayer* (1605), in *Works*, ed. W.T. Whitley, 2 vols (Cambridge, 1915), vol. 1, 27.

2   See Gareth Lloyd-Jones, *The Discovery of Hebrew in Tudor England: A Third Language* (Manchester, 1983).

3   *An Astrological Diary of the Seventeenth Century: Samuel Jeake of Rye 1652–1699*, eds Michael Hunter and Annabel Gregory (Oxford, 1988), 88.

4   *Records of a Church of Christ meeting in Broadmead, Bristol, 1640–1687*, ed. E.B. Underhill (London, 1867).

5   Samuel Hartlib, *Ephemerides*, Hartlib MS 31/22/39B. The stationer brother was probably T. Jackson, who published Raue's *General Grammar of the Ebrew, Samaritan, Calde, Syriac, Arabian and Ethiopian Tongues* (1648).

6   See Nigel Smith, *Perfection Proclaimed: Language and Literature in English Radical Religion 1640–1660* (Oxford, 1989), 328–9.

7   Bodleian Library, Ms Rawlinson D 828, fol. 31r.

8   William Aspinwall, *An Explication and Application of the Seventh Chapter of Daniel* (1654).

9   See the extensive discussion of this question in David S. Katz, *Philo-Semitism and the Readmission of the Jews to England 1603–1655* (Oxford, 1982), esp. 190–231.

10   Ibid., 175–6.

11   The importance of Raue's life and work is underestimated, even by Katz, who refers to him but once and very briefly. The best account is in *DNB*.

12   See William Robertson, *The First Gate, or the outward door to the Holy Tongue* (1653); . . . A key to the Hebrew Bible (1656).

13   T.B., *Observations Vpon Prince Ruperts White Dog, Called Boy* (1642).

14   Anon., *An Owle at Athens: Or, A True Relation of the Entrance of the Earle of Pembroke Into Oxford April xi. 1648* (1648).

15   Hanserd Knollys, *The Rudiments of the Hebrew Grammar* (1648). See also Johannes Buxtorf, *A Short Introduction to the Hebrew Tongue* (1656), trans. John Davies.

16   For examples of sectarian autodidacticism, see Smith, *Perfection Proclaimed*, 214–17, 299–307; Smith, 'The Charge of Atheism and the Language of Radical Speculation, 1640–1660', in M. Hunter and D. Wootton, eds, *Atheism in Early Modern Europe* (Oxford, forthcoming).

17   William Aspinwall, *Thunder from Heaven* (1655), Sig. A3r.

18   Alexander Ross, *A View of the Jewish Religion* (1656), 225. In the Old Testament, the menstrual issues of women is דָּוֶה (*dāhwĕh*), Isa. 30:22.

19   Christian Raue, *A Discourse of the Orientall Tongues* (1648), 15.

20   Hartlib understood that the learning of Arabic was part of an attempt to refute Islam in its own language. Proselytizing missions to convert the Sultan, as well as the Pope, by radicals occurred during the 1650s.

21   Raue, *A Discourse*, 17.

22   Ibid., 18.

23   Ibid., 19.

24   Ibid., 43.

25   See Keith Thomas, *Religion and the Decline of Magic* (London, 1971), 213.

26   For the use of Hebrew in non-extreme commentaries, see Joseph Caryll, *An Exposition with Practicall Observations upon the three first Chapters of . . . Job* (1643) (Caryll completed his commentary of the entire book of Daniel by 1666); Francis Roberts, *Clavis Bibliorum* (1st edn, 1649); John Robotham, *An Exposition of the Whole Booke of Solomon's Song* (1651).

27   Rogers was also using a different (and cruder) transliteration system to today's. The words from Hag. 2.6 would properly be transliterated as w ani mar ish . . . whir ashti.

70 NIGEL SMITH

28   John Rogers, *ΔΙΑΠΟΛΙΤΕΙΑ. A Christian Concertation with Mr. Prin, Mr. Baxter, Mr. Harrington* (1659), 62. See also Milton's translation of Psalm 88:15, 'That am already bruised, and shake/with terror sent from thee', with the marginal comment 'Heb. *Prae Concussione*', as opposed to AV 'I am afflicted and ready to die from my youth up.'

29   See Smith, *Perfection Proclaimed*, 79.

30   Rogers, *Ohel*, 45.

31   Knollys, *An Exposition*, 80; Rogers, *Ohel*, 425. The AV has the singular 'house', which is incorrect. For a further discussion of Rogers's dreams, see Smith, *Perfection Proclaimed*, 99–100.

32   Rogers, *Ohel*, 77.

33   Aspinwall had been a merchant, recorder, administrator, and explorer in New England. He had been a follower of John Cotton, was expelled from Massachusetts for siding with the Antinomians, and had played an important role in the founding of the Rhode Island colony. For further details, see R.L. Greaves and R. Zaller, eds, *A Biographical Dictionary of British Radicals in the Seventeenth Century* (3 vols, Brighton, 1982–4).

34   William Aspinwall, *An Explication and Application of the Seventh Chapter of Daniel* (1654), 3–4.

35   Ibid., 7.

36   Ibid., 4.

37   'Jegar-Sahadutha' (Gen. 31:47) means a heap of witnesses. The oiled pillar was set up by Jacob at Bethel (Gen. 28:18, 31:13).

38   Rogers, *Jegar-Sahadvtha*, title page.

39   Ibid., 1.

40   Ibid., 2.

41   *Perfect Occurrences*, 81 (14–21 July, 1648). Scourge (שׁוֹט) is properly transliterated as shôt.

42   *Perfect Occurrences*, 79 (30 June–7 July, 1648); *Perfect Occurrences*, 86 (25 August–1 September, 1648).

43   *Perfect Occurrences*, 84 (11–18 August, 1648). Hopsley has become חָפְסִילוֹ (hiph'il; root פָּסַל), 'they caused to be hewn out'. שֵׁר in פָּר לְשֵׁר (Middlesex) does in fact mean 'navel' or 'middle', so the Hebrew and English share a literal meaning for once, something which would have enforced the believability of the transliteration in the eyes of the credulous.

44   *Perfect Occurrences*, 80 (7–14 July, 1648).

45   Milton, *Complete Prose Works*, II (8 vols, New Haven, 1959), 553; *Perfect Occurrences*, 83 (28 July–4 August, 1648). לִין – 'to lodge, pass the night, endure'; דִין – 'judgement'.

46   *Perfect Occurrences*, 84 (4–11 August 1648). For iconography of Prince Charles, see Andrew Marvell, 'The Unfortunate Lover', and P.R.K. Davidson and A.K. Jones, *Notes and Queries*, n.s. 32 (1985), 170–2. כָבַר – 'to burn'; נָשִׂיא – 'cloud', and also 'lifted up' and hence 'princeps'.

47   *Perfect Occurrences*, 86 (25 August – 1 September 1648).

48   Abiezer Coppe, *Some Sweet Sips, of some Spirituall Wine* (1649), in N. Smith, ed., *A Collection of Ranter Writings from the Seventeenth Century* (1983), 52.

49   William Dugard, Diary, BL MS, Add. 23146, fol. 31v.

50   Coppe, *Some Sweet Sips*, 52–3. See also Noam Flinker, 'Ranter Sexual Politics: Canticles in the England of 1650', in Mark H. Gelber, ed., *Identity and Ethos* (New York, 1989), 325–41; Noam Flinker, 'Milton and the Ranters on Canticles', in Mary A. Maleski, ed., *Fine Tuning: Studies in the Religious Poetry of Herbert and Milton* (Binghamton, NY, 1989), 273–90.

51   Ibid., 52.

52   Henry Jessey, Baptist and influential Interregnum minister, involved in the negotiations with Menasseh ben Israel, thought that Hebrew would be universally spoken in the Millennium: E[dward] W[histon], *The Life and Death of Mr. Henry Jessey* (1671), 62.

53   Rogers, *Ohel*, 6.

54   Joseph Bauthumley, *The Light and Dark Sides of God* (1650), in Smith, *Collection of Ranter Writings*, 230.

55   Walker, בראשית, *The Creation of the World* (1649), 24.

56   Tany, *Theauraujohn his Theous Ori Apokolipikal* (1651), 20.

57   Katz, *Philo-Semitism and the Readmission of the Jews*, 110.

58   Tany, *Theauraujohn his Theous Ori*, 13.

59   Ibid., 47–8.

60   *The Nations Right in Magna Charta discussed with the thing Called Parliament* (1650), ed. A. Hopton (1988), 23.

61   Ibid., 24.

62   Ibid., 24.

63   Tany, *My Edict Royal* (?1655), 5.

64   Ibid., 24.

65   Joshua Garment, *The Hebrews Deliverance at Hand* (1651), 7.

66   Robert Bacon, *A Taste of the Spirit of God* (1652), 42. See also Henry Jessey's comparison of Sarah Wight's prophetic repetitions with the text of Plantin's Polyglot Bible (Rev. 4:8), Jessey, *The Exceeding Riches of Grace Advanced* (1647), 20.

67   For a more detailed account of 'Cole-venman's' orthography, see Smith, *Perfection Proclaimed*, 283–4.

68   See John Smith, *Of Prophecy*, in *Select Discourses* (1660), ed. Henry G. Williams (4th edn, Cambridge, 1859), 268; John Rogers, *Ohel*, 373.

I should like to acknowledge the generous assistance of Dr G. F. Nuttall, without whom this article could not have been completed.

3

From Shibboleth to Apocalypse: Quaker Speechways during the Puritan Revolution

HUGH ORMSBY-LENNON

I

In 1653 small groups of itinerant preachers began to leave their 'Quaker Galilee' – the Northern counties of Lancashire, Westmorland, and Cumberland – and quickly fanned throughout the British Isles, 'publishing the Truth' in fields, in marketplaces, and on hillsides. If the spiritual and ecclesiological situation which they encountered proved volatile, these 'First Publishers of Truth' rendered it even more explosive by interrupting formal worship in what they derisively dubbed 'steeple houses'. The Anglican church had been disestablished but it remained strong, albeit unofficially, in certain areas; the Presbyterian alternative proved neither so coherent nor so pervasive as its conservative Puritan designers had hoped; and established sects like the Baptists and Congregationalists were losing members to more radical sects which their own calls for freedom of worship had helped create. Increasingly disillusioned with all traditional modes of religious observance, English folk now gravitated towards sects like the Muggletonians, Ranters, or Fifth Monarchy Men. Some found temporary salvation with self-proclaimed messiahs like William Franklin, an adulterous rope-maker, and his celestial consort Mary Gadbury, a sometime brothel keeper, but most moved restlessly from sect to sect in pursuit of an authentic and spiritually satisfying revelation.[1] To such 'Seekers' on the antinomian fringe of Protestantism, a veritable smorgasbord of choices presented itself, choices of life-style no less than of spirituality or theology. One suspects, none the less, that most folk endured their daily tasks of getting and spending without any traumatic involvements or disengagements in either the 1640s or the 1650s. Yet however one quantifies (or qualifies) its extent, the nation's religious turbulence was extraordinary. If the plebeian cacophony raised by 'mechanic preachers' infuriated contemporaries – 'Tinkers bawled aloud, to settle / Church discipline, for patching kettle', sneered Samuel Butler: 'No sow-gelder did blow his horn / To geld a cat, but cried reform'[2]/ – historians must remain grateful for the blizzard of controversial tracts which has, for perpetuity, echoed the hubbub. At the eye of the storm, from its emergence in the early 1650s, was the Society of Friends.[3]

When George Fox began his own spiritual and geographical wanderings as a Seeker during the mid-1640s, he soon encountered one sect 'that relied much on dreams' and another 'that held women have no souls, adding in a light manner, no more than a goose'.[4] But whatever their theological vagaries, most sectaries and many Puritans still shared a conviction that hostilities with the Royalists would culminate gloriously with the millenial rule of the Puritan saints. Unfortunately the military triumph of Parliament and its allies was vitiated by intense strife among the victors. The trial and execution of Charles I (1648–9), events unprecedented in European history, sparked some wildly apocalyptic pamphleteering which continued unabated throughout the 1650s. For some, notably the Fifth Monarchy Men and certain Baptists, the death of Charles – who had so often been associated with the demonic figures in the Books of Daniel and Revelation – presaged the imminent return of King Jesus to rule over his saints. For others, including the Ranters and certain Seekers, the second coming was not to be anticipated as this outward culmination of 'history', but was to be experienced inwardly as a 'mystery'. With Cromwell's suppression of the Levellers, the passage of a Blasphemy Act designed to gag the Ranters, and the violent conclusion to the Diggers' experiment in utopian farming, it became clear that the country's new Puritan rulers, while more favourably disposed to religious liberty than their Royalist and episcopalian predecessors, would not readily cooperate with any millenarian schemes for social revolution. Increasingly, sectaries retreated into the security of a 'paradise within'; from here they excoriated the inadequacies of a 'godly rule' which they had dreamed of during the 1640s. The Fifth Monarchy Men, by contrast, called even more stridently and ferociously for the violent overthrow of all earthly government in preparation for the literal descent and direct rule of King Jesus.

Thus the situation which Fox and his fellow preachers faced at the start of the 1650s was different from that of the previous decade. More confused, dispirited, and contentious than heretofore, saints were now regularly at each other's throats as well as the government's. Certainly the array of religious options remained bewilderingly varied, so bewildering indeed that some saints succumbed to insanity. Yet the Quakers proved extraordinarily successful in their mission of 'convincement' (as they termed religious conversion), not simply as regards the numbers convinced but also because men like John Lilburne and Gerrard Winstanley, sometime leaders of the Levellers and Diggers, accepted the gospel as preached by Fox. Critical to the Friends' success was their strategy for distinguishing their own message from the din of rival sectarian claims and counterclaims. Quakers rendered themselves immediately identifiable by their speechways (passionately espoused and defended) rather than by their doctrines, which did not approach any fixity of definition until well after Charles II was restored in 1660. Yet, as we shall discover, Friends still manifested in their choice of shibboleths a version of the apocalypse wherein personal 'mystery' loomed larger than public 'history'.

II

In her spiritual autobiography Mary Penington records how, during the mid-1650s, she first 'heard of a new people called Quakers ... in the north' whilst she was herself 'in a state of being wearied in seeking and not finding'.[5] What little she learned concerned not the Friends' quiddities of Biblical interpretation but their choice of shibboleths, notably their determination to 'use thee and thou' rather than the respectful and honorific 'you' to all individuals. She also 'saw a book written in the plain language by George Fox' which she 'thought very ridiculous, so minded neither the people nor the book, except that it was to scoff at them and it'. Like most southerners, particularly the well born and the well educated, Mary initially despised the rustic speechways of preachers from the 'Quaker Galilee'. Yet she already sensed, quite correctly, that the Quakers preferred 'prayer' over 'doctrine', spiritual experience over the niceties of theology. 'Early Quakers', explains T.L. Underwood,

> focused their attention particularly upon religious experience rather than upon the elaborate and carefully reasoned exposition of that experience in systematic theology ... their emphasis fell upon the present, inward spiritual experiences, the immediacy, inwardness, and spirituality of the work of Christ, in contrast with outward, physical events, whether the crucifixion of Christ in the past or events expected in the future.[6]

Not long after she had waxed so contemptuous of the Society's pronominal quirks and plain language, Mary Penington and her husband Isaac, both ardent Seekers, were convinced by itinerant Quakers, who had first 'cried out against' their 'vain gay apparel'. Interestingly Mary found it easier to accept 'the doctrine preached by the Friends' – experiential precepts which included the light within, 'that of God in every one', and the reconstitution of Biblical narrative (or its apparent reconstitution) as allegory and psychodrama – than their directive to 'take up the cross' against 'the language, fashions, customs, titles, honour, and esteem in the world'. In the event, the Peningtons' cross proved heavy: because of their refusal to take oaths in court (a 'testimony' deemed crucial to upholding the plain language) much of their property was confiscated. Isaac's six imprisonments between 1661 and 1671 undermined an already delicate constitution, although ill-health and gaol did not prevent him from clinching a reputation as 'the Quaker Plotinus' with his many subtle meditations on the plain language. In due course, Mary's daughter by a first marriage, Gugliema, married William Penn, whose 'Holy Experiment' on the other side of the Atlantic blossomed into Pennsylvania. In colonial America the Society's 'plain language' – mandating honest negotiations in all commercial transaction – bore fruit in the counting house no less than in the meeting house. Even in England, where they were granted toleration rather than afforded liberty, Friends had already begun to prosper by the 1690s; for the next two centuries their economic success was phenomenal.[7]

When the Quakers first took up their cross during the 1650s, of course, they did so for spiritual reasons and with no thought of material gain. The privations endured by the Peningtons, both legal and economic, were typical, although their social position and income meant that they had far more to lose than most Friends. Certainly the Quakers' many critics could never have imagined that the objects of their scorn and detestation would subsequently become models of propriety and pillars of the nation's economy. 'There is a generation of people in our age called Quakers, which they disclaim as a nickname', Thomas Fuller complained in 1655, singling out for criticism their 'going naked as a sign' (in supposed imitation of Isaiah) and 'their other opinion that *thou* and *thee* is the omer of respect to be measured out to every single person, allowing the highest no more, the lowest no less'.[8] Against the Friends' literal-minded appeal to Biblical customs of pronominal usage Fuller deployed a relativistic argument: the 'custom of every country', he maintained, is 'the grand master of language, to appoint what is honourable and disgraceful therein'. His final fear – widely shared – was that 'such who now quarrel at the honour, will hereafter question the wealth . . . such as now introduce *thee* and *thou* will, if they can, expel *mine* and *thine*, dissolving all propriety into confusion.'

Were the Quakers social and economic revolutionaries – 'our Levellers new named', as George Wither feared[9] – intent upon dismantling the fabric of English society? Did their plain language signify for them what it signified for their many detractors? Alongside the plain language we must consider the Friends' distinctive social etiquette (or lack thereof) which ranged from forthright rejection of 'politeness phenomena' to odd symbolic actions, notably their going naked 'as a sign of the nakedness and shame that is coming upon the Church'.[10] 'When the Lord sent me forth into the world', Fox subsequently recorded in his Journal for the year 1649,

> he forbade me to put off my hat to any, high or low; and I was required to 'thee' and 'thou' all men and women, without any respect to rich or poor, great or small. And as I travelled up and down, I was not to bid people 'good morrow' or 'good evening', neither might I bow or scrape with my leg to anyone; and this made the sects and professions to rage . . .
>
> But oh, the rage that then was in the priests, magistrates, professors [i.e. ministers and preachers], and people of all sorts, but especially in priests and professors! for, though 'thou' to a single person was according to their own learning, their accidence, and grammar rules, and according to the Bible, yet they could not bear to hear it, and the hat-honour, because I could not put off my hat to them, it set them all into a rage. But the Lord showed me that it was an honour below, which he would lay in the dust and stain it, an honour which proud flesh looked for, but sought not the honour which came from God only, that it was an honour invented by men in the Fall and in the alienation from God . . . Oh, the rage and scorn, the heat and fury that arose! Oh, the blows, punchings, beatings, and imprisonments that we underwent for not putting off our hats to men![11]

Here Fox provides a helpful (if incomplete) summary of Quaker speechways and social etiquette, vividly suggesting the obloquy and physical violence they provoked. Like seventeenth-century conservatives, modern Marxists have interpreted such Quaker 'testimonies' as a calculated assault upon England's social and economic structures, structures threatened but not toppled by the Puritan Revolution.[12] Certainly the Quakers were not afraid to denounce oppression and exploitation, but the chief object of their polemic was 'exalted proud flesh which cannot bear *thee* and *thou* to a single person and is accursed with a curse and cast out from God'.[13] The twin demand by the well born and the well educated – whether parsons or justices, doctors or gentlemen – that the lower orders address them with the decorous *you* (rather than the intimate *thee*) and that hats be removed in their presence was furiously rejected by James Parnel, one of the first Quaker martyrs, as 'an invention of Proud Lucifer in man to exalt himself'.[14] In short, the most immediately offensive ingredient in the Quakers' plain language – their indiscriminate use of *thee* and *thou* – was administered as a corrective to postlapsarian human pride; any political implications of 'levelling' were secondary.

Plain language thus enjoined upon all Quakers the forceful rejection of what Mary Penington called 'the language, fashions, customs, titles, honour and esteem in the world'. In a fallen world, such capricious and mutable conventions bespoke human alienation from God, the spiritual surrender to carnal lures set by the devil. In effect, Friends agreed with Thomas Fuller that custom *was* 'the grand master of language' – other than their own plain language, of course – but viewed its governance as at best sinful, at worst diabolic. It was in the courtroom that the consequences of their affront to custom often proved most dramatic. In 1656, for example, before Fox and two companions were taken from Launceston gaol to Judge Glynne's courtroom, 'professors and priests' asked tauntingly: 'let's see whether they dare *thee* and *thou* and keep their hats on before the judge.'[15] Valiant for truth, the three Quakers (whom Fox compared to 'the three children cast into the fiery furnace by Nebuchadnezzar') did indeed dare and after a further nine weeks' imprisonment concluded that Judge and court 'objected nothing to us but about our hats'.[16] The original charges levelled against Fox and his travelling companions now seem nugatory (or trumped up), but even trials involving substantive accusations of blasphemy could quickly degenerate into wranglings about the formalities of pronominal usage and hat-honour. For the Friends, however, such formalities involved matters of substance, namely man's craving for 'the honour which god would lay in the dust'.

Fox further antagonized Judge Glynne by delivering 'a large paper against swearing to the grand and petty juries' in which he explained the Quakers' refusal to take the oath in court.[17] Citing Christ's injunction ('But I say unto to you . . . swear not at all . . . But let your communication by Yea, Yea; Nay, Nay; for whatsoever is more than these cometh of evil') Friends refused to take either political oaths of allegiance and against transubstantiation or the judicial oaths deemed integral to the verity of legal testimony.[18] Instead they sought permission to make a simple affirmation (the plain language of 'yea and nay'), a request which was not legally recognized until the Affirmation Act of 1696.[19] Since public order depended upon a subject's willingness to take political oaths (or, rather, since successive governments *claimed* that oaths were crucial to their exercise of legitimate authority), Friends continually found themselves in trouble; this was especially true after 1660 when rebarbative courts exploited this testimony to the plain language in order to punish a sect whose members were still eyed suspiciously as political revolutionaries.[20] Refusal to take judicial oaths was also turned against the Friends: Mary Penington, for example, lost much of her property when she refused to swear in Chancery against a relative's suit.

'If legal phrases, if promises and contracts were not regarded as something more than *flatus vocis*', observes Bronislaw Malinowski, 'social order would cease to exist in a complex civilization as well as in a primitive tribe.'[21] Certainly this was the position taken by English governments, both before and after the Restoration. Yet so inured had citizens become to taking oaths of loyalty and allegiance to each successive regime that their readiness to swear betokened a weary acceptance of chaos and mendacity rather than any commitment to social order and gospel truth. 'Oaths are but words, and words but wind, / Too feeble instruments to bind', asserts Ralpho, Samuel Butler's parodic Quaker, in defence of the Society's commitment to affirmation: 'they were only meant / To serve for an Expedient.'[22] Hence Friends objected not simply to the legal requirement that they swear but to the pervasive atmosphere of lying in which oaths were so expediently taken. 'We dare not swear because we dare not lie', explained Penn, more succinctly than either Fox or Penington: 'People swear to the end that they may speak truth; Christ would have them speak truth to the end they might not swear.'[23] Thus the Society's testimony on oaths was not primarily intended as a challenge to the legitimacy of government – ready to affirm, Friends were denied the opportunity – but was designed to recall folk to standards of veracity obtaining in Eden, upheld by Christ, and appropriate for England's Last Days. Then, as now, governments proved economical with the truth and resented the Quakers' spiritual challenge as a political one. The Friends' willingness to languish in gaol contrasted noticeably with the readiness of Ranters and other antinomians to sign oaths of recantation in order to win release. Doctrinally the Quakers resembled the Ranters (members of each group allegorized the scriptures, discovered a light within, and advocated human ability to overcome sin in order to attain perfection), but, once again, the Friends' commitment to the plain language served as a mark of distinction. To the wanton delight Ranters took in cursing and to their extravagant observance of contemporary etiquette, their 'extreme compliments' and 'bowing and scraping', Friends objected volubly.[24]

From where did the Quakers derive their plain language? Other dissident groups – Bogomils, Albigensians, Lollards, Taborites, Anabaptists, Baptists – had refused to take oaths and Friends followed in their tradition; to the Baptists their debt was immediate. In the late 1640s Levellers and Diggers rejected hat honour (as Lollards had before them); here, too, the Society had a direct precedent. From the Baptists, Quakers also learned how to purge the calendar of pagan names, replacing them with the plain language of 'first day', 'first month' etc.; 'popish' accretions were eliminated both from the Friends' calendar (Candlemas, Lady Day, Christmas were denounced, not celebrated) and from place names (just as 'churches' became 'steeple houses', Saint Paul's Churchyard became Paul's Yard, Grace Church Street became Gracious Street). Silence and paucity of words were advocated by Seekers (often) and by Ranters (sometimes), and Friends followed suit. 'They recommended silence by their example, having few words upon all occasions', Penn wrote of the early Quakers, who endeavoured (in theory if not in practice) to retain a staunch taciturnity when abused by professors and priests who 'fed upon words and fed one another with words' and 'endeavoured to bear [Friends] down with many words [and] kicked, and yelled, and roared, and raged'.[25]

Of all saints and mechanic preachers the Society proved most prolific both in speech and print, and gained such widespread notoriety for railing that objections to 'Quaker Billingsgate' became a topos in the propaganda of its adversaries.[26] 'It seems *thou* and *thee* is too good language for us [ministers]', noted Fuller, 'who are Cains, and Balaams, and dogs and devils in their mouths.'[27] Certainly Fox salted his plain language well when he told a Presbyterian minister that 'thou must eat thy own dung, and drink thy own piss, for all that is in thy book is but dung.'[28] Another of the Quakers' 'savage incivilities and turbulent practices' – that is, their repudiation of politeness phenomena – was their failure to give 'common respects' not merely to magistrates but even 'to any friends or old acquaintances. If they meet them by the way, or any stranger, they will go or ride by them as if they were dumb ... not affording a salutation, or resaluting though themselves be saluted.'[29] This rejection of salutations – of what James Nayler called 'heathenish high-way customs'[30] – comprised no gratuitous lack of politeness but another testimony in which the bankruptcy of wordly esteem could be rudely exposed. 'Nor could they humour the custom of "Good night, good morrow, Godspeed"', explained Penn, 'for they knew the night was good and the day good without wishing of either, and that the holy name of God was too highly and unthinkingly used and therefore taken in vain. Besides, they were words and wishes of course [i.e. custom] and are usually as little meant as are love and service in the custom of cap and knee.'[31] Thus the polite meaningless words of everyday communication proved no less objectionable to Friends than did the 'bowing and scraping' beloved by the Ranters and also by fantastical cavaliers (dubbed 'dammees' for their ranter-like propensity to extravagant swearing).

The shibboleth for which the Quakers gained most notoriety was, of course, their insistence (often self-sacrificial) upon using the intimate *thee* and *thou* to all individuals, regardless of birth, education, or rank. Here Friends seem not to have relied upon the crusading example of any other sect, although sectaries customarily emphasized the importance of spiritual intimacy and egality. Instead the direct origins of the Society's shibboleth appear to have been secular. It displays a distinct family resemblance to the speechways of yeomen which Shakespeare had characterized as 'russet yeas and honest kersey noes' in contrast to the 'taffeta phrases, silken terms precise' of courtiers and scholars.[32] Shakespeare's choice of sartorial metaphor – an expression of the topos that 'Language is the dress of thought' – reminds us that the Quakers dressed as well as spoke plainly. 'Let your lives speak', Fox exhorted Quaker congregations.[33] Thereby he suggested how their plain language could find a physical embodiment, its semiological correlate, not merely in the rejection of hat honour (intimately related as that was to an insistence upon *thee* and *thou*) but also in the elimination of ornament and frippery from garments.[34] Such forthright directives on the 'speaking' life certainly appealed to robust yeomanly independence and the class's innate dislike of unnecessary ostentation.

At the beginning of his *Journal* Fox evokes (if not without some hint of retrospective interpolation) the laconic speechways of God-fearing yeomen which he had, as a child, already resolved to emulate: 'For the Lord showed me that though the people of the world have mouths full of deceit and changeable words yet I was to keep to "yea" and "nay" in all things; and that my words should be few and savoury, seasoned with grace.'[35] Yet even in the Midlands where Fox grew up during the 1620s and 1630s employment of *thee* and *thou* appears to have been passing into desuetude. For England was gradually obliterating distinctions between T and V, still operative on the continent today, by dispensing with T almost entirely.[36] Only in the northern counties – notably the Quaker Galilee – does dialectology indicate that the widespread use of T was not yet verging on anachronism.[37] Among the small farmers and yeomen of the northwest – where Quakerism garnered its earliest converts – *thee* and *thou* constituted what linguists now describe as 'a social solidarity semantic'.[38] Of a comparable mentalité – that of the Russian peasantry during the nineteenth century – Paul Friedrich observes that 'a gregarious, fraternal spirit joined the peasants to each other' since they 'lived in what might be called a familial universe where almost everyone was addressed with the familial pronoun *ty*'.[39] Such was the context in which 'Friend' evolved as one of the several terms Quakers used to address each other.

In the south of England, however, where Friends began to proselytize in 1653, a 'non-reciprocal power semantic' prevailed: 'We maintain that *thou* from superiors to inferiors is proper as a sign of command', explained Thomas Fuller, 'from equals to equals is passable, as a note of familiarity; but from inferiors to superiors, if proceeding from ignorance, hath a smack of clownishness; if from affectation, a tang of contempt.'[40] That 'tang' had been given striking force when Sir Edward Coke turned on Sir Walter Raleigh at the latter's trial in 1603: 'All that he did was at thy instigation, thou viper; for I thou thee, thou traitor.'[41] Yet the phenomenon which Edward Sapir describes as 'linguistic drift' indicates that *thou* was beginning to disappear as a valid distinction of the type exploited by Coke and reasserted by Fuller.[42] But the Quakers' explicit emphasis upon its symbolism as a challenge to the pride of fallen man (and implicit use of its 'social solidarity semantic') dramatically, if temporarily, arrested its gradual elimination as a sociolinguistic marker. 'A man's consistent pronoun style gives away his status and his political views', modern linguists have concluded after examining societies in which the T–V distinction is maintained.[43] Certainly, as Friedrich indicates for nineteenth-century Russia,

> the extreme use of the *ty* of pronominal instability was part of hysteria; the onset of insanity was signalled by a neutralization of the distinction that sets off the two pronouns from each other ... The informal pronoun could serve as a one-sided expression of an extreme ideology which, from one point of view, was a lack of contact with 'reality' ... the exclusive use of the personal pronoun often symbolized an outlook on man and society characteristic of the insane, the senile, hermits, and extreme revolutionaries, notably terrorists.[44]

Quakers, too, were routinely accused of insanity, sometimes on legitimate clinical grounds, but more often because any challenge to the hegemony of social custom could, since the early days of Christianity, be construed as a madman's inability to come to terms with 'reality'.[45] But the Quakers' insistence on *thee* and *thou* ran far deeper than mental health, class status, or terroristic politics.

When Quaker preachers first arrived in London, they were indeed described as 'north country ploughmen who did differ in judgement to all other people', that is men whose speechways were as 'clownish', rustic, or 'agrammatical' as their ideas were heterodox.[46] Yet Quakers soon convinced several members of the southern gentry, notably Mary and Isaac Penington, William Penn, and Thomas Ellwood, Milton's future secretary and editor of Fox's *Journal*. For these friends a decision to 'take up the cross' of the plain language reflected not their class but a determination to reject the wisdom of the wise and join the 'agrammatical' poor who would inherit the earth. Ellwood vividly describes how he enraged his father by keeping his hat on and addressing him with the indecorously familiar *thou*: 'Though I had no hat now to offend him', Ellwood recorded after his father had forcibly removed three, 'yet my language did as much; for I durst not say [YOU] to him; but THOU, and then would he be sure to fall on me with his fists shouting *Sirrah, if ever I hear you say* THOU *or* THEE *to me again, I'll strike your teeth down your throat*.'[47] Thomas's father discerned in his son's linguistic recalcitrance that 'tang of contempt' mentioned by Fuller. Ellwood's younger friends seemed amused rather than angry – 'What, Tom! a Quaker!', they exclaimed – seeing in his dogged testimony to the plain language not calculated contempt or a threat to the political *status quo* but quixotic linguistic slumming with 'clownish' speechways. At any rate, the mockery and opprobrium which Fox and his companions provoked in Judge Glynne's courtroom was replicated throughout the nation as convinced sons, daughters, and apprentices made their own domestic contributions to the Society's assault upon the spiritual pride of 'Priests, People, Judges, Nobles, Kings, Fathers, Professors, and Rulers', all of whom 'when any *thee* or *thou*, you are them who are ready to murder.'[48] Insistence upon *you* to an individual Fox traced (not without some historical insight) to papal usurpations of authority; and, by the mid-seventeenth century, European observance of pronominal distinctions had come to symbolize (although somewhat more marginally in England until the Quakers dramatized the issue) respect for all authority whether construed politically, paternally (and the family functioned as a microcosm of the patriarchal state), or in terms of what custom had rendered decorous.[49]

Quakers wrote repeatedly and at extraordinary length in defence of their plain language, particularly their testimonies on oath-taking and on pronominal choice. Most Friends integrated their attack on false T–V distinctions (and their semiological correlate, hat-honour) into passionate diatribes against fallen humanity: 'this difference or respect of persons', explained Parnel, 'was never ordained by God, but by the Devil whereby he exalts himself in man.'[50] Richard Farnworth and Fox each devoted a complete treatise to the correct choice of pronouns. In *The Pure Language of the Spirit of Truth* – a short quarto printed no fewer than six times during 1655 and 1656 – Farnworth provided elaborate scriptural justifications for this Quaker shibboleth, although as his critics (including Fuller) pointed out, he was merely adducing examples of *verbal custom* during Biblical times rather than evidence of specific doctrinal injunctions (which could certainly be advanced in support of the Quaker testimony on swearing).[51] In *A Battle-Door for Teachers and Professors to Learn Singular and Plural* Fox (who relied heavily on the scholarly assistance of John Stubbs and Benjamin Furly) offered a folio continuation of Farnworth's arguments, bolstering Biblical precedents with examples drawn (and illustrated typographically) from languages as arcane as Aethiopick, Samaritan, and Coptick.[52]

Did Quakers begin to 'publish the truth' with the explicit intention of offering a testimony on *thee* and *thou*? Fox's claim that God had, in 1649, 'required [him] to "thee" and "thou" all men and women',[53] is contradicted by the earliest evidence which survives. In a manuscript letter of 1650 we see Fox still using "you" to Noah Bullock, mayor of Derby; indeed Ellwood tidied up Fox's deployment of T and V, when editing the manuscripts of the *Journal*, in order to make his pronominal usage conform to Quaker shibboleth.[54] What happened, I believe, was that the ardent peregrinations of First Publishers from the Quaker Galilee gave the area's speechways an immediate currency among newly convinced Friends throughout Britain. Indeed the Society's northern origins were continually mocked, and the ridicule provoked by the yeoman speechways of 'the 1652 country' (as Friends came to describe northwest England) surely came to function as a symbol, immediately and publicly recognizable, of their nationwide onslaught on spiritual pride.[55] Persecuted for their pronominal choices, Friends also resolved to endure punishment for a body of doctrines which was as yet not so clearly defined as their shibboleths. Like the early Christians who chose to die rather than acknowledge, before the magistrate, that 'Domitian is Lord', the Quakers validated their beliefs by suffering for them, even when those beliefs seemed merely cantankerous. Indeed such a comparison with early Christianity (and the Friends made many) steeled the Friends' resolve to be valiant for truth. Testimonies on speech also provided the Quakers with a highly visible means of differentiating themselves not simply from the world and its sinful predilection for 'changeable words' but also from rival sectaries: from Baptists (whose high standards of moral probity resembled the Friends'), from the Muggletonians who were addicted to cursing their adversaries (especially the Quakers!) for all eternity, but particularly from the Ranters, doctrinally so close to Quakerism but with a reputation for sexual licence the Quakers abhorred (not least because they themselves were tarred with the same brush).[56] 'And so all Friends, train up your children in the same singular and plural language', Fox exhorted the Society in 1660, conveniently forgetting his on own initial latitude on the shibboleth: 'keep to the proper, sound single language . . . So let Friends be distinct from all the world in their language, in their ways, in love, and in their conversations.'[57]

Passage of time confers objectivity, and twentieth-century commentators can reflect more dispassionately upon early Quaker speechways. But for their contemporaries the Friends' raucous interruption of church service, their noisy harangues in streets, courts, and marketplaces, their 'going naked as a sign', and their rejection of politeness formulae, all smacked of that extremism and terrorism with which Friedrich associates the Russian revolutionary's use of *ty*. Moreover, the apocalyptic rhetoric which the Quakers borrowed so copiously from Revelation brimmed with sanguinary and violent imagery. But unlike the bellicose Fifth Monarchy Men who, in 1661, rose in armed revolt to hasten the physical return of King Jesus, the Quakers eschewed violence and a militaristic reading of the Scriptures. 'All the Fifth Monarchy Men, that be fighters with carnal weapons', Fox wrote after their abortive uprising, 'they are none of Christ's servants, but the beast's and the whore's . . . they looked for Christ's coming outwardly.'[58] Whereas the Fifth Monarchists took their insurrectionary cue from Psalm 149, verse 6 ('Let the high praises of God be in their mouth, and a two-edged sword in their hand'), the Quakers seized from Revelation the 'sharp two-edged sword' which flames 'out of [Christ Triumphant's] mouth.'[59]

Unlike the Fifth Monarchists, who took up carnal weapons, the Quakers waged that they called 'the Lamb's War'

> against the beast and false Prophet, which hath deceived the nations; and we are of the royal seed elect, chosen and faithful, and we war in truth, and just judgement, not with weapons that are carnal; but by the sword that goes out of his mouth which shall slay the wicked and cut them to pieces.[60]

'Waging war with the sword of the mouth' was a favourite Quaker trope during the 1650s, and its provenance in Revelation was not fortuitous: yet if no less fervent than Fifth Monarchy Men as apocalypsists, Quakers espoused a *parousia* that was spiritual, not carnal or literal. 'They boast that Christ is come to them, neither look they for any other coming', a Baptist complained of the Quakers, 'that the world is ended with them, neither look they for any other end.'[61] Thus the Quakers adopted what has been variously described as a *vergeistigter Chiliasmus*, a realized eschatology, or an internalized apocalypse.[62] 'Christ hath been talked of, but now he is come and is possessed', Fox declared; 'the glory hath been talked of, but now it is possessed and the glory of man is destroyed ... Christ is come to teach his people himself.'[63] Espousing a doctrine of 'that of God in every one', Friends rejected practical expectations of the second coming in favour of the discovery of a paradise within, at once Edenic and millennial. Only utterance (or its semiological correlates: dress and behaviour) could give outward definition to inward states and convictions. Whereas rival sectaries took up weapons or fruitlessly calculated the end of an imminent millennium, Friends embodied the Word, made it flesh, let their lives speak. Hence their shibboleths functioned as much more than sociolinguistic markers or disparate testimonies; Friends envisioned their speechways as part of that great cosmic drama of language, which begins in Genesis and ends in Revelation, a drama inspired and directed by the Johannine logos. That the Holy Spirit had chosen the 1652 country for rekindling the light within endowed its speechways with a chiliastic edge. William Dewsbury declared that he served in an 'army which [God] has raised up in the North of England and is marching towards the South in mighty power to cut down high and low'.[64] 'Laying aside all carnal weapons, club and staff, force and compulsion', the Westmorland linen-draper John Audland brandished instead 'the eternal word of the everlasting God that is quick and powerful, sharper than any two-edged sword, which divides where no carnal weapon can divide.'[65] Thus it was that a shibboleth involving pronouns gained apocalyptic force.

III

'All languages are to me no more than dust', Fox declared in his 'Preface' to
A Battle-door:

> who was before languages were, and am come before languages were,
> and am redeemed out of languages into the power where all men shall
> agree: but this is a whip and a rod to all such who have degenerated
> through the pride and ambition ... men, crying up tongues to be the
> original, have degenerated from the tongues which they call the
> original, which be not the original ... For in the beginning was the
> word, which was before natural languages were.
> For speaking the word singular and plural we have been stoned and
> persecuted by the priests' and professors' generation, and our lives in
> jeopardy daily: what? sayest *Thou, Thou* to me?[66]

The ease and rapidity with which Fox passes from Johannine declaration to
advocacy of plain language will startle only those who neglect the imbrication
of Quaker shibboleth with realized eschatology. 'Plain language' is a
convenient term, the Quakers' own, with which to characterize their
pronominal principles as well as their other idiosyncrasies of speech. Yet
those shibboleths were inspired by a vision of what Farnworth calls 'the pure
language of the spirit of truth', a chiliastic language in which quotidian usage
is transfigured by a timeless apprehension of the logos. Most men were
condemned, because of their own pride and ambition, to grovel in the
postlapsarian dust of degenerate tongues, descended from the natural
languages first unleashed by the *confusio linguarum* at Babel.[67] By contrast,
those who recognized 'the light within' and 'that of God in every one' – as
did the Friends – could return 'before languages were' and recapture 'the
original' which was 'in the beginning'. Through the logos the world was
made: and God's creative *fiat* in Genesis 1:2, 'Let there be light', was
echoed, for the Quakers, in St John's peroration on word and light (John
1:1–14), in which their own experience of 'new creation' was grounded.
   From the Johannine logos Friends derived their experience of being in the
world and their strategies for representing it as 'plain' and 'pure' language.
During the Last Days – which Quakers, in common with other radical
sectaries, perceived in their own era – the 'pure language' constituted both
alpha and *omega*, both the original from which all creation had sprung and
the millennial glory that shone out from the Friends' *vergeistigten Chiliasmus*,
eclipsing the 'false glory' of fallen man. In this fullness of time, God would,
Zephaniah had prophesied, 'turn to the people a pure language, that they
may all call upon the name of the LORD to serve him with one consent'

(3:9). From this apocalyptic vision of linguistic unity Fox derived his own 'power where all men shall agree'. Quaker shibboleths thus represented the outward manifestation of an inner state in which the second coming had already occurred, spiritually not carnally, and in which the fallen world had arrived at its predestined end, the restoration within (and not without) of all things.

Celebrations of the 'pure language' were not confined to the Friends. Diggers like Winstanley, idiosyncratic saints like George Foster and Thomas Tany, and even the millenarian Baptist Hannah Trapnel all praised it.[68] From contemporary readings of the 'pure language of nature' John Webster – Independent preacher, educational reformer, and alchemical metallurgist – anticipated the imminent recovery, long prophesied, of 'all the rich treasury of nature's admirable and excellent secrets'.[69] But, as so often, Quaker meditations on the word, firmly rooted as those were in northern speechways, proved more resilient than the impressionistic and scattered paeans of other sectaries. Yet, for Friends, as for their contemporaries, the vernacular soil of the pure language was well fertilized by rich continental traditions of mysticism so rapidly absorbed during the Puritan Revolution.

In his *Liber de verbo mirifico* the great Renaissance Hebraist Johannes Reuchlin envisioned the '*sermo purus, brevis, sanctus, et incorruptus*' as the *lingua adamica*, the language in which God had conversed with our parents in Eden and which Adam had employed in giving names to all creation.[70] Thus the pure language, as interpreted by Reuchlin, served both as an ideal channel of communication between God and humanity (still available to St Paul as an 'angelical language') and as a paridisal semiology, a 'pure language of nature' in which words had a necessary or (what de Saussure calls) 'motivated' connection with what they signified.[71] Traditionally, this language was seen as a prelapsarian Hebrew reflected in the stars (first formed into the ideal shape of Hebrew letters), thereby providing Adam with a lexicon, one supplemented by a magic book brought him by the angel Raziel, from which he gained his onomantic powers as the original name-giver.[72] That Fox, untrained in the classical languages, or other more educated Quakers, ever consulted Reuchlin seems most unlikely, but mid-seventeenth century England comprised a veritable crucible of heterodox ideas on language – magico-mystical, cabalistic, alchemical – since many works by Renaissance polymaths, esotericists, and heresiarchs (Agrippa, Sendivogius, Paracelsus, Henrik Niclaes, Jacob Boehme, Oswald Croll, the Rosicrucians, et al.) were rapidly translated for a monolingual audience.[73] Notions of English itself as a *sermo purus* of the type canvassed by Reuchlin became widespread among antinomians and sectaries.

'Take notice scholars, I am not book learned, but I am heart learned by divine inspiration', announced the sectary Robert Norwood; 'no tongue on the earth can hold forth the Hebrew as the English tongue can render it to itself in the perfection. Richard Verstegan had already suggested, in a work that gained great popularity during the early 1650s, that Teutonic, immediate progenitor of English, was 'the first and most ancient language of the world, yea the same that Adam spake in paradise'.[74] For Quakers, also heart learned by divine inspiration, the vernacular served both as the key to Eden, unlocking the paradise within, and as an external symbol of their inward arrival at the New Jerusalem.

Boehme's rapturous and extensive writings on the *lingua adamica* – fully translated into English between 1644 and 1662 – must have proved especially attractive to Friends.[75] For Boehme transformed alchemical complexities and an abstruse Christian cabala into a theosophy which, if not without its own vagaries of style and doctrine, was experiential not discursive, spiritual not intellectual. 'Paradise is in the world', Boehme insisted: 'if our eyes were opened we should see it.'[76] Indeed Boehme's own trance-like recovery of the *lingua adamica* outside Görlitz in 1600 – once his eyes had been 'opened' by sunlight glancing off a pewter dish, he 'went forth into the open fields, and there perceived the wonderful or wonderworks of the Creator in the signature, shapes, figures, and qualities of all created things, very clearly and plainly laid open' – directly anticipated the 'openings' experienced by Fox during the later 1640s when the young Quaker-to-be spent much of his time wandering alone through the English countryside.[77] 'And the Lord's power brake forth', Fox wrote, 'and I had great openings and prophecies.'[78]

During the most memorable of these openings in 1648 Fox also gained mystical insight into the *signatura rerum* in the *liber creaturarum* or book of nature. 'Now was I come up in spirit through the flaming sword into the paradise of God', Fox wrote, endowing his experience of 'coming before languages were' with a dramatic and archetypal force which no other Friend could rival:

All things were new, and all the creation gave another smell unto me than before, beyond what words can utter. I knew nothing but pureness, and innocency, and righteousness ... I was come up to the state of Adam which he was in before he fell, in which the admirable works of the creation, and the virtues thereof, may be known, through the openings of that divine Word of wisdom and power through which they were made. The creation was opened to me, and it was showed me how all things had their names given them according to their nature and virtue. And I was at a stand in my mind whether I should practise physic for the good of mankind, seeing the nature and virtue of creatures were so opened to me by the Lord.[79]

Here Fox shakes the postlapsarian dust of 'tongues' from his feet and reacquires the *sermo purus*. From this Edenic semiology of a new creation, both inward and outward – a paradise 'beyond what words can utter' – he reacquires those wonder-working skills of thaumaturgy mastered not simply by Adam but also by patriarchs, prophets, and apostles who retained (or had reacquired like Fox) gifts of tongues and healing after the Fall.[80] Several years later, in conversation with the alchemist Edward Bourne, Fox spoke 'wonderfully ... of the glory of the first body, of the Egyptian learning, and of the language of the birds', a choice of topics which sheds further light upon his Adamic trance.[81] Illuminated by Eden, the cabalists' Adam conversed with (as well as named) 'the fowl of the air', a gift of tongues inherited by the *prisci theologi* (among others) who were proficient in the *hermetica* or 'Egyptian learning'. Moreover, such fluency in mystical birdsong inaugurates both the alchemist's labours with his *magnum opus* and the shaman's flight back to paradise: in the course of each spiritual discipline a 'secret language' is learned which enables its possessor to effect miracles of healing.[82] That Fox himself acquired a reputation as a thaumaturge – employing his insight into the *liber creaturarum* for the good of humanity – should come as no surprise; nor should the Quakers' deep-rooted and continuing interest in ornithology and botany.[83] Yet formal speculation on these esoteric dimensions of the 'pure language of nature' was, finally, alien to Quaker spirituality – unlike the English disciples of Paracelsus and Oswald Croll, Friends were practically rather than magico-mystically in-clined – and 'the pure language of the spirit of truth' was promulgated as chiliastic experience rather than as Edenic arcanum.[84]

After his attainment of Adamic insight into the *signatura rerum* and their paradisal pharmacopoeia, Fox was 'immediately taken up in spirit to see into another or more steadfast state than Adam's in innocency, even into a state in Christ, that should never fail'.[85] This final reintegration with Christ the primordial Word – 'before languages were', even the *lingua adamica* – Douglas Gwyn describes as a 'remarkable vista of apocalyptic fulfilment'.[86] What remains arresting about Quaker eschatology is its sophisticated elision of scriptural time-frames which to the quotidian and unconvinced eye must seem incommensurable. The creative *fiat* (what Fox calls 'the original'), the *lingua adamica*, and the pure language which Zephaniah prophesied for the last days all coexisted for the Friends in an eternal present. The flaming sword which excluded the unregenerate (but not the Quakers) from Eden was repossessed as 'the sword of the mouth' with which, in emulation of the Christic Word of God (Revelation 19:13), they waged the Lamb's War against latterday followers of the Great Beast and the Whore of Babylon. Like Boehme (whose reinterpretation of St John's imagery both as psychod-rama and as a perennial call to linguistic arms against 'Babylon' influenced early Quaker thought about language), Fox had 'great openings concerning the things written in the Revelations', openings from which he learned that the confusion of tongues in Genesis 11 was re-enacted as 'mystery' (if not as 'history') in Revelation.[87] How crucial this realization became to the Quakers' 'apocalypse of the word' a particular incident will make clear.

In 1658 Fox encountered a functionary of the Puritan government despatched to Durham in order 'to set up a college there to make ministers of Christ'.[88] Fox and some fellow Quakers remonstrated with the man to:

> let him see that this was not the way to make them Christ's ministers by Hebrew, Greek, Latin and the Seven Arts, which all were but teachings of the natural man. For the many languages began at Babel ... and they set them atop Christ the Word when they crucified him. And John the Divine, who preached the Word that was in the beginning, said that the beast and the whore have power over tongues and languages ... which are in mystery Babylon, for they began at Babel ... But [Christ] is risen over them all, who was before Babel was. And did he think to make ministers of Christ by these natural, confused languages, at Babel and in Bablyon, set a-top Christ the Life by a persecutor? Oh no![89]

For orthodox Christians, Hebrew, Greek, and Latin had each been ennobled by Pilate's decision to set them over the crucified Christ.[90] But Friends contrasted the Babylonian provenance of those languages with the fact that Christ the Word had not only preceded them (from 'the beginning') but also triumphed over them with the sword of his mouth. Indeed Babel/Babylon came to symbolize, for the Friends as for other saints, the fallen and diabolic state of mid-seventeenth century language – rendered falsely respectable in schools and universities – against which they waged an apocalyptic war of words. Fox's Edenic trance and his reacquisition of Adamic insight into the *signatura rerum* represented one strategy for 'repairing the ruines of Babel' (the phrase is John Webster's), a visionary enterprise which gripped the nation's imagination, resulting in panaceas as disparate as the *pansophia* of the English Rosicrucians, the pentecostal fits of many sectaries, and the universal language schemes of the Royal Society.[91]

During the *confusio linguarum* language had (supposedly) suffered in two ways. As an *ars significandi* (or semantics), words lost their Edenic capacity to function as true names, as a paradisal semiology. As a *usus loquendi* (or sociolinguistics), language forfeited its unity and unanimity – displayed when 'the whole earth was of one language and one speech' (Genesis 11:1) – to diversity and multiplicity; moreover, ideal communication between folk was ruptured not simply because they could no longer understand each other but because they could now lie, a development already signalled in Eden by the devil, traditionally reviled as the 'Father of Lies'. Dreams of 'repairing the ruines of Babel' have preoccupied folk ever since a consciousness of the inadequacies of language, both semantic and sociolinguistic, dawned upon them, but the intensity and scope of the Quakers' commitment to the task of repair is remarkable, even amidst the apocalyptic fervour generated by the Puritan Revolution.

Fox denounced the academic study of Hebrew, Greek, and Latin as degenerate: registering merely the *usus loquendi* which began at Babel, these 'tongues' did not reflect either the linguistic glory of the original *fiat* or the first body. Moreover, proficiency in tongues required a formal education which Quakers, like all sectaries, denounced volubly, maintaining that Christian ministry was conferred by the spirit, not by training in schools and universities, those outworks of Babylon.[92] For England's last days (particularly when viewed as psychodrama) the 'pure language' latent in the vernacular proved ideal, since, as Boehme remarked, 'every nation builds it out of its own materials, for in the right universal tongue we are altogether but one only people and nation even from Adam.'[93] And of all vernaculars, as we have seen, English was best fitted for the apocalypse of the word. Arrayed against the pure language, which had guaranteed unanimity before the *confusio linguarum* and in which men could now call again to God 'with one consent', were not simply dead languages like Hebrew, Greek, and Latin but the arbitrary customs which still governed vernacular usage. Custom, explained Thomas Fuller when rejecting Quaker shibboleths, was 'the great master of language', and it was against this tyranny of shifting conventions, people's 'changeable words' in Fox's memorable phrase, that Friends waged the Lamb's War.

When Friends 'took up the cross' against what Mary Penington called 'the language, fashions, customs, titles, honour and esteem in the world', they thus challenged the Babylonian hegemony of the grand master, custom: in conventions determining pronominal choice; in 'politeness phenomena' such as hat-honour, 'bowing and scraping',and the routine exchange of salutations; in gay apparel; and in pagan and popish relics in calendar and place names. Quaker infractions of customary usage were intended as outward signs of an inward state, just as those Friends who went 'naked for a sign' demonstrated their attainment of Adamic 'innocency' or their determination to offer an apocalyptic reproach to the threadbare conventions of Anglicanism and Presbyterianism, 'signifying to you that the day was near at hand, even at the door, in which the Lord would strip you naked and bare'.[94] The Quakers' rejection of oaths and their decision to use the pure language of 'yea and nay' also revealed, Isaac Penington explained, their inner attainment both of Adam's 'state of innocency' and of a chiliastic 'state of true redemption' in which oaths were unnecessary because lying was unimaginable; 'brought back from the death, from the fall, from the deceit, and from the shadows into the truth, into the pure life, into the innocency', Isaac Penington continued, Quakers were 'new formed in Christ's new image, and

become a new creature' with a 'new spirit and conversation'.[95] After James
Nayler rode into Bristol in 1656 in symbolic *imitation* of Christ's entry into
Jerusalem (and *not* as Christ himself, as his persecutors claimed), he offered
the vindication that 'it pleased the Lord to set me up as a sign of the Coming
of the Righteous One . . . as to the outward, as a sign.'[96] Christ, the second
Adam, had returned – as a mystery and not as history – to teach his people:
not merely in the person of Nayler but in everyone who rejected ceremonial
observances (pronominal, liturgical, calendrical, juridical) in order to participate in 'the everlasting day, the Day of Christ Jesus'.[97] Hence any adherence
to 'vain customs and fashions', a *usus loquendi* initiated at Babel, was a sign of
postlapsarian weakness: 'Touching good even and good morrow, spoken
without fear of the Lord, we do deny', Fox declared, 'but good to all men we
wish and the good day that they may be brought into it . . . we witness the
happy day of the Lord is come, the good and happy day, the day of Christ.'[98]

Fox's rediscovery in 1648 of the *ars significandi* employed by Adam, 'how
all things had their names given them according to their nature', also
contributed to Quaker perceptions of the debased role of language in a
postlapsarian society. But unlike Webster and other alchemically minded
sectaries, Quakers did not work experimentally on the task of restoring 'all
the rich treasury of nature's admirable and excellent secrets', the paradisal
semiology. Instead Friends embarked on a moral and experiential critique of
fallen names, contrasting them with 'Christ, whose name is above every
name . . . and by this you come to fathom all other names under the whole
Heaven'.[99] Indeed Babylonian semantics had menaced Quakerism from its
moment of origin as a *named* sect. The sobriquet 'Quaker' was imposed in
mockery ('because we bid [men] tremble at the name of the Lord') by Justice
Gervase Bennett in 1650, a sinful abuse of language which Fox denounced
vehemently: 'A Justice to wrong name people! What may the brutish people
do, if a justice of the peace gives names to men? But thou art lifted up proud
and haughty, and so turnest against the just, and misnamest the Saints.'[100]
Inhabiting a 'familial universe' where *thou* and *thee* were appropriate,
Quakers preferred the more neutral term 'Friend' or spiritual designations
like 'the royal seed of God'. When they themselves employed the term
'Quaker' they prefixed it with 'a people called', as Thomas Fuller noted,
since they regarded it as a 'nickname'; that is, as one applied not according to
the *ars significandi* of Adam or of Christ the Word but according to the
mendacious principles of 'Old Nick', the Father of Lies who had tempted
Justice Bennett into 'wrong naming' them.[101]

'I am not one of them, which call themselves Papists, Anglicans, nor
Presbyterians, Independents, Anabaptists, Puritans', declared Fox, 'but that
which God called me to, the elect before the world began.'[102] Here Fox
draws not upon the Edenic achievements of his 1648 trance but upon his
subsequent return to an eternal moment before names, even Adamic names,

'before languages were ... out of languages into the power where all men shall agree'. Divided and reified by postlapsarian names, Christians will never agree: only when they return to the pure language and call upon the name of the Lord with one consent, as Zephaniah had prophesied, will unity and unanimity replace multiplicity and disagreement. 'All they that are in the Light are in unity', explained Fox,

> all who know the word which is a mystery are come to the beginning ... for this word is as a fire, burning up all corruption, as a hammer that beats down all high minds, high nature, that the pure seed may be raised up; as a sword that cuts to pieces, and divides asunder the precious from the vile ... and this is the word of reconciliation, that reconciliation together to God, and gathers the hearts of his people together, to live in love and unity one with another.[103]

The paradoxical energies of the pure language – on one hand an apocalyptic sword, on the other an outward sign of the Friends' loving unity – register the paradox of Quakerism itself. For in order to preach 'the light within' Friends acted as a chiliastic *force de frappe*, savagely attacking (albeit with words and not swords) the sinfulness of men and women they were determined to save.

'The battle is begun, the Beast is raging mad', Farnworth thundered in 1653: 'but fear not, come into the battle.'[104] Once enlisted in the Lamb's Army that descended on England from the north, Quakers were guaranteed 'new names' from the Lamb's 'Book of Life' (Revelation 2:17; 3:5), which provided talismanic security when they waged war on those who bore the mark of the Beast and mouthed 'changeable words'. This 'secret language' of new names – we recall the secret languages acquired by alchemist and shaman – conferred a chiliastic authority on the Friends and distinguished them still further from those who were yet in bondage to the 'old names' of the Fall and postlapsarian creation. Farnworth styled himself 'one whom the world calls a Quaker / But is of the divine nature made partaker' and declared, in what was perhaps the fullest Quaker exposition of new names, that he was

> redeemed out of all kindreds, tongues, and nations, one whom the world knows not, neither me, nor my name: I am a Soldier and if any inquire after me or my name, they may find it in the spiritual muster-roll or Book of Life; saith the Lord, I will give them new names which none can know but those that have them, and I witness that name given me, and is unknown to the world. The old man, the old name; the new man, the new name; he that is in Christ is a new creature, old things are passed away; and all things are become new ...

those that are born again and are in Christ know both me and my name; and those that are in the Fall, and the old nature know neither me nor my name.[105]

If the pure language constituted an outward sign – directed at those still inhabiting a fallen world and the old nature – of the Friends' new creation within, then their new names comprised a secret language comprehensible only to God and to other members of their community who had experienced a *vergeistigten Chiliasmus*.[106] Exactly how this secret language could be shared – other than by an experience of phatic communion – was never disclosed.

On the title and end pages of their many publications, Friends forcefully contrasted the new names which they had learned from the Lamb's Book of Life with the old names by which they were known in the world. The most frequently used construction was 'by one known to the world as . . .', but often a baroque ingenuity prevailed. Edward Bourne, Fox's alchemist friend, styled himself 'a follower of the Lamb who makes war with the sword of his mouth known amongst men by the name of Edward Bourne'; Marmaduke Stephenson wrote from Boston gaol as 'a friend of truth, and a sufferer for the Seed's sake which is kept in bondage under Pharaoh and his Taskmasters, my name in the flesh is Marmaduke Stephenson'; and Charles II received 'a Noble Salutation . . . from the council and nobility of the Royal Seed, the Lion of the Tribe of Judah, the Everlasting King of Righteousness who reigneth in George Fox the Younger'.[107]

The world, the flesh, and the devil still presided over those arbitrary and customary names which had been confirmed upon children during the pagan ceremony of baptism; but reintegration with the Word released Quakers from such postlapsarian traditions. Generalizing from individual to community, Farnworth repeatedly assailed his contemporaries for employing 'the nickname of *Quakers*'. Farnworth's litany of examples was unusual only for the frequency and intensity of its qualifications – 'those thou reproachest and revilest under the nickname of Quakers'; 'thou judgeth the Quakers (by thee so called)'; 'those thou reproachest and revilest under the nickname of Quakers' – and the mannerism gained widespread favour.[108] From such linguistic entrapments of the Fall the pure language promised release. But with a 'new song' on their lips and 'their Father's name written upon their foreheads', Friends confidently issued 'A Call out of Egypt and Babylon', declaring that the pure language would release men from the bondage of the old words and ensure their triumphant arrival in the New Jerusalem.[109]

The final paradox was that the New Jerusalem, as envisaged and visited by Fox, was devoid of words: 'So here is the city within the Light where there is no place nor language, but there his voice may be heard.[110] In its original and final manifestation the 'pure language' comprised a silence broken only by the eternal voice of God, the creative logos and 'the first speaker in

Paradise'.[111] 'The end of words', explained Isaac Penington, 'is to bring men to a knowledge of things beyond which words can utter.'[112] With the absence of words – experienced by Fox at the beginning as well as at the end of time – people became reunited with the eternal Word: 'I saw into that which was without end, and things which cannot be uttered, and of the greatness and infiniteness of the love of God, which cannot be expressed in words.'[113] The most distinctive feature of Quaker worship was its long periods of silence. 'Sometimes after they are congregated', complained one critic in 1653, 'there is (altum silentium) not a whisper amongst them for an hour or two or three together.'[114] When Fox preached in Yorkshire in 1651, he recorded how he 'sat on a haystack and spoke nothing for some hours for I was to famish them of words'.[115]

At most of the great 'threshing' meetings, of course, when new Friends were gathered in, there were those 'raptures, ecstasies, swoonings, groanings, tumblings, and prostrations, skreekings, murmurings, trances' to which contemporaries objected so forcefully.[116] Silent meetings were customarily designed for those from whom the world's words had already been winnowed, that is for the convinced. Fox reminded the faithful that they should leave 'the wandering whirling tempest' of human language in order to share 'the fellowship where there is no words spoken ... drinking at the springs of life where they do not speak words'.[117] Long before Fox preached the dawning of the Lord's Day, Zephaniah had also famished his auditory: 'Keep silence at the presence of the Lord God; for the day of the Lord is at hand' (1:7). In Revelation, 'there was silence in heaven about the space of half an hour after the opening of the seventh seal' (8:1). Fox claimed to preach when 'the time of silence was known': 'such as know the seven seals shall know silence in heaven.'[118] At this climactic juncture it was no longer necessary to provide an outward verbal manifestation of one's arrival in paradise and the New Jerusalem. After the Lamb's War had been won, the pure language became wordless: 'new songs' unheard were sweeter than those heard. 'Let all flesh be silent before the Lord, amongst you', wrote Charles Marshall as late as 1677: 'cease from a multitude of words, that is not from the guidance of the Word, which was in the beginning; and cease from those discourses that draw the mind out from an inward, deep sense of the invisible, immutable power of the Lord God Almighty.'[119]

IV

When Quakers endeavoured to sustain and protract their experience of realized eschatology – their inner sense that 'Christ has come to teach his people himself', that 'the everlasting day, the day of Christ Jesus' has dawned – they faced difficulties which were to prove well-nigh insurmountable, both for the individual and for the community. During the 1650s, as the Lamb's War raged, Friends espoused a christology which bears an uncanny resemblance to the first Christians', as that has been reinterpreted by some twentieth-century scholars. 'Jesus proclaimed the incarnation of God, the mystery of the heavenly father coming to dwell among his people', observes Thomas Sheehan, constrasting early Christian *experience* with later hypostatizations by established churches: 'Jesus preached that God was arriving in the present–future', a complex apocalyptic arrival which betokened both 'a radical sense of time' and 'God's presence among men and women'.[120]

The Quakers' vision of this present–future – as manifested in their elision of scriptural time-frames – is directly comparable to the early Christian grasp, as can be seen from Douglas Gwyn's fine exposition of 'the World's time versus God's'.[121] So too is their awareness of 'that of God in every one', provocatively re-enacted by Nayler, whose ride into Bristol 'as a sign of the Coming of the Righteous one' demonstrated the present (and mysterious) fact of indwelling rather than the anticipations of a second coming infinitely deferred throughout the course of history.[122] For issuing a semiological challenge so subversive of orthodox Christology – a Christology in which, Sheehan contends, the Church 'has surrendered the present–future and in its place constructed the mythical past–present–future of a cosmic "salvation-history" according to which God had become man in the past, was reigning in heaven at present, and would return to earth in the future'[123] – Nayler was savagely punished by Parliament in a travesty of justice: his forehead was branded, his tongue was bored, and he was whipped through the streets of London and Bristol. Friends repudiated Nayler not for his theological doctrines (such as those were) but for the extravagance with which he and his claque of female supporters had dramatized the Quaker experience of indwelling. Nayler's fate sent tremors of anxiety through Quakerism; yet Friends continued to wage the Lamb's War. Extrinsic acts of persecution posed less of a threat to their *vergeistigten Chiliasmus* – adversity only rendered them more valiant for truth – than did its intrinsic untenability over extended periods of time.

The Quakers' reading of Revelation, like their Christology, also approximated to what has been posited for the early Christians. 'The moral strategy of the Apocalypse', observes Wayne A. Meeks,

is to destroy common sense as a guide for life. Prudential morality is based on the taken-for-granted consensus about the way things are . . . So long as one does not disturb the public order or wilfully affront one of the symbols or agents of her sovereignty, Rome is a powerful but benign presence. That is the common sense view and from it follows a quiet and peaceable life. The vision of the Apocalypse shreds and rips away that common sense.[124]

For Rome as embodiment of Babylon, the Quakers substituted Puritan England, shredding the common sense and prudential morality of their contemporaries no less vigorously than did the first Christians. Custom as 'the grand master of language' – the *usus loquendi* of Babel which was taken for granted in the vernacular – they assailed with an especial ferocity, affronting public order with their symbolic refusal to abide by the established consensus on pronominal usage. Agents of authority – justices, ministers, local gentry – were infuriated when they were addressed as *thee*, when hat-honour was denied them, when the customary order of courtroom and church service was broken by Quaker outbursts and harangues. Once we comprehend the bellicosity with which the Friends waged their apocalyptic war of words, it is not difficult to see why many members of the establishment believed that Quaker rhetoric was merely a prelude to terrorism and insurrection in which distinctions between mine and thine would also be obliterated. But despite the Friends' onslaught on the status quo – aspects of which, like their refusal to pay tithes, had genuine economic consequences – their radicalism was, ultimately, spiritual rather than political.[125] For if the Friends' 'linguistic politics' – words as swords 'dividing the precious from the vile' – was designed to cauterize darkness and Babylonian pride from the human heart, it also functioned as communal psychodrama, its goal the dawning of a light within rather than the outward establishment of a communist polity.

As universalists, Quakers were determined that the whole world should bask in the light of love and unity – their 'word of reconciliation' – which had first illuminated their own community; their rejection of a sectarian identity (and name) reflected this drama of world-wide convincement. Tireless and resourceful as evangelists overseas – the extraordinary journeys undertaken by Lamb's Warriors have not received the separate study they deserve[126] – Friends emulated the Apostles who had fanned throughout the Mediterranean once they had received the gift of tongues at Pentecost. Some Quakers also laid claim to this gift – in which Babel's *confusio linguarum* was again transcended – and in 1657 two 'were found in the streets [of Paris] so starved with cold and hunger, that one would have thought the spirit had been dead in them ... what their message was is unknown, but they despaired not of the gift of tongues';[127] needless to say, they knew no French! In another elision of time-frames, the Society's pure language thus became a pentecostal manifestation of Acts 2 as well as of Genesis, Zephaniah, the fourth gospel, and Revelation. Of course, unity and unanimity – as linguistically figured forth at Pentecost – represented an ideal rather than actuality: thus the Quakers insisted on a public definition of the Society through shibboleth even as they worked towards their dream of world-wide convincement. Overseas, as at home, their endeavours were pacifistic and symbolic rather than militaristic: convincement demanded verbal not physical violence.

During the 1640s the New Model Army had marched to the beat of a different millenial drum – Cromwell's fiery chaplain Hugh Peters carried a Bible in one hand, a pistol in the other[128] – and even as late as 1661 Fifth Monarchists seized the literal sword of Psalm 149. Yet the Quakers remained true to Revelation as that was understood by the early Christians.[129] 'Military images abound in John's depiction of "what must soon take place"', explains Meeks,

> but the active combatants are primarily superhuman: Christ and the angels against the forces of the great dragon. The metaphoricity of their combat is also emphasized by some of the biblical language: Christ conquers by 'the sword of the mouth' and by his sacrifice as the slain Lamb. The humans who 'conquer' do so by remaining faithful, perhaps also to the point of death, not by taking up arms against the government. The Revelation is no call for revolutionary action, but for passive resistance, for disengagement and quietism.[130]

Unlike their antinomian predecessors of the 1640s, the Quakers were metaphoric iconoclasts who broke social and linguistic conventions – politeness phenomena – rather than stained glass windows, market crosses, and medieval statues.[131] Thus bizarre behaviour – going naked as a sign was but one example – replaced the desecration of physical objects which had characterized the earlier decade. And, like early Christians, the Lamb's Warriors were faithful unto death, as Christopher Hill grimly notes when he records 'the extraordinary mortality rate among [Quaker] leaders in the early 1660s – great tribute to the English gaols in removing "undesirables".'[132] The Lamb's War wound down after the Restoration of Charles II in 1660, but not simply because so many soldiers had been eliminated (at least in this world) from Farnworth's 'spiritual muster-roll'.

To sustain for long the spiritual excitement of a realized eschatology is intrinsically impossible: in general, human kind cannot bear very much 'unreality' and will yearn, once the pinnacles of apocalyptic experience have been scaled, to descend back into the quotidian routines of a quiet and peaceable life. At the height of the Lamb's War, Friends sustained a passionately rhetorical mimicry of Christ's superhuman struggle with the Great Beast and Whore. After 1660 they came increasingly to wage 'not war but diplomacy' – as Richard Bauman aptly characterizes their overall retreat from a gratuitously confrontational use of shibboleths[133] – and moved steadily towards that disengagement and quietism which proved the hallmark of their spirituality for the next century.

To be sure, the Restoration witnessed continued persecution, which intensified after Parliament's passage of the repressive Quaker Act in 1662. Passive resistance continued unabated, notably in the Friends' refusal to swear either judicial or political oaths; Solomon Eccles paraded naked through Westminster Hall and Bartholomew Fair, and engaged in such semiological bizarrerie as lighting a bonfire of books and musical instruments on Tower Hill.[134] But the pure language was no longer wielded with the military ardour of the 1650s. Historians have occasionally lamented the gradual advent of the Lamb's diplomacy and contrast the majestic frenzy of Quakers' testimonies during the Puritan Revolution with their Restoration prudence, which rendered even valour in the face of persecution (still a quixotic valour when judged from a worldly consensus 'about the way things are!') long-suffering and patient rather than provocatively wilful or antagonistic. Clearly many Quakers had begun to aspire to a quiet life in which they could worship peaceably, an aspiration finally realized, albeit by a grudging Parliament, in the Toleration Act of 1689 and the Affirmation Act of 1696. Such a goal demanded not merely judicious diplomacy with successive Stuart governments but a moderation, both linguistic and semiological, of uncontrolled hostility to the agents and symbols of England's latterday Babylon.

The consolidation of a 'gospel order' by Friends involved discouragement of 'imagined, unseasonable, and untimely prophesyings'.[135] 'Going naked as a sign' was frowned upon, although Fox did not repudiate his friend Eccles. The incantatory and passionately 'agrammatical' style chosen by the Lamb's Warriors and First Publishers of Truth gradually gave way to a genuinely *plain* language, which lacked the chiliastic edge and justification that I have limned in early Quaker rationales for the *pure* language. Indeed Quaker idiosyncrasies of speech – once their apocalyptic purpose had slackened – began to appear as one linguistic custom amidst the many current in England, the mark of a peculiar people rather than a defiant challenge to postlapsarian human pride.

'The prophets of a new age of the Spirit had become inoffensive bourgeois eccentrics!', concludes Horton Davies: 'Revolution and rapture had been succeeded by retirement, innovation by innocuousness.'[136] With the publication in 1678 of Robert Barclay's *Apology for the True Christian Divinity: Being an Explanation and Vindication of the Priciples and Doctrines of the People Called Quakers*, doctrine clearly began to vie with experience for supremacy. This was in marked contrast to the early 1650s when Mary Penington rightly intuited that Friends preferred prayer to theology. Dedicated to Charles II and first published in Latin (1676), Barclay's *Apology* constitutes a classic of theology, a claim which cannot be made for earlier tracts by the Lamb's Warriors who had denounced Latin as 'the language of the beast'. The old freedom to publish – once the gauntlet of state censorship had been run – any vision of the truth, however antinomian, had already been eroded. With the establishment of the Second Day Morning Meeting in 1672 to review manuscripts, it has been argued that the practice of 'Quaker censorship' was formally instituted.[137] One work was 'delivered back for waste paper', another was deemed 'very difficult to read and to distinguish the matter, by reason it is not right English'; a work dealing with Jacob Boehme was judged 'a mixture of light and darkness' and neither 'suitable nor safe' for publication; two treatises by Isaac Penington were 'not judged meet to be printed'.[138] The Meeting's minutes certainly reflect Quaker anxiety about heterodox or ecstatic works which could bring the Society into disrepute, but careful inspection does not disclose a marked tendency towards thought control. In the most noteworthy of these moves towards prudence and common sense as a guide for life, Fox's *Journal* first appeared in an edition discreetly censored by Thomas Ellwood; its ancillary 'book of miracles' – the thaumaturgic legacy of Fox's Edenic trance of 1648 – was eliminated.[139] Even so, twelve of Fox's 'miracles' were indexed and the folio volume provoked a firestorm of conservative criticism.[140]

During the 1660s Fox had himself proved instrumental in the successful establishment of a 'gospel order', demonstrating thereby his brilliance not only as a charismatic leader (so evident in the 1650s) but also as an organizer who was determined that outbursts of waywardness like Nayler's should not endanger the spiritual legacies of the Lamb's War and its realized eschatology. The task of reconciling individual liberty with the needs of the community was a delicate one and Fox's endeavours provoked lively opposition, his detractors mocking the 'Foxonian unity' which, they complained, would lead Friends 'from the rule within to subject us to a rule without'.[141] Given Fox's new emphasis upon communal decisions – the meeting house replaced hillside and marketplace as the locus of worship – internalized apocalypsism was dislodged as the *quidditas* of Quaker faith and practice, the critical experience which transformed and convinced Friends' comprehension of language and reality. Or, rather, the dawning of Christ's Day within became a spiritual transformation which required some monitoring from the believer's local meeting and no longer demanded that he or she confronted Babylon's agents with the sword of the mouth.

In a Restoration world which resolutely refused to end – a world, moreover, of such encroaching and recognizably 'modern' phenomena as insurance policies, fire brigades, and the Royal Society[142] – even internalized apocalypsism and its pure language seemed less plausible than they once had during the high drama and magico-mystical ferment of the Puritan Revolution. Quaker eschatology moved closer to orthodoxy as rendered by Thomas Sheehan, an orthodoxy which Albert Schweitzer identifies with 'the delay of the *parousia*, the non-occurrence of the *parousia*' and finally 'the abandonment of eschatology, the progress and completion of the de-eschatologising of religion'.[143] By 1660 Fox had already begun to chide some Quakers for their willingness to 'speak half the confused language of the world, and half the true language', namely their readiness to adapt pronominal shibboleths, when not amongst Friends, to the postlapsarian norms of contemporary usage.[144] 'No cross, no crown', declared Penn with characteristic brevity, and the willingness of most Quakers to shoulder the cross and suffer for their linguistic convictions still helped give the movement its firm definition.[145] Curiously it was the schismatics opposed to Foxonian unity who advocated appeasement of, rather than diplomacy with, the government, so that they could follow the promptings of their own spirit without state repression. Mainstream Quakers stuck to their linguistic principles, but when they took up their cross in English gaols they accepted a fate as the Lamb's hostages rather than as His warriors. After 1660 most Quaker commentaries on the pure language remained formally compatible with those issued during the previous decade, as an examination of the dates of quotations in this essay will confirm; when changes occurred, they were gradual and not consistently unidirectional.[146]

After the Restoration, Quakerism succumbed to what Max Weber describes as 'the routinization of charisma', a development as inevitable to every branch of Christianity as the loss of the present–future and the de-eschatologizing of belief.[147] From Weber's perspective as a sociologist, the Lamb's diplomacy and the establishment of gospel order would represent aspects rather than causes of this predictable routinization. Both charismatic leadership and discipleship, Weber explains, are 'undiminished, consistent, and effective only *in statu nascendi* ... When the tide that lifted a charismatically led group out of everyday life flows back into the channels of workaday routines, at least the "pure" form of charismatic domination will wane and turn into an institution.'[148] Weber was anticipated – more passionately and with specific reference to the waning of the pure language – by Stephen Crisp, who in 1666 waxed melancholy when he saw 'the words and speech again corrupted and run into the old channel of the world, and the single pure language learned in the light, in the time of their poverty and simplicity, almost lost and forgotten'.[149] Always indefatigable as talkers and writer, Friends have also striven energetically to ensure that none of their spiritual heritage is lost or forgotten, an endeavour to which their remarkable libraries bear witness. Without the advent of a secure gospel order during the 1660s, it is doubtful whether their vision of the single pure language learned in the light could have survived as living inspiration rather than as a historical curiosity like the tracts of Ranters or Muggletonians. During the 1960s Quaker opponents of the Vietnam War raised again the standard of the Lamb's War; when faced by the threat of nuclear catastrophe – a potential apocalypse wrought not by divine but by human hands – some Quakers have rediscovered 'the courage to be' from the *vergeistigten Chiliasmus* of Fox and the First Publishers of Truth. The pure language may well flow back into worldly channels of workaday routine, but Quaker history suggests that spiritual tides will always return to an original and undiminished light.

V

The tumultuous birth of Quakerism and its growing respectability are not unique phenomena in the history of Christianity – *vergeistigter Chiliasmus* and the routinization of charisma will be with us until doomsday – but never have the early years of a religious movement been so exhaustively documented, either by its adherents or by its detractors. And the Friends' striking ability to reconcile economic triumphs with a continuing moral witness also ensures the Society a unique place in history. Yet the importance of 'plain' and 'pure' language cannot be confined to denominational or even to religious history. When Quakers challenged custom as grand master of language and behaviour, they revealed an innate kinship with contemporaries ostensibly as different as Thomas Hobbes and Fellows of the Royal Society. For all of them strove to rearticulate the links binding *res et verba*, whether these were construed in terms of *usus loquendi* or of *ars significandi*. In each of the period's cultural domains – from literature, philosophy, and law to science, medicine, and magic – comparable endeavours yielded revolutionary consequences, sociolinguistically no less than semantically. Mid-seventeenth-century England was racked by semiological and linguistic crises – indeed, given the revisionist historiography of the Puritan Revolution which currently prevails, these may soon constitute the sole revolutionary changes left to document! – but the dialectic between Quaker speechways and national crises must remain matter for a future study.

ACKNOWLEDGEMENTS

The substance of this essay was delivered as the annual T. Wistar Brown Lecture at Haverford College on 19 November, 1987. A printed version subsequently appeared in Italian as 'Dallo Scibboleth all'Apocalisse', in *Lingua Tradizione Rivelazione: Le Chiese et la comunicazione sociale*, eds Lia Formigari and Donatelli Di Cesare (Casale Monferrato: Marietti Università, 1989). All texts in the present revision have been modernized. I am grateful to Haverford College for the award of its T. Wistar Brown Fellowship, 1987–8, and to the staff of its library's Quaker Collection, particularly Edwin Bronner, Elisabeth Potts Brown, and Diana Alten, for their invaluable assistance. I am also grateful to Dick Brown and his staff at the Newberry Library (where I held a Newberry/NEH Fellowship) and to Malcolm Thomas and his colleagues at Friends House Library (where I worked under the aegis of an ACLS Grant-in-Aid) for their efficiency and hospitality.

Comments and encouragement from Kenneth Carroll, Vincent Cherchia, Charles Cherry, Douglas Gwyn, Christopher Hill, Craig Horle, Dell Hymes, Jo Martin, Nigel Smith, and Vivian Salmon have also proved indispensable. All errors of fact and interpretation remain my own.

NOTES

1　For the strange adventures of Franklin, Gadbury, and their disciples see Humphrey Ellis, *Pseudochristus: Or, a True and Faithful Relation of the Grand Impostures, Horrid Blasphemies, Abominable Practises, Gross Deceits Lately Spread Abroad* (London: Luke Fawn, 1650).

2　Samuel Butler, *Hudibras*, ed. John Wilders (Oxford: Clarendon Press, 1967), I, ii, 535–8.

3　Not until the late eighteenth century did Quakers become the Religious Society of Friends, although 'Society of Friends' had already gained currency during the Restoration. To avoid monotony, I have used 'Quaker', 'Friend', and 'Society' interchangeably.

4　John L. Nickalls, ed., *The Journal of George Fox* (London: Religious Society of Friends, 1975), pp. 8–9. All quotations come from this edition unless otherwise noted.

5　Norman Penney, ed., *Experiences in the Life of Mary Penington* (Philadelphia: The Biddle Press, 1911), pp. 38–40. All the ensuing quotations from Mary come from pp. 38–42 and 52–3.

6　T.L. Underwood, 'Early Quaker Eschatology', in *Puritans, the Millennium and the Future of Israel: Puritan Eschatology 1600 to 1660*, ed. Peter Toon (Cambridge: James Clarke, 1970), p. 96.

7　A convenient overview may be found in David Burns Windsor, *The Quaker Enterprise: Friends in Business* (London: Frederick Muller, 1980).

8　Thomas Fuller, *The Church History of Britain* (London: John Williams, 1655), dedicatory epistle to Book VIII (unpaginated). Fuller penned this dedicatory epistle to Francis Greville, Baron Brooke, immediately prior to the publication of his large folio history. All quotations from Fuller come from this six-page epistle.

9　George Wither, *Vaticinia Poetica* (London: Edward Blackmore, 1666), p. 10. This work was written in the mid-1650s; Wither subsequently warmed to the Society.

10　Penelope Brown and Stephen Levinson, 'Universals in Language Usage: Politeness Phenomena', in *Questions and Politeness*, ed. Esther N. Goody (Cambridge: Cambridge University Press, 1978), pp. 56–289; William Simpson, *A Discovery of the Priests and Professors, and their Nakedness and Shame which is coming upon them* (London: Robert Wilson, 1660), p. 8. See also: Norman Penney, *The First Publishers of Truth: Being Early Records (Now First Printed) of the Introduction to Quakerism into the Counties of England and Wales*

(London: Headley, 1907), pp. 364–9. Kenneth L. Carroll, 'Early Quakers and "Going Naked as a Sign"', *Quaker History*, 67 (1978), pp. 69–87; Richard Bauman, *Let Your Words Be Few: Symbolism of Speaking and Silence among Seventeenth Century Quakers* (Cambridge: Cambridge University Press, 1983), pp. 84–94.

11 Fox, *Journal*, pp. 36–7.

12 See, for example, Christopher Hill, *The World Turned Upside down: Radical Ideas during the English Revolution* (New York: Viking, 1972); Barry Reay, *The Quakers and the English Revolution* (New York: St Martin's Press, 1985). Yet denominational historians, it must be noted, customarily underemphasize the radical thrust of Quakerism.

13 Richard Farnworth, *The Pure Language of the Spirit of Truth ... or Thee and Thou in its Place* (London: no publisher given, 1655), p. 5.

14 James Parnel, *A Shield of the Truth* (London: Giles Calvert, 1655), p. 28.

15 Fox, *Journal*, p. 242.

16 Ibid., pp. 244–6.

17 Ibid., pp. 244–5.

18 Matthew 5: 34–7. In Launceston, Fox chose to cite the other key text, James 5:12. For a discussion of the Society's testimony on oaths see Bauman, *Let Your Words Be Few*, pp. 95–119, and for its grim legal consequences Craig W. Horle, *The Quakers and the English Legal System: 1660–1688* (Philadelphia: University of Pennsylvania Press, 1988).

19 See J. William Frost, 'The Affirmation Controversy and Religious Liberty', in *The World of William Penn*, ed. Richard S. Dunn and Mary Maples Dunn (Philadelphia: University of Pennsylvania Press, 1986), pp. 95–119.

20 Recently Richard Greaves has uncovered some evidence that Quakers were engaged in anti-government plotting: *Deliver us from Evil: The Radical Underground in Britain, 1660–1663* (New York: Oxford University Press, 1986), pp. 50–7; 'Conventicles, Sedition, and the Toleration Act of 1689', *Eighteenth-Century Life*, 12 (1988), pp. 11–13.

21 Bronislaw Malinowski, *Coral Gardens and Their Magic: A Study of the Methods of Tilling the Soil and of Agricultural Rites in the Trobriand Islands* (London: Allen and Unwin, 1935), II, p. 234.

22 Butler, *Hudibras*, II, ii, 107–8, 188–90. For specific discussion of Quaker testimonies see lines 219–32. Butler derides the Society's testimony on oaths, but his treatment indicates, willy-nilly, its moral coherence amidst so much expediency and lying. For more on the heated Restoration context see Susan Staves, *Players' Scepters: Fictions of Authority in the Restoration* (Lincoln, Nebr.: University of Nebraska Press, 1979), pp. 191–251.

23 William Penn, *A Treatise of Oaths* (London?: no publisher, 1675), pp. 14, 24.

24 See, for example, Fox, *Journal*, p. 195.

25 William Penn, *A Brief Account of the Rise and Progress of the People Called Quakers* (London: T. Sowle, 1694), p. 45; Fox, *Journal*, pp. 23, 70.

26 For a discussion of Quaker Billingsgate see Hugh Ormsby-Lennon, 'Swift and the Quakers: I', *Swift Studies*, 4 (1989), pp. 34–62.

27 Fuller, *Church History of Britain*, dedicatory epistle to Book VIII.

28 George Fox, *The Great Mistery of the Great Whore Unfolded* (London: Thomas

Simmons, 1659), p. 120. That Fox's source was 2 Kings 18:27 did not, one suspects, make the recipient of his invective, Gyles Fermin, any the more comfortable. For a discussion of other examples of the Society's 'emetic language', see Nigel Smith, *Perfection Proclaimed: Language and Literature in English Radical Religion 1640–1660* (Oxford: Clarendon Press, 1989), pp. 334–5.

29   Francis Higginson, *A Brief Relation of the Irreligion of the Northern Quakers* (London: H.R. at the sign of the Three Pigeons, 1653), p. 28.

30   James Nayler, *An Answer to the Book called The Perfect Pharisee under Monkish Holiness* (No place, no publisher, no date), p. 21.

31   Penn, *Rise and Progress*, p. 46.

32   *Love's Labours Lost*, V, ii, 406–13.

33   This ringing admonition is recorded on the memorial tablet on Firbank Fell where Fox delivered his great Whitsunday sermon in 1652: see Fox, *Journal*, pp. 108–9.

34   See Amelia Mott Gummere, *The Quaker: A Study in Costume* (New York: Benjamin Blom, 1968 [1901]); Joan Kendall, 'The Development of a Distinctive Form of Quaker Dress', *Costume*, 19 (1985), pp. 58–74. For the melodramatic rituals during which Friends divested themselves of 'the Antick Fantastical Fashions of the World', see Ormsby-Lennon, 'Swift and the Quakers: I', pp. 42, 54.

35   Fox, *Journal*, pp. 1–2.

36   For representative studies of T and V see Joan Mulholland, '"Thou" and "You" in Shakespeare: A Study in the Second Person Pronoun', *English Studies*, 48 (1967), pp. 1–9; and Charles Barber, '"You" and "Thou" in Shakespeare's *Richard III*', *Leeds Studies in English*, n.s. 12 (1981), pp. 273–89. Continuing developments during the seventeenth century (with the exception of those relating to Quakerism) have not received the attention they deserve.

37   The best treatment remains Hugh Barbour, *The Quakers in Puritan England* (New Haven: Yale University Press, 1964), pp. 163–4.

38   Roger Brown and Albert Gilman, 'The Pronouns of Power and Solidarity', in *Style and Language*, ed. Thomas S. Sebeok (Cambridge, Mass.: MIT Press, 1960), p. 257.

39   Paul Friedrich, 'Structural Implications of Russian Pronominal Usage', in *Sociolinguistics*, ed. William Bright (Mouton: The Hague, 1971), p. 222.

40   Brown and Gilman, 'Pronouns of Power and Solidarity', p. 255; Fuller, 'Epistle', *Church History*, VIII.

41   Quoted by Brown and Gilman, 'Pronouns of Power and Solidarity', p. 275.

42   Edward Sapir, *Language* (New York: Harcourt Brace, 1921), pp. 146–70.

43   Brown and Gilman, 'Pronouns of Power and Solidarity', p. 253.

44   Friedrich, 'Structural Implications of Russian Pronominal Usage', pp. 248–9.

45   See Hugh Ormsby-Lennon, 'Metaphor and Madness', *ETC: A Review of General Semantics*, 33 (1976), pp. 307–18; Charles L. Cherry, *A Quiet Haven: Quakers, Moral Treatment, and Asylum Reform* (London and Toronto: Associated University Presses, 1989), pp. 24–50. Christopher Hill has, of course, suggested that ostensibly mad behaviour served a socially subversive function: see *The World Turned Upside Down*, pp. 223–30.

46   William Spurry, 'To the Friends appointed to collect the first publication of the Lord's everlasting truth in London in this age', in Penney, *The First Publishers of Truth*, p. 163. On the spiritual resonance of 'agrammaticality' see Jackson I. Cope, 'Seventeenth Century Quaker Style', *PMLA*, 71 (1956), pp. 725–54.

47   Thomas Ellwood, *The History of the Life of Thomas Ellwood* (London: J. Sowle, 1714), pp. 56–7. Although Ellwood himself did not favour the 'agrammatical' mannerisms favoured by almost all the First Publishers (even when they were schoolmasters) and deployed a style which would not have been amiss in *The Spectator*, his determination to adhere to the plain pronominal style influenced his corrections of manuscripts for the posthumous edition of Fox's *Journal* (1694).

48   Farnworth, *The Pure Language*, pp. 1–2.

49   See Fox, *A Battle-Door for Teachers and Professors to Learn Singular and Plural You to Many, and Thou to One: Singular One, Thou; Plural Many, You* (London: Robert Wilson, 1660), pp. 16–18 (separate pagination at end); Brown and Gilman, 'Pronouns of Power and Solidarity', p. 256 (for the Freudian dimensions).

50   Parnel, *A Shield of the Truth*, p. 28.

51   That several imprints carried 'Nakednesse a signe or figure' suggests that Quakers saw a direct parallel between 'going naked for a sign' and their use of *thee* and *thou*.

52   Fox, *A Battle-Door, passim*. Benjamin Furly was one of the most learned of the early Quakers. See William Hull, *Benjamin Furly and Quakerism in Rotterdam* (Lancaster, Pennsylvania: Lancaster Press, 1941).

53   See note 11.

54   For a facsimile of the relevant manuscript, Ellwood's revisions, and a commentary (which does not, however, embark upon an explanation) see Joseph Pickvance, *A Reader's Companion to George Fox's Journal* (London: Quaker Home Service, 1989), pp. 14–15.

55   On the profound significance of northern England for the Society and for its detractors see: Christopher Hill, 'Puritans and the "Dark Corners of the Land"', *Change and Continuity in Seventeenth-Century England* (London: Weidenfeld and Nicolson, 1974), esp. pp. 40–1; and Hugh Ormsby-Lennon, 'Swift and the Quakers: II', *Swift Studies*, 5 (1990), pp. 54–89.

56   On the saints' alleged propensity for sins of the flesh see Hugh Ormsby-Lennon, 'Raising Swift's Spirit: Das Dong-an-sich', *Swift Studies*, 3 (1988), pp. 9–78; 'Spirit' was a cant term for penis and semen.

57   Epistle 191 in George Fox, *A Collection of Many Select and Christian Epistles* (London: T. Sowle, 1698), p. 149.

58   Fox, *Journal*, pp. 410–20. For a recent discussion of Quakers and Fifth Monarchists see Greaves, *Deliver us from Evil*, pp. 52–9.

59   See variously Revelation 1:16; 2:12; 16; 19:16. See also 2 Corinthians 10:4 ('For the weapons of our warfare are not carnal, but mighty through God') and Ephesians 6:17 ('the sword of the Spirit, which is the word of God').

60   Edward Burrough, 'The Epistle to the Reader', in Fox, *The Great Mystery*, sig. B^2 r.

61   Joseph Wright, *A Testimony for the Son of Man* (London: Stephen Dagnal, 1661), p. 78. Remarkable not for its novelty but for its succinctness, Wright's criticism was restated, incessantly, throughout the rest of the century.

62   Theodor Sippell (1911) quoted by Geoffrey Nuttale, *The Welsh Saints 1640–1660* (Cardiff: University of Wales Press, 1957), p. 53. Nuttall refers to 'what is now called a "realized eschatology"', a phrase he derives from C.H. Dodd's important work, *The Parables of the Kingdom* (London: Nisbet, 1935); on 'internalized apocalypse' see M.H. Abrams, *Natural Supernaturalism: Tradition and Revolution in Romantic Literature* (New York: Norton, 1971), pp. 47–55, with specific reference to Boehme and Winstanley; and, further, Abrams, 'Apocalypse: Theme and Variations', in *The Apocalypse in English Renaissance Thought and Literature*, ed. C.A. Patrides and Joseph Wittreich (Ithaca, NY: Cornell University Press, 1984), esp. pp. 353–6 on 'The Apocalypse Within'. See also Maurice A. Creasey, *'Inward' and 'Outward': A Study in Early Quaker Language* (London: Friends' Historical Society, 1962). For a recent exposition (and critique) see Clayton Sullivan, *Rethinking Realized Eschatology* (Macon, Georgia: Mercer University Press, 1988).

63   Fox, *Journal*, pp. 232, 236–7. This was a theme to which Fox and all Friends returned.

64   William Dewsbury, *A True Prophecy of the Mighty Day of the Lord, which is coming and is appeared in the North of England, and moving towards the South and shall overspread all the Nations of the World* (London: Giles Calvert, 1654), title page.

65   John Audland, 'The Suffering Condition of the Servants of the Lord at this Day, Vindicated', in *The Memory of the Righteous Revived: Being a Brief Collection of the Books and Written Epistles of John Camm and John Audland*, eds Thomas Camm and Charles Marshall (London: Andrew Soule, 1689), p. 197. Worn out by proselytizing and persecution, Audland died of consumption in 1664.

66   Fox, 'Introduction', *A Battle-Door*, sig. A^2 v.

67   The myth (and reality) of Babel is one of immense significance in Western culture; backgrounds relevant to the Quaker contribution may be found in Arno Borst, *De Turmbau von Babel: Geschichte der Meinungen über Ursprung und Viefalt der Sprachen und Völker*, 6 vols (Stuttgart: Anton Hiersemann, 1957–63); Claude-Gilbert Dubois, *Mythe et Langage au Seizième Siècle* (Bordeaux: Ducros, 1970); George Steiner, *After Babel: Aspects of Language and Translation* (London: Oxford University Press, 1975).

68   I shall discuss non-Quaker visions of the pure language (and other related topics) in a separate essay tentatively entitled 'Shamans, Cargo Cults, and Quakerism: Pentecostal Phenomena during the English Revolution'.

69   John Webster, *Academiarum Examen, or The Examination of Academies* (London: Giles Calvert, 1654), p. 32.

70   Johannes Reuchlin, *Liber de verbo mirifico* ([1494]; reprinted Leiden, 1533), p. 124.

71   On the angelical language see 1 Corinthians 13, 2 Corinthians 12:1–4, and the discussion by Webster, *Academiarum Examen*, pp. 27–8. See also James D. Tabor, *Things Unutterable: Paul's Ascent to Paradise* (Lanham, Md.: University Press of America, 1986), which sheds considerable light on the linguistic

mysticism of mid-seventeenth century sects. See also Michel de Certeau, 'Le parler angélique', in *La Linguistique fantastique*, eds Sylvain Auroux, Jean-Claude Chevalier, Nicole Jacques-Chaquin, and Christiane Marchello-Nizia (Paris: Clims/Denoël, 1985) pp. 114–36. Ferdinand de Saussure, *Course in General Linguistics*, trans. Wade Baskin (New York: Philosophical Library, 1959), pp. 131ff.

72   See my discussion in 'Renaissance Curiosa', *Modern Philology*, 82 (1985), pp. 417–19, and in 'Rosicrucian Linguistics: Twilight of a Renaissance Tradition', in *Hermeticism and the Renaissance: Intellectual History and the Occult in Early Modern Europe* (Washington, DC: Folger Shakespeare Library, 1988), pp. 311–41.

73   See generally Keith Thomas, *Religion and the Decline of Magic* (New York: Scribner's 1971); and Charles Webster, *The Great Instauration: Science, Medicine, and Reform 1626–1660* (London: Duckworth, 1975); David S. Katz, *Philosemitism and the Readmission of the Jews to England: 1603–1655* (Oxford: Clarendon Press, 1982); James Grantham Turner, *One Flesh; Paradisal Marriage and Sexual Relations in the Age of Milton* (Oxford: Clarendon Press, 1987); Smith, *Perfection Proclaimed*. The general context is further discussed in Ormsby-Lennon, 'Rosicrucian Linguistics', in which documentation for the ensuing paragraphs may be found.

74   Robert Norwood, 'Epistle' to Thomas Tany, *Theauraujohn His Aurora in Tranlagorum in Salem Gloria* (London: Giles Calvert, 1655), sign. A² r. Verstegan, *A Restitution of Decayed Intelligence* (Antwerp: R Bruney 1605), p. 190. Here Verstegan relays, if not without some scepticism, the theories of the eccentric Flemish polymath, Goropius Becanus (Jan van Gorp): for the sources of Verstegan's bizarre etymological proofs, see Becanus, *Origines Antverpianae* (Antwerp: Plantin, 1569), pp. 539–541. The *Restitution* was reprinted in 1652, 1653, and 1655.

75   See generally Serge Hutin, *Les disciples anglais de Jacob Boehme* (Paris: Denoël, 1960). No full-scale study of Boehme's influence upon the Quakers has been attempted: but see, in the interim, Smith, *Perfection Proclaimed*, pp. 185–225.

76   Boehme, *Forty Questions concerning the Soul*, trans. John Sparrow (London: Matthew Simmons, 1647), p. 149.

77   Abraham von Franckenberg, *The Life of one Jacob Boehme* (London: Richard Whitaker, 1644), sig. A² r; Fox, *Journal*, pp. 7, 9: 'I would get into the orchard or the fields, with my Bible by myself . . . I fasted much, and walked abroad in solitary places, and often took my Bible and went and sat in hollow trees and lonesome places until night came on.'

78   Fox, *Journal*, pp. 8, 9, 16, 21.

79   Fox, *Journal*, p. 27. For the climate of ideas see Jacob Boehme, *Signatura Rerum: or the Signature of all Things shewing the Sign, and Signification of the several Forms and Shapes in the Creation*, trans. John Ellistone (London: Giles Calvert, 1651).

80   On Fox's career as a healer see Henry J. Cadbury, ed., *George Fox's 'Book of Miracles'* (Cambridge: Cambridge University Press, 1948). See also Amelia Mott Gummere, *Witchcraft and Quakerism: A Study in Social History* (Philadelphia: The Biddle Press, 1908).

81   'Journal' of Edward Bourne as reprinted by Penney, *The First Publishers of Truth*, p. 278.

82   See Mircea Eliade, *The Forge and the Crucible: The Origins and Structures of Alchemy*, trans. Stephen Corrin (New York: Harper and Row, 1962), esp. pp. 164–8. Eliade, *Shamanism: Archaic Techniques of Ecstasy*, trans. Willard R. Trask (Princeton, NJ: Princeton University Press, 1964), *passim* but esp. pp. 93–9.

83   For seventeenth-century contexts see E. Jean Whittaker, *Thomas Lawson: North Country Botanist, Quaker and Schoolmaster* (York: Sessions Book Trust, 1986).

84   See for example, *A Treatise of Oswaldus Crollius of Signatures of Internal Things* (London: John Starkey and Thomas Passenger, 1669). See also Owen Hannaway, *The Chemists and the Word* (Baltimore, Md.: Johns Hopkins University Press, 1975).

85   Fox, *Journal*, p. 27.

86   Douglas Gwyn, *Apocalypse of the Word: The Life and Message of George Fox (1624–1691)* (Richmond, Ind.: Friends United Press, 1986), p. 63.

87   Fox, *Journal*, p. 8.

88   Fox, *Journal*, p. 333. For the background see Richard Greaves, *The Puritan Revolution and Educational Thought: Background for Reform* (New Brunswick, NJ: Rutgers University Press, 1969), pp. 56–7; Webster, *Great Instauration*, pp. 232–42.

89   Fox, *Journal*, pp. 333–4. Fox continually returns to his Babel/Babylon theme: e.g. *To the Protector and Parliament of England* (London: Giles Calvert, 1658), pp. 38–9.

90   See Philippe Wolff, *Western Languages AD 100–1500*, trans. F. Partridge (New York: McGraw Hill, 1971), p. 113.

91   Webster, *Academiarum Examen*, p. 25. See the discussion by Hans Aarsleff, 'Language, Man and Knowledge in the 16th and 17th Centuries', unpublished lectures 1964, Ch. 3, manuscript on deposit at the Warburg Institute, London, and the Newberry Library, Chicago.

92   For the background to disputes over the qualifications for ordination see Greaves, *The Puritan Revolution and Educational Thought: Background for Reform*, pp. 16–19, 24–5.

93   Boehme, *Mysterium Magnum: or An Exposition of the First Book of Moses called Genesis*, trans. John Ellistone and John Sparrow (London: H. Blunden, 1654), p. 213.

94   Penney, *First Publishers of Truth*, p. 213.

95   Isaac Penington, *The great question concerning the lawfulness or unlawfulness of swearing under the Gospel* (London: Robert Wilson, 1661), p. 7.

96   As recorded by Thomas Burton: cited in Emilia Fogelklou, *James Nayler: The Rebel Saint 1618–1660*, trans. Lajla Yapp (London: Benn, 1931), p. 191. For insight (within Quaker-like contexts of a distrust for linguistic custom) into 'the use of the body as an intentional sign' and 'the trope of the walking hieroglyph', see Roger Poole, *Towards Deep Subjectivity* (New York: Harper and Row, 1972), pp. 18, 25. Many mid-seventeenth century sectaries used their bodies as hieroglyphs or engaged in strange symbolic behaviour: I shall

discuss these phenomena as symptoms of the nation's 'semiological crisis' in the essay mentioned in note 68.

97 Fox, 'Wheeler Street Sermon' (1680), reprinted in *Early Quaker Writings 1650–1700*, eds. Hugh Barbour and Arthur O. Roberts (Grand Rapids, Mich.: Eerdmans, 1973), p. 508.

98 Fox, 'To all who love the Lord Jesus Christ', *Several Papers: some of them given forth by George Fox, others by James Nayler* (no publisher or place given: Printed in the year as the world accounts, 1654), pp. 11–12.

99 Fox, *A General Epistle to be Read in all the Christian Meetings in the World* (London: no publisher given, 1662), p. 1.

100 Norman Penney, ed., *The Journal of George Fox* (Cambridge: Cambridge University Press, 1911), I, p. 5.

101 Such folk-etymologies were much favoured by sectaries as they dismembered the English language during the Puritan Revolution.

102 Penney, ed., *Journal of George Fox*, I, p. 333. This seems to be a topos; it can also be found, a century later, in the Methodist sermons of George Whitefield. Further research is necessary.

103 Fox, 'To all who love the Lord Jesus Christ', in *Several Papers*, p. 6.

104 Farnworth, 'To the valiant Souldiery of the Army of the Lamb', in *An Easter Reckoning, or A Free-will Offering* (London: Giles Calvert, 1653), sig. A3v.

105 Ibid., second leaf of title page.

106 See Barbour and Roberts, *Early Quaker Writings*, p. 127. Many of the sectaries were accused of devising 'secret languages', particularly the Ranters.

107 Bourne, *A Warning from the Lord God out of Sion* (London: Robert Wilson, 1660), title page; Stephenson, *A Call from Death to Life, and out of the dark ways and worships of the world where the seed is held in bondage under the merchants of Babylon* (London: Thomas Simmons, 1660), p. 18; Fox 'the Younger', *A Noble Salutation and a Faithful greeting unto Thee Charles Stuart* (London: Giles Calvert, 1660), title page.

108 Farnworth, *Anti-Christs Man of War, Apprehended, and encountered withal, by a Souldier of the Armie of the Lamb* (London: Giles Calvert, 1655), *passim*. On p. 11 alone there are seven instances of this verbal tic.

109 Fox, *A Testimony of What we believe of Christ* (London: no publisher given, 1677), p. 59. In 'A Call out of Egypt and Babylon', in *An Easter Reckoning*, pp. 29–33, Farnworth provides an adumbration of his own pamphlet on the 'pure language' and one of the first organized Quaker statements on pronominal usage. On the 'new song' see Revelation 14:3 and 15:3; also Psalms 40:3. See further Kenneth L. Carroll, 'Singing in the Spirit in Early Quakerism', *Quaker History*, 73 (1984), pp. 1–13.

110 Penney, ed., *Journal of George Fox*, II, p. 171.

111 Fox, as quoted by Bauman, *Let Your Words Be Few*, p. 24. But contrast Henry J. Cadbury, ed., *Narrative Papers of George Fox* (Richmond, Ind.: Friends United Press, 1972), p. 8.

112 Quoted by Cope, 'Seventeenth Century Quaker Style', p. 729.

113 Fox, *Journal*, p. 33.

114 Higginson, *Irreligion of the Northern Quakers*, p. 11.

115 Fox, *Journal*, p. 88.

116 Ralph Lupton, *The Quaking Mountebank: Or the Jesuit Turned Quaker* (London: E.B. at the Angel in Paul's Churchyard, 1655), p. 7.

117 Fox, *Something Concerning Silent Meetings* (no place, no publisher, no date), broadsheet.

118 Fox, *An Epistle to all People on the Earth ... shewing that it was the practice of many to wait in silence upon God* (London: Giles Calvert, 1657), p. 9.

119 Charles Marshall, 'An Epistle to Friends in and about Bristol', in *Sion's Travellers Comforted and the Disobedient Warned* (London: T. Sowle, 1704), pp. 222–3.

120 Thomas Sheehan, *The First Coming: How the Kingdom of God became Christianity* (New York: Random House, 1986), pp. 221–2. But see Sullivan, *Rethinking Realized Eschatology*, for a traditional perspective.

121 Douglas Gwyn, '"Into That which Cannot be Shaken": The Apocalyptic Gospel Preached by George Fox', in *The Day of the Lord: Quaker Eschatology in Perspective*, ed. Dean Freiday (Newberg, Oreg.: Barclay Press/Faith and Life, 1981), pp. 91–2.

122 For the fullest account of the context and meaning of Nayler's momentous ride see William G. Bittle, *James Nayler 1618–1660: The Quaker Indicted by Parliament* (York: William Sessions, 1986). The most incisive account remains Leonard W. Levy, *Treason Against God: A History of the Offense of Blasphemy* (New York: Schocken, 1981), pp. 265–96.

123 Sheehan, *The First Coming*, p. 221.

124 Wayne A. Meeks, *The Moral World of the First Christians* (Philadelphia: Westminster Press, 1986), p. 145.

125 But see Barry Reay, 'Quaker Opposition to Tithes, 1652–1660', *Past and Present*, 86 (1980), pp. 98–120. Nicholas J. Morgan emphasizes spiritual rather than political motives, 'Lancashire Quakers and the Tithe, 1660–1730', *Bulletin of the John Rylands Library*, 70 (1988), pp. 61–75.

126 Michael R. Watts describes these Quaker journeys (which ranged from the Middle East to the New World) as 'one of the most dramatic outbreaks of missionary enthusiasm in the history of the church' (*The Dissenters. Volume I: From the Reformation to the French Revolution* [Oxford: Clarendon Press, 1978], p. 198).

127 As quoted by Barbour, *The Quakers in Puritan England*, p. 151. 'Speaking in tongues' often accompanies outbreaks of missionary enthusiasm, especially among folk who are not formally educated. We must distinguish 'xenoglossia' (the mystical acquisition of foreign languages as in Acts 2) from 'glossolalia' (as treated in 1 Corinthians). Mid-seventeenth-century saints like George Foster and Thomas Tany were undoubtedly glossolalists, but the Quaker evidence remains ambiguous. Bauman rejected my argument (advanced in a reader's report) that Friends spoke in tongues (*Let Your Words Be Few*, pp. 82–3), but I shall re-examine the evidence in the essay cited in note 68. Certainly Boehme's suggestion that 'the holy Ghost did open on the day of Pentecost ... in one language all languages; and this was also Adam's language whence he gave names to all creatures' (*Mysterium Magnum*, p. 233) sheds enormous light on Fox's Edenic trance and on Quaker attitudes to the pure language as hidden in the vernacular.

128 For this (and other examples), see Antonia Fraser, *Cromwell: The Lord Protector* (New York: Knopf, 1974), p. 100. For an account of the New Model Army which emphasizes its apocalyptic aspirations, see Leo Solt, *Saints in Arms: Puritanism and Democracy in Cromwell's Army* (Stanford: Stanford University Press, 1959); for a revisionist account see Mark Kishlansky, *The Rise of the New Model Army* (Cambridge: Cambridge University Press, 1979). The Lamb's Warriors replaced Peters's pistol with the sword of the mouth; and in their reaction to literal-minded Biblicalism employed the light within to irradiate the Bible's dead letter, a strategy which infuriated their adversaries.

129 But see the recent work of Richard Greaves, cited in note 20.

130 Meeks, *Moral World of the First Christians*, p. 146.

131 Margaret Aston does not include such 'metaphoric iconoclasm' in *England's Iconoclasts. Volume I: Laws against Images* (Oxford: Clarendon Press, 1988).

132 Christopher Hill, *The Experience of Defeat: Milton and some Contemporaries* (New York: Viking, 1984), p. 164. For the dire statistics see Hugh Barbour and William Frost, *The Quakers* (New York: Greenwood Press, 1988), p. 66; and Ronald Hutton, *Charles the Second: King of England, Scotland and Ireland* (Oxford: Clarendon Press, 1990).

133 Bauman, *Let Your Words be Few*, p. 146.

134 For the strange career of Eccles, see Ormsby-Lennon, 'Swift and the Quakers: I', pp. 44–5.

135 Robert Barclay, cited by Bauman, *Let Your Words be Few*, p. 146.

136 Horton Davies, *Worship and Theology in England: From Watts and Wesley to Maurice, 1690–1850* (Princeton, NJ: Princeton University Press, 1961), p. 123. But Kathryn A. Damiano has recently argued that eighteenth-century Quaker quietism actually constituted a 'realized eschatology', affording a basis for social action as part of the realization of the Kingdom of God on earth: '"On Earth as it is in Heaven": Eighteenth Century Quakerism as Realized Eschatology' (Ph.D. Diss.: Union of Experimenting Colleges and Universities, Cincinnati, Ohio, 1988).

137 Luella M. Wright, *The Literary Life of the Early Friends 1650–1725* (New York: Columbia University Press, 1932), pp. 97–109.

138 Minutes of the Second Day Morning Meeting (ms. in Friends House, London), pp. 7, 8, 31–2.

139 See Rufus Jones, 'Foreword', in *George Fox's 'Book of Miracles'*, p. ix.

140 See Ormsby-Lennon, 'Swift and the Quakers: I', pp. 48–9.

141 See William Mucklow, *The Spirit of the Hat* (London: F. Smith, 1673), p. 11 and *passim*. For discussions of early Quaker schism and Fox's 'gospel order' see William C. Braithwaite, *The Second Period of Quakerism*, 2nd edn (Cambridge: Cambridge University Press, 1961), pp. 215–396; Kenneth L. Carroll, *John Perrot: Early Quaker Schismatic* (London: Friends' Historical Society, 1971); and Michael J. Sheeran, SJ. *Beyond Majority Rule: Voteless Decisions in the Religious Society of Friends* (Philadelphia: Friends' Yearly Meeting, 1983).

142 Thomas, *Religion and the Decline of Magic*, Ch. XXII, esp. pp. 647–56.

143 Albert Schweitzer, *The Quest of the Historical Jesus*, trans. W. Montgomery (1906; repr. New York: Macmillan, 1961), p. 361.

144   Fox, 'Epistle 191' (1660), in *Collection of Many Select and Christian Epistles*, p. 149.

145   The fuller title for Penn's short treatise – *No Cross, No Crown; or, several sober reasons against hat-honour, titular respects, you to a single person, with the apparel and recreations of the times* (London: Publisher not given, 1669) – indicates his readiness, like that of his mother-in-law Mary Penington a decade earlier, to become a 'patient Bearer of the Cross of Jesus', thereby re-endorsing the testimonies witnessed by the Lamb's Warriors during the 1650s. The intensity of the Friends' apocalypsism may have waned, but Quakers stood valiantly by their testimonies.

146   In response to Max Weber's hypothesis of a 'disenchantment of the world', historians and sociologists of religion have frequently employed a paradigm of progressive despiritualization and inevitable secularization. Such a paradigm fits some (but by no means all) of the facts of Quakerism after 1660; see Damiano, '"On Earth as it is in Heaven"'. For a contemporary example (which bears close comparison with the Society's development) see Margaret M. Poloma, *The Assemblies of God at the Crossroads: Charisma and Institutional Dilemmas* (Knoxville: University of Tennessee Press, 1989).

147   Max Weber, 'Charisma and its Transformations', *Economy and Society: An Outline of Interpretive Sociology*, eds Guenther Roth and Claus Wittich (Berkeley, Cal.: University of California Press, 1978), II, pp. 1111–58.

148   Ibid., p. 1121.

149   Stephen Crisp, *An Epistle to Friends Concerning the Present and Succeeding times* (1666) in Crisp, *A Memorable Account of the Christian Experiences* (London: T. Sowle, 1694), p. 123. Crisp, of course, is using 'channel' with its seventeenth-century meaning of 'gutter'.

Part II

Language and Social Authority

4

'New World of English Words'[1]: John Ray, FRS, the Dialect Protagonist, in the Context of his Times (1658–1691)

JO GLADSTONE

We offer a hundred banquets to true philosophers, whose concern is to gaze with their own eyes on the nature of things and to listen with their own ears to natural voices; who prefer quality to quantity, and usefulness to pretension; to their use, in accordance with God's glory, we dedicate this little book and all our future studies.

John Ray, preface to *Catalogus Cantabrigiam*, 1660[2]

John Ray, FRS (1627–1705), the focus of this study, was a seventeenth-century English botanist. Guided by his own lively version of the philosophy of Puritan individualism, and against heavy odds (for he was of comparatively humble social origins for his day for a man of learning), he made significant contributions to the study not only of plants, of which he was master, but also of geology, entomology, ornithology, and fish, contributions that held good from the time of the Glorious Revolution until well into the 1840s. He was a distinguished taxonomist of the animal and vegetable kingdoms. He published a number of learned works on the subjects both of biological classification and of Christian comfort, in standard English and Latin.[3] It would be true to say that his contribution to the development of the biological sciences was of major importance, even though his 'loose-knit' taxonomies of nature were later superseded by those of Linnaeus and Darwin.

In addition to his scientific and theological works, which are closely interlinked, John Ray published a collection of proverbs[4] and a refined and complex checklist of rare plants by county.[5] These topographic plant lists have never been reassembled and reprinted. They were commissioned for Edmund Gibson's 1695 folio edition of Camden's *Britannia*. If they were to be reprinted in entirety and re-identified so that the plants listed by locality could be recognized by modern field botanists, Ray's catalogues of wild flowers would provide as good a list as could be assembled even today of the rare flora of the British Isles by county. Ray was right to pride himself on the accuracy of his field botany.

This observant and immensely industrious scientist simultaneously edited a pair of minor but widely used lexicographic works no social historian of the English language should overlook. They were published a year apart, for sale to the general public after two of Ray's most important patrons had died. One of these works was a classical dictionary, the *Dictionariolum*, modelled on one by Comenius (1592–1671).[6] The other, which he tended to play down, was a dialect glossary. The country words it is made up of, with their significations, he collected in the northern and southern counties of England, using the same methods and travelling over the routes that he used for his botanical and fauna collecting tours, his 'simpling journeys' after 'native' plants. The dialect usage he studied was the everyday speech of country people. It is to Ray's first glossary of 'native' English proverbial phrases and nominative usage, his *Collection of English Words*, that this study is dedicated.[7]

The *Collection* was an important glossary. It raised questions about the validity of the English language in its minority forms. These questions still occupy people who speak English today as children, adults, and old people in the multilingual speech community that has always contributed a certain freshness and vitality to the English language. Ray's *Catalogus Cantabrigiam*, a catalogue of Cambridge plants, was published towards the end of the Interregnum. In his introduction he expressed the need for philosophers like himself, the New Men of the scientific revolution, to 'listen with their own ears'. The sound Ray persuaded them to listen to (indeed, he stated in the same introduction that he felt impelled 'to entice my friends to share my pursuits')[8] was the lexicon of spoken country English.

This lexicon he published fourteen years after his Interregnum Cambridge plant catalogue. Its introductory manifesto announced the method of a loose-knit cataloguing tradition that survived him. The English dialect-collecting tradition, in this historic sense, was an integral part of the empirical impetus that also fired the natural sciences. The cereal grains for which Ray gave technical Latin names, topographically and alphabetically listed for fellow field botanists as useful entries alongside the wild plants of Cambridgeshire in 1660, for example, were listed in their most general grassroots dialect terms in the *CEW 1* and *2* glossaries of 1674 and 1691.

The separate listing of these three codes, standardized scientific English and Latin nomenclature, and dialect English, was part of Ray's contribution to the history of English botany, but this did not mean he believed that the common language should be ploughed under. For a span of at least three observational generations, this was a fruitful and rewarding field for eighteenth-century dialect lexicographers in the learned tradition he founded. John Ray (like William Withering, Adam Sedgwick, Robert Willan, Edward Jenner, James Hutton, and many other natural philosophers in his empirical tradition) was loyal to a code of dialect usage in which he was proficient, and he was prepared to seek out like-minded colleagues to assist in his tabulating enterprise. That corresponding group of interpreters communicating in the printed word about the signification of dialect words provides a definition of the seventeenth-century dialect protagonism adequate for this study.

Poetic Individualism in the Long Eighteenth Century and Ray's Lexicographic Lists

The poetic liveliness of dialect English words may have delighted readers of the first, and apparently very popular, lists tabulated by the Ray group. The poetics of environment they recorded was later glossed, for example, by Captain Francis Grose on his rural peregrinations with Robert Burns a century later. These words are still moving as expressive country evocations. 'Early light of day' was listed by Ray in Norfolk dialect as *cobweb morning*, which he identified with misty mornings (*CEW 1*:61). *Very Tarky* was a Suffolk expression for 'very dark' in his first published list. (*CEW 1*:77). *Fairy sparks* or *shelfire* were East Anglian words describing the kind of sparks static electricity may generate in the dark out of doors on people's clothes when it is very dry, and were described by Ray for Suffolk as 'often seen on clothes at night' (*CEW 1*:65). *Sheld* indicated birds' feathers or animal pelts that were, in Ray's words 'flecked and partly coloured'; the word is from rural Sussex (*CEW 1*:76), where, too, 'to *shimper*' meant 'to shimmer or shine'. Gerard Manley Hopkins devoted a sonnet to the observation these dialect terms reflected: Ray simply recorded the words. They were memorable. They were rational. They were under threat.

Later collectors, especially in East Anglia, delighted most in the ebullience of country words for beasts and flowers. It is pleasant to know a blackbird is a *black uzzle*; *spink* is a chaffinch; *flitter mouse* is a bat. *Star-slubber* is the pretty and evocative name for frogspawn. *Tewfet* is a lapwing, and *miredrum* is a bittern. *Modder* in herd-loving Norfolk, Suffolk, Essex, and even Cambridgeshire meant a country 'girl or wench' in Ray's listings (*CEW 1*). Later, collectors heard the word used of cows and mares as well, or instead. Keith Thomas has emphasized the problems this ebullience caused biological systematists from this period onwards.[9] But these may have been natural philosophers less linguistically tolerant than Ray himself.

Ray's country words have more sound-track to them and are noisier, more down-to-earth, more earth-bound than the less engaged standard equivalents. Their taxonomic purchase is far more generalized and loose than the later, Latin binomial classifications of plants and animals in the Linnean system, so loathed by John Clare.[10]

That dialect English word usage should abound with evocative words for wildlife in nature should not surprise us. It is, however, evidence for the powerfully internalized documentary realist capacities of Ray's dialect inventories. But were these lively codes capable of the expression, say, of emotions, such as human affection? Again, the words are not wanting.

The poetics of affection in the northern and southern English dialect lexicon as collected or used by John Ray, Robert Burns, John Clare, Ann Wheeler, and others, is far from the grinning (*girning*) death's-head caricature of the dialect scolding-literature, best known in middle Georgian dialect narratives like *The Exmoor Scolding*, first published in the *Gentleman's Magazine* in the 1760s, or in the hybrid pages of John Collier's *Tim Bobbin*, Lancashire's much-loved Simple Simon dialect cycle about a journey through the countryside round Oldham.[11] *Dilling* was Ray's southern expression for 'a darling, favourite child'. *Cutter* was to fondle, to make much of, 'as when a goose her young', and to *croodle* was 'to creep close together like chickens under a hen'. Clare extended this definition – he did not know of Ray's dialect lists but followed his botanical and bird classifications avidly. Clare in the 1820s also listed *croodle* as 'to huddle for warmth or protection'.[12] The collections of both great East Anglian dialect lexicographers, John Ray, whose botanical works Clare admired, and John Clare himself, though independently made, show considerable overlap in their chosen glossarial listings. East Anglia has a fine dialect writing tradition; it is perhaps the English locality where the regional muse, for sheer sophistication, was most fully explored by dialect protagonist writers.

The poetics of hardship endured were also powerfully expressed in Ray's word lists, as they were in those of Clare after the 1820s.[13] Long-eighteenth-century dialect literature, prone to self-mockery and low on character development in its satirical Restoration and Augustan modes, acquired gravity and serenity in two very different literary movements. Seventeenth-century Puritan individualist dialect users like Ray deployed dialect usage for its sombre directness. So did the very different group of Thresher Poets in what has been defined as the late Georgian 'anti-pastoral' tradition.[14] *Deam, deafely*, 'lonely, solitary, far from neighbours', and *dowly*, 'melancholy, lonely', are northern listings collected by the Ray group (*CEW 1*:26, 27). *Dare* is an Essex word for grief and hardship defined by Ray as 'pain, as in "It *dares* me" – "It pains or grieves me."' (*CEW 1*:64). Most telling, perhaps, of all is the overlap in sound and signification that Ray indicates between the word for 'work' and the word for 'pain'. In northern dialect usage both terms are encompassed by the word *wark*. The meaning of this word in Ray's collected northern word definitions was 'to ake, (or) to work' (*CEW 1*:51).

The literary potency of these eighteenth-century dialect word lists, 600–900 words strong, coincided with the expressive needs not only of non-conforming, often standard-fluent, ministers who began the country-word collecting tradition, but also of dialect-using poets like John Clare and Robert Burns and their fellow writers of the Georgian dialect enlightenment. These writers, men and women, contextualized what Ray and his contemporaries inventoried.

It is time to explore the limited practical and self-defining world of dialect English usage as published in the long eighteenth century, and to examine its value as a source of empirical, qualitative information about daily life at the village level. To give the word lists their due, it is best to stack them in categories by topic and try to become familiar with them. The lexicon quoted throughout the rest of this essay will be from the first or second edition of the original Ray *Collection of English Words* (*CEW*).

Two variables had, as an editorial responsibility, to be weighed up by Ray himself with caution and intensity of purpose. This balancing was an integral part of the exercise of dialect protagonism as he conducted it. The variables are the richness of the lexicon itself, which was entirely oral, and the skill of the transcriber, which was by its very nature susceptible to circumstantial biographical and literary skew. Ray's dialect opus shows in a good light on either of these counts if rural naturalism is made the standard of the historian's textual searches.

Ray's Dialect-collecting Initiative in the Context of his Times

The long-eighteenth-century, single-word, dialect-collecting tradition, now superseded,[15] has left for the social and cultural historian a series of empirical and poetic inventories of considerable *heft* (weight when held up in the hand for examination). There was little artifice – in Ray's words, 'no pretension' – about them. These lists, generally under a thousand words long, each word bearing its own signification, are part of a tradition initiated by Ray in his attempt to codify, to 'catalogue', the necessary economic underpinnings of everyday rural life.

On the assumption that the dialect lexicon is rich in the description of country matters, as the lists Ray and his correspondents accumulated certainly were, what empirical inventories stand out? There were, in particular, agricultural, mining, and dietary inventories. These concerned the New Men of the Commonwealth period, Samual Hartlib, Ray himself, and Secretary Oldenburg's language purist correspondent from Suffolk, Nathaniel Fairfax.[16] Few at the Royal Society were equipped observationally or by social background to penetrate these closely guarded country codes with so sure a touch as Ray, so he did the work on them without the encouragement of the Royal Society.

Ray formed a corresponding group of dialect collectors and lexicographers with whom he maintained a level of social and scholarly trust. His correspondents' function was to segregate, then alphabetize, category after category of material inventory stacked in the rural dialect lexicon. In this essay, a single category of inventory, a part of the dietary norm, has been selected. Animals, which in his scientific work Ray inventoried as a zoologist, in his dialect word list appear as livestock on the farm. Plants, of which Ray was one of the world's great classifiers in his day, provided a dialect shortlist of commonly used country names for food crops and weeds.

Ray's role as a scientist intruded into his work as a dialect lexicographer. Yet no list of equivalent length in the dialect lexicons since constructed has held up so compact or reflective a mirror to eighteenth-century, rural, empirical life and thought. Before some of Ray's dietary entries are reviewed as an example of the efficacy of the way he explored dialect usage, as vindication of his own philosophical empiricism, it will be necessary to observe the collector himself as pilgrim, setting out on his word-collecting journeys. He carried them out from 1658 to 1691.

Ray, Restoration Scholar of the Vernacular

For Ray's *Dictionariolum* of 1675, Comenius had paved the way. The *Dictionariolum* was a schoolchild's dictionary in three languages.[17] It was designed by Ray to introduce each young classics scholar fortunate enough to have his early learning enhanced by such a text to the day-to-day practicalities of Roman and Greek life. It encapsulated Ray's version of life as recorded by the ancient Roman and Greek republicans. This little work was ahead of its time.[18] It introduced English children to the adult world of the Greeks and Romans as part of an everyday seventeenth-century child's experience.

More advanced in concept was Ray's duodecimo red-letter dictionary, the *Collection of English Words*. This his former pupil from Trinity College, Cambridge, Thomas Burrell, had published in London a year earlier. The little book, ill-paginated, with amateur but lively layout, is very rare today. Its columns are striking for the vigour and originality of Ray's own preferences in the virtually virgin field of the vocabulary of rural English local and regional usage. In his foreword to this and to the subsequent edition of this fascinating 'middle period' work *CEW 1* and *CEW 2*,[19] Ray appeared to wish to introduce the polite travelling reader, moving through the English shires and byways, to the thought, not of the Romans or Greeks, but of northern rural dialect speakers. Who here is the child, the reader intended to be educated by the dictionary? Who here is the expert, the one who understands the language that is being imparted? Who here commands the words being taught – the language with which to control the rural environment? The republican questioning of authority – that is to say, standard authority – is implicit in this work. It is an implicitly oppositional code.

In a brief note in his foreword to *CEW 2*, Ray warned his readers that contact with dialect speech was hard to come by, that university men in particular might have difficulties in gaining access to normal local usage, and that readers should guard against presumption in the assignment of significations to word lists without a great deal of local knowledge.[20] The thought behind the earlier edition, *CEW 1*, is similar: here the collector is the child, the dialect-speaker the man, in Ray's way of looking at the task of field collection.

Ray's first *Collection of English Words* cited no lexicographic work earlier than a dictionary which Edward Phillips (1630?–96) published, a good deal of it plagiarized. It was *A New World of English Words or a General Dictionary*.[21] The publication of Phillips's dictionary had coincided with Ray's first important botanical trip into the west Midlands and Wales, on which occasion he may have begun to collect dialect terms, on a comparative basis, from the areas through which he travelled. Cheshire, Lancashire, and Cumbria were three of his most often mined regional speech areas; East Anglia was also a favourite. In each of these, his botanical knowledge, based on field trips in the summers, was unmatchable at that time.

The *Collection of English Words* was written about the language of country people in the north (who provided the bulk of its dialect word inventory), but is also rich in dialect terms then in current use in rural Essex and Sussex and other parts of the south. Ray and one of his patrons, Peter Courthope the ironmaster, seem, by Ray's account, to have held enthusiastic discussions about this 1670s project.[22] Ray knew Courthope at Cambridge as one of his own students in the 1650s. Their relationship was crucial to Ray by 1662, when he became proscribed as a Restoration tutor of Cambridge under-graduates (with his own assent), as a former Cromwellian fellow of Trinity. At this point he needed shelter, confidants, and actual financial help. His Cambridge fellowship had ended and he had to live.

It was to Courthope alone, according to the seventeen Danny Letters that Ray wrote to Courthope, that Ray confided his sense of revulsion and defiant dismay at the return of the 'Old Order' to Cambridge after 1661.[23] Ray saw his own version of knowledge and didacticism during this troubled time as part of the New Order that would ultimately prevail, in spite of temporary setbacks. The roots of the dialect collection 'hastily gathered up' by Ray in 1674 are to be found in his search, as a younger academic in the 1650s, for an orderly new polity, perhaps on Fairfaxian lines.

Courthope was Ray's personal confidant. In a sense, therefore, the dedication to him of the dialect collection must be viewed as a 'political' tribute of a kind Courthope himself would have endorsed; for the economi-cally self-sufficient Courthope knew details of the choice Ray had had to make when he was obliged on grounds of conscience to leave academic life. So did Bishop Wilkins, another patron: he excused Ray his subscription to the Royal Society of London when Ray became a member.

The balance of the country word collection was made up from words collected 'live' in many provincial parishes where Ray himself (or like-minded, rurally based correspondents, whose definitions he cited) had spent a little time. He required of his correspondents that they should live in a local area long enough to report with confidence on meanings otherwise impenetrable to standard speakers. He furthermore expected of them an emotional commitment to particular, local, dialect regional speech forms.[24] Such a sense of affinity with a local word repertory made its exponents to some degree expert in local meanings. Ray himself was such an expert for the Braintree area of Essex, by birthright and long-term residence. As a scholar dependent on the patronage of others after he lost his Interregnum fellowship, Ray also seems to have penetrated the local Northamptonshire dialect of Middleton, that of Cheshire, and that of Sussex during periods of residence there at the homes of at least three of his patrons besides Peter Courthope.

The first and foremost of these provincially based patrons was his student and colleague, the younger Francis Willughby. Second (though Ray had reservations about his lack of flexibility as a biological thinker), there was the eminent patron of science, John Wilkins. By the time Ray was approached by him, through Willughby, to act as Latin Secretary to Wilkins's Royal Society *Essay towards a Real Character and Philosophical Language* in 1666,[25] Ray's membership of the Royal Society of London was assured; for this great organiser of science was about to become a Restoration bishop of Chester, and considered Ray's classical linguistic skills the finest of his generation of natural philosophers. The parallel development of Ray's rural language interests at this time is made the more remarkable, perhaps, for this.

Then there was a Suffolk patron, Ray's student, Philip Skippon the Younger, Ray's travelling companion on collecting trips to Scotland and to the Mediterranean. Skippon was the son of a prominent Cromwellian major-general, and his presence as a travelling companion on Ray's collecting trips might have embarrassed the less Cromwellian-associated Francis Willughby politically during the Restoration. Ray was as diplomatic in such matters as he could be, given his zeal for the well-furnished summer field trip, and his very limited means. It does seem, however, from his biographer and follower Derham's account of the reasons for Ray's refusal to accept the conformity required of him by the Bartholomew Act in 1662, that he did keep occasional company with extreme Nonconformists, regardless of the civic danger, a real one from 1662 until his word lists were published.

There is no indication that any of Ray's patrons objected to Ray's enthusiasm for the integration of dialect usage into a single nationwide listing. Indeed, it would seem that Courthope actively perusaded his friend to set about his innovative task, a task Ray believed had never before been attempted. There is no possibility that they would have objected to his scholarly sources. Besides Phillips, there was Thomas Browne, the Icelandic scholar Hickes, Spencer the poet, and above all his field correspondents, Brokesby, Nicolson, Tomlinson, Thoresby and a number of others.

The *Collection of English Words* is mainly made up of internally consistent sets of brief dialect word lists, principally identified by Ray with rural usage in northern (three-quarters of the usage listed) and in southern parishes of England and Wales. The two little dictionaries Ray published in the mid-1670s *CEW* and the *Dictionariolum*, had been preceded by a more conventional work, *English Proverbs* (1670), an elaborate list of topographically ascribed proverbs in the tradition of Fuller's *Worthies*.[26] The earlier proverbial and the later, philosophically more poised and integrated, country word collections were usually published in tandem throughout the eighteenth century. They served as a joint set of homilies and lexicon of country nominative wisdom. They were widely read, and were collated by Ray with his customary modesty. Compared with the stuffy commentaries of Ray's earlier *Proverb* assemblages, however, his *CEW* inventories have an irrepressible freshness about them. He was drawing attention to a new world of words, local variants of words he himself had known only in their Black Notley, Essex, dialect setting, and relishing the task.

The collection was a minor work of the day, and also a very minor work of Ray's, but both editions, *CEW 1* and *CEW 2*, sold well. They opened people's eyes to the richness of their source material. And they were written with a personal emphasis laced with that affirmative 'we', the seventeenth-century dialect protagonist affirmative, declaring 'We say . . .'. This was not to survive Ray's generation. Perhaps his was a generation fortunate enough to have experienced an easing of prejudice against dialect usage at many social and intellectual levels during the English Revolution. It was more complicated for later, eighteenth-century dialect lexicographers, many of whom were only too ready to deny the validity of the vernacular code.

The Cromwellian connection in Ray's case may be important in the legitimation of his self-appointed task as dialect lexicographer. Coming of age closer than his Georgian successors to the time when it is thought that the chasm between standard and dialect (popular) English widened,[27] Ray may merely have experienced a fortunate insulation, as a grammar-schoolboy from the country, from the notion of any innate superiority of standard codes over his vernacular mother tongue: he used both. He may also have code-switched when collecting.

The facts are that a humanities lecturer in Cromwellian Trinity College Cambridge was funded, without aristocratic patronage, for the small-press publication of country word lists collected between 1658 and 1674. Thomas Burrell, the publisher, with his brother, William, a prosperous Sussex farmer, had studied under Ray at Trinity in the Interregnum. The Burrells were cousins of the ironmaster, Peter Courthope, Ray's patron in Danny, Sussex. The publication history of *CEW* is by any standards an unusual one for a newly created botanical Fellow of the Royal Society of London where strictures against the kind of metaphorical usage on which the irrepressible flexibility and vigour of country word lists depends were strong at the time.

Ray's own intellectual justification for his espousal of country inventories at such a juncture appears to derive from the internally satisfying ideology he implanted in them. His rural word lists show compatibility both with the Cambridge Platonism of Henry More and Ralph Cudworth in the 1650s, and with the Royal Society's experimentally directed Restoration reduction-ism, which set out to strip back the English language to direct, not inferential, usage. At a more superficial level, Ray remained a linguistic preservationist, against the current of his intellectual peers, perhaps because he was such a fine field biologist. He was not willing to risk the loss of plain common sense from the English language, broadly viewed, because a standardizing linguistic edict, 'Nullius in Verba', had been issued by the Royal Society of London.

The first edition of the country word collection was published with help from patrons and correspondents who were each and every one Noncon-forming Anglicans, with the exception of William Nicolson, later Bishop of Carlisle. The rest had a wary attitude (as Ray did himself) to the restored monarchy and its supporters. The dialect word list sold out quickly, and the greatly extended second edition, published in Ray's lifetime in the more favourable intellectual climate of the Act of Toleration, sold just as well, even though Christopher Wilkinson, his second edition publisher, showed less respect for its learned author than had the good Burrells. By then, the rehabilitation of Ray's English Revolutionary sermons, his unpublished and unrecorded commonplaces, had triumphantly taken its course.

By 1691, Ray, the scholarly recluse from Black Notley in Essex, had himself survived the flattery of a period of rediscovery of his work. He rejected, by more than one reliable account, the secretaryship of the Royal Society, several livings, and a bishopric. It was more in his personal style to bring to press at this juncture his most influential theistic work, *The Wisdom of God in the Creation*, following the publication of his greatly augmented second edition of the *CEW*. In this edition, the Fairfaxian undertones of Ray's explanatory texts and those of his younger correspondents (in particular, Edward Lhwyd, the Oxford Celtic scholar and naturalist, and William Nicolson of Carlisle)[28] emerged a little more clearly. There was no reason why they should not by this time, locally or nationally. The climate had grown safer for notions of the desirability of the democracy of the parish pump.

The dialect dictionary was highly pragmatic. This can be seen from the aid it might have given a newly incumbent parson who needed to know the country vocabulary with which the tithe collector had to be familiar. Its help to the provisioner on a route march is clear from the oaten bread listings Ray put for the first time into the published record. Its power to define the symptoms of the dermatological ills of ageing countrymen, or of their livestock, may have a relevance to the history of dermatology.

In itself, Ray's impenitent commitment to dialect lexicography, over the thirty years following his first great field trip into Wales in 1658, was a lonely act. He travelled only with his pupil, Philip Skippon (he paid Thomas Willisel, a veteran of the New Model Army, to collect for him in Snowdonia, as Willisel had collected for the Royalist botanist Thomas Johnson in Kent before the Civil War). In an often-quoted letter to Secretary Oldenburg about the Royal Society's commitment to the Baconian experimental method, Ray praised the scheme for the protection its practice might afford, 'to ease those that are oppressed'.[29] Ray's disclaimer to Secretary Oldenburg in September 1675, about his inability to perform experiments for the diversion of members of the Royal Society, serves as an affirmation of his strong adherence, against the world, to his own collating and collecting skills, of which the *CEW* formed part: 'To speak the truth I have neither ability nor leisure to make experiments of any kind – by ability I mean neither wit nor purse, having no good projecting or inventive faculty. But if something I have observed in the History of Plants or Animals may be accepted, I shall not be wanting to do my part.'[30]

He did play his part. Even as a dialect collector, Ray, the revisionist taxonomist of nature, explored dialect usage, as he explored natural history and the ancient languages: Hebrew, Greek, Latin, and Icelandic (through

Hickes's brand-new dictionary of 1689).[31] He sought to retexture standard English too, for the teacher's sake and for the learner's.[32] This democratizing ideal of Ray's must be borne in mind when a perspective is sought on his intellectual persistence in the wish to 'translate' the dialect codes of the rural counties.

Dialect English, it must be emphasized (lest the twentieth-century historiography of cultural innovation as opportunism obscure Ray's perceptiveness as a linguistic analyst of mid-seventeenth-century English as it was spoken), was one of the strands of the New Learning Ray wished to perpetuate. The spelling reform he urged, for didactic reasons, on standard English was part of a more fully participatory linguistic programme for the new culture he envisaged, an exploratory one in which regional usage and its taxa would play a part. In his in-depth knowledge of its southern inventories, of which he had been a user from birth, the code had experiential soundness. A language pessimist, like others of his intellectually tumultuous generation, Ray (and his circle of collectors locally affiliated by cultural accommodation or deep knowledge) saw the dialect repertory as an includable lexicon. Many other lexicographers viewed the forms of self-expression of these locally hallowed regional codes through prurient or disdainful filters. These codes were seen by the 'denial' school as forms of excludable English. Ray played the first significant counter-move in an ultimately lost battle against disdain, with unshakable purpose. Thanks to his resolute linguistic intentions, it was not during the long eighteenth century that the battle was lost.

Ray's Dietary Entries

Ray's dialect word lists serve as a window on to their compiler, the Trinity sizar's, view of the rural, day-to-day world all round England. The lists reflected Ray's adult regional experience, a controlled Interregnum one, of the England of the brief sway of the majors-general, whose sons became the patrons with whom he travelled the shires as a teacher, an intellectual, and a reporter. This chronological experience can be said, indeed, to have allowed Ray to stand above the necessarily atomizing localism of many dialect protagonists, and see the topic in the round.

Early modern rural speech must begin with food, and first of all with bread, the staff of life. A qualitative picture of the English rural diet, antedating the work of the great Enlightenment economic dietary compilers (whose work was so closely linked to prison and agricultural reform) emerges. The bills of fare collected by Ray can be fleshed out with a little help from the records of surviving recipes, all of which remain intact in British 'self-sufficient' regional dietaries. Such recipes re-emerge particularly in times of scarcity. Dialect, not standard English, codes for them and guards the secrets of their survival value; hence the survival of the language itself, in spite of the casualties of war and peace that were Ray's personal social experience. In what follows, breads and meats listed by Ray will be reviewed in their regional setting. A forthcoming paper will set out his 'wild food' and 'white meat' – dairy food entries.

'Oatcake kneaded with water only': Ray's northern and southern bread entries

Early modern rural dietary usage in the dialect inventories collected by the Ray group is well-stocked with breads and the wherewithal to *lithe* (thicken) broths and to stiffen to slicing point the communal country porridges and field *stithes* (mixed peasen and oat porridges and their local and regional variants). Teas, sugars, and white breads, late Georgian mainstay of the labouring diet, are absent. Cheese and skimmed milk are a continuum; so probably was thin, home-brewed beer. As one exception to all his other first edition word entries, Ray's northern breads were de-alphabetized: six types of bread, all baked from oaten flour, were listed under the single entry, *bannock*. Ray himself was impatient at what he considered the lack of finesse surrounding this northern bill of fare. He was familiar with it, for he frequently travelled through Cheshire northwards to Cumbria or westwards into Wales on his collecting journeys before 1672.

Cumbria and the Borders still pride themselves on their crisp local oat bakery, as Lancashire prides itself on its soft, limp oakcakes. Given that the northern word lists were intended for a southern patron, and for travellers, including clerical and botanical amateurs sojourning in wild corners of the oat-eating parts of Britain, (such as the mountains of Cumbria, Snowdonia, and the Wastes of Bewcastle), Ray's oat-bread entries can be assumed to have been taken seriously. To a southern traveller used only to the white loaf – the fine-flour, yeast-baked 'manchet' of the day – the heavy, bran-loaded oat breads of the northern English and Celtic countryside, with their thirst-inducing dryness, may have seemed close to plebeian 'brown crops', as the pulses, beans, and peas (corn-flour substitutes in necessity) were named. Wheaten and barley entries, the 'white crops' of the southern standard bill of fare, were not listed among Ray's particularizing northern grain lists.

Ray's regional flours have a country ring about them. *Pillerds* (Cornish barley) is listed, as is *meslin* or *mashelson*, a mixture of wheat and rye. *Haver* is the northern oat entry Ray gives in his dialect word list, together with its flour, *haver meal*, and its baked form, *haver bread*. *Yets* is an oat grain dialect term from Northumberland. Roughest of all these is *chimping*, rough ground oatmeal, or grits, *greets*, the grain of oats. The entry *chizzell* (bran) in Sussex and Kent is one of several which Ray discovered to be common to the north and south. *Brots*, broken crops, were added by Nicolson for Northumbrian dialect foods. *Orts*, tail ends, the refuse of the grain not saleable in the market but kept by farmers for their own consumption and that of their hired men or animals, helped to maximize the quantity of the oats harvest that was utilized for human consumption. *Chimping* or *chizzell*, northern and southern bran, and *brots* or *orts*, northern and southern remnant grain supplies, were terms which were synonyms in husbandry practice. This was in accordance with the Puritan view of language – for it was the realities that language represented, not the words themselves, that were in the image of God.[33]

Poverty grain substitutes in Ray's southern lexicon were *brank* and *crap*, now pejorative but then dialect words for buckwheat in Suffolk, Norfolk, and Worcestershire. In Essex, *crap* was the dialect term for the weed darnel. Mixed cereal grains were also sown, though Ray's entry implies that former weak cultivation and cropping methods of such hybrid plantings were becoming outdated – an instance of the crucial reformist element in his conservationist work as a dialect recorder. He was an 'improving' antiquarian, in the Hartlibian sense: one entry runs '*Dredge*. A mixture of oats and barley now very little sown.'

Before discussing Ray's important composite entry for *bannock*, the contrast between his *haver* entry for northern usage and his standard botanical cereal and pulses entries for the Cambridge area, catalogued in 1660 in the Cambridge catalogue of wild flowers, his first significant botanical publication,[34] should be summarized. Ray, an expert observer of rural agronomy, isolated the generalized dialect words in his country word collections. He did not allow his own standard expert knowledge of country cropping patterns to flood the simple usage in the rural dialect lists he collected. He was, as it were, capable of scholarly double-think, knowing extensively, but limiting the rural lexicon he recorded to a representative list.

In the Cambridge *Catalogus*, Ray's own broad-based taxa prevailed. Cultivars he listed round Cambridge were *avena*, either common or manured oats, and *secale*, 'rie', rye. Winter and summer hemp, *cannabis*, he listed as an entry from Ely, Cromwell's home town. *Hordeum* (barley) and *distichum* (sprit or battledore barley), together with winter square barley, were listed among the 'coarser' cereals. These cereals were still central to the diet of the rural poor in East Anglia as well as the north when Clare wrote *The Shepherd's Calendar* in the 1820s.[35]

Of 'brown' crops in the fields round Cambridge, Ray entered three kinds of field pea. He also listed two *fabas*, the field bean, a major and a minor. Most important was wheat, of which he listed seven varieties: white lammas, red lammas, white-eared red-bearded, white-eared red, bearded Kentish, grey, and red-eared bearded. The colour of the grain and the presence or absence of marked awns appear to have been the variables. Ray picked these out as they were visibly apparent and used them as taxonomic markers in common English, his long-drawn-out but reliable style of classification. This was possibly an exhaustive list. It would have suggested sources for flour and anticipated levels of great tithes by wheat yield, levels that every farmer working the glebe knew he must pay under threat of excommunication.

Ray's composite entries for northern oat breads

Haver, the northern oat flour, Ray recorded as a staff-of-life entry. From it was baked a medley of popular breads. These were classified by their size, rising, texture (from soft to hard), bolting, and a plurality of other, somewhat slippery diagnostic features. It must be admitted in the matter of Ray's entry for oaten breads that the systematics of their nomenclature eluded him. Some of these breads were sieved, some were not; some were a little leavened, but most were not; some were crisp, some were floppy; some were bulked into huge loaves, while others were casually constituted from a half-handful of meal plucked in the field and baked in the oven.

Tharcakes Ray listed as baked from oat flour 'ground at the mill, and fair water, without yeast or leaven, and so baked. In Lancashire and other parts of the North, they make several sorts of oaten bread.' *Tharcakes* were the first of the oat breads he listed, then came '2. *Clap Bread*: thin hard oatcakes. 3. *Kitchiness Bread*, 4. *Riddle Cakes* and *Hand hoven bread* and 5. *Jannocks*'. A little yeast inexpertly used entered into the preparation of Cheshire and Lancashire *hand-hoven* bread. *Hoven* in dialect usage seems to have had a negative aspect in cheese and bread preparation. It indicated the swelling of the great loaf or wheel of cheese, product of food preparation in danger of miscarrying. The largest oat loaf Ray listed was the *jannock*, 'oaten bread made into great loaves,' for communal and durable consumption. He also listed *riddle cakes*, 'thick northern sour oaten cakes, which differ little from that which is called *hand hoven* bread, having but little leaven and being kneaded stiffer'. *Kitchiness bread*, still available in Clwyd and Lancashire today, consists of 'thin soft oatcakes made of thin batter', in Ray's good description of them. This northern oat bakery was indigestible but nutritious. It was the staff of life for thousands of communities in the northeast, in the northwest, and on the Celtic fringes of the British Isles, which are also dialect aware. It is a fine hardy diet, but was probably inadequately supplemented, by any modern standard, by protein and fats from other sources.

Bouted bread was a Northumberland entry for a bread made of wheat and rye. The loaf would have been made out of *blen corn*, wheat mixed with rye; no pure wheat loaf was entered in Ray's northern list. The field meals in his dietaries stand out: *shag* was a piece of bread and cheese; *butter-shag* (also known as *thoomb shag* in Cumbria) was a slice of bread very thickly larded with butter. *Stife* bread was a very strong bread made with pea and bean flour, which give it a robust smell and taste. 'A great *hunch*' was a great piece of bread. In general, the vocabulary signals that field meals consisted of oat bread loaded with great smears and slices of butter and cheese. These were the backbone of the rural diet, the cold field meals sustaining rural labourers on the six working days of the week when there was agricultural work to be done, throughout the long eighteenth century.

With their lively interest in the history of their subject, namely the British traditional regional bill of fare (a little of it, to judge by the Ray lists, going back virtually unchanged to the Restoration), Theodora Fitzgibbon, Jane Grigson, and the children's writer Alison Uttley, to name a few, have recorded and experienced (in the Ray tradition, at first hand) recipes that remain by name, content, and regional speciality as direct survivors of the seventeenth-century diet.[36] One of these recipes in brief will suffice to supplement Ray's Puritan, laconic significations, frustrating as they are to the historian of diet.

Jane Grigson gives details for *riddle bread* from West Yorkshire. This is compounded of a pound of fresh oatmeal and half an ounce of yeast. A ladleful of the mixture is thrown onto a bakestone, and the resultant damp, flexible strip of oaten dough, which will become the 'cake' is hung on a wooden clothes rail before the fire to dry, or on lines across the kitchen ceiling. It is crisped quickly, immediately before eating, and the flavour is bitter. *Riddle bread* is eaten with soups, cheese, butter, and so on. Ray's description is precise. This *riddle cake* held its form right through the long eighteenth century and beyond, Jane Grigson recording it in Derbyshire in the mid-1920s.

The very act of gathering, collating, publishing, making lists of dialect categories relating to the staff of life, bread, had its own affirmative power. Bolted or undersifted, the staff of life of the country poor is indicated formally, since a word and a praxis exists for it. People's dietary entitlement is made normative by the dialect words they used when they indicated what they expected to eat. To ignore the words for the normative diet is to deny the entitlement, as those who tolerated derisive standard Poor House dietaries were to prove in late Georgian times. Authors like William Cobbett, in advocating the use of rye and barley in loaves and for feeding farm animals, supported the vernacular norm of the rural inventories.[37]

As characteristic as the thin, baked oatcake parts of Ray's bill of fare were the soft, swelled, *creed* or 'boiled' oat entries. These include not only *frumenty* but also *drummock* ('oatmeal and water mixed raw'), '*sowings, sowans, oatmeal flummery*', and '*suppings*, broth, spoon-meat'. Alison Uttley published a fine recipe for *frumenty*, John Clare's favourite harvest dish. It was eaten in Clare's memory, from a hardwood bowl, communally.

Frumenty or *flummery* was a dish of whole wheat ears, with the husks blown away. They were put in a big earthenware casserole, covered with water and put in a warm oven for three days. They became soft and jellied and delicious. We ate this with new hot milk and sugar on top. The slow cooking was called *creeing* and applied to wheat, barley, oats or any corn. This word *creeing*, is from the French word *crever*, to burst 'now forgotten in all but country places.'[38]

Soaked, fermented, swollen grain recipes formed the basis of the eighteenth-century medically prescribed 'low diet', and it is probable that the diet of the rural poor throughout the period would have been so classified. The lower-class diet was a middle-class invalid diet, by and large, and it incorporated at least one possible famine food *waybread* (plantain), 'so called because growing everywhere in streets and ways'. Soups were *lithed*, their liquors thickened with oat flour, to produce *kale* or *keal*, the cabbage-and-leek-rich broth of the north and west. The favoured dish of the American Puritan fathers is recorded by Ray. 'To *lithe*: To stir the oatmeal into the *gulls* or *hasty pudding*.'

Pies baked in the baker's oven enter Ray's lists. A *quested pie* is one 'whose sides have crushed by each other and so joined to them as to be less baked'. A *sad* loaf or pie is a 'heavy' one. There is no exact antithesis listed, but lest the reader, like Ray, despair of seventeenth-century northern culinary skills, a *smopple* pie crust is defined as one that is 'short and crisp'.

It was with yeast bakery at an expert technical level that Ray was at his ease. He was partial to white wheaten bread, served as his due as a poor Cambridge scholar of distinction. In the sort of personal reference that is one of the diversionary charms of historical English lexicography, Ray's entry in the *CEW* list for the Cambridge university dietary staff of life is presented as a southern bakery term: '*Size of bread*. Size comes from "scindo", I cut, one fourth part of a half penny loaf.' The size was the origin of the term for Ray's college status, 'sizar', a scholar poor enough to be compensated for his teaching in part by the food he was granted gratis by the College Foundation. (Ray also defined the *cue of bread*: 'Cue is "Q", the abbreviation of a quarter, the half of a halfpenny loaf'. Yeast entries were given an extra spiritual investment in Ray's lists: *gosgood*, yeast or barm, 'is nothing but God's good, the *Bonum divinum*'. Of yeast terms, of which there are a number, as there are of field meals, Ray used the first person plural, 'we in Essex'. He added, 'In Sussex and Kent where it is in use, it is also called *beer good*.' *Newing* is a Norfolk term for yeast. *Rising*, *sizzing*, and *barm good* are also listed. *Sizzing* was explained as onomatapoeia by Ray, when he referred to the Sussex term, 'from the sound of beer or ale in working'.

The Kentish household bread, *revel bread*, was described by Grose as 'whitey brown bread': it was wheaten but coarse. *Hufkins* were Kentish muffins, and *dowlers* or *dumplins* were Norfolk dumplings. They were *daw* if they were undercooked. A *pudding pie doll* in Norfolk was a toad-in-the-hole made of meat boiled in a crust. A *huff* in Gloucestershire was a light yeast paste enclosing fruit or meat whilst it was stewed – it huffed up in the operation. A *stull* was a *luncheon*, 'a great piece of bread and cheese or other victual in Essex'. A *stuckling* was an apple pasty or pie in Sussex.

A contrast was openly drawn between the dour northern dietary and repast entries and the more lush southern ones, a difference later to be used as leverage against the 'improvident' newly poor agricultural labourers of Ray's southern counties. By stereotype, life in the north, as the poetics of northern dialect inventories suggest, appears harder and the northern dietary 'lower', in the *CEW* and other long-eighteenth-century dialect lists, than they do in the south. This same difference persists by and large today. In Ray's day, this was seen as a difference, perhaps as a great divide: in the late Georgian period, it was seen as a difference to import forcibly to the south, however much against customary southern dietary practice such a northern import might appear.

'Red meats' in Ray's country word lists

Ray came from beef country. The butchers round Chelmsford, Essex, who supplied the London markets, were buried in such splendid monuments that they had their own architectural term for them – 'carnifices', the tombs of dead fleshers. Ray listed 'a *nail* of beef' for Sussex, 'a weight of eight pounds'. He gave the Norfolk term *'ice bone'* for 'a rump of beef'. In Devon, a *kearle* of veal or mutton was 'a loin of those meats'. There was the *pestle* of pork from Exmoor, and Grose recorded the *bolting* of pickled pork by ravenous farm servants in Kent and Sussex, a behavioural rather than a dialect word listing. Ray recorded the Devon expression for being stuffed with food: '"C'have eat so much, c'ham quit a quot" i.e. "I have eat so much I am cloyed"' (*CEW 1*:80). By contrast to these bountiful butcher's-meat listings, meat entries in the northern lists are few. There was the *snack*, a morsel of meat taken hastily; there was *soused pork*, 'the ear of a hog, pickled and soused'; there were the *warisons* (the stomach and its contents), and the *nears* or *conniers* (the kidneys). *Saim, samme, seame* and *sallis* (hog's lard) was a crucial dietary ingredient. So were *harns*, ox brains in Cumbria, and *hinge* or *hange*, the liver, heart, and lungs of sheep. The inwards of the hog were the entrails, *chitterlings*. The *kimnel* was a powdering tub for salting meat.

The wild wood pigeon was a *quice* in Gloucestershire and a *cushat* elsewhere. For the northwest, Ray listed the butchery term *whoave* for Cheshire (to overwhelm, used when a pig or chicken was smothered before being killed). To *sweal* was to singe a hog in Sussex. Sausages and blood pudding were widely eaten in the north and well prepared by filling *tharns* or *ropes*, 'guts prepared to receive pudding'. Ray continued, 'The *haggis* or *haggass* so prepared, consisted of the entrails of a sheap minced with oatmeal and boiled in the stomach or paunch of the animal.' The *groyne* was the swine's snout and the *fix fax* of the north was a butchery term for the sinews, the neck tendon of cattle and sheep, called in Norfolk the *paxwax*.

The northern involvement with the southern high-animal-protein dietary preferences was primarily along the drove roads south and east, where the small black cattle from the Scottish Borders and beyond would be driven on the hoof by oat-eating north country drovers.

Meals and drinks of the seventeenth-century labourer in husbandry

Captain Francis Grose, who was a hearty Georgian eater and drinker, though an unreliable lexicographer, gave *fitchet pie* as a northern and Cheshire entry. The pie was a 'meal given to the reapers at harvest home, composed of apples, onions, and the fat of bacon in equal quantities'. A *flacket* was a small barrel taken out to the haymakers for their refreshment. No tea and no potatoes enter these lists until the period of Ann Wheeler, the Cumbrian dialect writer, when they appear in her short tales about Cumbrian life from a country upper servant's point of view.[39] These date from the 1790s, by which time these two key innovations in the working-class diet had registered in the dialect listings. '*Bever*, *bit*, and *supper*' are other field meal terms, several of which were first listed by Ray but preserve their terminology unchanged (and regionally variable) in present-day dialect usage.

Customary commensualism is not treated here, but a brief mention should be made of three customary feasts Ray listed: '*Rushing*, feasting. *Upzetting time*. A gossiping and christening feast held when the newly delivered mother was ready to get up.' (*Bed-ale* and *groaning-ale* was served on these occasions.) *Footing time* in Norfolk was the time when a lying-in woman was delivered, was shrived, and got up. In south Wales, this occasion was known as a *bidding*, and *help ale* was drunk, as the *Gentleman's Magazine* reported in May 1784.[40]

Having reviewed some of the qualitative entries in Ray's lists of dialect repertories, in this case for the regional rural red meat and bread dietary, it is possible to contemplate those quantitative ones that might appear relevant to a parson in his northern parsonage, preparing to inspect his share of the God's tenth, the compulsory legal tithe levied on each family. It was to the grain allowance and the high-protein animal fare that the rural parson, greedy or impoverished, was primarily entitled, whether or not the local farmer agreed with his customary claims. The on-the-spot negotiations over the elusive right to the tithe that have taken place in rural areas are a fascinating chapter in Church economic history,[41] but the dialect record throws little light on the subject. Ray would probably have assumed that the garnering of the great and lesser tithes was a holy office, and indeed have been obliged himself in the Interregnum, when he was still a college steward or domestic officer, to have policed it if necessary. He would have endorsed the right of the encumbent parson to God's tenth in kind of the parish produce.

Ray had rejected the offer of a parish in Cumbria during the Common-wealth and the offer of a bishopric at the end of his life after the Glorious Revolution. Whatever his view of his own fitness to the vocation of parish priest, that view was probably imbued with a strong sense of stewardship, in his case manifested in part in his concern for the intellectual storehouse of the language of the poof. The hard-nosed parish farming and pluralism of Bishop Nicolson of Carlisle, who persecuted Cumbrian Quakers and other non-jurors with rigour, Ray would have rejected. (It seems certain that Ray never met Nicolson, but incorporated Nicolson's important Cumbrian dialect word lists very late in the day in *CEW 2* through the mediacy of Ray's commercially minded second edition publisher, Christopher Wilkinson.) Perhaps George Herbert's moving poem, written in the voice and from the experience of stewardship of an early seventeenth-century rural parson reflects Ray's cautious attitude to parish tithing. The sense of Christian stewardship in Herbert's dedicatory verse is elusive, but dwells on the conscience. The poem is from Walton's *Lives*, and Herbert dedicated it 'To my successor':

> If thou chance for to find
> A new House to thy mind,
> And built without Cost:
> Be good to the Poor,
> As God gives thee store,
> And then, my Labour's not lost.[42]

The burden of the tithe in marginal areas, where Nicolson's Cumbrian tithemen pressed hard, could in *CEW 1* times within living memory have pushed the poor over the brink of poverty. These upland areas experienced the last true subsistence crisis of the seventeenth century. Ray's adult informants from 1658 to 1660 in Cumbria had experienced as children the horror of death from famine.[43] By John Clare's day, the dialect word *clemm'd* had come to mean 'parched with thirst'[44] like thirsty gleaners on the summer harvest fields. Ray's definition was from an even grimmer age, and perhaps explains the preponderance of country words with dread and tired overtones in his Northern dialect listings: '*Clem'd* or *clam'd*: Starved, because by famine the guts and bowels are as it were clammed or stuck together. Sometimes it signifies thirsty, for we know in thirst the mouth is very often clammy' (*CEW 1*:10).

Marginal nutritional status was no deterrent when there were tithes to be gathered in, even in poverty-stricken parishes. The connection between tithe-gathering by scholarly, rural Anglican parsons and access to published knowledge of local words has necessarily been uncomfortably close.

Long-Eighteenth-Century Great and Lesser Tithe Terms in Ray's CEW Lists

The parish customary right that was of key economic importance to dialect users was that of *leasing* – 'to pick up corn left by the reapers, called in some counties *gleaning*'. *Seel* was the dialect term for the season for cropping. The gleaners' family had rights over the incompletely garnered harvest. These rights extended in glebe lands over the *haver seel*, the *hay seel*, the *barley seel*, the *bark seel*, and in the rural south the *wheat seel*. Such user-rights were inviolable and, if they were negotiable, few records of negotiations survive in the written record, except when rural violence erupted on a scale wider than that of the village.

In Ray's first comprehensive *CEW* list, users' common rights over minerals like lead and salt were also inventoried. Ray's entry for *walling*, the boiling of salt in the great Cheshire salt pans of Nantwich, Northwich, Droitwich, and so on, identified salt rights in dialect with *walloping*: 'In some boroughs persons who boil a [salt cauldron] there are called pot-wallopers and are entitled to vote for representatives in Parliament.' Customary rights of access to the riches of the land, including minerals, preoccupied no few Commonwealth dialect protagonists, and Ray's dual interest in vocabulary and English common law in its customary aspect is typical of them.

The gleaners took what was left after the harvest, but the parson had been there before them. To him, as God's parish emissary (on cited Old Testament precedents), was due a tenth of all the harvest before the gleaners were let loose on the fields. The payment was usually in kind; the parishioners were mostly illiterate or near illiterate, and the parish clerk supervised the levy with the tithe men. Not surprisingly, a trace of rural anti-clericalism, surviving in rural Catholic north Wales in a stream of 'black cow' jokes (the black cow is usually the parson, and harm is unwittingly committed against his person in the jokes), was recorded by Ray. '*To bishop*' in Ray's northern list is used 'for milk that is burned in boiling, as "The bishop has set his foot in it".' This is harmless enough, but uncomfortable reading to the archidiaconate.

So, too, is Ray's one actual tithe entry, which implies a massive ambiguity over which cleric was entitled to the tithes in one possibly Interregnum Norfolk dialect-speaking area. Ray's term is *catchland*, defined by him as 'Land which is not certainly known to what parish it belongs, and the minister that first gets the tithes of it enjoys it for the year'. Ambiguity over claims to the living, be they claims over praedial tithes (lesser tithes, paid on produce grown or grazed on the parish like hay, flax, and wood) or great or corn tithes (levied on grain crops), probably created many rights entitlement skirmishes at harvest time.

Many of Ray's other dialect terms would have served as a *vade mecum* to the tithe gatherer unused to northern or southern locutions. There follows Ray's record of the quantities and crops that would be brought in by the parson or his tithe gatherers to the *teen barn*, a right in kind abolished as dialect usage subsided along with the Tithe Commutation Acts of 1836–60:

A *quartern*. A Quarter of a peck. [This was used to measure loaves as well as flour and grain, so that it is possible that an incumbent had a right over some of those great oaten loaves in Ray's *bannock* listings.] *Seame*. A Quarter. Eight bushels. Also known as a 'horseload', and used of wood as well as grain. *Comb*. Four bushels or half a quarter. A *cop*. A pea and bean measure. Fifteen sheaves in the field and sixteen in the barn. [The reason for the augmentation when stored is not explained]. A *bole*. Four *kennings*. Three new *boles* make an old *bole* in oats and barley only. [Several of these self-defining, closed-off entries are given, especially by Captain Grose.] *Leap*. *Lib*. (Suffolk). Half a bushel.

In Essex, this last measure was used for seed corn, more valuable than the rest.

Most of these quantitative terms were collected in the south, where Ray was on his own ground and may have collected dues for Trinity on rural college lands in the Interregnum. Some of these dues were measured by the *neiful* (the fistful) or by the single or double handful, the southern dialect *yepsen* or *yapsen* or the northern *gowpen*, being countrymen and women's subsistence measures. Or they were measured as a *nitch*, a small quantity of hay or corn, 'less than a *jobbet*'. The parson also required his tenth of the *rathe* fruits and *fimble and carl* hemp. These early ripening crops among the praedial tithes that were his due were of the greatest monetary value. 'Mixed' tithes were payable on animals nourished on parish grounds, including colts, lambs and their wool, geese, piglets, chickens, eggs, and so on. It is hard to believe that dialect users parted easily with such produce to standard-speaking vicars and bishops, whether or no they were dialect collectors, especially if the parishioners were Catholic or Nonconformist country folk from the 1660s onwards. William Nicolson, the most active tithe collector in the second edition Ray group, and later a holder of a plurality of sees and seats in Ireland as well as on the Scottish borders, added to his terriers for Cumbria and Northumbria 'personal' tithes on the labour of felling, fishing, and milling. They were his due, but he was indefatigable in his extension of that due, preferring to invest in ecclesiastical stone rather than feed the parish.[45] (A more sharing, Christian attitude towards the parish obligation of the incumbent is recorded in the George Herbert poem of the generation before Ray, quoted at the end of the previous section.)

William Nicolson's terrier returns for the Cumbria–Roxburghshire border, part of his great rebuilding of the eastern ward of Westmorland for the Anglican Church (1680–99), were made in a province with a tax assessment of £92 a year. Westmoreland, another dialect-speaking area was assessed even lower at this time, at £63. This was during the Interregnum. Ray's 'southern' region of Norfolk was assessed at £3000 a year and Devon at £2500 at this period, as is to be expected from the dietary contrasts Ray's inventories present. Nicolson's tithing terrier was precise: he wanted the northern parishes on a sound financial footing from the 1680s, when Ray's original dialect vocabularies were extended to *CEW 2*. The parishioners could keep the first two lambs born to a ewe; then, Nicolson wrote, 'we take the third', using the very same 'we' (Nicolson preferred the Latin 'nostrates' in his own definitions) that Ray used to define identity with dialect users. Wool and lamb *tilths* were taken in June. The tithe was recompensed in Melmerby with a thank-offering from the parson of six-pennyworth of ale. Denton shepherds were less amenable than Melmerby ones: 'They were obliged as they call [the tithe] to run their lambs and to hide their wool in dark places.' Pity the Denton vicar who needed his church vestibule reroofed.

Kine tithes were due at Easter: 'A *skip* and a *cwy* each a half penny. A fallow cow one penny. A new milked cow twopence halfpenny. A new calved cow three pennies.' Here, relative monetary values imply that pennies must have been in circulation, but the system was primarily one in kind. The *tith-hen* or *reckhen* was the poultry levy paid at Martinmas 'from every house in the village poor and rich'. A farthing was the tithe on 'six of any of the following, turkies, hens, ducks and other tame poultry'. Two eggs a year for every laying hen was owed to the parson by every villager from the borderland between Scotland and England, the remote 'debatable lands'. One egg was owed for a young hen, a reasonable grace levy which did not involve the complexities of commutation to cash.

As sizar for Trinity under Cromwell and Wilkins in 1654–9, Ray himself may have been to inspect Trinity lands as far north as rural Felmersham in Bedfordshire, a Great Ouse parish of some profitability to the college. He, like Nicolson and Ray's other dialect contributors, might therefore have had practical insight into the regulation of tithes in kind. Quite properly, the *CEW* word lists reflect this rural expertise, and would have served as a dialect learners' checklist for needy or perplexed incumbents looking for their yearly subsistence out of their dialect area. Ray's general tithe terms include:

> *Bud.* A weaned calf of the first year. (Suffolk) *Cadma. Winnock.* The least pig of the litter. *Cade lamb.* A tame lamb. A *gow* or *gilt.* Hog or sow pigs in the North. A *gimmer* lamb. A two year old lamb. A *fare* of pigs. All the pigs brought forth by the sow at one litter. *Cleckin.* A young chicken. A *steg.* A gander. A *staffe* of cocks. A pair of cocks. A *lafter* or *laster* of eggs. Thirteen eggs set under a hen.

Nicolson's enquiries into 'ye condition of ye place, pastor and people' in the Borders hill country stemmed from less scholarly roots than those of Ray and Lhwyd. These two inadequately funded travelling scholars both believed that the systematic recording of the wealth of the countryside would provide a bank of knowledge necessary to a commonwealth of cognoscenti. Indeed, they put out programmes for the collation of such knowledge (regarded with some suspicion by the authorities), though they died too soon for any of them to be implemented.[46] It was the Enlightenment agricultural economists who had fulfilled their endeavour, but from a more self-seeking point of view. Enlightenment topographic economists and statisticians, still dialect collecting, set out their findings in the interest of landowners and the land acquisitive. Ray's initiatives, nevertheless, pinpoint the underlying sense in which the ideas of the English Revolution bore late fruit during the Enlightenment. The continuum is underemphasized to the demerit of our historiography of dialect English and the broader intellectual advances its cultivation represented.

Social Affirmation and Linguistic Assertion in Ray's CEW

William Nicolson's worldly tithe-collecting motives for the publication of Cumbrian and Scots Borders' hill-farming dietary and livestock terms have been compared with those of the travelling scholar Ray and his companions, especially Courthope and Philip Skippon the Younger. From this comparison, it can be inferred that Ray's tenacity in the matter of dialect word collection sprang from a personal involvement in the code when he was young, and a sympathy for its empirical and metaphorical reach when he was at the height of his intellectual powers as a scholar. Ray's interest in country usage in its empirical sense was a double one. First there was his conservationist search for signification; secondly there was the implicitly social entitlement that the code he published affirms. The pursuit of English dialect as a valid medium of communication outlived him. For us, as for him, the 'New World of English Words' is at its powerful best when reflected through multiple lenses.

By his recognition of alternative English word repertories, this gentle, pedantic, preaching, Interregnum botanist from rural Essex felt he had contributed one more jot of wisdom to a Commonwealth – dialect-speaking as well as standard – which might have a chance to grow to full stature. As an early member of the Royal Society, banned from academic life because of his integrity as a man of God, Ray persisted, in academic and religious exile in Black Notley, in building the Commonwealth he had always stood for by his scientific, religious, taxonomic, and linguistic endeavours. They could not and cannot, as socio-intellectual contributions, be separated, reflecting as they do his own modernizing integrity.

John Ray, a rural intellectual in semi-banishment at the height of his career, a deacon who never preached out loud again after the Restoration, remained linguistically and empirically faithful to the speakers of country tongues who had raised him: it was his wish, rather than that of his grieving followers, that he might be buried in open ground at his death, outside the walls of that grassy backwater of a natal parish church at Black Notley, Essex. Earlier, when death removed his collector companions and his patrons one by one, with his tasks still incomplete, it was his free-riding collector companion, the Cromwellian dialect-speaking veteran Thomas Willisel, that he most mourned.

John Ray required of his dialect word lists, as he did of his science, his taxonomies, and his theology, that they should retain the uncircumscribed, personally attributable style of all the work he published. His correspondents' lists must be their own, but ones wholly in accordance with his own experience as a collector over like ground. These country words were communally collected, reflective of country life as it was then lived. Ray's good name as a scholar is their vindication in the national archives. The irony is that it was the period of government by the majors-general (whose more scholarly sons and heirs were Ray's direct responsibility *in statu pupillari*) that instituted the mixing of tongues and tithes that was finally fatal to dialect usage. But that same period, the Interregnum, also gave Ray's impetus public impact and popularity, in the dual sense indicated in Peter Burke's crucial study, *Popular Culture in Early Modern Europe*. Dialect usage did not ultimately survive the mingling of codes. Ray's timing for the publication of *CEW 1* and *CEW 2* is highly significant.

It is not possible to write a history of the English language in the long eighteenth century, or indeed that of its science or its literature, without giving full scholarly attention to the published dialect record of the country English usage the Ray group set in train (for all its shortcomings). That newly recorded lexicon, built up, in Ray's self-effacing term, of 'words seldom used', was to him and must be to us a generative matrix, which stands, Janus-faced, at the bifurcation of the ways.

BIBLIOGRAPHY

ABBREVIATIONS OF RAY TITLES CITED

These are given in order of year of publication.

CC	*Catalogus Cantabrigiam*, 1660
Real Character	*Essay towards a Real Character and Philosophical Language*, 1668
EP	*English Proverbs*, 1670
Obs.	Observations, Topographical, Moral and Physiological ..., 1673
CEW 1, 2, 3, 4	First, second, and third editions of *Collection of English Words*, 1674, 1691, 1818, 1874
Dictionariolum	*Dictionariolum Trilingue*, 1675
Wisdom	*The Wisdom of God in the Creation*, 1691
Gibson	Edmund Gibson's folio edition of Camden's *Britannia*, 1695
FC	*Further Correspondence of John Ray*, 1928
Danny Letters	Letters to Peter Courthope (written 1658–74)

WORKS OF RAY PRINCIPALLY CITED

Ray, John, Fellow of the Royal Society, *A Collection of English Words Not Generally used, with their Significations and Original in two Alphabetical Catalogues, the one of such as are proper to the Northern, the other to the Southern Counties. With catalogues of English Birds and Fishes: and an account of the preparing and refining of such metals and minerals as are gotten in England.* (H. Bruges for Thomas Burrell at the Golden Ball under St Dunstans, Fleetstreet, London, 1674).

All significations and dialect words cited in the text are from this source unless otherwise identified.

The title of the first edition (cited here as *CEW 1*) is in red and black type and there are 84 small octavo leaves. The dedication is to Peter Courthope, Esquire. The 'collection of local words' occupies pp. 1–80, the entries for northern words being twice as numerous as those for the 'south and east country'. These two regional English dialect lexicons, chosen because they were words 'not generally' (i.e. only regionally) used, are followed by bird, fish, and mineral listings. There are 15 pp. of bird listings, 15 pp. of fish listings and 35 pp. of descriptions of vernacular mineral extraction customary practice and lexical usage. The last 6 pp. are misnumbered and the typesetting is crude throughout.

On 17 January 1674, Ray advised his patron, Peter Courthope, that the country word glossaries 'have sold very well, and that your cousin Thomas Burrell has disposed of almost the whole impression, which for his sake I am glad of'. (*FC*, 37). Robert Hooke, FRS's diary entry for 26th November 1673 indicates he bought his copy for a shilling on that day. The title page date of 1674 would appear to post-date the time by which the small octavo country word hand-book had almost sold out, suggesting Ray already had a considerable following, on the strength perhaps of the success of his *Collection of English Proverbs* and the Cambridge catalogue of plants of 1670 and 1660, both of which were sold in Cambridge by William Morden and printed by John Hayes, the University printer. The dialect dictionary was a London venture.

In 1737, Ray's *Proverbs* were combined with the *Collection of English Words*, and they were reprinted in 1768 and 1818. This popular joint edition circulated throughout the long eighteenth century. The most accessible copy of the country word list is the 1818 combined edition, *A Complete Collection of English Proverbs . . . to which is Added by the Same Author . . . a Collection of English Words*, T. and J. Allman, London (cited as *CEW 3*). The Linnean Society of London, among other collections, has a few copies of the rare first edition, but the simplest way to read Ray's second edition is as a sequel to the *Proverbs* in joint editions.

The second edition was expanded by the contributions of a younger generation of collector-correspondents whom Ray trusted. Ray eliminated the birds and fish because, in his introductory words, 'they were very imperfect, and since much more fully given in the histories of birds and fishes published by us' (that is to say, Francis Willughby and Ray). He added, 'Besides, if God grant life and health, I may put forth a particular methodical synopsis of our English animals and fossils . . . which will swell to a considerable volume' (*CEW 2*: end of preface). The importance of the built-in obsolescence of the zoological entries, as of the mineral ones, is that it in a sense implies that the 'scientific' lists prepared by the group of systematists including 'John Ray of Essex', working to Wilkins's direction during the 1660s on the *Essay towards a Real Character*, and the popular-knowledge dialect compendia published independently by the Ray circle between 1673 and 1691, might themselves be refined and extended at some future date.

As well as omitting birds and fish, the second edition adds the title page wording 'The Second Edition, augmented with many Hundreds of Words, Observations, Letters, etc.' The subscription runs: 'London: printed for Christopher Wilkinson at the Black Boy over against St Dunstans in Fleetstreet, 1691' (cited here as *CEW 2*).

In this second edition, Edward Lhwyd's 'British or Welsh' dialect parallels are included, as is a brief, able Cumbrian list sent to Lhwyd by Mr Tomlinson of Edmund Hall. A more formidable, scholarly, Latin list of Northumbrian dialect from the young William Nicolson, sent directly to the publisher, was also commented by Ray as editor. As a substitute for the fish and bird lists, Ray published 'An account of some Errors and Defects in our English . . . Manner of Spelling'. This edition is 173 pp. long and advertises Ray's popular *Dictionariolum Trilingue* in the end matter, by this time in its third 1689 edition. It seems that a third edition of *CEW* might have been planned by the Ray group since Francis Brokesby sent in some notes on

Yorkshire dialect pronunciation (followed in 1703 by a Yorkshire list from Ralph Thoresby) using the first person plural for dialect usage, as Ray did. The identificatory first person plural is a badge of style for the Ray group: Brokesby, for example, wrote of Yorkshire East Riding pronunciation 'in that many words, we leave out the aspirate both at the beginning and at the latter end.' This letter is published in *CEW 3*: 292.

The combination of standard English spelling reform, access to the ancient languages, and fluency in English dialect lexical signification underlines John Ray's belief in the value of each of these strands, learned, standard, or popular, of the tongue of the nation whose interest he wished to serve with his learning.

The rest of John Ray's publications cited here (a very small selection of his total opus) are listed chronologically by year of publication. His great botanical works are discussed by Charles Raven and others, and are not discussed here. The vernacular word list is the least known and *The Wisdom of God* was the best known of this short list. Both epitomize the intellectual freedom granted to Ray during his sole period of established tenure of office as an innovative Interregnum tutor with a scientific bent, in Cromwellian Cambridge. The proof of this lies in his surprising disparagement of his old Alma Mater in the 1691 *Wisdom*. He did not feel the scientific enterprise had yet taken root in the very Great Court to which he had transplanted mountain herbs for his garden patch with such keen assiduity until 1662.

During the Bentley Debates at Trinity, at the time of the preparation of the second edition of the *CEW*, the younger Lhwyd and the elder and weightier thinker Ray prided themselves on their converse with shepherds and miners rather than academics. Their pride, that of the displaced, was one in intellectual independence. They believed they were in touch with reality, with 'things' rather than with 'tongues', and there is little reason, from a cursory reading of either edition of *CEW*, to doubt that this was so. The surprising thing was that the *CEW* was ever written at all. I owe it to a reading of Keith Thomas's book *Man and the Natural World* to have appreciated that political exile in the country (in Essex, where Ray was born and bred) may have been a crucial catalyst for the enterprising philological and biological experiments in the tabulation of everyday matters that Ray made.

Ray, John, 'Letters to Peter Courthope'. Of these letters, the twenty-one written between 1658 and 1674 have survived. They appear in *FC*, but are inaccurately transcribed there. The original mss are kept in the Danny Archive, housed in the East Sussex record Office at Lewes (cited as Danny Letters).

(W)Ray, John, *Catalogus Cantabrigiam*, Cambridge, 1660. The Cambridge catalogue is most easily read in modern English translation (*Ray's Flora of Cambridgeshire*, trans. and ed. A.H. Ewen and Cecil Thomas Prime [Hitchin, Wheldon and Wesley, 1975]). The *Appendix* to this important local plant catalogue was published three years later. Ray had already journeyed alone into Derbyshire and north Wales by this time, and was about to leave for the north of England and the Isle of Man, then under Cromwellian rule, with Willughby. He was ordained by Sanderson at the Barbican just before Christmas of that year. In 1661, Skippon and he travelled to York and north to Scotland, where the common northern bill of fare did not impress him favourably, and returned to Cambridge via Carlisle and Cumbria. Willisel was collecting for him by this time. In the following year, Ray travelled round Wales with Skippon and Willughby, and went on to Cornwall with Skippon. The preface of the catalogue is programmatic for the rest of Ray's work. (Cited as *CC*.)

Ray, John, artificial taxonomies designed for the biological tables for John Wilkins's *Essay towards a Real Character and Philosophical Language* (London, Royal Society, 1668). A folio edition, this was ready for the printers by 1666 (see Stearn below). John Ray wrote the botanical tables for Wilkins's artificial classification of knowledge, of which he later disapproved. See *JR*:182. (Cited as *Real Character*.)

Ray, John, *Collection of English Proverbs*, Cambridge, 1670, best read in *CEW 3*.

Ray, John, *Observations Topographical, Moral and Physiological* ... (Printed by Andrew Clark and published by John Martyn in 1673, at a cost of 6 shillings). Six times the price of the *CEW*, this was bound up with *A Catalogue of Foreign Plants*. The work is dedicated to Philip Skippon, Ray's fellow traveller (with Willughby) on his tour of Italy, Switzerland, and France, on the pattern later followed with the *CEW*, which was dedicated to Courthope. The patron-dedicatee was, as in that instance, an Interregnum student of promise trained as a fellow-travelling observer of the vernacular in man and animals. The European tour, which was prolonged, preceded the decision to put full scholarly effort into the first edition of the *CEW* and in part, perhaps, provided the European perspective that made its objectivity possible. (Cited as *Obs.*)

Ray, John, *Dictionariolum Trilingue*, London, 1675. The facsimile published by the Ray Society, London, 1981, is available at the Natural History Museum, and has an invaluable introduction by William T. Stearn. This facsimile is dedicated to Sir Geoffrey Keynes, whose 1951 and 1976 bibliography of John Ray's works supplement Raven's biographical references in *JR*. (Cited as *Dictionariolum*.)

Ray, John, *Historia Piscium*, London, 1686. Dedicated to Willughby's memory.

Ray, John, *The Wisdom of God in the Creation*, London, 1691; also *Collection of English Words*, 2nd edition, 1691. The second edition of *Wisdom* appeared in the following year, followed by fresh editions in 1701 and 1704. (Cited as *Wisdom*.)

Ray, John, in Edmund Gibson's folio edition of Camden's *Britannia*, 1695 (Published for A. and J. Churchill, Black Swan, Pater noster Row, London), 'More Rare Plants Growing Wild' entries, recounting local rarities that are still unique to the counties traversed on Ray's earlier regional 'simpling voyages'. These are interspersed with other county entries, some of the Welsh ones being by Lhwyd, and can be read throughout Gibson. Included in the Bedfordshire entries (292) is an elaborate description of the preparation of woad, with complete vernacular manufacturing and price terms. Ray's pragmatic enterprise as a serious field naturalist is set in period by the fact that his ungarnished 'rare plant' entries always succeed, county by county, the reiterated aristocratic pedigree listings entitled 'More Earls'. (Cited as *Gibson*.)

Ray, John, *Further Correspondence of John Ray*, ed. R.W.T. Gunther, Ray Society Publication 114, London, 1928. (Cited as *FC*.)

BIOGRAPHICAL WORKS CONSULTED

Arber, Agnes, 'A seventeenth century naturalist, John Ray', *Isis*, 34: 319–24.

Derham [William], *Memorials of John Ray, consisting of his life by ... Derham; with Biographical and critical notices by Sir J. E. Smith*, ed. Edwin Lankester, The Ray Society, London, 1846: 16.

Raven, Charles E., *John Ray, Naturalist, his Life and Works* (Cambridge University Press, Cambridge, 1942). This invaluable source is a *chef d'oeuvre* and is especially interesting in its theological, systematic, and regional botanical detail, which is unmatchable. It was reprinted by Cambridge University Press in 1990. (Cited as *JR*.)

Stearn, William T., 'John Wilkins, John Ray and Carl Linnaeus' (The Royal Society of London Wilkins Lecture, 1985), *Notes and Records of the Royal Society*, 40, no. 2, May 1986: 101–24. Important on the influence of Wilkins, made a bishop by Charles II for the *Real Character* volume, on the independent but developing thought of Ray in the sphere of biology and language. (Cited as 'John Wilkins'.)

Webster, Charles, entry on Ray, John. In C.C. Gillispie (ed.), *Dictionary of Scientific Biography 11* (Charles Scribner, New York, 1976), 313–18.

GENERAL BACKGROUND

Burke, Peter, *Popular Culture in Early Modern Europe* (Temple-Smith, London, and Harper, New York, 1978). 'The Triumph of Lent: The Reform of Popular Culture' places the 1650s at a pivotal point in the withdrawal of polite from popular culture. Ray in a sense, in his dialect lexicography, sought less to reform popular dialect culture than to bridge a widening gap before it was too late. (Cited as *Popular Culture*.)

Hill, Christopher, *Intellectual Origins of the English Revolution* (Clarendon Press, Oxford, 1965). Especially 125–30 on Wilkins on language and society, and the appendix, 301–13, on puritans and scientists at Oxford and Cambridge during the Interregnum. Ray's 1660s–90s doubts as to the capacity of Restoration Cambridge to institute the modernization of the curriculum (by the inclusion of science in a central role), as set out clearly in *Wisdom*, conform to Christopher Hill's analysis. Like his dialect lexicography, Ray's espousal of botanical science was oppositional, as it was later to be for Rousseau.

Obelkevitch, James, 'Proverbs and Social History', in Burke, Peter, and Porter, Roy, *The Social History of Language, Volume 1* (Cambridge University Press, Cambridge, 1987). A unique contribution to the analysis of English class usage in the seventeenth and eighteenth centuries. 'Dialect' proverbs are not discussed as such, but Ray's collection falls well into Obelkevitch social analysis. (Cited as Obelkevitch, 'Proverbs'.)

Potter, Simeon, and Sargent, L., *Pedigree: Essays on the Etymology of Words from Nature* (Collins, New Naturalist Series, London, 1973). This work is very much in the Ray tradition and is on the subject of the unique strengths of dialect words in English usage.

Sloan, Phillip R., 'John Locke, John Ray and the Problem of Natural System', *Journal of the History of Biology*, 5, no. 1, Spring 1972: 1–54. Useful on the influence of John Locke on shifts in Ray's taxonomic views from the time he joined the Royal Society of London in 1667. (Cited as 'John Locke'.)

Thomas, Keith, *Man and the Natural World: Changing Attitudes in England (1500–1800)* (Penguin, Harmondsworth, 1984). Especially 251–4 on the celebration of the countryside by those whom political failure had driven from the city in the 1650s, and 281–2 on the seventeenth-century English clergymen-naturalists and their amateur helpers.

Willey, Basil, *The Eighteenth Century Background: Studies on the Idea of Nature in the Thought of the Period* (Penguin, Harmondsworth, 1960). 'The Wisdom of God in the Creation', 32–47. Ray and Derham are treated as Enlightenment thinkers. Ralph Cudworth and Henry More, Ray's philosophical mentors among the Cambridge Platonists, figure in Willey's earlier volume, *The Seventeenth Century Background: Studies in the Thought of the Age in Relation to Poetry and Religion* (Penguin, Harmondsworth, 1962). Especially 123–55, 'Rational Theology: The Cambridge Platonists'.

Wright, C.J., *Comenius and the Church Universal* (Herbert Barber, London, 1942). A useful introduction to this important Commonwealth figure, an influence on Ray undiscussed by Raven in *JR*. The *Orbis pictus* of Comenius was the first children's dictionary published, and was illustrated to assist language learning by the young child.

NOTES

This essay is dedicated to William T. Stearn, botanist, author, and embodiment of the enduring vitality of John Ray's belief in the commonwealth of scholars. It owes a profound sense of gratitude to Dr Roy Porter for his encouragement, and to the librarians of the Harvard Library, the Linnean Society of London Library, and the Society of Antiquaries Library for unfailing scholarly assistance.

1   Edward Phillips, *A New World of English Words: or a General Dictionary, containing the terms, etymologies, definitions and perfect interpretations of the proper significations of hard English words throughout the Arts and Sciences, liberal and mechanic* (London, Nathan Brooke, 1658, reprinted by Scolar Press, 1969). Phillips was nephew to John Milton, and tutor to John Evelyn's son 1663–72. His English translation of his uncle's Latin letters of state, written for Cromwell, were published in 1694. His dictionary was derivative, plagiarizing in particular the 1656 *Glossographia* of Thomas Blount of Orleton, Hereford-shire, a zealous Roman Catholic and a lexicographer of distinction, who indignantly denounced Phillips's borrowings between 1658 and 1673. However-er, Phillips's folio dictionary was popular and Ray cited it rather than Blount's dictionary in his definition of the Cheshire drink *bragget*.

Blount (1618–79) first used the title term 'hard words' and sought to categorize, by his listings, usage in 'our refined English tongue'. Blount was a Worcestershire Royalist and suffered greatly for his Roman Catholic integrity, not least by being plagiarized by Puritans during the Interregnum. Phillips's substitution of usage 'throughout the Arts and Sciences, liberal and mechanic' was nevertheless, ideologically speaking, a positive product of the intellectual ferment of the Commonwealth period, in which the young Ray participated.

It is for this reason that Phillips's title has been chosen to provide the title for this paper, in spite of the plagiaristic and therefore dubious text to which it was originally attached. It was to the 'empirick' tradition of Phillips's dictionary, to which the Royal Society of London was also committed, that Ray, with his *CEW* and *Dictionariolum* listings, contributed. Ray, and after him Nathan

Bailey, the East End of London Nonconformist lexicographer of the 1730s, emphasized, rather than 'hard words' in the English language, all words in good usage, including the words of 'empiricks' at a popular level, a tendency spurned in print but not in fact in the 1750s by Dr Johnson and James Boswell.

2   End of preface, trans. Raven, *JR*:83.

3   See Phillip R. Sloan, 'John Locke', and William T. Stearn, 'John Wilkins', for the development of Ray's criteria for botanical classification, from the time he was patronized to compile Wilkins's botanical Tables and to translate Wilkins's artificial language into Latin. See Raven, *JR*, for Ray's botanical and theological works.

4   *EP*, 1670. Some preference for the Braintree area of Essex and for the university where his intellectual life unfolded is apparent in these collections. Ray, however, was frank in his espousal of the editorial privilege of partiality. Scottish and Hebrew proverbs are included.

5   In Gibson, 1695. The lists of 'More rare plants' by county, as commented by Ray, Lhwyd, and others, would make a lively present-day publication, with present-day surveys to ascertain survival rates. It should be noted that the same is true of the lexical usage lists. Ray's collections of regional plants are of the highest standards.

6   The *Dictionariolum* (1675) must owe its origin as a concept to the Czech writer Comenius's lively *Janua linguarum*, his *Gates of Knowledge*, and to his illustrated children's dictionary of the 1640s, but Comenius, the internationalist scholar, invited to England by Hartlib, never attached importance to the signification of rural dialect. 'Mother tongue' to Comenius was the standard language of a person's country of origin, as opposed to the other standard and ancient tongues acquired through education, through refugee status, or through the profound linguistic influence of extensive travel.

7   *CEW 1* and *2* (1674 and 1691). The scholarly reprint of 1874 (*CEW 4*) by the Rev. W.W. Skeat is marred by Skeat's ahistorical impatience with Ray's etymological naivety. Because of his philological outrage, Skeat omits to comment on the unusual nature of Ray's identificatory approach to usage and signification. Skeat's edition marks, however, the first time the two editions were compounded, indexed, and annotated since Ray first published them. To this collection is added an account of Yorkshire words by Ralph Thoresby, the Leeds antiquarian, sent to Ray in 1703 and published with Ray's *Philosophical Letters* by his literary executor, the Essex clergyman William Derham.

    The entire list of the invaluable reprint series of English Dialect Society Publications provides interesting reading for the social historian of language.

8   John Ray's *CC* preface, which, as his first introduction to his first book, enjoyed by Hartlib and others, was programmatic for all future published works.

9   Keith Thomas, *Man and the Natural World*.

10   John Clare's anti-Linnean views are clear from his published *Autobiographical Fragments* (Mss. B3: 73) reprinted by Eric Robinson (*John Clare's Autobiographical Writings*, ed. Eric Robinson, Oxford University Press, Oxford, 1986). Clare noted, 'I have puzzled wasted hours ... to understand a shadow of the system, so as to be able to class the wild flowers peculiar to my own neighbourhood, for I find it woud [sic] require a ... second Solomon to

understand them in Lennis [Linnaeus'] system. Modern works are mystified by systematic symbols' (a movement initiated by Wilkins, rather than Ray). 'When one turns to the works of Ray, Parkinson and Gerrard where there is more of nature and less of art, it is like . . . a balmy summer of a dewy morning after the troubled dreams of a nightmare'. (49)

11 Of the Georgian successors to Ray as a dialect lexicologist, the dialect writers most valuable for the empirical loading of their glossaries include William Marshall, Robert Burns, Ann Wheeler, the Lancashire author John Collier, and John Clare. The dialect contributions, most of them anonymous, to the *Gentleman's Magazine* now need to be written up, as the women writers have been by Alison Adburgham, *Women in Print: Writing and Women's Magazines from the Restoration to the Accession of Victoria*, Allen and Unwin, London, 1972: 79–109. Women contributors of standard English to the *Gentleman's Magazine* included Jane Hughes, Catherine Cockburn, and Elizabeth Carter from the 1730s. There is no mention at all, however, in Adburgham's text of provincial women dialect writers, who may have had a statistically predominant dialect reading following.

The difficulty, as with all minority identification in the eighteenth century, is the anonymity surrounding the work. The editorial and literary discernment of editors like Roger Lonsdale has begun to throw light on the historiography: see his introduction, selection, and brief biographies in *The New Oxford Book of Eighteenth Century Verse*, Oxford University Press, Oxford, 1987.

12 Clare, glossary to the *Shepherd's Calendar* (1821), Eric Robinson and Geoffrey Summerfield, eds, *Collected Verse of John Clare*, Oxford University Press, Oxford, 1967. (And see n. 35 below.)

13 The greatest stanzas of the best verse of Clare, in the *Shepherd's Calendar* and the 'Lament of Swordy Well', were written between 1820 and 1832. These remarkable anti-pastoral works reflect the physical hardship of life on the land as it was actually experienced. The texts of Tusser and Ray's rural glossaries both reproduced dialect common wisdom. Clare in the 1820s read Tusser with interest, noting the shift in meaning of rural East Anglian dialect words since the sixteenth century. Thomas Tusser's *One Hundred* and *Five Hundred Points of Good Husbandry* were first published in 1557 and 1573. They contain rural saws of a practical nature for the southern farmer. A good recent edition is Thomas Tusser, *Five Hundred Points of Good Husbandry*, ed. Geoffrey Grigson, Oxford University Press, Oxford, 1984.

14 An attitudinal periodization of the literary traditions of English pastoral verse is authoritatively established by John Barrell and John Bull in the *Penguin Book of English Pastoral Verse*, Penguin, Harmondsworth, 1974. Their introduction and selections provide an invaluable orientation to a mainly standard English (rather than dialect) pastoral literary heritage. John Barrell's *The Idea of Landscape and the Sense of Place* is a key Clare study (Cambridge University Press, Cambridge, 1972), as is his contribution to the history of Georgian pastoral art, *The Dark Side of the Landscape* (Cambridge University Press, Cambridge, 1980). There is a danger, however, of the literary overview crowding out movements other than the poetic literary, which were also fundamentally 'anti-pastoral'. Ray, for example, deliberately eschewed any

fancy journalism, though his paeans to Cromwell from Cambridge in Latin show he was capable of such. By the 1690s, Ray preferred hard lists – witness the 'list' style he persisted in using for Gibson in what was, after all, a generally read and elaborate folio edition of Camden's *Britannia*: 'Truly I have indeed by me some observations made in my simpling voyages . . . but I have neither skill nor leisure to contribute anything considerable' (Raven, *JR*: 267).

15   The publications of the Leeds-based Survey of English Dialects (Leeds Dialect Society, *Survey of English Dialects (The Basic Material)*, E.J. Arnold for the University of Leeds, Leeds, 1963–) provide essential follow-up reading to the texts of the long-eighteenth-century dialect compilers. There appears to have been a survival rate for some of the English dialect inventory by 1950 in anticipated local speech areas such as Norfolk and Cumbria, though the impact of television, film, and radio on old and young in such rural areas may be terminal.

16   Nathaniel Fairfax's letters to Secretary Oldenburg through the period of Oldenburg's imprisonment in the Tower make interesting reading. He was persuaded to desist, perhaps, by Oldenburg's political difficulties, which language purist letters from a Suffolk Nonconformist could merely have served to deepen, as implied in the Halls' full edition of the Oldenburg correspondence. Rupert A. Hall and Marie Boas Hall, eds, *The Correspondence of Henry Oldenburg, Vol. III, 1666–1667*, University of Wisconsin Press, Madison, 1986: 321, 491). Nathaniel, ejected curate of Withisham, Suffolk, and his son were both language purists. The stilted style of Fairfax's prose, to be read *in extenso* in his purist book *The Bulk and Selvedge of the World* (London, 1674) is to be noted in a letter he wrote to the beleaguered Oldenburg in September 1667: 'Being so much a stranger to all concerns of yours but ye of philosophy, I thought it too unwary to give you ye workings of my breast as a friend, when affairs were too techy, yt my way was not open as a Philosopher.' There is no indication that Ray had any connection or sympathy with the language purist movement, of which William Morris was a late adherent. However, the coterminal existence of such a movement with the first effective dialect lexicon in the English language is not a coincidence. Alternative speech forms were momentarily coming into print and into public favour. On Nathaniel Fairfax, see Charles Barber, *Early Modern English*, Andre Deutsch, London, 1976: 90–6, 'The Language Purists'.

17   Comenius, the Czech refugee, and Ray, the displaced Englishman, both fell to lexicography to relieve painful intellectual exile, and to educate others.

18   See the facsimile of the *Dictionariolum*, with an introduction by William Stearn.

19   Ray's prefaces, *CEW 1* and *CEW 2*.

20   Ray's deprecatory warning that university men might not make good ethnographers comes in the second edition *CEW* preface (1691). Referring to the inability of Hickes, the Icelandic scholar, and Nicolson, the Northumbrian prelate, to tell what usage was exclusively northern and what were more generally used dialect terms, Ray suggested that 'these gentlemen being north-countrymen and during their abode in the universities and elsewhere not happening to hear those [dialect] words used in the south, might suppose them to be proper to the north.' (*CEW 2*, preface: 3)

21 See n. 1 above.

22 See Ray to Courthope, Danny Letters, which remained in Courthope family hands until the 1920s, when they were donated to the Lewes Record Office, Sussex.

23 Ray mistrusted Trinity Cambridge academics who had gained their fellowships at the expense of exiles of conscience like himself after 1662. It appears from Derham's statements that he could have been saved from losing his fellowship in 1662 if he had had fewer religious scruples. The question then arises of whether Ray's dialect collecting, which was original and oppositional, was the intellectual product of a generally adversarial, oppositional world view. In this case, like that of Clare, language loyalty seems a more solid explanation.

24 Ray's honest preface to *CEW 1* suggest that he felt regional bias to be a natural part of scholarly enthusiasm, not a badge of disabling prejudice.

25 See Stearn, 'John Wilkins'.

26 Ray's comments in the proverbial listings are nevertheless shrewd and err on the side of justification of the folk inventory, a practice he was to follow with *CEW* fourteen years later. See, for example, Ray's vitalist entry for 'Proverbial Observations belonging to Health' (*EP*: 21) 'When the fern is as high as a ladle, [summertime] / You may sleep as long as you are able. / When the fern begins to look red, [autumn] / The milk is good with brown bread.' Ray's bachelor, ex-sizar's comment on this complicated idiomatic assertion runs, 'It is observed by good housewives, that milk is thicker in the autumn than in the summer, notwithstanding the grass must be more hearty, the juice of it being better concocted by the heat of the sun in the summertime. I conceive the reason to be, because the cattle drink water abundantly by reason of their heat in summer, which doth much dilute their milk.' The complexity of the idiom includes the notion that you sleep (in lieu of drinking rich milk) in summer. Ray sees his editorial role as a justificatory one. The vernacular, by his interpretation, had rationalist underpinnings.

27 See Peter Burke, *Popular Culture*.

28 Edward Lhwyd was a Celtologist and polymath at the Bodleian Library, Oxford. The illegitimate son of a disreputable scion of an old dispossessed north Wales landed gentry family, he forged an independent path as an intellectual, which the older and wiser Ray appears to have cherished and approved of. They never met.

William Nicolson, at the time of the Ray dialect word-collecting an archdeacon and shortly to become a pluralist, was another of the younger generation of correspondents whom Ray attracted without actually meeting. An avid tithe-gatherer, Nicolson, like the other Cumbrian and Scots Border bishops, left terrier accounts of the dues in cash and kind exacted from the hill-farming families in their bishoprics. These are reprinted in the *Transactions of the Cumberland and Westmorland Antiquarian and Archaeological Society I*, ed. R.S. Ferguson, Bell, Carlisle, 1877: 'Miscellany Accounts of the Diocese of Carlisle with the Terriers delivered in to me at my primary visitation': 120. The manuscript is housed in the library of the Dean and Chapter at Carlisle Cathedral. Nicolson was an FRS by 1685. Ray's foreword to *CEW 2* indicates the 'live' nature of his correspondents' collecting activities. He wrote: 'I desired

my friends and acquaintances living in several countreys to communicate to me
... what they should afterwards gather up out of the mouths of the people,
which divers of them accordingly did ... I am confident I am not mistaken as
for the sence and importance of these words, having received it from persons
that well understand the force and meaning of them in the places where they
are used' (*CEW 1*:2).

29   Ray's 1674 letter to Oldenburg is quoted in *FC*: 67. Raven pointed out that it
was written coincidentally with Ray's 'hastily gathered up' dialect word lists
(*JR*: 271).

30   Ray reiterated in *Wisdom* that he considered mathematics a gentleman's
pastime which all ought to be trained in but to which only a very few might
contribute usefully (*Wisdom*: 174). Biology, perhaps, came into a more general
category, as shown by his pragmatism as far as dialect inventories were
concerned. He wished the new knowledge 'were able to compass and
comprehend the whole latitude of learning' (*Wisdom*).

31   George Hickes, *Grammaticae Anglo-Saxionae et Moese-Gothicae* (Oxford University Press, Oxford, 1689).

32   Ray, 'Defects in our English Alphabet ... and manner of Spelling' (*CEW 3*:
286–90).

33   Wilkins advocated classification by means of an artificial language, as exemplified by his *Real Character* artificial sign replacements for English and Latin
proper names. Milton's view was quoted by Dr Johnson in Johnson's great
dictionary as an aid to the signification of the word 'lexicon': Ray's *CEW*
appears to participate in this intellectual climate almost pedantically. The
Milton quotation Johnson selected was: 'Though a linguist should pride
himself to have all the tongues that Babel cleft the world into. Yet if he had not
studied the solid things in them as well as the words and lexicons, he were
nothing so much to be esteemed a learned man, as any yeoman wise only in his
mother dialect' (Johnson's *Dictionary*, 1755). Ray paid tribute to Wilkins for this
same view in an unusually elaborate passage in *Wisdom*: 'That learning, saith a
wise and observant prelate, which consists only in critical notions on words and
phrases, hath in it this intrinsical imperfection ... Words being but the images
of Matter, to be wholly given up to the study of these, what is it but Pygmalion's
frenzy, to fall in love with a picture or image? Let us ourselves examine Things
as we have opportunity ... No knowledge doth so satisfie the soul as this in
comparison, whereto that of words and phrases seem both insipid and jejeune'
(169). Ray evidently felt that dialect inventories were capable of forming an
accurate picture of 'matter', and this should on this account not be excluded
from the counsels of the learned. The philosophical basis of his rejection of the
artifice of Wilkins's 'real character' effort at the Royal Society was the
distortions Wilkins's artificial ranking placed on empirical biological reality.
Wilkins himself was falling into 'Pygmalion's frenzy'. The dialect dictionary is
in a certain sense a rejection of the artificial in favour of the 'natural' and
indeed the 'primitive', Adamite tongue of England.

34   Seventeenth-century pulses are discussed with all other food crops lists in *CC*
in Raven, *JR*: 96–7.

35   John Clare's food listings are sparse, one-line entries, always emphasizing

dearth: the meagre Christmas fare of Helpstone in December, the empty larder in January with all the cheese eaten, the starved stock in spring, the July mower slaking his thirst on sorrel in the field. These entries gain their poignancy by contrast with the lyricism of nature all around. The boy's food raids are typical.

36 These three writers on what amount to the long-eighteenth-century bill of fare all choose a strong regional and historical focus. This note cites one book out of many by each of them. In Theodora Fitzgibbon, *Irish Traditional Food* (Pan Books, London, 1983) the entries on *colcannon*, *brotchan Roy*, and other ancient Celtic foods (158) are key to the leek and oatmeal basis as well as the very high butter intake of the early Celtic dietary of Ireland, Wales, and Scotland. Fitzgibbon's Scottish, Welsh, West Country, Lake District, and Yorkshire Crockery Pot bills of fare are useful present-day entries from which to project back to the dialect literature. Jane Grigson, *English Food* (Penguin, Harmondsworth, 1974), maintains that the *jannock* came in with the clog to Bolton le Moor in 1337, brought in by refugee Flemish weavers. She includes a meatless heavy pancake recipe for eighteenth-century harvesters, made of wheat flour, milk, ale, eggs, ginger, and lard, commenting 'They were reckoned to be an adequate if heavy substitute for both meat and bread' (278). *Farls* (quarter *bannocks*), oatcakes, and *riddle bread* are well described, with full technical dimensions and drying and hanging procedures (266–8). For riddle bread see also Alison Uttley, *Recipes from an Old Farmhouse* (Faber, London, 1966). Barm dumplings (51–2), whigs (88), hayfield drinks (89–90), *tharcake* (17–18), and hasty puddings (31–2) are all meticulously described as being in the bill of fare of Lloyd George's Derbyshire in the Garsington area. Ray's dialect inventories of 1674 are exemplified in this small, hill-farm household bill of fare.

Of the historic texts used for this study, Samuel Bamford's edition of the 'Tummus and Meary' tales of John Collier, and the Cumbrian late Georgian balladeers, carries the same independent evidence of a stable rural dietary, low in animal protein, high in milk and oat entries. A good edition is John Collier, *The Works of Tim Bobbin in Prose and Verse with a memoir by John Cary*, John Heywood, Manchester, 1862. (The glossary is necessary for non-dialect speakers: 74–114.) *Clemmed*, *manchet*, *haverbread*, *tharcake*, *afterings*, and other dietary entries Ray made familiar are in these listings. Bamford the Radical was the key reviver of the Tim Bobbin tales as a historical, satirical text, in Lancashire dialect. Samuel Bamford, *Dialect of South Lancashire or Tim Bobbin's 'Tummus and Meary' with an enlarged and amended Glossary of Words and Phrases Chiefly used by the Rural Population of the manufacturing districts of South Lancashire* (John Heywood, Manchester, 1850).

37 Ray's southern dialect-speakers continued on time-honoured lines to bake barley and meslin loaves when wheat was dear, a pattern encouraged by dietary reformers, who invoked customary rural usage and who were wary of innovative potato monoculture through the hard times of 1793–1824. See, for example, the pro-customary dietary invocations of a southerner: 'One third wheat, one third rye, one third barley make bread that I could be very well content to live upon all my lifetime . . . Indeed the fact is very well known that our forefathers used barley bread to a very great extent' (William Cobbett, *Cottage Economy, containing information relative to the brewing of beer, making of Bread . . . and other*

matters deemed useful in the conducting of the affairs of a Labourer's Family,
C. Clement, London, 1822: 55). John Clare's Northamptonshire labourers in
husbandry, depicted in the *Shepherd's Calendar,* subsisted on barley loaves in
the 1820s.

It is useful to test Ray's 1660–70 northern bread word listings (as opposed to
his southern ones) against Arthur Young's 1760s observations. These were
observations in the Ray tradition, extended by the addition of local price at
purchase for these rural provisions, a matter the Ray group did not address in
their word lists. Specifically, Young noted 'much oat bread' in the Leeds area of
Yorkshire, where Ralph Thoresby had collected dialect words for Ray. Rye
bread alone or rye meslin breads baked with rye–wheat–pease flours or
barley–pease blends were consumed in the rural areas from Durham to
Tyneside dialect-speaking Newcastle. Local consumption patterns in Cumbria,
where Ray and his Cumbrian correspondent, Tomlinson, a 'statesman' from
Edmund Hall, collected dialect words and rare plants, were slow to change. A
hundred years after Ray's collecting journeys, oat breads were still the
traditional staple food of the Garstang district of Cumbria. Oat cakes were
staples in Kendall and Shap Fell. Oat–barley meslin loaves were traditional to
Keswick, and Penrith specialized in subsistence barley–rye and bean–oatmeal
blends. These were never 'hunger foods': they were locally grown and baked
staples of northern life.

In the Cheshire districts round Knutsford and Altrincham, the 'southern'
pattern, advocated later by Cobbett, of wheat–barley meslin or pure barley
loaves begins. It seems probable from Young's evidence that Ray used the
Cumbrian oat bread dietary, which he knew well as an Essex traveller in the
north, as a normative inventory for the dialect-speaking north.

Young summarized his northern provision tables of 1766–70 in his *A Six
Month's Tour through the North of England containing an account of the Present State
of Agriculture, Manufactures and Population in Several Counties of this Kingdom,
Volume IV* (W. Strahan, London, 1770), 424–6, Letter XXXVIII, Provisions
Tables. A good general account of the Georgian as opposed to the Restoration
rural dietary (about which less is known), using sources such as Arthur Young,
Sir Frederick Morton Eden and David Davies, is George E. Fussell, *The
English Rural Labourer: His Home, Furniture, Clothing and Food from Tudor to
Victorian Times* (Batchworth Press, London, 1949), 84–91.

38   Uttley, *Recipes*: 12–13.

39   Ann Wheeler's ingenious transcription of polite Cumbrian dialect usage was
published in Kendal by Branthwaite in 1790, 1802, and 1821. It is entitled *A
Westmoreland Dialect . . . in four familiar dialogues.* The first three tales are set
locally, and in the fourth a young Cumbrian girl reports on her first visit to rich
relatives in London, rejecting their exaggerated town manners. The central
figure in the tale is a housekeeper (perhaps Mrs Wheeler herself), breaking off
work to chat and give advice to her friends on their personal relations with men.

40   Women, with their generally lower standard-education levels and high domestic skills, were often adept dialect users, whether as first or second language.
Their problem was not only finding a publisher, but finding a dialect
readership.

41 The dispossessed, landless Clare implied that Northamptonshire tithing disputes in the 1820s were merely a matter between hostile farmers and greedy parsons (the *Shepherd's Calendar*: 71, July, lines 11–18. A parson's own record of his anger and indeed physical violence when denied tithe in the field is recorded by John Skinner in his *Journal of a Somerset Rector (1830–1834)*, foreword by Virginia Woolf, Oxford University Press, London, 1971: 272–5. This entry for the harvest of 1824 is interesting because the same parson, John Skinner, was in search of a primitive language as a major preoccupation, while suffering all the signs of violent paranoia over open tithe-resistance on the glebe.

42 George Herbert, *Poems*, ed. Helen Gardner (Oxford University Press, London, 1969), 198.

43 See A. Appleby, *Famine in Tudor and Stuart England* (Stanford University Press, Stanford, Cal., 1987).

44 John Clare, *Selected Poems*, eds J.W. Tibble and Anne Tibble (Dent, London, 1965), John Clare's glossary: 253.

45 Ms of Nicolson's terrier returns, Carlisle Cathedral; reprinted Ferguson, *Transactions I*.

46 William Baxter and John Ray encouraged the subscriptions for *Archaeologia Britannica*, ten fascicles of which (in one volume) were published by 1707 before Lhwyd's early death. Baxter reviewed it for Sir Hans Sloane in the *Philosophical Transactions of the Royal Society*, September 1707. See also 'William Baxter and Edward Lhwyd's *Archaeologia Britannica*, 1707', John Kenyon, *Bulletin of the Board of Celtic Studies 34*, 1987: 118–20.

5

The People's English: Language and Class in England *c*.1840–1920

PATRICK JOYCE

For almost a century after the opening of Queen Victoria's reign there flourished in the industrial districts of the north of England a literature that claimed to represent 'the inner life of the people'.[1] This claim was based upon the belief that it was only in the people's own tongue that this life could be adequately rendered. The people's tongue was dialect, and it spoke their true identity. The foremost examples of this literature were to be found in the industrial districts of Lancashire and Yorkshire. With the exception of the northeast, though dialect literature was a phenomenon nationwide in its scope in this period, nowhere outside the textile districts did it achieve the depth of response found there. None the less, the creation and reception of this literature reveals much about attitudes to language and class widely prevalent in English and indeed British society at this time.

What it perhaps tells us most about is the creation of social identities among the labouring poor. In this respect its significance is much more than regional or indeed national. At roughly the same time, and in similar social if not political conditions, there emerged in the textile districts of France a similar dialect literature. In considering its role in handling communal and class identities William Reddy has rightly observed that,

Interpretations of social class are still confidently put forward that are utterly mythical in form. Groups are characterised by describing the outlook or mentality of a typical member of the group ... as if such a thing could exist. All signs of rhetorical effort to make, mould or alter community identities are systematically ignored ... An entirely different view of working-class identity is possible, however, as soon as one begins to treat records of working-class experience as instances of a continuous effort to create identity, as interpretations, as tentative proposals about self and others, with no particular authority and finality.[2]

This study is in large part about that rhetorical effort to create identity, an effort in which language was not only a means but a symbol. Until relatively recently in historical work, language has been strangely and sorely neglected. The recent literature on class in nineteenth-century Britain begins to redress this neglect. There is a growing recognition that language is not a simple reflection of 'experience' and 'consciousness' but actively constitutes these categories, and a growing debate on how this in practice occurs.[3] Yet so far there has been relatively little said about language itself, or for that matter about the processes by which social identities are formed, and the content of such identities. A literature that purports to be about 'languages of class' often has curiously little to say about language or class. New work on national identities has more to say on these matters,[4] as does a nascent social history of language.[5] What is becoming increasingly apparent is the simple but important point that collective identities are indeed socially constructed and are not somehow immanent in social formations and processes. What is also apparent is just how important language itself is in this. Yet in relation to the size of the field the modesty of the labour expended must be recognized.

One way forward would involve attention to contemporary work in sociolinguistics. The discipline has much to offer historians, alerting them to aspects of the past which have either been ignored or taken for granted. Sociolinguistics reveals the active role of language in the formation of group and individual identities. It also indicates how linguistic phenomena are social realities, the outcome of social changes which they both reflect and shape.[6] It is in the discipline's attention to spoken usage that it is especially valuable, particularly in relation to dialect. A consideration of dialect literature is incomplete without attention to the spoken language in which it was rooted. An account of spoken usage itself involves some treatment of prevailing attitudes to language use, as well as to the practices of use. Such attitudes are themselves inexplicable without an understanding of the wider discourses that invested the English language and English literature. Thus, before the literature can be approached, it is necessary to dwell on these matters. In this way the social and intellectual contexts in which the literature developed will be apparent. Consideration of the people's English reveals a good deal more about the English people than the proclivities of the labouring English alone.

I

Sociolinguistic studies have gone far to correct the evolutionary biases of an older dialectology. Instead of linear notions of dialectical change, in particular the supposedly inexorable decline of dialect in the face of linguistic and cultural standardization, what is apparent is that spoken dialect was and is undergoing constant change.[7] Amidst this change there may be considerable continuity, and where older forms recede these are often replaced by other non-standard varieties which may be similarly localized and have similar sorts of value attached to them. Older notions of dialect have in fact become part of received common sense, and in this form have strayed into historical writing. In regarding urbanization and internal migration as having eroded local dialects by the 1820s, Colley is not untypical of this somewhat Whiggish interpretation of language.[8] In the nineteenth century, as in the present, if it is not these forces that are ritually invoked then it is the supposed levelling techniques of education, print, or the developing mass media. When one turns to the evidence from the industrial north it is apparent how frequently the premature obituary of dialect has been written.

As early as 1850 Samuel Bamford bemoaned the decrease in dialect use and popular custom.[9] However, if we move forward to 1917, the sentiments of Bamford are again echoed, this time for the 1850s and 1860s: people were then held to be more 'parochial', and dialect terms then in use were reported as no longer current.[10] A shrewd observer of Black Country dialect in the 1930s recognized this constant tendency to exaggerate the decay of dialect, a tendency closely related to the mythologizing of the past as the 'good old days', of interest in itself but not especially revealing about actual usage.[11] Some sixty years after the institution of mass elementary education, daily use among the Black Country working classes strongly reflected nineteenth-century patterns.[12] Even as early twentieth-century observers mourned the passing of older forms of dialect, it was recognized that in Lancashire alone there were at least twenty different dialects, especially individual town ones, which were not only strong but markedly different one from another.[13] Actual change probably owed more to the processes of migration into the factory towns than to education or the media. Modern dialectologists indicate the rapid mixing of surrounding dialect in urban speech.[14] Given the nature of migration into the textile districts, often short-range and by a series of steps, an element of continuity in styles of speech seems likely.

The 1861 parliamentary reports on the state of popular education offer considerable insight into spoken use and attitudes to it.[15] Among the education commissioners the culture of the populace is regarded as a species foreign and exotic to educated opinion. Popular manners are invariably depicted as rude and barbaric. Language is very often presented as the index of this cultural state: in Rochdale, for example, speech is represented as being blunt and abrupt. Primitive customs were said to abound in the district, particularly the inclination to dispense with surnames in favour of dialect patronyms and similar forms. For two miles around the centre of Milnrow, a district of Rochdale reputedly the centre of the Lancashire dialect, it was said that a stranger would find it almost impossible to understand the 'broad, unadulterated provincialisms' of the natives.[16] The attitude of 'educated opinion' is clear enough here, as it was some three decades later in the town when an unusually progressive school inspector maintained that dialect should be used in elementary education. This drew down the wrath of the educated classes of Rochdale, for whom the rootedness of dialect was the greatest difficulty in the way of advancing 'a good English education'.[17] The more common attitude among school inspectors seems to have been one of contempt for dialect, a contempt that was framed in what for Lancashire people was the 'foreign language' of the inspector.[18]

The association of strong dialect attachments and thriving local cultures apparent in the case of Rochdale, and evident also in the sociolinguistic literature, is reflected in the other districts considered in the 1861 reports. In the case of the Cumberland lead miners, and the smallholders of that county known as 'statesmen', these attachments went hand in hand with long traditions of literacy and book ownership. Where literacy was less marked, and where the social distance between the classes was greatest, as in the colliery villages of Durham and Cumberland, it was said that 'the language of books is an unknown tongue to the children of the illiterate, especially in remote situations. It is utterly unlike their vernacular dialect, both in its vocabulary and construction, and, perhaps, not less intelligible than Latin was to the vulgar of the middle ages.'[19] It is indeed striking how little formal schooling eroded dialect.[20] The commissioner for Durham and Cumberland noted that educational success was achieved only in the Sunday school, where teaching was done in 'one of the most uncouth dialects it was ever my lot to hear'.[21] The link between modes of thinking and modes of language was perceived by the commissioner: Scots teachers in the far north of England had the best success, as through their language they had access to the minds and the culture of the children, and he noted of himself that without a familiarity with Lowland Scots he would have had no free or satisfactory discourse with the labouring classes of the region.[22]

These latter instances serve to indicate how dialect, as with other aspects of spoken use, might cross class boundaries as well as accentuate them. There were considerable variations within standard and dialect forms, variations which had much to do with the social settings of usage.[23] It is clear that many ostensibly 'middle-class' people spoke (and speak) forms of dialect, or else had the dialect as a resource to be called upon. The cultural and linguistic roots of many later nineteenth-century employers, for example, were decidedly local.[24] If, on the whole, pronunciation and class have been more closely allied in Britain than in any other Western nation, there has always been a degree of movement from one linguistic ethos to another, and historically this seems to have been more marked than is often supposed. Correspondingly, the social identities worked out in dialect were complex, as were their uses. In the nineteenth-century industrial north, for instance, employers and other middle-class elements constructed a demotic style, drawing much on demotic speech, which was of great importance for the maintenance of factory paternalism and in the management of party politics.[25]

None the less, if attention to the strategies and settings of spoken use complicates the class picture in a productive fashion, one cannot ignore the increasing class differentiation of standard and dialect in the nineteenth century. Moving beyond questions of use to what may loosely be termed ideologies of language, this pattern is reflected in valuations of popular language: the attitudes of the 1861 education commissioners were widely characteristic of English society, and were perhaps the dominating pattern of response. But they were far from comprising the only response. On the contrary, dialect literature emerged in an intellectual and social *milieu* which was often open and sympathetic to the culture of the people. Indeed, the literature can in part be understood as a reaction to these two major ideological currents, the negative and the positive, and it is therefore necessary to take a closer look at each, however briefly.

In terms of the development of the national language, the late eighteenth century saw a marked acceleration of the process of codification. The elaboration of a prescriptive grammar, an obsession with logical rule, and a clearer separation out of the 'vulgar' and 'polite' tongues were all characteristic.[26] In the nineteenth century this was reflected in oral terms, 'received pronunciation' consolidating itself through its various manifestations as 'the Queen's English', 'the King's English', and, later, 'Oxford' and 'BBC' English. Pronunciation became slowly allied to power, learning, and authority, and it is clear that many people have lived with the corrosive illusion that their own tongue is somehow 'ignorant' or 'wrong'. These developments were early on reflected in educational practice. David Vincent shows how the teaching of literacy for most of the nineteenth century involved the rejection of the home environment of the child, particularly the child's linguistic community. 'Intelligence' was defined in terms of 'established knowledge', contrary to the 'sensuality' of the home and the local community.[27]

An examination of nineteenth-century school textbooks, as of elocution books and manuals of usage, indicates how these attitudes, amounting to a deliberate attempt to destroy the linguistic worlds of the 'lower orders', were reflected not only in but beyond the schoolroom.[28] The outlook of the 'educated classes' noted earlier was implemented in terms of the grammars, readers, and composition books provided for schoolchildren. These were concerned at every turn to maximize the distinction between 'vulgar' and 'polite' language, to exalt written over spoken English, and to associate 'correct' English with superior breeding and social success. One example of the dissemination of these values beyond the schoolroom must suffice, the extraordinary *Enquire Within Upon Everything*, which had sold 592,000 copies by 1877.[29] This compendium of advice on all matters of social skill is a classic in the voluminous literature of Victorian self-improvement. It contains a large section with hundreds of rules and hints about correct speaking and writing. It is at once absurdly prim, hyper-correct, and extaordinarily supercilious about popular usage. Imitation of the 'educated' is the key to success. Imperfect grammar, the misuse of words, and incorrect pronunciation are all corrected with reference to the hideous errors of dialect, the most reprehensible form of which is Cockney. The tone is taken from *Punch* and its guying of popular speech. Nine versions of Cockney are identified and denounced, including 'Low', 'Genteel', 'Cockney Flunkey', 'Feminine', and 'Domestic'. Similar treatment is meted out to the Irish and the Scots, and to provincial 'brogues', 'provincialism' being the most characteristic form of abuse. The most pressing of all dilemmas in this agonized world is '"H" or "No H"? That is the question.' The reader is finally assured that though he or she may not be educated, he or she may yet become 'cultivated' through the proper exercise of language.

However, precisely at the time when the divergence of 'high' and 'low' cultures was becoming increasingly apparent in the early nineteenth century there emerged an attempted reconciliation of the two. Burke has described 'the discovery of the people' evident from the late eighteenth century across Europe.[30] This new and more positive attitude to the culture of 'the people' dwelt upon language as perhaps the central means by which the historical unfolding of cultures was to be revealed. The scholars of the German Enlightenment were crucial: for Michaelis, for example, etymology was 'the voice of the people', the people's 'archive'; and in Herder language is the revelation of the spirit of the 'folk'. There was a new interest in spoken as well as written language, in the illiterate, and in dialect.[31] In terms of language study in England these approaches bore fruit in the Philology Society (1842), which was in turn the inspiration for that great totem of English cultural identity the *New English Dictionary*, later the *Oxford English*

Dictionary, the first volume of which was issued in 1886. In England the historicist and evolutionary aspects of the new ideas of language and culture were from early on associated with the idea of English and British national identities. They were also closely related to the idea of English literature as the symbol of national identity. Language and literature were both seen in historical terms, and the historical principle most actively at work was a national one. Among the popularizers of the new language study, the spiritual and moral life of the English was disclosed in their language.[32] In Macaulay's widely influential *History of England*, it was disclosed in their literature. As with class attitudes to language study and teaching, this identification of language and literature with the nation was popularized with increasing energy in the second half of the century.[33]

Thus the intellectual climate in which dialect literature developed was one in which language and literature carried versions of nation and people that offered the labouring classes the possibility of inclusion in the body of society rather than the exclusion so evident in other respects. Among those most closely involved with words, especially dialect words, this sense of language as inclusive is particularly marked. For James Murray, editor-in-chief of the *New English Dictionary*, the English language is inseparable from the nation's history, especially its political institutions. Like the constitution, the language was not the creation of one generation or of one class. Its unwritten profundities were echoed in a rich, unsystematized language. In Murray (a Scot) these linguistic characteristics are attached to an idealized Britain rather than to England, and one is aware of the invention of Victorian Britain at this time as well as the perhaps more deep-seated associations with England and Englishness.[34]

Yet in the figure of Murray one is also aware of cultural influences quite outside the established intellectual community. Murray was, among many other things, not least a child of radical, plebeian dissent. In this he was very similar to Joseph Wright, his collaborator and the editor of the great *English Dialect Dictionary*. Both were products of the artisan, domestic economies of rural-industrial Britain, one from lowland Scotland, the other from the Yorkshire Pennine uplands. Both carried into their labours a deep sense of their own oral cultures, which was closely linked to the outlook of radical Nonconformity. Their strong sense of local history and custom was thus wedded to a radical interpretation of the wider national history.[35] In both men the sense of the independent traditions of 'the people' gained in youth was an energizing force throughout their lives. In their time popular, oral culture was being understood anew through the prism of a literate, autodidact culture, and it is to the provincial centres of this culture that one must turn in order to discern the full meanings of English in their day.

Vincent has considered the ways in which working-class authors utilized print and standard English in the first half of the nineteenth century to establish a class presence; one which extended, explored, and authenticated their own culture.[36] In this process their attitude to the past was an ambiguous one, as was that of the autodidact working men who more generally were such a vital leaven in popular society. The thrust of their endeavour involved the belief that reason and its employment in the acquisition of 'useful knowledge' would make them and their fellows free of the legacy of the ancien regime. The association of knowledge with progress was close, as was the belief that by mid-century they had lived through a period of change unprecedented in the whole of history. Vincent has described the mingled rejection and sense of loss involved when the light of reason was directed upon their own culture.[37] The attitudes of mind they rejected were symbolized by custom, and not least by the dialect language they took to be an integral part of the irrational in the old order. And of course, as William Cobbett among others often saw, in order to establish a presence in public, political discourse the people would themselves need to appropriate print and standard English. Yet, as the examples of Wright and Murray indicate, rejection was not the only nor the primary response. In the north of England from the 1840s one sees emerging in dialect literature a much more positive attitude to their own past and langauge on the part of autodidact working men.

This involved a meeting of their own cultures and the new valuations of language and culture that have been described. These intellectual currents, taking form in folklore, local history, and literary activity as well as the study of language, were in fact at their most lively and effective in local and provincial society, developments there often preceding those at a national level. However, before considering how the more positive outlook on the people's culture was worked out in its provincial centres, it is necessary to give an account of the development, audience, and major characteristics of the dialect literature which was at the centre of this outlook. This account will quickly make it evident that, if influenced by intellectual currents from outside popular society, dialect writers were above all speaking to the values and mores of the great mass of the working poor from which they came. In the end dialect literature worked because it articulated the needs and self-images of this majority. It was their own perceptions of their own language that finally mattered, rather than others' ideas of the people's English.

II

Dialect literature written by working men and read by a mass working-class audience emerged in the course of the 1840s in industrial Lancashire and Yorkshire.[38] In the industrial northeast of England this emergence was earlier, and authorship and audience were less distinctively proletarian than they were later to be in that region, or in Lancashire and Yorkshire.[39] None the less, throughout the north, authorship and audience were never exclusively working class. The sources of this literature lay in the long tradition of broadside ballads in dialect and standard English, covering national but especially regional and local themes and developments.[40] It was thus heavily indebted to the very important oral elements in the older culture, elements which it indeed did much to perpetuate into the new. It also drew on more distinctly literate and literary influences. Later dialect writers owed much to John Collier of Rochdale ('Tim Bobbin') whose dialect work, especially his comic dialogue *Tummus and Meary* (1746), helped to establish a tradition of conscious literary endeavour in that mode. Collier's fictions, and his *nom de plume*, invoked the motifs of the wise fool as everyman and the dominant industry of the region, which were to be important later. On a more exalted literary level Mrs Gaskell's novels were important in establishing a public space for dialect in the mid-century, just as her husband provided encouragement to dialect study and literature. From as early as 1840 in Manchester, somewhat later in the West Riding, local literary cultures emerged that embraced different class elements in the fostering of dialect. In dialect and literary journals, as in associations of dialect writers and friends of the dialect, this sort of inter-class cooperation continued into the twentieth century. Thus the contexts out of which dialect literature emerged were never exclusively proletarian.

From around the mid-century an oral-cum-written culture gave way to a written-cum-oral one as authors became aware of a large reading audience. Edwin Waugh, along with Ben Brierley and Samuel Laycock in Lancashire, and John Hartley and Ben Preston in Yorkshire, were the leading but not at all the only early writers. Hartley's father was a Halifax tea merchant, though Hartley himself spent his early working life as a pattern maker in an engineering works. The others came from the manual working class, and knew poverty at first hand in their early days. Waugh was a printer; the others worked as textile operatives, Laycock and Preston failing to emancipate themselves from the factory for most of their working lives. Waugh, Brierley, and Hartley were exceptional among dialect writers in managing to earn some sort of living from their writing. It was chiefly this group that extended the range and subject matter of dialect so that it became a literature addressing the everyday nature of popular life. If the formative influences upon dialect were in no simple sense 'working class', its subject matter and most of its audience were.

In the third quarter of the century it is the labouring poor that themselves become the heroic subject of the literature. This is especially apparent in the dialect almanacs of the West Riding, the names of which bear out their social ethos (in existing accounts of dialect literature their significance has been neglected): *T' Bag o' Shoddy Olmenac* (Batley), *The Weyvers Awn* (or *Pudsa*

THE PEOPLE'S ENGLISH   163

[Pudsey] *Annewal*), *Dewsbre Back at Mooin Olmenac, The Barnsla Foaks Annual* or *T' Leeds Loiners Comic Olmenac.*[41] By 1877 there were forty dialect almanacs currently published, all but four in the West Riding. The most famous of these, John Hartley's *Halifax Illuminated Clock Almanac*, was selling 80,000 annually by 1877, and continued its unbroken run until after World War II. The heyday of the almanacs was before 1914, though others continued later as well as the Halifax one. The writers of these intensely local publications were either autodidact working men or small printers and stationers. They were hawked, or sold in a range of outlets such as pubs and grocery shops. They represent an extraordinary outpouring of 'penny capitalist' production. In a sense, however, authorship is irrelevant: the uniformity of method, tone, and content in the almanacs reflects intertextual influences, but far more than this it reflects a uniformity of expectation in their audience. To sell they had to correspond to the people's self-mythology, though in responding they also shaped that mythology. They dwell on the minutiae of daily life, offering a comic and moral commentary on the pleasures and sorrows of daily existence. Honesty, hard work, dignity, helping one's fellows, avoiding the hypocrisies of the rich are the stuff of the morality; a sense of decency and of the moral worth of individuals and communities. Authors' *noms de plume* established the right to speak for particular localities (amongst the poets to function as the 'bards' of particular locales), and this representative function was as characteristic of Lancashire and the northeast as of Yorkshire. In turn particular localities established long-lived reputations, such as Rochdale, the woollen districts around Huddersfield, or the village of Failsworth outside Manchester.[42] Significantly the latter two were among the last bastions of hand production in textiles in the third quarter of the century. With the growth of the provincial press in the 1850s, newspapers became a major venue for dialect writing, and this further enforced the notion of the author as local spokesman.

The Lancashire dialect annuals and journals were very similar to the Yorkshire almanacs. Embroidered with sayings and proverbs, filled out with tales, skits, and poems, they enjoined a similar fortitude and jollification. Rather more significant than the better-known *Ben Brierley's Journal* is the large crop of holiday annuals that began to appear towards the end of the century. The most notable exemplar of the late nineteenth-century dialect journal or annual founder was Allen Clarke, the operative and later journalist, socialist, and full-time dialect author. Between 1889 and the 1930s his long line of Bolton-based journals sold in large numbers, establishing him as the foremost of the second generation of writers, and Bolton as another regional capital of dialect (indeed one whose pedigree went back almost a century from the 1930s).

The forms of dialect were therefore various. One very distinct strand, that of dialect in the music hall of the northeast, cannot be pursued here. Along with almanacs, journals, and newspapers, dialect reached a mass audience in the long-continuing broadside ballad form, in penny pamphlets and cheap booklets, and in reciters. There was also a market among the better-off for expensive and specially annotated editions of the leading writers, some of whom achieved a limited fame outside the north partly through these means. Most of all, dialect literature was a spoken as well as written form, a staple item in the ritual and convivial occasions of the great constellation of institutions set up by working people about this time: the cooperative society, the trade union, the social and political club, the friendly and burial society, but also the religious and especially the Sunday school gathering. The leading dialect writers also went on tour with the penny reading so characteristic of the first age of mass literacy. Thomas Wright, journeyman engineer, stated in 1867 that penny readings, whether amateur or professional, were greatly popular in the manufacturing districts, frequented by all classes of working people, and free of oppressive patronage.[43] At such times, and on many other occasions, women were present, and it seems clear that if not usually written by women dialect was read and listened to as much by women as men. Home life and family affairs were indeed a staple of a literature in which barriers of gender seem to have been as little marked as those of status within the working class. The private arena was as important as the public: dialect recitation at home and among neighbours was common practice among the northern working classes.[44] In Lancashire and Yorkshire, amateur dialect theatre was another venue for the orality of dialect (dialect sketches were also acted at the usual convivial public occasions).

The oral reproduction of dialect makes us aware that figures for sales are not an especially good guide to the popularity of the literature: a single pamphlet or broadsheet might pass through many hands, many listened if they did not read, and of course the newspapers gave a readership it is impossible to measure. What figures there are, largely based on the claims of the authors, suggest large sales: the figures for Hartley's *Almanac* are revealing, and Clarke claimed to have a regular sale of his *Teddy Ashton's Northern Weekly* of 35,000 in the 1890s, and a sale of over one million of his penny *Tumfowt Sketches* by the early twentieth century.[45] While most publications did not scale these heights a mass market was there, and it must be remembered that the circulation of much of this material was very local and hence its impact especially intense. The period between the 1840s and about 1920 seems to have been the high point of the literature: before then there were limitations of technology, distribution, literacy (and need); after it were the limitations posed by the counter-attractions of the popular press and new forms of the mass media which were less shaped by local and regional interests. This outpouring of dialect seems to have been regionally localized in Cumberland, Durham, Northumberland, Yorkshire, and Lancashire.[46] Other English regions did see dialect publication in this period, particularly in the West Country, but there does not seem to have been anything approaching the example of the northern counties.

A fuller account of the later development of the literature than the necessarily truncated one presented here would certainly need to dwell on the differences of generation between authors, say between a Waugh and a Clarke. The early generation, born between c.1780 and 1820, drew directly on rural and domestic-industrial culture, also on the traditions of popular radicalism. Hartley was a kind of intermediate figure, utilizing the pastoral-industrial but locating most of his fictions in the factory present, and so imparting to the Yorkshire almanacs an earlier engagement with the urban and industrial than was perhaps the case in Lancashire. The later generation of writers, such as Clarke in his *Tumfowt Sketches*, much more directly figure the present occupational life of the worker, and the life of the factory, at the centre of their writings: 'factory foak' are not only the object of the appeal but the subject, as can be seen in the pages of the textile operatives' journals, *The Cotton Factory Times* and *The Yorkshire Factory Times*. The extent to which dialect had become an integral part of popular culture can be gauged in the pages of the former journal. When the unions wished to mount a mobilization of popular opinion around a particular issue it was to dialect, and the cartoon form, that they turned. For decades *The Cotton Factory Times* ran a column, 'Mirth in the Mill', in which ordinary readers themselves returned their speech to print, commenting on mill life in the conventions of a literature that had so become part of their mental outlook.[47] The later generation of writers thus used dialect for trade union ends (indeed the staff of the union journals were often themselves dialect authors), and many of the leading socialists of Lancashire and Yorkshire such as Clarke, Ben Turner, and Joseph Burgess were steeped in the dialect.[48] They also quite consciously used the dialect in the business of making socialists. Thus the identities dialect dealt with were plastic, malleable, utilized by employer paternalism and party politics as we have seen, but also and very effectively by socialist politics as well.

This appropriation and redirection of dialect-influenced social identities indicates that even if dialect literature itself fell from its earlier prominence between the wars, the social archetypes and motifs in which it dealt were themselves utilized in different modes and presentations, but with a striking degree of continuity as well, after the First World War. This can be seen in the standard English books of local humour and jokes which dealt with a specifically regional sense of humour, figuring as their heroes and heroines 'ordinary' working people.[49] Music hall, cinema, radio, and later television made inroads upon dialect, yet rather than seeing the eclipse of these earlier identities it is their reconstitution that is apparent; in Gracie Fields, in the Formbys, father and son, in Stanley Holloway, in the long line of northern comics, perhaps indeed in that most popular of all celebrations of a mythologized proletariat, *Coronation Street*.

The figure of Gracie Fields, for example, offers insight into the ways in which earlier representations were reconstituted. 'Our Gracie' or 'Sally in Our Alley' carried on in this light what may be seen as a distinctively Rochdale tradition (with due qualifications, even 'Tim Bobbin' of Rochdale may be seen as an ancestor). The Rochdale mill girl, through her various manifestations in music hall, records, radio, and films, came to have powerful resonances among the entire British working class of the inter-war years.[50] And not only the working class, of course, for Fields was 'Our Gracie' to many among the more exalted in British society, not least the British monarchy. The career of Fields, and the other examples, show not only how myths of identity were persistent and proletarian, but how also they were appropriated and reforged in ways that blurred and transformed class identities.

This account of the literature, though brief, none the less conveys something of its considerable longevity and range, and provides a context in which to place other historians' accounts of dialect.[51] These deal with selective and narrow aspects of a multifarious phenomenon, or else use a much foreshortened chronological framework which leaves out many of the most important developments. They thus fail to appreciate the considerable significance dialect has for an understanding of popular culture and class attitudes. They do this also because they deal in anachronistic and idealized notions of class consciousness, measured against the assumptions of which dialect literature is seen to represent somehow inadequate forms of class outlook. Even the most subtle of these approaches[52] deals in a false polarity of protest and consolation, failing to realize that dialect was about the generation of meanings and identities, the management of change and daily life. The crudest of these accounts runs into the realms of the bizarre,[53] dealing in a fantasy world inhabited by 'class traitors', 'labour aristocrats', and other examples of 'false consciousness'. All accounts, to one degree or another, deal with a realm of 'real' or 'authentic' class or personal experience anterior to its verbal significations, rather than seeing that language is itself constitutive of this experience, and in a relation to it anything but passive or reflexive. The point of this essay is to escape from such anachronistic interpretations of class, and to do so by attending to its actual historical forms, forms which to a very important extent are produced imaginatively. These imaginative and symbolic forms are not the icing on the class cake, they are the cake itself, or at least a very big part of it.

III

Yet dialect literature discloses much about the relationships between groups and classes, as well as about the imaginative forms of social identity. The new openness on the part of higher social elements to the language and culture of the 'people' represents the ground upon which such class relations were worked out. And this ground was at once ideological and territorial, the English provinces figuring as both the venue for cultural influences that crossed social boundaries, and a principal symbol of what these influences helped create. The myths of belonging that dialect elaborated worked at many levels; at those of town and neighbourhood, of class and nation, but particularly at the level of the region, which was the prism through which these other aspects were so often refracted. In these respects dialect worked in parallel with other developments.

From around the middle of the century in the manufacturing districts, town histories emphasizing a newly elaborated civic and industrial heritage began to appear in increasing number. The Lancashire and Cheshire Historic Society was formed in 1848, and already its concerns were imbued with the new learning: language was seen as the means of understanding a popular culture which in its industrial aspect continued unbroken and unsullied down from Elizabethan times.[54] Local history, folklore, and language study were indistinguishable in these early initiatives, which in the third quarter of the century resulted in a voluminous literature on regional folklore, song, and language. Developments in the provinces often predated nationally coordinated ones. The English Dialect Society was not founded until 1873, the Folklore Society only in 1878. In the activities of these societies, as with the publication of folklore collections and, later, with the *Victoria County History of England*, the county figured not only as a principle of classification but as an ideological counter in its own right. Samuel has recently noted how the county was second only to the nation itself as the focal point around which Englishness was constructed in the second half of the nineteenth century[55] (the county was as potent in Whig interpretations as in the Tory ones he describes). In terms of dialect literature Beetham has discerned a similar process, the nation being realized *through* the region. The provincial folklorists' and others' emphasis on the continuity and integrity of local cultural traditions fed powerfully into the idea of a national culture supposedly rooted in these traditions.[56]

This indeed is true, and there is a sense in which metropolitan culture was strongest precisely where regionally based enthusiasts were most determinedly local. However, this understanding may miss important aspects of tension between metropolitan and provincial cultures, and may also underestimate the active and creative aspects of the latter. In this regard one may remark, necessarily *en passant*, the considerable degree of local autonomy in the disposition of power in the nineteenth century, reflected, for example, in the implementation of the poor law and in urban self-government. The rise of the local, provincial press from around the 1850s also represented a distancing from the centres of privilege and metropolitan cultural domination, especially when it was linked to the spikey independence of popular and Nonconformist local Liberalism. It is also from the 1840s and 1850s that in the political and social strategies of the propertied classes one may discern a similar reassertion of anti-metropolitan tendencies. So much is apparent in later nineteenth-century employer paternalism and political activism, as well as in the spheres of urban patronage, urban social policy, and civic culture.[57] It was with some justice that the likes of Arnold, Ruskin, and Carlyle feared the fate of 'culture' and of metropolitan domination at the hands of the provincial, 'barbarian' middle classes.

Thus the inter-class sympathies represented in dialect might be rather complex in operation, involving not a subsumption of autodidact and popular culture in some supposed hegemony but a shifting pattern of alliances, in which class perspectives were retained in the common pursuit of what were, anyway, often markedly radical political and social causes. Bonds of sympathy between the classes were evident, for instance, in the attack upon an idle, profligate, non-industrial and aristocratic England. Stereotypes of the 'real England' as the industrial north were much in evidence, counterposed as they were to the perceived condescension of the effete and privileged south, and its domination of power and culture. The contempt felt by much 'educated opinion' for dialect was not characteristic of all social elements outside the labouring poor, which, as we have seen, might themselves have access to and sympathy for dialect. Beetham has recently considered the institutions, and the social and intellectual mediations, involved in the emergence and encouragement of dialect literature in mid-Victorian Manchester.[58] These institutions and individuals were certainly influential in marking dialect with a number of the prevailing assumptions concerning language and literature, especially the emphasis in contemporary discourse upon language as the repository of national identities that were held to subsume or negate class identities. This emphasis on a classless realm of tradition and 'culture' was certainly important (even if, as suggested, a common fund of cultural symbols might be very differently appropriated by different social groups, and inter-class sympathies might mask continuing differences of class outlook). The early dialect writers were an integral part of the world of the folklorists, and similarly venerated a national tradition of language and literature of which dialect was held to be an important part.

It is necessary to attend to the points of concordance between 'high' and 'low' culture, and to the intellectual *milieu* in which dialect developed. However, the example of a few leading authors and the public discourse that surrounded the literature should not be confused with the multifarious phenomenon dialect was, nor with the manifold ways in which its large popular audience received and in turn shaped it. The significance of dialect, of course, inhered also in how people from outside the labouring poor used it to construct images of themselves and of the poor, especially the poor they most desired to see. These uses of dialect are of great interest (they cannot be pursued here), but they were of a different order to the desired self-identities that did most to shape the literature, namely those emanating from the working poor themselves. What is in the end most striking, given the powerful repulsive and seductive influences present in the two major higher-class ways of seeing popular language, is how dialect literature drew on its own indigenous roots.

Comparison with the French example helps show how this was done. In both examples what seems to have been involved was a similar kind of exploration, a probing of new identities through the handling of older themes and values in popular life. As Reddy observes of the French case, such loyalties do not emanate from 'a simple, mythical, fully realised communal identity'.[59] Rather, 'community' and the class loyalties with which it is so deeply interwoven, are made up of the materials to hand, and if these are not solely rhetorical in character then they are very importantly so. Comparing the two examples of the textile districts, English dialect seems less tentative, more emphatic, also more complex, composed as it was of a greater variety of themes, authors, and contexts of performance and use. The reworking in the French case of the old popular spirit of farce is analogous to the English reworking of popular traditions; for instance, the themes and functions present in the ballad tradition. As in France, dialect is not chiefly a vehicle of complaint, though it carries forward a similar hope for justice and fairness. In some appropriations – in its trade union and socialist uses, for example – it becomes a literature of protest, but in the main it is not this. It is not a heroic literature; or rather its heroism resides in a bodying forth, as in the French example, of the steadfastness, knowingness, and resilience of the poor. Above all, in both cases, it was about the finding of wisdom and self-respect. Its irony was understated and indirect, and in the English example the comic mode was greatly important.

But there were marked differences as well. Domestic life is treated positively in the English literature, indeed the virtue of 'homeliness' is perhaps the fundamental one. Unlike the French example, where work is taboo and the machine hated, work is much more central; at first what may be termed mythical work as the motifs of domestic industrial culture are used to negotiate the present, and after this real work. This difference was perhaps in part due to the much stronger trade union traditions present, at least in Lancashire. In turn, the French example suggests the necessity of comparison between different English regions.

The failure of dialect literature to emerge elsewhere on anything like the scale it attained in the north cannot be due to the destruction of dialects in other regions: as far as one can tell, dialect usage continued strongly in most parts of England. Developments in the standard language were, however, important for the emergence of dialect literature. The linguistic conventions and uniformities upon which dialect depended, such as a widely comprehensible orthography, themselves depended on the consolidation of the standard. With the explosion of both literacy and print from the early nineteenth century, standard English had a new prominence in popular life. The increase of the standard, in its spoken as well as written forms, may have contributed to a desire to maintain what was felt to be under threat. Yet something much more positive was at work than these defensive reactions. Print and standard language were themselves taken over to serve a still-lively oral culture and its non-standard forms. Even as dialect represented the increasing power of the standard form in print it offered new opportunities to undercut this power. A growing market for popular literature was also important. In the third quarter of the century in the industrial north a more literate and settled urban population, and one with greater spending power than previously, created a commercial market for dialect which was amply met by provincial publishing firms such as those of the Heywoods in Manchester, and Nicholsons in Wakefield, covering the West Riding. The same may be said for the northeast, though there a nascent music hall was another response to the new demand. Demand and supply met in the new conditions of community life in these regions. These conditions are amply reflected in the themes of home and family life so marked in the literature.

Yet if these conditions were not exactly the same in other regions of England, the national picture in these respects was not dissimilar, and it is necessary to look further for the reasons behind dialect's northern popularity. The significance of particularly influential authors should not be minimized, nor the influence of those outside the labouring populations, especially when it took the potent form of a populist antiquarianism. The reasons, however, go deeper and it seems needful to turn to the particular blend of change and continuity in the economic and social structure of Lancashire and Yorkshire. Dialect was made necessary by the degree of change undergone, and made possible by the still powerful continuities of structure and memory that obtained. In adverting earlier to the link between centres of dialect literature and older forms of industrial production, the unevenness of the development of mechanized factory production becomes apparent. Within mechanized trades, such as cotton spinning, continuity was also more marked than is sometimes supposed, in work practices, for instance, or in craft outlook.[60] Yet there was considerable upheaval as well, nowhere more than in the case of the handloom weavers. This blend of industrial change and continuity was in process around the mid-nineteenth-century, just at the time when dialect emerged. Continuity is above all evident in the simple fact that textiles, albeit in often radically altered forms, still continued as the dominant industry of these regions. In the northeast, the changing social geography of mining, attended by increases of scale and an altered pattern of location,[61] represented a rather similar blend of change and continuity.

This pattern of changes in work organization and outlook was reflected in the character of population movement. Contrary to older notions of industrialization as synonymous with the breakdown of previous patterns of community and family life, recent research has emphasized the phased movement to large towns, the cellular growth of towns around earlier settlements, the similarity of environment between different urban-industrial situations, and above all the role of the family in mediating the transition to urban, factory life.[62] It is perhaps surprising to discover that mid-nineteenth-century Lancashire retained more of its native-born population than any other English county.[63] Yorkshire was slightly less retentive, but for both counties – as in the northeast – immigration was mostly from contiguous counties. None the less, the pace of population increase and the degree of demographic flux should not be minimized: there were differences between the cities and the factory towns, and everywhere the new scale and problems of urban life were apparent. Men like Edwin Waugh and Ben Brierley were indeed children of their time: nurtured in a hand-working, part-rural culture they lived to see the proliferation of factories and the octopus growth of Manchester. Thus people adapted to change and created new identities, but they did so with a cultural legacy which was still a living one.

As with Joseph Wright and James Murray, this may be seen in the close association of dialect with towns and areas where such social and economic continuities were marked. The sense of the past involved was often a radical one, for it was in 'proto-industrial' north Britain that Nonconformity made such inroads from the late eighteenth century.[64] The vitality of the popular culture of domestic-industrial communities has often been remarked,[65] but far less considered is the translation of this legacy into the new conditions of later nineteenth-century industrial Britain. Even as the handloom weaving village of Failsworth was engulfed by Manchester in the second half of the nineteenth century it gave rise to perhaps the single most notable group of dialect writers, of whom Ben Brierley was the most renowned. The woollen districts of Huddersfield, among the last to transfer fully to mechanized factory production, were an important location for dialect. From the late nineteenth century there also issued from the area a stream of local histories that testify to the keen sense of a customary, oral past evident in the likes of Wright and Murray.[66] In northeast Lancashire demographic stability and continuity in the structural organization of industry, as well as in family structures themselves, all indicate the existence of strong community cultures similar to those of the mining villages of Durham remarked upon by the 1861 education commissioners. In the mining villages, analogous to domestic-industrial communities, attachment to the spoken dialect was translated into the music hall form; in northeast factory Lancashire into the form of dialect literature. Recent work on industrial conflict in the north Lancashire of the 1870s indicates not only the link between tight community structures and such cultural continuities but also the exercise of communal codes of conduct, akin to an earlier 'moral economy', in the prosecution of industrial disputes.[67] Dialect represented a range of cultural practices extending beyond the rhetorical sphere alone.

In appropriating the past, however, dialect also ordered the present. It spoke to 'working folk' of all occupations and geographical locations, conferring upon them citizenship in the nationalities of 'Lanky', Yorkshire 'Tyke', or northeast 'Geordie'. The substantial numbers of Irish immigrants were included, but in their own way: their linguistic and cultural peculiarities were rendered in the very popular tales, skits, and monologues figuring 'Pat', 'Mick', or 'Brigid' as comic heroes and heroines. Given the venom of anti-Catholic and anti-Irish feeling in Lancashire popular politics, the tone of these is strikingly affectionate.[68] Though dialect authors operated as the spokesmen of particular communities, and this was one of their strengths, the language they used was conventionalized in ways that made it accessible to wider audiences. Working people thus had a new form of communication in print that created somewhat different communal associations to those going before, ones broader and less localized in scope. People read, or listened, in different and more standard dialects than those in which they spoke. The locality, the area within the region (such as the clearly identifiable southeast and northeast Lancashire dialects), the region itself, and the exchange between regions (as with the popularity of Lancashire dialect in Yorkshire and vice versa); all these represented different social and linguistic levels which were yet knit together in inclusive social mythologies. Differences were recognized but, around the central image of the region and its cultural and industrial identity, they were subsumed in a unitary voice that was one of the first and most enduring of the English working class.

At the centre of these mythologies was language, which in this context may clearly be understood as not the form of culture but its substance. This was so in two senses. The earlier consideration of spoken usage indicated how social identities are created in the everyday contexts of use. In a more conscious and deliberate sense than this, working people at the time identified their language as perhaps the central aspect of their culture. Much else changed, but language persisted as part of the symbolic structure of the old culture and as the defining characteristic of the new. Time and again dialect authors returned to the significance of their own language. For Bamford in 1850 dialect is the representative form of the old historical identity of Lancashire.[69] For Joseph Ramsbottom in 1866 dialect expresses what he called 'the inner life of the people': it articulated the silent heroism of the poor, and was a voice demanding to be heard.[70] For Brierley it is the defence against a deadening and repressive metropolitan cultural hegemony.[71] And for Allen Clarke in 1923 it is the people's 'father' and 'son' both, soldering them together, and giving voice to the innate character of Lancashire – its honesty and straightness, the openness of its moors, and the mighty contribution of Lancashire working folk to the industrial and political life of the nation.[72]

Dialect use was in fact varied, and within the extremes of actual spoken use and the literature itself came a range of forms which are of interest and importance. Dialect was, for instance, frequently used in the street literature of Victorian political elections,[73] or in trade union actions,[74] and these uses were, as we have seen, revived in the late nineteenth century. Such uses often owed much to the ballad form and the rich ballad tradition. Between dialect literature and the ballads there were in fact considerable similarities of form and function.

Besides its role in the formation of social identities, dialect also functioned as social commentary and social morality. These three functions were distinct though closely linked, and they were present in the ballads as well. In the almanacs and journals, as in the prose tales of, say, Brierley or Oliver Ormerod, the 'Rachda' Fellay',[75] there is a running commentary on events like elections, exhibitions, and royal visits. The tradition of commentary on events was closely integrated with that of social morality, occasions such as exhibitions and the visits of comic characters outside the region offering the venue for moralizing commentary upon the changing modes and manners of popular life; for instance, upon holidays, excursions, temperance and drinking habits, also domestic life. However, contrasting the first with the second half of the century, in dialect the functions of commentary and reportage fade with the development of the popular press, and the function of identity correspondingly increases. In contrast, the dialect and standard English ballads, continuing to be popular into the 1870s (much later than is often thought), had a far less oblique and more direct role of commentary and reportage. Though they cannot be considered as substitute newspapers, they did take up some aspects of reportage. But they too, if less directly and systematically than the dialect literature, were involved in the generation of social identities, and what is especially revealing are the continuities that obtained between the two forms in this respect.

A very significant instance of this is the ballad 'Jone O' Grinfilt' (John of Greenfield, near Oldham). The collector John Harland gives six versions of the song, and mentions at least thirteen in total.[76] The original recounts the enlistment of a starving handloom weaver to fight in the French Wars. He fights willingly, if under the spur of poverty. The evident patriotism is balanced by the ironic realization of poverty, and by John's attachment to his town and trade.[77] Subsequent versions, appearing as late as the Crimean

War, took up all manner of political and other themes and causes.[78] One version, 'Jone O' Grinfilt Junior', seems to have been especially popular.[79] This was a searing indictment of the effect of the post-war depression on the handloom weaver. Harland recorded, in 1865, that the last three lines of this had become 'household words' in the Lancashire of the present: 'Hoo [she] says ho'od begin, un feight blood up to th' e'en. / Hoo's nowt agen th' king, bur hoo loikes a fair thing, / Un' hoo says hoo can tell when hoo's heawrt.' This song, re-christened 'Th' Owdham Weyver', continued to be very popular into the late nineteenth century, as did the original (they were sung in the Cotton Famine, for instance, and much preferred over the usual 'dole' songs sung on the streets).

They were not alone in this respect: there are numerous examples of early nineteenth-century dialect ballads that survived powerfully. But 'Jone' is a central figure. His extraordinary popularity clearly relates to his function as everyman, the working man as hero, the poor weaver who knew poverty at first hand and survived it by a comic and ironic mastery. The debt of later dialect literature to this rendering of everyman is clear, but even more significant is that generations of factory workers emblemized their outlook with reference to the figure of the handloom weaver and the trade of hand-loom weaving. Between the ballads and the dialect literature one can thus see the invention of mythical work, an invention that, in figures like Waugh and Brierley, was not romantic or nostalgic, but a way of understanding and judging the great changes they and multitudes more had experienced.

Side by side with the continuing popularity of the older ballads, Brierley evolved his most representative and popular comic character, 'Ab o' th' Yate' (Abe of the Gate). Within Ab's home village of Hazleworth is lodged 'Walmsley Fowt', and it is within the home 'Fowt' (fold), a symbol central to the whole literature, that he experiences the freedom of the loomhouse, the fellowship of the pub, and – with some upsets – the 'gradeliness' of home life.[80] 'Gradely' is a fundamental dialect term, connotating contentment, enjoyment, the fittingness of things. Waugh's principal character, Besom Ben, inhabits the same rural-industrial world, and there is the same stress on freedom of movement and self-sufficiency in the old order.[81] The literature as a whole was heavily influenced by Waugh and Brierley, and was characterized by a similarly detailed and loving recreation of custom and linguistic usage. The freedom of earlier days is used as an implied comment upon and measure of the greater confinement of present urban, industrial life, just as representations of Nature interrogate present urban conditions.[82] Sim Schofield wrote at length of Failsworth, and the rich and varied popular culture in which Brierley and the local coterie of writers grew up.[83] Brierley's work drew heavily on this background; one in which, it is clear, the autodidact tradition complemented rather than contradicted its customary aspects. The tension between the two elements was noted earlier. In the north it seems to have been less marked, though it is likely that the contrast is itself overdrawn: these writers did not reject the customary past of their communities, and the symbiosis of custom and self-education that has been noted for the early part of the century[84] seems to have survived later on, despite the mid-Victorian ethic of progress and improvement, and its attempt to drive a wedge between the two traditions.

Ultimately, this evocation of the freedom of a vanished Eden of the handloom weaver and rural artisan is anything but nostalgic. In the literature it sits cheek-by-jowl with a bitter realization of the poverty and dependence that are also seen as characterizing the old days. Brierley in fact explicitly inveighs against the tendency to sentimentalize 'the good old days'.[85] The symbolism of food and hunger (starving is 'clemming' in Lancashire dialect) is extraordinarily powerful in the literature, and the realities of progress are acknowledged in this and many other respects.[86] Many of the dialect authors were radicals and Liberals, and the liberal dream of progress and reason is strong in them, but it is also balanced by a keen sense of loss which itself distances and questions bourgeois versions of improvement.[87] Right down to the later period of dialect, for instance in Allen Clarke's socialist versions, the old rural-domestic industrial order continues to be celebrated as a means of criticizing the industrial present.[88]

By these means, drawing on older traditions, dialect forged new representations of popular identity. The dialect almanacs of the West Riding and other parts of Yorkshire dwelt on the everyday concerns of neighbourhood life, and presupposed in their audience a detailed knowledge of localities, their history, industry, and individuals. This is so from the earliest days: the *Barnsla Foak's Annual*, begun in 1839, treats Barnsley as an intimate, extended village. The village figures prominently in the almanacs, both as the site of current life and as the reader's birthplace; one left with regret, a place of old customs, youth, and family happiness.[89] The public life of communities is also registered, as with the *Weyvers Awn*'s listing of forty-two feasts, fairs, and 'clashes' in the Bradford, Leeds, and Halifax district between March and November 1881. This engagement with present life is earlier and more direct in Yorkshire, but is still very evident in Lancashire, as in Staton's Bolton journals in the 1850s, or in booklets of recitations centred upon intimately known neighbourhoods, such as Benjamin Wood's work on Bury.[90]

Images of weaving and the weaver are central, reflecting in a wider context that creative reworking of the past seen in Waugh and Brierley. In the northeast the same kind of symbolic activity is very characteristic of the literature, including its indigenous music hall variety. There the key occupational identities are those of the pitman and keelman, the former functioning as the major symbol of continuity, the latter, much as the handloom weaver, as the symbolic *locus* of a reworked past. In the northeast these occupational motifs were closely related to the 'Geordie' and the 'hinny', or 'canny' lad, in the same way as in Lancashire and Yorkshire they are related to 'Lanky', the 'Tyke', and regionally appropriate versions of the 'canny', such as the 'gradely'. In Lancashire and Yorkshire there are numerous symbolic utterances about life and weaving; for instance, the way that the joys and sorrows of life are woven together by God the great weaver. *Noms de plume* summoned up for generations of factory workers the days of hand production: the names are legion, among them 'T' Owd Weyver', 'Owd Shuttle', 'Owd Throstle', and the oldest of all, 'Tim Bobbin'. Along with these are the figures of the wise uncle and the knowing fool, such as 'Uncle Owdhem', 'Bob Stubbs', or 'Tommy Toddles'.[91] Names are also drawn from the naming practices of communities. The disdain with which the 1861 education commissioners referred to people dispensing with surnames has been noted. This practice, reflecting a plurality of similar surnames many of which were linked in kinship, was a common practice in the choice of bardic name; for instance, Tom o' Dick o' Bobs (Joseph Baron of Rochdale) or Bill o' Jacks (William Baron of Blackburn). Such terms were invariably used for characters in the literature, especially by Brierley. The choice of name both reflected and recreated the mores of community life in a similar way to that in which the choice of the 'fowt', so widely prevalent in the literature, figured as the symbolic centre of home and neighbourhood life.

Certain key poems, widely popular at the time, may be briefly considered (the text of these is given in the appendix), 'Waugh's 'Eawr Folk' celebrates his own family and by inference the families of his readers. Their varied characters and (considerable) accomplishments are lovingly recorded. In Laycock's 'Bowton Yard' kin and community are related in a similar depiction of the immediate locale of the home. In his 'Quality Row' and 'Second Visit to Quality Row' (not given here) he returns to the same theme: the poorest and the most stoical are the real heroes, though high and low are all part of the same human brotherhood. Health and a contented mind are to be prized above wealth. The theme of the street, yard, or row reproduces in the context of the factory town neighbourhood the motif of the older 'fowt'. In Sam Fitton's 'Cotton Fowd' there is a conscious reworking of this old constituent of mythological neighbourhood, also a reworking of Laycock which reflects the strong inter-generational debts in the literature. The tone towards the better-off is sharper but still muted. 'Cotton Fowd' is a kingdom of its own, of 'fowks' good and bad who in the end are 'nobbut human after all'. As with the representations of the past these portrayals are not sentimental and uncritical. They are accompanied, as in Brierley, by a sharp sense of the drawbacks of such life in the conditions of prevailing poverty; for instance, the self-interest and intrusiveness of neighbours. None the less, the dominant role is one of celebration, and of triumph over near-impossible odds.[92]

Dialect was very often about family life, children, lodgers, marriage itself, and the joys and discords of the home. These are as present in the *Halifax Illuminated Clock Almenac* of the 1940s as in the literature of a century earlier. It is clear that the dialect, if written by men, was read and received by women. Much of it was indeed written for a family audience, and this is echoed in its content and form, the recitation being a private as well as public event. The representations of women do indeed draw on the dominant gender stereotypes of the age, but the picture of women that is presented is without neither subtlety nor sympathy, as it would have to have been in regions where many women worked and comprised part of a paying audience. But, as with all other aspects, gender differences are subsumed in the glorification of 'working folk' and their community life. The home, as the centre of this life, is not a sentimentalized retreat but always part of the wider setting. One is some distance from middle-class depictions of 'home sweet home'. Waugh's famous 'Come Whom To Thy Childer An Me' enjoyed great popularity with all classes. Yet it is very characteristic of the literature that it drew forth a string of parodies, the most renowned of which was Brierley's 'Go Tak Thi' Ragged Childer An Flit', a piece far removed from the conventional pieties.[93]

These accounts of the virtues of 'ordinary', 'poor', or 'working' folk broach the matter of the character of the social identities created in dialect. A full account of the content of these representations would need to place them with reference to other discourses in which representations of the social order were made, such as those of work and politics.[94] This is not possible within the scope of this study. None the less, something of this content will be evident. They certainly amounted to a class reading of society in which the term 'working class' makes much sense. The 'people' or 'ordinary folks' were importantly defined in terms of attributes emanating from the world of labour. But to say that the outlook was a 'working-class' one is to say something at once significant and unrevealing. The 'class' reading of society suggests the need to attend closely to the actual terms in which class was described, which were as much to do with the couplet 'rich or poor' as with the attributes of labour. Indeed, the central notions that come out of the literature are ones in which economic criteria are secondary to moral ones. The peculiar mix of work, region, history, and community rendered through the prism of language gave rise to valuations of the social order that might best be termed 'popular'. The terms 'working-class' or 'populist', while adequate in some respects, do not properly convey the whole. 'Popular' notions predominated over class ones, in the sense that class made up the former but did not exhaust their meanings. In the literature, as with Laycock and Fitton, the one an avid Liberal and the other an avid Socialist, one constantly detects a universalist and moralizing conception of the social order in which class is ultimately a selfish negation of the aspiration to human brotherhood of all 'folks', of all of 'the people'. While the 'people' may most often be seen as working folk, all men and women may be included if they behave in ways that are fair and respectful. It seems to me that the idea of the social order evident in dialect is widely representative beyond that literature, and is indeed very near the heart of popular class attitudes in England.

People, class, nation, together with region and locality, were in fact not discrete social categories but ways in which composite and sometimes ambiguous social identities were built up. Each acted upon the others. It might be through the idea of the nation that class perspectives were gained, or through class perceptions that visions of the nation were enunciated. Beneath these abstractions one is aware, through an understanding of popular language, how important perceptions of place and community were. It was out of these that the values of class and nation were so often built, though again the process was not one-directional. In the case of the industrial heartlands of England, language was perhaps the major element holding these various elements together. The ambiguity of my title will be apparent. The 'people's English' was at once a class assertion of the integrity of the people's own language and culture against the condescension of the higher classes, and a reflection of the popular nature of class. Just as much as the King's or the Queen's English, the people's English has played a central role in creating the outlook of what remains among the most class conscious of all nations.

NOTES

1   Joseph Ramsbottom, 'Writing in Dialect', *Country Words*, 15 December 1866.
   The research upon which this article is based was funded by a Nuffield Foundation Social Science Research Fellowship, and I should like to thank the Nuffield Foundation for its support. My thanks are also due to Dick Leith and Lesley Milroy for their comments on an earlier draft of this article. To David Vincent and John Seed I owe a special debt of gratitude, for their encouragement and their perceptive advice.

2   W. Reddy, *The Rise of Market Culture: The Textile Trade and French Society 1750–1900* (Cambridge 1984), p. 259.

3   G. Stedman Jones, 'Introduction' and 'Rethinking Chartism', in *Languages of Class* (Cambridge 1983); R. Gray, 'The deconstruction of the English working class', *Social History*, 11:3, Oct. 1986; J. Foster, 'The declassing of language',

New Left Review, 15, 1985; see also P.A. Pickering, 'Class without words: symbolic communication in the Chartist movement', *Past and Present*, 112, Aug. 1986.

4   R. Colls and P. Dodd (eds), *Englishness: Politics and Culture 1880–1920* (London 1986); R. Samuel (ed.), *Patriotism: The Making and Unmaking of British National Identities* (London 1987), 3 vols., esp. vol. 3; see also B. Anderson, *Imagined Communities: Reflections on the Origins and Spread of Nationalism* (London 1983), ch. 5; E. Weber, *Peasants into Frenchmen: The Modernisation of Rural France 1870–1914* (London 1977); T.O. Ranger and E.J. Hobsbawm (eds) *The Invention of Tradition* (Cambridge 1983); and for the often complementary nature of class and nation, L. Colley, 'Whose nation? Class and national consciousness in Britain, 1750–1830', *Past and Present*, 113, Nov. 1986.

5   D. Leith, *A Social History of the English* (London 1983); P. Burke and R. Porter (eds), *The Social History of Language* (Cambridge 1987); D. Vincent, *Literacy and Popular Culture in England 1750–1914* (Cambridge 1989). The literature on the different dimensions of linguistic communication and on their cultural consequences has much to offer historians. See the lively and stimulating introduction by W.J. Ong, *Orality and Literacy: The Technologizing of the Word* (London 1982).

6   There is a useful introduction by P. Burke in Burke and Porter, *The Social History of Language*. Certain approaches, contentious but illuminating, have directly concerned themselves with the structuring of models of the social order through language acquisition. See, for example, M.A.K. Halliday, *Language as Social Semiotic* (London 1978). In empirical sociolinguistics the work of W. Labov has been seminal, in particular *The Social Stratification of English in New York City* (Washington 1966), and *Language in the Inner City* (Oxford 1977).

7   W. Labov, 'The social motivation of a sound change', in W. Labov, *Sociolinguistic Patterns* (Oxford 1977); L. Milroy, *Language and Social Networks* (Oxford 1980), ch. 1.

8   Colley, 'Whose Nation? class and national consciousness in Britain 1750–1830', p. 102.

9   S. Bamford, *The Dialect of South Lancashire or Tim Bobbin's 'Tummus and Meary' Revised and Corrected . . .* (Manchester 1850).

10   *The Record* 25:2, Aug. 1917, p. 9. This was the journal of the Lancashire Authors' Association.

11   There are revealing resemblances between the perceived decline of dialect and the shifting historical threshold held to mark the demise of the English countryside. Both involve myths of a vanished golden age. See R. Williams, *The Country and the City* (London 1973).

12   T.H. Gough, *Black Country Stories* (reprinted from *Dudley Herald*, 1935–7), 5 vols (Dudley 1937), vol 5, pp. 30–2, 71–2.

13   *The Record* 2:25, Aug. 1917, and 'Lancashire life', 100, June 1936.

14   L. Milroy, 'Urban dialect in the British Isles', in P. Trudgill (ed.), *Language in the British Isles* (Cambridge 1984), p. 214.

15   Reports on the State of Popular Education in England, *Parliamentary Papers*, 1861, XXI; Pt. II (on Rochdale and Bradford), Pt. II (on Dudley, Stoke, etc.), Pt. II (on Durham and Cumberland).

16   Ibid., Pt. II (J.S. Winder on Rochdale and Bradford), p. 175.

17   See the Introduction to J. Trafford Clegg, *The Works of J. Trafford Clegg (Th'owd Weighver)* (Rochdale 1898).

18   J. Barlow Brooks, *Lancashire Bred* (Stalybridge 1926), 2 vols, vol. 1, pp. 137–8.

19   *Parliamentary Papers*, 1861, XXI, Pt. II, p. 339.

20   The compiler of the great *English Dialect Dictionary*, Joseph Wright, knew nothing of standard English, little indeed of reading and writing, on leaving school around 1870; E.M. Wright, *The Life of Joseph Wright* (London 1932), 2 vols, vol. I, ch. 1.

21   *Parliamentary Papers*, 1861, XXI, Pt. II, p. 340.

22   Ibid., p. 340.

23   A proper account of the strategies and contexts of everyday use is beyond the scope of this study. This area is as important as it is elusive. Nineteenth-century novels are often very revealing; for example, the works of Arnold Bennett and H.G. Wells (especially Wells's *Kipps*). There is a useful but wholly unsystematic study in this area, K.C. Phillips, *Language and Class in Victorian England* (Oxford 1984).

24   P. Joyce, *Work, Society and Politics: The Culture of the Factory in later Victorian England* (London 1982), ch. 1.

25   Ibid., esp. p. 188–91, 285–8.

26   Leith, *A Social History of English*; J. and L. Milroy, *Authority in Language: Investigating Language Prescription and Standardisation* (London 1985), esp. ch. 1, 2; B. Strong, *A History of English* (London 1970); but see especially one of the few serious works on the social history of language, O. Smith, *The Politics of Language 1791–1819* (Oxford 1984), esp. ch. 1.

27   Vincent, *Literacy and Popular Culture in England 1750–1914*, 'Education'.

28   The claims made in this paragraph rest upon a reading of the hundreds of schoolbooks and related texts contained in the Marmion Collection, John Rylands Library, University of Manchester.

29   Published by Houlston and Company, London.

30   P. Burke, *Popular Culture in Early Modern Europe* (London 1978), ch. 1, 9.

31   H. Aarsleff, *The Study of Language in England 1780–1860* (Princeton 1967), ch. IV.

32   Charles Chevenix Trench, *English Past and Present* (1855), pp. 8–9; also *On the Study of Words* (1st edn London 1851).

33   On the idea of a literary *history* and on the development of English studies at the level of 'high' culture see T. Davies, 'Education, ideology and literature', in T. Bennett and S. Martin (eds), *Culture, Ideology and Social Process* (London 1981); B. Doyle, 'The invention of English' in Colls and Dodd, *Englishness*; on the dissemination of the new concern with language and literature in the education system of the late nineteenth century, and for the historical–national caste of this, see D.J. Palmer, *The Rise of English Studies* (London 1965), chs 3 and 4. Lower down the educational ladder, the Marmion Collection of school textbooks has many examples of the influence of the idea of a national language

and literature in elementary education.

34 See the interesting remarks of T. Paulin, *A New Look at the Language Question* (Field Day Theatre pamphlet, Derry 1983).

35 Wright, *Life of Joseph Wright*, vol. I, ch. 1; vol. II, pp. 438–43, 606, 608. K.M.E. Murray, *Caught in the Web of Words: James A.H. Murray and the Oxford English Dictionary* (Yale 1977), chs I, III–V.

36 D. Vincent, *Bread, Knowledge and Freedom* (London 1981), esp. chs 2, 8 (pp. 190–3), 9.

37 D. Vincent, 'The decline of oral tradition in popular culture', in R. Storch (ed.), *Popular Culture and Custom in Nineteenth Century England* (London 1982).

38 Readers are referred for a fuller account of dialect literature to M. Vicinus, *The Industrial Muse* (London 1974), ch. 5. My own account departs from and adds to this account in many respects.

39 On the northeast see R. Colls, *The Colliers' Rant: Song and Culture in the Industrial Village* (London 1977); D. Harker, 'Thomas Allan and "Tyneside song"', introduction to 1972 edition of *Allan's Illustrated Edition of Tyneside Songs* (Newcastle-upon-Tyne), first published 1862; D. Harker, 'The making of the Tyneside concert hall', *Popular Music*, 1, 1981.

40 For a selection of dialect ballads, B. Hollingworth (ed.), *Songs of the People: Lancashire Dialect Poetry of the Industrial Revolution* (Manchester 1977).

41 The best collection of these is in Leeds Central Library.

42 B. Brierley, *Home Memories and Recollections of a Life* (Manchester and London 1886); Brierley, 'Failsworth my native village', in J. Dronsfield (ed.), *'Ab o' th' Yate' Sketches* (Oldham, 1896), 3 vols, vol. III.

43 T. Wright, *Some Habits and Customs of the Working Classes* (1867), Pt. II, pp. 174–5.

44 For the great impact of dialect on Ben Turner, perhaps the foremost turn-of-the-century Yorkshire union leader and socialist, see B. Turner, *About Myself 1863–1930* (London 1930), pp. 19, 24, ch. II, 32–3.

45 *Teddy Ashton's Lancashire Annual*, December 1924.

46 W.W. Skeat and J.H. Nodal, *English Dialect Society. A Bibliographical List* (London 1877). This shows the regional balance but underplays the significance of the northeast: Lancashire and Yorkshire were by far the most productive centres. Of course this shows the situation only down to 1877, but the regional balance did not change much after this. The dialect literature of the English regions outside the north forms the subject of a study separate from this present one. See P. Joyce, *Visions of the People: Industrial England and the Question of Class 1848–1914* (Cambridge 1991), ch. 11.

47 *The Yorkshire Factory Times* ran a similar column. See, for example, *The Cotton Factory Times*, Jan., Feb. 1911.

48 Turner, *About Myself*; J. Burgess, *A Potential Poet? His Autobiography and Verse* (Ilford, n.d.); Brooks, *Lancashire Bred*; S. Fitton, introduction to his *Gradely Lancashire* (Stalybridge 1929); H. Mitchell, *The Hard Way Up* (London 1968), p. 116; K.E. Smith, *West Yorkshire Dialect Poets* (Wetherby 1982).

49 For example, F. Ormerod, ('Owd Throstle'), *Lancashire Cracks* (Manchester n.d., c.1920s?), written for 'gradely folks wearing clogs'.

50 M. Burgess and T. Keen, *Gracie Fields* (London 1980).

51   Vicinus, *The Industrial Muse*; M. Beetham, 'Healthy reading: the periodical press in late Victorian Manchester', and B. Maidment, 'Class and cultural production in the industrial city: poetry in Victorian Manchester', both in A.J. Kidd and K.W. Roberts (eds), *City, Class and Culture: Studies of Social Policy and Cultural Production in Victorian Manchester* (Manchester 1985). In addition to the works of Harker cited above, see also 'Joe Wilson', in P. Bailey and J. Bratton (eds), *The Victorian Music Hall* (Milton Keynes 1986), 2 vols, vol. 2.

52   That of Maidment, 'Class and cultural production in the industrial city', pp. 149, 151, 161, in which class is 'not far enough developed at the time', or else is 'confused'.

53   That of Harker in all the works cited. Beetham's account, while subtler, tends to stereotype the literature as sexually chauvinist.

54   *Historic Society of Lancashire and Cheshire, Proceedings and Papers, Session 1, 1848–9*, inaugural address by Rev. A. Hume (Liverpool 1849).

55   R. Samuel, 'The Tory interpretation of history', paper presented at the History Workshop Centre for Social History workshop, 'Patriotism: Ideology and Myth in the Making of English National Identity', Oxford 1984.

56   Beetham, 'Healthy Reading', p. 174.

57   Joyce, *Work, Society and Politics*; A. Howe, *The Cotton Masters 1830–1860* (Oxford 1984), chs VII, VIII; on the rise of a distinctively regional school of novelists after Mrs Gaskell, and the elaboration of a middle-class regional identity, see T. Thomas, 'Representation of the Manchester working-class in fiction, 1850–1900', in Kidd and Roberts, *City, Class and Culture*.

58   Beetham, 'Healthy Reading', esp. pp. 173–5.

59   Reddy, *The Rise of Market Culture*, p. 264.

60   P. Joyce, 'Work', in *The Cambridge Social History of Great Britain 1750–1950* (Cambridge 1990), 3 vols, vol. 2, ed. F.M.L. Thompson.

61   A.E. Smailes, *North England* (London 1960), ch. 9; D.J. Rowe, 'The population of nineteenth-century Tyneside', in N. McCord (ed.), *Essays in Tyneside Labour History* (Newcastle 1977).

62   M. Anderson, *Family Structure in Nineteenth-Century Lancashire* (Cambridge 1971); R. Dennis, *English Industrial Cities in the Nineteenth Century: A Social Geography* (Cambridge 1984); Joyce, *Work, Society and Politics*, chs 3, 5.

63   J.T. Danson and T.A. Welton, 'On the population of Lancashire and Cheshire 1801–1851', *Transactions: Historic Society of Lancashire and Cheshire*, XI (1858–9).

64   A.D. Gilbert, *Religion and Society in industrial England* (London 1976), pp. 110–15.

65   E.P. Thompson, *The Making of the English Working Class* (London 1968), chs 8–10, 12; see also R. Elbourne, *Music and Tradition in Early Industrial Lancashire 1780–1840* (London 1980).

66   J. Sykes, *Slawit in the 'Sixties* (Huddersfield n.d., 1920s?); J. Sugden, *Slaith-waite Notes of the Past and Present* (Manchester 1905): D.F.E. Sykes, *History of the Colne Valley and its Vicinity* (Huddersfield 1897); A. Wrigley, *Rakings Up* (Rochdale 1949). Ammon Wrigley was a notable dialect poet as was David Lawton: Lawton, *Webs from Fancy's Loom* (Manchester 1918).

67   J.E. King, '"We could eat the police": popular violence in the north Lancashire

cotton strike of 1878', *Victorian Studies*, 28:3, Spring 1985, esp. pp. 463, 466–70.

68   The oral-mimetic was a vital part of contemporary popular culture, and indeed extended to all classes. In the second half of the century the publishing house of Abel Heywood in Manchester turned out large numbers of reciters featuring the linguistic traits of the Scots, the Dutch, American Negroes ('niggerosities'), the Germans, and many more.

69   Bamford, *The Dialect of South Lancashire*.

70   *County Words*, 15 Dec. 1866.

71   *Ben Brierley's Journal*, December 1871; 'Goosegrove Penny Readings', in Dronsfield, *Ab o' th' Yate Sketches*, vol. III.

72   'In praise o' Lancashire', *Teddy Ashton's Lancashire Annual*, 1923.

73   B. Grime, *Memory Sketches* (Oldham 1887), pp. 168–9.

74   H.I. Dutton and J.E. King, *'Ten Per Cent and No Surrender.' The Preston Strike, 1853–1854* (Cambridge 1981), pp. 43, 100, 125.

75   Oliver Ormerod, *O Ful, Tru, Un Pertikler Okeawnt, O Bwoth Wat Aw Seed Un Wat Aw Yerd We Gooin Too Th' Greight Eggshibishun E Lundun . . . by O Fellay Fro Rochdale* (Rochdale 1856). Sales of 12,000 were claimed since the first edition of 1815.

76   J. Harland, *Ballads and Songs of Lancashire Ancient and Modern* (3rd edn, London 1882).

77   The ballad may be found in Hollingworth, *Songs of the People*.

78   These versions may be found in the Pearson Ballad Collection, Mancheter Central Reference Library.

79   Under the title 'Th Owdham Weyver' this may be found in Hollingworth, *Songs of the People*.

80   Brierley, 'Bein Gradely', 'Walmsley Fowt Goose Club', in Dronsfield, *Ab o' th' Yate Sketches*, vols II, III or see Brierley, *Daisy Nook Sketches* (Manchester and London 1881); 'Treadlepin Fold', in Brierley, *Tales and Sketches of Lancashire Life* (Manchester and London 1884).

81   G. Milner (ed.), E. Waugh, *Besom Ben Stories* (Manchester n.d. 1880s?).

82   K.E. Smith, *The Dialect Muse* (Wetherby 1979).

83   S. Schofield, *Short Stories About Failsworth Folk* (Blackpool 1905).

84   Thompson, *The Making of the English Working Class*, pp. 312–6.

85   E.g., 'Old Times and New', and 'Hard Times', in Dronsfield, *Ab o' th' Yate Sketches*, vols II, I.

86   B. Brierley, 'Ab . . . An Chep Beef', 'Shoiny Jim's Kesmas Dinner', 'Hard Times', in ibid., vols III, I; J. Barnes, 'We couldno' stand it neaw', in *Heywoods Samples of Lancashire Verse and Prose* (Manchester n.d., 1885?); this is very evident throughout Laycock also S. Laycock, *Warblins Fro' An Owd Songster* (Oldham 1893).

87   J. Hartley, 'What Aw Want', 'Me Grandfayther's Days'; prose pieces on 'Progress' and 'Machinery'; also 'Done agean', on food and happiness, in *Yorkshire Ditties*, 2nd series (Wakefield n.d.); J. Staton's *Bowton Loominary*, e.g. for 1857, is very characteristic here; see also B. Brierley, 'A Day at Bolton Abbey', in Dronsfield, *Ab o' th' Yate Sketches*, vol. III.

88   *Teddy Ashton's Lancashire Annual*, 1927.

89   *The Chimney Nook*, 1908.
90   B. Wood, *Sparks From the Smithy: Lancashire Rhymes and Recitations* (Bury 1879).
91   E.g., *Bob Stubbs Yorksher Awmanack*, 1914; *Tommy Toddles Comic Almanac*, 1862, 1863–75.
92   J. Baron (Tom o' Dick o' Bobs), 'Naybers', in *Short Studies on Important Subjects* (Manchester 1892); B. Brierley, 'Dooin One's Own', in Dronsfield, *Ab o' th' Yates*, vol. II.
93   The ironic caste of Brierley's work, and of dialect itself, is very much evident in the entries for B. Brierley, *Ab o' th' Yate's Dictionary; or the Walmsley Fowt Skoomaster* (Manchester 1881), e.g., 'Archbishop: One who looks more after the fleece than the flock', 'Atheist: A man who doesno' believe as another believes', 'Historical: Deautful'.
94   For a full discussion see Joyce, *Visions of the People*; and for a treatment of work, P. Joyce (ed.), *The Historical Meanings of Work* (Cambridge 1987).

APPENDIX

'Eawr Folk', Edwin Waugh

Er Johny gi's his mind to books;	
Er Abram studies plants, –	
He caps the dule for moss an' ferns,	*devil*
An' grooin' polyants;	*polyanthuses*
For aught abeawt mechanickin',	
Er Ned's the very lad;	
My uncle Jamie roots i' th' stars,	*searches*
Enough to drive him mad.	
Er Alick keeps a badger's shop,	*grocer's*
An' teyches Sunday schoo';	
Er Joseph's welly blynt, poor lad;	*almost blind*
Er Timothy's – a foo; –	
He's tried three different maks o' trades,	
An' olez miss'd his tip;	*throw*
But, then, he's th' prattiest whistler	
That ever cock'd a lip!	
Er Matty helps my mother, an'	
Hoo seews, an' tents er Joe;	*looks after*

At doin' sums, an' sich as that,
My feyther lickes them o;
Er Charley, – well, – there connot be
Another pate like his, –
It's o crom-full o' ancientry,
An' Roman haw-pennies!

Er Tummy's ta'en to preitchin' –
He's a topper at it, too;
But then, – what's th' use, – er Bill comes in,
An' swears it winnut do;
When t' ones bin strivin' o' he con
To awter wicked men,
Then t' other may's some marlocks, an'   *mischief*
Convarts 'em o'er again.

Er Abel's th' yung'st; – an' – next to Joe, –
My mother likes him t' best;
Hoo gi's him brass aboon his share,
To keep him nicely drest; –
He's gettin' in wi' th' quality, –
An' when his clarkin's done,
He's olez oather cricketin',
Or shootin' wi' a gun.

My uncle Sam's a fiddler; an'
Aw fain could yer him play
Fro' set o' sun till winter neet
Had melted into day;
For eh – sich glee – sich tenderness!
through every changin' part,
It's th' heart that stirs his fiddle, –
An' his fiddle stirs his heart.

An when he touches th' tremblin' string,
It knows his thowt so weel,
It seawnds as if an angel tried
To tell what angels feel;
An', sometimes, th' wayter in his e'en,
'At fun has made to flow,
Can hardly roll away, afore
It's blent wi' drops o' woe.

Then, here's to Jone, an' Ab, an' Ned.
An' Matty, an' er Joe, –
My feyther, an' my Mother; an'
Er t' other lads an' o;
An' thee, too, owd musicianer,
Aw wish lung life to thee, –
A man that plays the fiddle weel
Should never awse to dee!

'Bowton's Yard', Samuel Laycock

At number one, i' Bowton's Yard, mi gronny keeps a skoo,
Hoo hasna' mony scholars yet, hoo's nobbut one or two;   *she's only*
They sen th' owd woman's rayther cross, – well, well, it may be so;
Aw know hoo boxed me rarely once, an' poo'd mi ears an' o.

At number two lives Widow Burns, hoo weshes clooas for folk;
The'r Billy, that's her son, gets jobs at wheelin' coke;
They sen hoo cooarts wi' Sam-o'Neds's 'at lives at number three;
It may be so, aw conno tell, it matters nowt to me.

At number three, reet facin' th' pump, Ned Grimshaw keeps a shop;
He's Eccles-cakes, an' gingerbread, an' traycle beer an' pop;
He sells oat-cakes an' o' does Ned, he 'as boath soft an' hard,
An' everybody buys off him 'at lives i' Bowton's Yard.

At number four Jack Blunderick lives; he goes to th' mill an' wayves;
An' then, at th' weekend, when he's time, he pows a bit an' shaves;   *cuts hair*
He's badly off, is Jack, poor lad! he's rayther lawm, they sen,   *lame*
An' his childer keep him down a bit, aw think they'n nine or ten.

At number five aw live misel', wi' owd Susannah Grimes,
But dunno like so very weel, hoo turns me eawt sometimes;
An' when aw'm in ther's ne'er no leet, aw have to ceawer i' th' dark;
Aw conno pay mi lodgin' brass becose aw'm eawt o' wark.

At number six, next door to us, an' close to th' side o' th' speawt,   *downspout*
Owd Susie Collins sells smo' drink, but hoo's welly allus beawt;   *without*
An' heaw it is, ut that is so, aw'm sure aw conno' tell,
Hoo happen mak's it very sweet, an' sups it o hersel'.

At number seven ther's nob'dy lives, they laft it yesterday,
Th' bum-baylis coom an' marked the'r things, an' took 'em o away;
They took 'em in a donkey-cart – aw know nowt wheer they went –
Aw reckon they've bin ta'en an' sowd becose they owed some rent.

At number eight – they're Yawshur folk – ther's only th' mon an th'
woife,   *Yorkshire*
Aw think aw ne'er seed nicer folk nor these i' o mi loife!
Yo'll neer see 'em foin' eawt, loike lots o' married folk,   *quarrelling*
They allus seem good-temper't like, an' ready wi' a joke.

At number nine th' owd cobbler lives, th' owd chap ut mends mi shoon,
He's gettin' very wake an' done, he'll ha' to leeov us soon;
He reads his Bible every day, an' sings just loike a lark,
He says he's pratisin' for heaven – he's welly done his wark.

At number ten James Bowton lives, he's th' noicest heawse i' th' row;
He's allus plenty o' summar t' ate, an' lots o' brass an' o;
An' when he rides or walks abeawt he's dressed up very fine,
But he isn't hawve as near to heaven as him at number nine.

At number 'leven mi uncle lives, aw co him Uncle Tum,
He goes to concerts up an' deawn, an' plays a kettle-drum;
I' bands o' music, an' sich things, he seems to tak' a pride,
An' allus makes as big a noise as o i' th' place beside.

At number twelve, an' th' eend o' th' row, Joe Stiggins deols i' ale;
He's sixpenny, an' fourpenny, dark-colour't, an' he's pale;
But aw ne'er touch it, for aw know it's ruin't mony a bard,
Aw'm th' only chap as doesn't drink 'at lives i' Bowton's Yard!

A neaw aw've done, aw'll say goodbye, an' lov yo' for a while;
Aw know aw haven't towd mi tale i' sich a fust-rate style;
But iv yo're pleas't aw'm satisfied, an' ax for no reward
For tellin' who mi neighbours are ut live i' Bowton's Yard.

'Cotton Fowd', Sam Fitton

We han some funny folk i' Cotton Fowd.
We'n big an' little folk, an' young an' owd;

We'n short an' tall uns too, an' fat an' smo;
So if yo' like I'll write abeawt 'em o.
Eawr Cotton Fowd ull bow the knee to noan,
It has a sort o' kingdom of its own;
We'n thick yeds, bawd yeds, bacon-yured an' curled.
It tak's o sorts o' folk to make a world.

Well, first of o, i' th' middle house,
Next dur to Rovin Joe,
There lives a chap wi' tons o' sense,
He thinks he has it o.
Yo'll never find him worchin' hard,
He's swanky, yo' con see.
He's what they coen – howd on a bit –   *call*
I think that beggar's me.

I' th' corner house there lives a chap
Who's never tasted boose.
For, when he isno' mindin' mules,   *i.e. spinning mules*
He minds his P's and Q's.
He's gettin rayther wake i' th' yed,
An' wackery at th' knees.
He's brass enough to live retired;
He will do when he dees.

Next dur to him lives Bob o' Sups,
He's allus seekin' trouble,
He conno' see mich good i' life,
Unless he's seein' double.
Last week he supped his Sunday shoon,
It's time he geet some new uns.
He conno' keep his spirits up:
And what he has are blue uns.

I' that big heawse at top o' th' hill,
There lives a millionaire.
He's o his loaves an' muffins baked,
His mind is free fro' care.
There's some think he's an angel, an'
He looks it, yo' con bet.
He happen wears a halo, but
I havno fun it yet.

He wears tay-party whiskers an'
They hand deawn on his chest.
They say he's quite a gentleman,
I reckon he's knows best.
He never looks at sich as me,
He's one o' th' upper class.
I dunno like his whiskers, but I weesh I had his brass.

A poor owd widow lives next door;
Hoo's welly seventy-eight.   *almost*
To keep hersel' alive at o,
Hoo fairly has to feight.
Hoo does a bit of charrin', then
Hoo goes round sellin' barm.   *yeast*
Of course hoo gets her pension, so
Hoo winno' tak' mich harm.

At number nine, next dur to t' church,
There lives a nice owd maid.
Hoo's very fond of gossipin',
Hoo mak's it in a trade.
Hoo's what they coen religious, an'
Hoo goes to t' Sunday schoo'.
If onybody plays her tricks,
Hoo'll curse 'em till they're blue.

Hoo's allus havin' bits o' fraps,   *arguments*
Wi' thoose at number seven.
By th' way hoo gets her dander up,
Hoo'll never go to Heaven.
Hoo towd a woman t' other day,
Hoo'd knock her off her perch,
But this owd maid's a chapeller,
While t' woman goes to t' church.

We han a little shop an' o,
It's kept bi Mester Cant;
He'll sell yo' owt yo' may require,
And things yo'll never want.
O' th' folks i' th' Fowd look up to him,
They sen he's gettin' rich,
It's not becose he's clever, it's
Wi' chargin' folks too mich.

O' keeping friends wi' every one
He seems to have a knack.
When onybody goes i' th' shop
He smiles o down his back.
Yo' owt to yer him singin' hymns,
He gets 'em off his chest;
An' like a good church warden, he
Con sing 'Amen' wi' th' best.

A widow woman lives next dur,
They coen her Mrs Green.
Hoo has a lot o' childer too,
I think hoo's seventeen.
If childer are a blessin', well,
Moor sweet 'ud be their cup,
If poor folks childer o were born
Wi' brass to bring 'em up.
We'n funny folks i' Cotton Fowd,
Some wrong, an' others reet,
They're nobbut humans after o,
There's noan of us so breet.
There's clever Dick an' crazy Joe,
An 'others I could tell.
But what's the use o' sayin' moor,
Yo'n o met sich yo'rsel'!

All annotated Lancashire dialect in this appendix is taken from Hollingworth, *Songs of the People*.

6

Languages and Conquerors

VICTOR KIERNAN

Humanity, wandering over vast areas and living for much of the time in small, scattered communities, has displayed an inexhaustible gift for devising languages. Invention of new ways of turning thoughts into words might be called in early times its principal occupation, giving employment to mental powers vastly in excess of any practical requirement. It may even be surmised that only when human beings came together in such numbers, as in the Nile valley, that they had no need of more languages, could energy be released for the building of civilization. Of the thousands of tongues people have spoken, many have disappeared, or are dying now like the forests. Half a century ago S.K. Chatterji remarked on how Bengali, easternmost of all Aryan or Indo-European languages, was encroaching on aboriginal speech along its borders.[1] A quarter-century ago it appeared that a score of Turki dialects, most of them in southern Siberia, were receding before the spread of Russian.[2]

Historians as a rule have paid oddly little attention to how the people they write about talked. But war and conquest, it can be said, have been the most powerful arbiters of the fates of human languages. Two brought into close contact by force always influence each other in some degree. In subject territories much depends on whether they are being controlled from outside, for the exaction of tribute in some shape, or occupied for settlement. In the latter case the intrusive language may supplant the native one, as English did in Ireland, or be exchanged for it, as that of the Northmen was for the French of Normandy. Or the two may, after long interaction, merge into a new compound language. This has happened rarely, at least in historical times; far the most important example is the English that evolved from the Norman conquest. A more obscure one may be the 'Neo-Punic' into which the Semitic language of Carthage was rapidly changing, through intermingling of its people with the native population of north Africa, by the time of the Roman conquest. Typically, 'for official purposes and in religious rites the original forms were still adhered to.'[3]

A converse to the process of settlement or colonizing has been forcible removal and relocation of a people, or part of it, by a conqueror. This was practised by Babylonians and Assyrians, and in the New World by the Incas, who systematically carried off recalcitrant villagers and replaced them with more docile subjects from other quarters of their swelling empire.[4] This forwarded assimilation, and diffusion of Quechua, everywhere the official language, which otherwise could scarcely have spread so widely during the fairly brief lifetime of the empire. Mongol rulers carried off from captured cities artisans, builders, and artists, who could be usefully employed in their own capitals. As compensation of a sort the threat of sack and massacre by their armies drove a multitude of refugees out of Central Asian cities like Samarkand into India, where their coming reinforced the Sultanate of Delhi set up by Muslim invaders not long before. Roman conscription had the effect of shuffling servicemen between provinces, with pidgin-Latin for their common speech. Armies in Asia, and in Europe into the eighteenth century, and their shadow-armies of camp-followers, were always of a cosmopolitan sort. A victorious host like Timur's snowballed as it advanced. Soldiers of fortune abounded nearly everywhere.

Countless others were carried off for sale as slaves, up and down the Roman empire, all over the Muslim world, and above all, from the sixteenth to the nineteenth century, across the Atlantic. Angola as a Portuguese colony was chiefly valued as a source of forced labour for Brazil. Even in such extreme situations, linguistic influences were not altogether one-sided. Spanish underwent changes when it crossed the ocean.[5] In late colonial days 'Carolina gentlewomen talked "like Negroes"', it was said. 'This seems to have been the origin of the "Southern drawl"'; there was something akin to it in Jamaica.[6]

On the enslaved the effect was naturally far more drastic. Many ethnic groups as well as unnumbered individuals all through history suffered traumatic disruption, and cultures along with their languages were crippled. From this chronic instability of the human lot some guesses might be made about humanity's chronic lack of mental equilibrium. Colonial conditions like those in French Algeria made for an incoherent mixture of low-grade French with colloquial Arabic, which must, it has been argued, have disturbed the working patterns of the mind. In the *colonisé* everywhere thinking is liable to be disoriented, and may disconcert observers by an elementary, even infantile quality.[7]

Women have a good claim to be classed as *colonisées*, or at any rate through most epochs have belonged to the inferior strata of society: very probably they were its earliest working class. They were regularly carried off as part of the spoils of war; even when this did not befall them, they were victims of men's physical strength, disguised by philosophers and preachers as men's superior wisdom. Their mode of talking might be affected by their exclusion from the public life carried on by men, though little record of this remains. Athenian women had a stock of words of their own; some, conceivably, inherited from a previous race, others perhaps devised to veil their meaning from masculine ears. Zulu women belonged to a much more polygynous society, and to a conquest-state devoted to capture of women and cattle. In a large homestead dialects must often have been various, and have made female talk almost a new mixed one. 'At the king's kraal, indeed', it was reported, 'it is sometimes difficult to understand the speech of the royal wives.'[8] Often in Africa and elsewhere, in New Guinea for example, the homestead was an economic unit of production as well as a place of recreation for the owner; and wives collected from here and there would have to find ways of organizing their tasks.

When two peoples are brought together by the sword, the linguistic outcome will depend on their respective social structures, chiefly that of the dominant partner, and on their marriage and family customs. There may be apartheid, as in later British India and South Africa, or polygamous appropriation, or anything in between. Africa and eastern Asia had a secular current of migration from north to south; middle Asia too, though also another from east to west. Migrants must, it is recognized, have been less often whole peoples than war bands, travelling with few women and eager to acquire others on the way or where they settled. It has often been too readily assumed that the incoming language would then succumb, because, in Basil Davidson's words, 'it was the mothers who decided what the children spoke.' He sees a need for caution over this, but gives the example of the Fulani overrunning Hausaland in northern Nigeria, early in the nineteenth century, and subsequently accepting the Hausa language.[9] On the other hand the alien click sounds in Zulu and other Bantu languages can only have come from the Hottentots and Bushmen, by way of women taken from them. Polygamy can multiply speakers of the 'male' language, when these have a motive, such as religion, for preserving their identity. Muslim feudal societies, in contrast with European, drew little distinction between offspring of wives and of concubines, and in new territories, like early Muslim India, needed to augment their numbers rapidly.

In any fairly complex, but still pre-national, society under long-continuing foreign occupation, a slowly quickening drift towards adoption of the intrusive language can be expected. Learning it can throw open many opportunities, especially to the literate. It is the higher strata of the conquered people, mostly town-dwelling, who will make the change first, especially if the new tongue is accompanied by an attractive new culture. A new religion can have a wider magnetism, and in time reach all classes. Islam benefited in an exceptional way from the fact that the language of the first Muslim conquerors was the sacred tongue in which the *ipsissima verba* of Heaven had been delivered. A magic virtue attached to them; talismans inscribed with them abounded, whether the wearers could read them or not. There was seldom any enforced conversion to Islam, seldom any active preaching of it to unbelievers; it could wait for them to turn to it of their own accord.

A theatre of special interest is the 'Near East', or western Asia, where three continents meet, and its southward and eastward neighbours or appendages. This cradle of ancient civilizations shows a bewildering kaleidoscope of tongues, to account for which the Tower of Babel furnished a picturesque myth. Egypt was Hamitic. Hittites and others of Indo-European speech came to occupy parts of Asia Minor – if indeed Anatolia was not, as suggested lately, its starting point[10] – and, later on, Persia. Sumerian, in southern Mesopotamia, has no known origin or affinity. The rest belonged to the Semitic family, whose members were more closely related than those of the Indo-European, and since being first recorded have changed much less,[11] like the societies and cultures they belonged to.

Much of the Near East was Semitic as far back as the eye can see. As Roux says, not all Semitic speakers can have come out of a half-empty Arabia;[12] still, Arabia's less infertile regions and northern fringes formed what has been called 'the great Semitic reservoir',[13] out of which a steady trickle of migration can be assumed, turning at times into a flood. Over a great part of the Near East there must have been a continual flux, a pattern of mostly short-range change of place, with nomads turning into semi-nomads and part-cultivators, and these into regular farmers, and rustics into townsmen. Each mutation would involve more or less of social or ethnic friction; and 'annual seasonal migrations of nomads for summer grazing after harvest became periodically mass settlement or armed invasion.'[14]

As a natural outcome of land-hunger and population shifts, the Near East and its environs were a confusion of peoples living not only side by side but often on top of one another. In Greece the Dorian invaders seem for centuries to have felt different from the natives they had overcome; the Hittites too may have been a dominant minority.[15] In the later second millennium BC there was a Hittite empire. This whole region was the stage on which the world's first empires were reared; civilizations and empires seem to have arisen concurrently, as if two aspects of the same thing. Amenhotep of Egypt in the fifteenth century BC boasted (no doubt with some exaggeration, always indulged in by fishers of men as well as by fishermen) of having deported from northern Palestine and southern Syria very large numbers of their inhabitants; his figures add up to nearly a hundred thousand.[16] Sumeria was swallowed up in a Semitic Mesopotamia; first the Akkadians to its north took the lead, and then successive Babylonian and Assyrian war-lords carried their standards abroad.

Canaan or Palestine, a narrow corridor between the northern edge of Arabia and the Mediterranean, always had a polyglot though basically Semitic population. Most important among later arrivals there and in Syria were Aramaean tribes. In Canaan their dialects were soon encroaching on their forerunner and cognate, Hebrew; what seems to have set the seal on the latter's decline was that memorable episode of ancient imperialism, the Babylonian Captivity following the fall of Jerusalem in 586 BC. From that time Hebrew, limited to a district of Judaea, was giving way more quickly to Aramaic; well before the birth of Christ it was, as a spoken language, extinct. Time's whirligigs have brought Hebrew back from the grave, while Aramaic today clings to life only in a few corners of Syria and Iraq. In another area, the marshlands of southern Iraq, it has had a ghostly afterlife. Marsh Arabs, an explorer tells us, have a religion containing elements of Manichaeism, and its ceremonial language is Aramaic.[17] In such fashion a departed tongue may come to serve new generations, as Latin was to do for so long.

Aramaeans settled in city-states of their own, but kept enough of early wandering habits to be addicted to long-distance trade, and carried their language with them along the trade routes of the Near East. Its diffusion was powerfully aided by the empires, sometimes heavy-handedly. During the ninth and eighth centuries BC several Aramaean enclaves in northern Syria were seized by the Assyrians, who to forestall rebellion deported a good part of the population and scattered it over their dominions. Neo-Babylonian rulers, supplanting the Assyrians in the next two centuries, found Aramaic, now widely known, a convenient medium of diplomacy and administration, and thereby helped it to become the general vernacular of Mesopotamia and Syria–Palestine. It was a classic case of imperialism utilizing a foreign language instead of trying to impose its own. When Babylon was overthrown by Cyrus the Persian in 539 BC and the Achaemenid dynasty (sixth to fourth centuries BC) took over the hegemony, Aramaic was the only language by means of which their patchwork empire could be run. Still more completely than by the previous ruling power, it was employed officially throughout the provinces.

From the time when 'civilization' began (in the Old World at least) there have been two interwoven strands of linguistic history, spoken and written.

Languages have been very numerous, modes of writing extremely few. Yet the latter have been, for human evolution, in some ways the more important, because writing is the vehicle of people's efforts to think, to exchange ideas, to plan. Egypt devised its hieroglyphs. Sumeria had a script composed of signs, each denoting a monosyllabic word, and these were borrowed by the Akkadians and their successors, and developed into the cuneiform system, suited to incision on clay tablets. Along with them many Sumerian deities were adopted, and for ages after it ceased to be spoken 'prayers and incantations continued to be recited by the priests in Sumerian.'[18] But what civilization was waiting for was an alphabet.

'There is only one alphabet, which has spread over almost all of the world',[19] though it has proliferated into an extraordinary variety of shapes. It has often been supposed that it derived from simplified late Egyptian characters. This remains to be proved; at any rate, the alphabet made its appearance, about the first half of the second millennium BC, among speakers of northwestern Semitic dialects on the Mediterranean coast, a region of small city-states engaged in long-range commerce. Multiple contacts with far-off peoples might well jolt the inventors out of the grooves of habit, and their business vocation would impress on them the value of written records, and of time. Prominent among them were the Phoenicians, whose sea-roving eyes were turned westward, but the alphabet was also being used, not later than 1000 BC, by the Aramaeans, well qualified to appreciate the importance of the 'simple, practical script of the future'.[20]

Their language was familiar, and their script followed it, dislodging the cumbrous old cuneiform from its long-held position: a surprising triumph, as Rostovtzeff said, but explainable by the simplicity of the new method, which gave it an entry even into Egypt, and by the indispensability of the language for everyone engaged in commerce.[21] It had one foot in Canaan, whose peoples were above all intermediaries between Mesopotamia and Egypt, and hence were in a good position to popularize 'their greatest contribution to human progress'.[22] The alphabet was a creation of small, free peoples – not without 'merchant princes' – but its worth, like that of Aramaic, was quickly comprehended by more powerful governments. Rulers needed written records to organize their administrations round, and the alphabet represented an immense economy of effort. It relieved them of dependence on the narrow class of scribes who alone could master cuneiform. A minister, even a monarch, could now learn to read reports for himself. There was, needless to say, much modifying and improving of the new script to be done as time went on. No Semitic alphabet could be equally well suited to languages of other descent.

The later annals of the alphabet and its metamorphoses are another Babel-story, linked at many points with the rise and fall of kingdoms. The Uighur Turks on the confines of China adopted a Sogdian form which they abandoned in favour of the Arabic after their conversion to Islam; meanwhile it was taken over from them by the Mongol conqueror Genghiz Khan (d. 1227), with whom they allied themselves, and who wanted a means of writing the commands of his new empire: after this broke up the script went on being used until the fifteenth century by both Mongol and Turk heads of the successor states.[23] Subsequently all branches of the Turki-speaking family used the Arabic script, like good Muslims, in spite of its unsuitability to their own phonetics.

Long before this an earlier version of the alphabet had found its way to India, where it underwent a 'remarkable adaptation' into Brahmi,[24] and enabled Sanskrit to be written down for the first time. Here again, it was brought by traders, but made use of by elite classes to bolster their political and cultural ascendancy, always in the last resort based on military strength. A dominant class likes to have its own mode of speech, as a badge of status. Writing can be called the mother of speech, instead of its child, where elaborate, artificial fashions are in question. The Latin of Cicero and Horace, the Sanskrit of Kalidasa, would be impossible without writing, unable to elevate themselves above the miscellaneous Italic or Indic dialects. Once formed, and moving further apart from the chatter of the marketplace, they would add further distinction and prestige to the ruling class.

In Sanskrit drama, kings and grandees speak in high-flown Sanskrit; their underlings talk a Prakrit or vernacular. However, the alphabet unlike the older scripts is easy enough to have a democratizing influence, which might turn against the elites. In India it must have helped to stimulate business activity and sharpen the wits of the trading classes, and to fill the sails of two new religions which appealed chiefly to them, Buddhism and Jainism. Buddha and his disciples taught in Pali, the vernacular of the lower Ganges valley, and this was given wider currency by the conversion to Buddhism in the third century BC of Asoka, who clearly felt the need of an ideology for his new-built empire. There could be no better advertisement of his power than the famous columns set up here and there in his territories, carved with his edicts. From India Buddhism carried its language over southeast Asia, where many of its words found permanent homes; with it went its script, ramifying as it spread into variants adapted to regional tongues. In southern Burma the early Mon inhabitants, who turned Buddhist, were overrun by Burmans from up the Irawaddy, who adopted their religion and script while keeping their own language;[25] an example of the different fortunes that spoken languages and their written forms have often had.

The tide of conquest, for long running westward from Mesopotamia and then Persia, was reversed by Alexander's defeat of Darius. Alexander died in 323 BC, and his acquisitions at once broke up, but remained under

Macedonian rule; even after Greece fell before the Romans in 146 BC the Hellenistic kingdoms survived for a while longer, Egypt until 30 BC. In what was now becoming the eastern wing of the Roman empire, Latin might be the official medium, but Greek continued to be the channel of culture. A strange dearth of curiosity about other languages has been pointed to as a feature of the inquisitive Greeks.[26] They had no notion of learning any of them; it was for barbarians ambitious of rising in the scale to learn Greek. In the Hellenistic kingdoms this was necessary for any natives wanting a share of their good things; many no doubt became bilingual. Hellenistic life, as something new and fresh, had an irresistible appeal to the higher classes, and Alexander himself had set the example of intermarriage. Greek had a potent influence on economic life too, like Aramaic before it. It was 'an immense convenience for exchange' to have 'one great market controlled by the Greek or Hellenized merchant and the Greek manufacturer'.[27] Growth of large cities was one testimony.

Another consequence was felt by the Greek language itself. To perform its new functions it had to be standardized. Hitherto it had been a medley of dialects. 'Now a common Greek language, the *koiné*, a modified form of Attic, was adopted by the royal governments and became universal throughout the Greek world.'[28] There was no thought of extending it to the rustic masses, just as no government until very recent times thought it any part of its duty to teach commoners to read or write. There is really nothing surprising about a neglect which Kohn attributes to lack of Roman 'political energy'.[29] Some old tongues, like Lydian, may have died out, but on the whole 'the native languages were extremely persistent', and Phrygian, for one, seems to have revived with the aid of Greek script.[30] An analogy can be seen here with the preservative effect on languages previously unwritten of being provided with alphabets by modern missionaries, or Soviet educators. Some attempts were made in the early centuries AD to adapt Greek script to Egyptian; but not much progress was made with this 'Coptic' until the fourth century, with Christian missionizing and translations.

No new blended speech was arising; there were no pidgin-Greek patois with any such vitality as the pidgin-Latin destined to grow into new languages in the Roman West, part of the raw material for new nations. Primarily this was because of the gulf between town and country. Latin in the West was mostly the vulgar tongue of common people, easy for foreigners to pick up; Greek in the East was more the literary medium of urban elites. Greek and Latin were in competition, moreover, and both were more completely alien from the native languages there than Latin from Celtic. A further weighty factor was the chequered rise of Christianity. Outlawed, in opposition, the new faith could find expression through the submerged dialects of the masses; after its adoption by the imperial government, discontents among the masses could find expression through heretical movements, linked with the old languages and representing a primitive nationalism.

Mazzarino quotes a Christian poet of the second century who longed for the empire to end and freedom to return to every *ethnos*, or nationality – 'a concept which was always connected in the Roman world more or less with language'.[31] In the next century Mazzarino can speak of the birth of Syriac and Coptic '"national literatures", bred almost by the religious demands of the masses'.[32] After the conversion, unrest in northern Africa, where Punic as well as Berber was still alive, came more into the open, in the guise of Donatism. But the empire could never bring itself to broaden its base by granting such languages a status alongside that of the Graeco-Roman culture;[33] much as, it might be added, the Dual Monarchy before 1914 could not resolve to save itself by admitting its Slav and other peoples and languages to an equality with the German and Magyar.

When the Roman West collapsed the East struggled on for another millennium, as the Byzantine empire. Asia Minor was still 'Rum', or Rome, when the Muslims reached the town they called 'Erzerum'. Greek had been gaining ground over Latin well before Justinian in the sixth century carried the use of it for official and legal business further, as being more familiar to the educated classes. A civil servant, John Lydus, condemned this, citing an antique prophecy that when the Romans gave up their language Fortune would desert them.[34] Here is an unusually early display of linguistic patriotism, but it was clearly inspired by a professional wish to have employments reserved to men skilled in Latin. Lydus accused those responsible for the changes of a revolutionary desire to throw posts open to men who knew only the language known to all of any education, and who could not be fit for them.[35] He might have been a Victorian Englishman insisting on Homer and Virgil as a vital requirement for posts in the Treasury or in India.

Already before Islam came to unfurl the banner of conquest, Arabia was showing familiar symptoms of overcrowding and restlessness. Small Arab border states cropped up in Syria and Jordan; they adopted the Aramaic of their neighbours, and became Hellenized, some later Christian. Islam was the climax of the age-old movement outward from the desert, before the Arabs came to a halt and the Turks succeeded to their role. Politically it brought no more than repetition once more of the old routine of Near Eastern empire, despotism in alliance with religion; as Lapidus says, it was 'a new guise for a more ancient civilization'.[36] In linguistic terms the way was made smooth for Arabic by the fact that in most of the adjoining lands Semitic speech was still, in spite of Macedon and Rome, current among the masses. These dissatisfied masses were separated from those above them by the alien culture that the upper classes had long since embraced. Christianity, or the now official Church, had signally failed to close the gap between the educated and those it called 'pagans', or yokels. Acceptance of Islam, and with it of Arabic, by high and low alike, could restore a kind of social unity, however imperfect.

This process was a long-drawn-out one, though least so close to the centres of empire, first Damascus and then Baghdad, where Arab settlers would be most numerous. One contributor to change, very active in the Roman empire, the army, was less so here, because military service was normally reserved to Muslims; of course some will have joined the fold in order to qualify for it, and Muslims from all lands served together and needed a lingua franca. Many ordinary folk must have been encouraged to change religions by the levelling tendency which had a place in Islam. In Egypt Coptic continued to be spoken for another century or two, in Upper Egypt much longer: a writer of about 1400, quoted by Lane, says that women and children there spoke hardly anything else.[37] In all such situations there must have been a lag between the learning of a new language by men and by women. In Lane's own time, about mid-nineteenth century, Coptic was a dead language even among the Christian minority, although church services were conducted entirely in it;[38] another case of the accents of a defunct tongue embalmed and preserved by religion.

Such culture as pre-Islamic Arabia could boast was mainly poetry, a blend of primitive and sophisticated of the type composed by clan bards under many skies, in Wales and Ireland for instance; verse highly professional, caged in intricate metres and conventions which later Arabic literature was never able to escape from. They were perfected in its golden age, the sixth century,[39] on the eve of the great eruption. This conferred on them imperial prestige, and the making of poems was viewed more as craft than as inspiration.[40] Medieval Arabic literature belonged almost exclusively to 'the small privileged ruling minority'.[41] For the masses, religion had to suffice.

For the educated, however, in the earlier and better days of the Caliphate, a civilization Arabic-speaking rather than Arabian was quickly called into being 'by the collaboration of many peoples', and of individuals not all Muslim.[42] It can be thought of as a new edition of the cosmopolitan Hellenistic culture, with Arabic instead of Greek for *koiné*, or lingua franca of the pen, and with the storm of the invasions to clear the musty Byzantine air. As a natural consequence of its wide diffusion, Arabic soon underwent a simplifying tendency, making it at least rather less difficult to master,[43] much as Greek had been reduced to uniformity after being carried abroad by Alexander. During the springtime of the new order, before its oxygen in turn was used up, men of the sort formerly bilingual with Greek as acquired language now learned Arabic instead of or in addition to Greek. Muslim states were habitually set up by conquest and organized for further conquest, so that they seldom possessed only one language. 'Throughout Islamic history many of its leading literary figures have been bilingual, and not a few of them trilingual.'[44] Omar Khayyam wrote mathematics in Arabic, for scholars everywhere to read, poetry in his native Persian. Under Arab rule Persians wrote poetry in Arabic also, but in a very different spirit from that of their later national literature.[45]

Arabic as a spoken language died out in the remoter regions of conquest. In Sinde, in the eighth century the first Muslim foothold in India, Islam went on (as in Persia, not always in orthodox form), but Arabic faded. Through trade and religion it could influence languages still further afield, like Malay and Swahili, 'not only in vocabulary but also to a certain extent in phonology and syntax'.[46] Modern Swahili is said to be 40 per cent Arabic, and may be counted a genuine new language arising from fusion. Perhaps the same may be said of Maltese, a mixture of colloquial Arabic with vulgar Italian. Of very great importance in the cultural history of the Muslim world was the influence of Arabic on Persian. In all these cases Arabic was introduced by Arab occupation.

So it was also in Spain, the westernmost colony, though there the number of Arabs was very few, and most of the invaders were their Berber followers.[47] How far colloquial Arabic displaced 'Romance', or nascent Spanish, especially in Andalusia, has been a much disputed issue. Questions about the family come to the fore. It has been customary to think of the invaders bringing no women with them, and therefore having to set up house with native women, obtained at first by force. It is easy to believe that Arabs arrived without wives, but it is not obvious that Berbers, from nearby Africa, would find it hard to bring them. As in other such contexts it has been maintained that native mothers would pass on their language to their children;[48] but Muslim religious education might counteract this, at least at higher social levels. The Reconquest left Spain in the end with a language basically Romance, but owing more words to Arabic than to any other source except Latin.[49]

Words from Arabic related chiefly to spheres where the Muslim occupation had brought higher standards. One of these was agriculture, with irrigation, though it does not seem to have been sufficiently realized that this is a quite puzzling fact. Islamic civilization everywhere has been essentially urban. Neither Arabs nor Berbers, nor the many Jews in Moorish Spain, were farmers. Somehow improvements must have filtered in from Muslim Sicily and Egypt, those two old granaries of Rome, and served as inducements to cultivators to turn towards Islam and Arabic. In Christian Spain there was left behind a large residue of 'Morisco' peasants whom it took a long time to persecute into Catholicism or out of existence.

In Persia under the Caliphate the administration was carried on in Arabic, and the people, who may have been as weary of Zoroastrian priestcraft as some Byzantine provinces of Christian, went over to Islam. But the old Pehlevi language fundamentally survived. It was enriched, or sometimes burdened, with a plethora of Arabic terms, governmental and religious or philosophical, and, more surprisingly, literary: the metrical system of Arabic verse was to remain permanently fixed on Persian poetry, despite its manifest unsuitability. But as Arab power decayed, Persian feeling revived, with a literary reawakening as one of its signs. This began in eastern areas where Arab control was more easily shaken off. It found a champion in the great poet Firdausi (941–1019), a rebel against both Arab oppression and Arabic cultural dominance.[50] His new 'Islamic Persian' was 'a modified form of Pehlevi with a large element of Arabic in its vocabulary'.[51] All cases like this of linguistic fusion have meant a vocabulary largely foreign on a native grammatical base simplified by the wearing-down effect of a long coexistence, as Anglo-Saxon was simplified by Danish invasion and Norman conquest. Persian retained an Arabic script but gave it the artistic form of *nasta'liq*, which was to pass into India and other countries, and, in some measure, into Pitman's shorthand.

Persia never had an empire again as in antiquity, but instead it achieved a cultural and linguistic supremacy over Islam in Asia, and in particular over its Turki neighbours. The kingdom itself has always included a bevy of minorities, most of them of Turki stock. Other peoples, related to these, were flowing through northern Persia in the course of a protracted movement of expansion that left them stretched out between eastern Asia and the Balkans; their destinies intertwined with Persia's in diverse ways. T'ang China knew them as the Uighurs. They gained control of the oases of central Asia, stifling its partly Buddhist culture and partly Indo-European speech. In the late eleventh century when the Seljuq Turks were a strong power in Asia Minor their Persian councillor Nizam al-Mulk was a leading expounder of medieval Muslim statecraft.

His book on this, written in Persian, had nothing to say about languages, but expatiated on the advantage of checks and balances in an army recruited from different races.[52] Muslim conquest of India had been initiated in 1001 by Mahmud of Ghazni, and was being pushed on by forces of the conglomerate sort recommended by Nizam al-Mulk. Turks from central Asia formed their backbone, but their leaders were more or less Persianized. What is now Afghanistan was a wild multiracial expanse, through which the invaders marched, picking up soldiers of fortune on the way. It was really an eastward extension of Persia, with Persian for one of its chief languages, and Pushto, related to it, the other. Down to the eighteenth century a steady influx of Persians helped to keep the language alive in India; many were would-be courtiers, office-seekers, or patronage-seeking poets, of whom Persia always had superfluous swarms.

Turkish gave way to this higher culture, as Berber in Spain gave way to

Arabic; the pen was showing itself mightier than the sword. As in Spain the newcomers were garrison forces, mostly settling in cities old or newly founded, an environment more congenial to Persians than to Turks, for whose pastoral life there was little room in India; and they had even less allegiance than the Persians to any motherland outside. Very few words of theirs have survived on Indian lips, among them *chabuk*, for whip, and titles like *khan* or *begum*. It might have been expected that the second deluge of Muslim conquest, in the sixteenth century, would bring fresh vitality to Turkish. Babur, the first Mughal emperor, an exiled prince from Farghana in Turkestan, and one of many descendants of the heroic butcher Timur, wrote memoirs which are a monument of eastern Turkish, or Chagatay, literature. All his own descendants were taught the language of their ancestors in childhood, as a mark of dynastic pride; but his great-grandson Jahangir wrote his memoirs in Persian, the medium of all court business and culture. Turks of the Uzbeg branch now in command in central Asia were still flocking in as mercenaries in the eighteenth century, but they in their turn were soon absorbed into the now large Muslim minority.

Large-scale conversion to Islam took place, for special reasons, in two out-of-the-way regions, the western Punjab (now the chief province of Pakistan) and eastern Bengal (now Bangladesh). The former lay in the path of Islamic influences coming from Persia and Central Asia through Afghanistan; it was more arid, pastoral, tribal, than the eastern Punjab, and its clans were often converted – nominally at least – *en masse*. Eastern Bengal had been largely Buddhist, and Buddhism there had come under forcible pressure from revivalist Hinduism; so that Islam might be welcomed as a deliverance. These regions attracted little foreign settlement, and lacked the magnetic pull of a royal court; their mostly rustic dwellers kept their own languages, though the Punjabi and Bengali of the Muslim areas drew more than the rest on the Persian-Arabic lexicon. A much closer parallel can be seen between the influence of Arabic on Persian and that of 'Islamic Persian' on the dialect of Hindi in the vicinity of the capital, Delhi. While the Muslim elite spoke and wrote in Persian, and high-caste Hindus still for many literary as well as religious purposes used Sanskrit, in this area from the early days of Muslim conquest a new medium was developing for the use of common people. A blend of the local vernacular with Persian words in common use, it came to be known as Urdu, the lingua franca of the 'Orda' or army, or royal camp (the Turki word from which the English 'horde' is derived). Here once more, the grammatical foundation was native, the superstructure largely foreign.

Urdu grew up in and round Delhi, and travelled with the army, a moving town of tents with a vast train of camp-followers. It could make not only Indians and foreigners, but Indians of different provinces, intelligible to one another. As time went on it came to exert 'a tremendous influence on all the

Aryan languages of the country', and in a lesser degree even on the Dravidian, in the south, and some of the aboriginal.[53] On another level it may be supposed to have played a part in intermarriage between foreigners and women of families converted to Islam, and in the huge harems and households of the nobility, stocked with women and slaves from here, there, and everywhere.

For a very long time it was scarcely required for writing. India was well furnished with literate skills, and it was easy for governments to find men ready to learn Persian and serve as assistants or translators. Regular sub-castes, the Kayasths, grew up, specializing from father to son in this profession. When the British came they were as prompt to learn English. Theirs could be rewarding work; in the province of Bihar in very recent times, Kayasth families that came up through it rivalled the landowners in wealth and influence.[54] Urdu, however, was acquiring a new, literary dimension from the eighteenth century, with the waning of the Mughal empire and Persian culture. It found a place more quickly in verse than in prose; Persian was still being used for official business in the early British period. Somewhat similarly, Anglo-Norman showed more aptitude for verse than for prose, because, we may guess, official matters were left so largely to Latin.

To fit itself for its new station Urdu incorporated many more Persian and Arabic words and poetical images, with their exotic overtones, and Urdu poets made free use of Persian syntactical usages. Before long Hindi, likewise hitherto a simple vernacular, or rather string of dialects, was turning itself into a literary medium, and multiplying its stock of Sanskrit words. Urdu, or as it was often called Hindostani, still in conversation a lingua franca, on paper was dividing itself into two languages, which might be tied to rival religions and class interests. They were written in separate scripts – very remote cousins – the Persian-Arabic and the Devanagiri or Sanskritic, which did still more to make them mutually incomprehensible. It was a dichotomy akin to that of Serbo-Croat, with the Slav or Cyrillic alphabet in use in Serbia and its Orthodox church and the Latin in Catholic Croatia, a dependency of Hungary within the Habsburg empire.

Competition between the rival scripts, and their claims in education and employment, was growing fierce in later nineteenth-century India, especially in the provinces along the Ganges where they clashed most sharply. How much it was inflamed by British divide-and-rule tactics is a question highly controversial. A foreign government faced with mounting nationalist opposition was not likely to forget its own interests altogether. One point that may be made in its favour is that it needed and fostered simple Hindostani in the sepoy army, with its soldiers from all over the country; and when an army newspaper, the *Fauji Akhbar*, was started, it was printed in neutral Roman type.

Meanwhile Indian languages were taking over more and more English words and expressions, to an extent that Jawaharlal Nehru – a master of both Urdu and English – censured as unnecessary and deforming. Years ago I heard a socialist student orator, wanting to express in Hindostani the idea: 'We shall bring about a healthy evolution in the development of the proletariat', do so with the words: 'Ham *proletariat* ki *development* men *healthy evolution* karenge.' With this might be compared a line of Urdu verse by the great twentieth-century poet Iqbal:

$$Khilaf-i-ma'ani-i-ta'alim-i-ahl-i-din\ main-ne,^{55}$$

where the final word is Hindi, the rest all Arabic but also to be found in the Persian dictionary, and the syntax Persian. Iqbal wrote half his poetry in pure Persian, for his international public, his religious lectures and political speeches in English; his mother-tongue was Punjabi.

A traveller in Kirghizia in the 1930s found himself on one journey with a 'characteristic Central Asian polyglot party: seven different nationalities', and an individual of mixed blood. Living in proximity, such people find it easy, he remarks, to work out 'a jargon understandable by all', and his party 'quickly evolved a common tongue ... a sort of pidgin Turkish'.[56] By jumbling peoples up together the conquerors who every now and then swept across the steppes must have helped to keep dialects from drifting too far apart. Islam, shared by all, endowed all tribes with the same religious terminology. As some of the Turks moved on westward, settling in northwest Persia and on the Anatolian plateau, they often preserved the linguistic identity that in India they lost. In the principalities set up across Asia Minor 'essentially Turkish cultural traditions' survived for long within their Islamic context, and Turkish predominated both in state affairs and in the literary activities that began in the later fourteenth century.[57]

Still, Persian and Arabic models exercised an increasing fascination on elite classes drawing apart from the common herd, until Turkish court-poetry could do no more imitate them, and true native inspiration was left to folk-poets. This was not remedied, but worsened, by the establishment of the great Ottoman empire, sprawling into three continents. It conquered Arabia, and was often at war with Persia, but it was destitute of any national sense, and in its palmiest days drew its best soldiers and all its higher officials from European war-captives or renegades, and tribute-children brought up as Muslim fanatics – all classed as slaves of the sultan's household. As has happened not seldom, empire negated nation.

An imperial throne must surround itself with the trappings of a culture of high repute. All the greater and lesser courts of the Muslim world competed in enlisting writers, mostly Persians, who could shed lustre on them. In business of state the sultans wrapped themselves in the purple patches of a jargon known as 'Osmanli'. 'In this, distinction of style came to mean a heavy encrustation of Arabic and Persian and a reduction of purely Turkish elements to little more than a few syntactical devices',[58] to hold together sentences of staggering length and minimal meaning. Traditional English civil-service gobbledegook has been nurtured by a similar psychology; the further removed a bureaucracy is from ordinary life, the more instinctively it screens itself from reality by spinning a cobweb of words. As late as the nineteenth century the anthropologist Tylor was deriding the Turks for 'enriching their own barbarous language' with Arabic and Persian – quite recently with terms for, of all things, 'man' and 'father'.[59] (All the same, a well-born British schoolboy of that date often referred to his father as 'the pater', or 'governor'.) Only at the end could imperial pride be transposed into national self-respect. When their empire vanished in 1918 the Turks discovered for the first time that they were a nation, and one of the Kemalist reforms was to purge its language of unwanted accretions.

Where a solid community under Ottoman rule turned Muslim, as in Albania and Bosnia, it retained its native speech, though entrants into official service would acquire Turkish as a second language. Albania, indeed, which gained a prominent place in army and state, and Armenia with its scattered trading classes, borrowed a great many words from or through Turkish, so many as to hinder Western scholars from identifying their languages as Indo-European.[60] It has been noted that all Slav languages preserve their complex case system, except Bulgarian.[61] This seems to resemble the experience of Anglo-Saxon under foreign pressures. Bulgaria was more thoroughly occupied than any other part of the Balkans, with colonies of Turks round the garrison stations and an appreciable number of converts. Ordinarily intercourse between Turks and others was limited; the 'millat' system gave each people, or rather each creed, a partial autonomy, and the government was usually content to leave them alone so long as they kept quiet. Greek Orthodox communities, Armenian, Jewish, were allowed to make their own arrangements for administering their own codes of private law (that of the dominant Muslims being essentially religious), and for collecting the taxes due from them to the government.[62] Unless Albanian is to be regarded as an exception, there was no likelihood of Turkish entering into their lives thoroughly enough to give birth, like Latin, to a brood of offspring.

In European empires contemporary with the Ottoman, as in far older ones, some local languages received promotion. In the Americas missionary activity, encouraged for political purposes by Spanish rule, played a part here. Franciscan preachers made use of the Aztec language, Nahuatl, and broadcast it over Mexico. Further south the Jesuits similarly gave a wider currency to Guaraní by employing it in their 'Reductions' or settlements. Guaraní showed itself capable of accommodating Spanish words and sounds, and also turns of syntax. Today it is, with Spanish, one of Paraguay's two national languages, and most Paraguayans speak both.[63] Aztec and Maya seem to have been written down in Latin script quite soon after the conquest, and this must have favoured their survival. Like Guaraní these two, and the Quechua of the Incas, 'still show great vitality', combined with much borrowing from Spanish.[64] In Africa the Hausa of northern Nigeria and the central Sudan spread far and wide in colonial times as a means of communication. Swahili was used for teaching under several colonial flags, and is now the national language of independent Tanzania, overriding all local, tribal tongues.

On the other hand the modern state in Europe, and European empires in their later stages, have frequently shown hostility to languages of ethnic minorities or colonies. They have wanted to accelerate the processes, more gradual and natural under Roman or Arab rule, that deprive subject peoples of their leading elements. In the Habsburg empire it was a policy of the landed oligarchy of Hungary, to which Slovakia belonged, to immobilize the Slovaks politically by compelling all those who hoped for a post in any service to learn Magyar and turn themselves into Hungarians. In their colonies the French practised somewhat similar tactics. To secure their confidence and the jobs they dispensed their subjects had to learn French, cut themselves off from their own people, become black or Asian Frenchmen. In Algeria, which in legal fiction was not a colony but part of metropolitan France, teaching in Arabic was not allowed. The ban fitted in with the racialist thinking common in modern Europe, for which as Edward Said has pointed out 'language and race seemed inextricably tied.' Renan, an authority on the Semitic languages, considered them proof of Semitic mental inferiority.[65]

Fanon saw colonialism as seeking to destroy native culture in order to safeguard its own position; colonial revolt he saw as in part the defence of this culture.[66] Memmi in his *Portrait du colonisé* accused colonialism of wanting to convince native people that their language was poor and inadequate, and that for all higher purposes they must rely on European speech. For him, recovery and development of his own tongue, with all its emotive associations, was an essential of his 're-discovery of himself'.[67]

Ironically, when Arnold Toynbee visited Algeria in 1964, he found that it had been easier for the country to throw off French military domination than French culture: 'political emancipation from France and cultural assimilation to France' had been going on simultaneously. A joke was going round Cairo that the first task of a group of Egyptian teachers invited to Algeria would be 'to help the Algerians to re-learn their ancestral Arabic language'.[68] In spite of decolonization English, in particular, is still the lingua franca of many Third World elites, like those of both India and

Pakistan, the language that everyone aspiring to enter the ruling or the affluent classes must know. It is a double-edged legacy of the days of empire, mentally stimulating, socially divisive. At the end of 1989 the Sri Lankan government, in an attempt to disarm the violent resentments of the unprivileged, decided to make English a compulsory school subject for all.

NOTES

1   S.K. Chatterji, *The Origin and Development of the Bengali Language* (Calcutta University Press, Calcutta, 1926), pp. 1–3.

2   W.P. Lehmann, *Historical Linguistics: An Introduction* (Holt, Rinehart & Winston, New York, 1962), p. 45.

3   B.H. Warmington, *Carthage* (1960; Penguin, Harmondsworth, 1964), p. 256.

4   J.A. Mason, *The Ancient Civilizations of Peru* (Penguin, Harmondsworth, 1957), p. 197.

5   J. Trend, *The Language and History of Spain* (Hutchinson, London, 1953), p. 166.

6   A. Calder, *Revolutionary Empire* (Hutchinson, London, 1981), p. 505.

7   E. Sicard, in Anouar Abdel-Malek, ed., *Sociologie de l'impérialisme* (Éditions anthropos, Paris, 1971), pp. 707–10.

8   J.G. Frazer, *The Golden Bough* (abridged, Macmillan, London, 1922), pp. 257–8.

9   Basil Davidson, *Africa in History* (Weidenfeld, London, 1968), pp. 94–5.

10   Colin Renfrew, *Archaeology and Language. The Puzzle of Indo-European Origins* (Cape, London, 1987), ch. 11.

11   F. Bodmer, ed. L. Hogben, *The Loom of Language* (Allen and Unwin, London, 1944), p. 421.

12   G. Roux, *Ancient Iraq* (1964; Penguin, Harmondsworth, 1966), pp. 137–8.

13   J.M. Roberts, *History of the World* (Hutchinson, London, 1976), p. 80.

14   John Gray, *The Canaanites* (Thames and Hudson, London, 1964), p. 25.

15   R.A. Crossland, 'Indo-European Origins', *Past and Present*, 12, 1957, p. 25.

16   Gray, *The Canaanites*, p. 37.

17   W. Thesiger, *The Marsh Arabs* (1964; Penguin, Harmondsworth, 1967), p. 127.

18   S.H. Hooke, *Middle Eastern Mythology* (Penguin, Harmondsworth, 1963), p. 38.

19   A.C. Moorhouse, *Writing and the Alphabet* (Cobbett Press, London, 1946), p. 36.

20   Roux, *Ancient Iraq*, p. 250; cf. M. Cohen, *The Art of Writing* (Unesco, Paris, 1965), introduction and p. 11.

21   M. Rostovtzeff, *A History of the Ancient World* (2nd English edn, Clarendon Press, Oxford, 1930), vol. 1, p. 132.

22   Gray, *The Canaanites*, pp. 17, 144.

23   Jack Chen, *The Sinkiang Story* (Macmillan, New York, 1977), pp. 103–4;

R.F. Hosking and G.M. Meredith-Owens, *A Handbook of Asian Scripts* (British Museum, London, 1966), p. 20.

24 Hosking and Meredith-Owens, *Asian Scripts*, p. 27.

25 Ibid., pp. 36–7.

26 J.T. Waterman, *Perspectives in Linguistics* (University of Chicago Press, Chicago, 1963), p. 8.

27 Rostovtzeff, *Ancient World*, vol. 1, p. 370.

28 A.H.M. Jones, 'The Hellenistic Age', *Past and Present*, 27, 1964, pp. 6–11.

29 Hans Kohn, *The Idea of Nationalism* (Macmillan, New York, 1945), p. 63.

30 Jones, 'Hellenistic Age', p. 9.

31 S. Mazzarino, *The End of the Ancient World* (1959; English edn, Faber and Faber, London, 1966), pp. 159–60.

32 Ibid., p. 163.

33 Ibid., p. 164.

34 P.N. Ure, *Justinian and his Age* (Penguin, Harmondsworth, 1951), pp. 119–20.

35 Ibid., pp. 211–12.

36 I. Lapidus, *A History of Islamic Societies* (Cambridge University Press, Cambridge, 1988), p. 121.

37 E.W. Lane, *Manners and Customs of the Modern Egyptians* (1836; Dent, London, 1908), p. 542.

38 Ibid., p. 544.

39 B. Lewis, *The Arabs in History* (1950; 4th edn, Hutchinson, London, 1966), p. 131.

40 J. Kritzeck, ed., *Anthology of Islamic Literature* (Penguin, Harmondsworth, 1964), p. 24, citing G. von Grunebaum.

41 Lewis, *The Arabs*, p. 140.

42 Ibid., p. 131.

43 Lane, *Modern Egyptians*, p. 213n.

44 Kritzeck, *Islamic Literature*, p. 161.

45 Lewis, *The Arabs*, p. 133.

46 S. Potter, *Language in the Modern World* (Penguin, Harmondsworth, revised edn 1961), p. 114.

47 P. Guichard, *Structures sociales 'orientales' et 'occidentales' dans l'Espagne musulmane* (Mouton, Paris, 1977), pp. 124, 126.

48 Trend, *Spain*, p. 53.

49 A. MacKay, *Spain in the Middle Ages* (Macmillan, London, 1977), pp. 88–9.

50 G.-R. Sabri-Tabrizi, *Iran: A Child's Story, a Man's Experience* (Mainstream, Edinburgh, 1989), p. 106.

51 Reuben Levy, *An Introduction to Persian Literature* (Columbia University Press, New York, 1969), p. 2.

52 Nizam al-Mulk, *The Book of Government*, trans. H. Darke (Routledge, London, 1960), ch. 24.

53 Chatterji, *Bengali Language*, p. 13.

54 Information from Dr P.D. Tripathi, of Patna, in 1967.

55 From the poem 'Life-story of Man', in Iqbal's first Urdu collection, *Bang-i-Dara* (Mohamed Ashraf, Lahore, 1924).

56   E. Murray, 'With the Nomads of Central Asia', *National Geographical Magazine*, Washington, Jan. 1936, p. 20.

57   H. Inalcik, in M.A. Cook, ed., *A History of the Ottoman Empire to 1730* (Cambridge University Press, Cambridge, 1976), p. 20.

58   C.V. Findley, *Bureaucratic Reform in the Ottoman Empire ... 1789–1922* (Princeton University Press, Princeton, 1980), p. 91.

59   Sir E.B. Tylor, *Anthropology* (1881; Watts, London, 1930), vol. 1, p. 122.

60   Bodmer, *Loom of Language*, p. 406.

61   Ibid., p. 414.

62   Findley, *Bureaucratic Reform*, pp. 20–4.

63   Trend, *Spain*, p. 167.

64   Potter, *Language*, p. 128.

65   E.W. Said, *Orientalism* (Routledge, London, 1978), pp. 99, 141.

66   Frantz Fanon, *The Wretched of the Earth* (1961; English edn, Penguin, Harmondsworth, 1967), pp. 190ff.

67   Albert Memmi, *Portrait du colonisé* (1957; Payot, Paris, 1973), pp. 162–3.

68   A.J. Toynbee, *Between Niger and Nile* (Oxford University Press, London, 1965), p. 116.

Part III

Meaning and the Self

7

Towards a Semiotics of the Nerve: The Social History of Language in a New Key

G. S. ROUSSEAU

Nerves are in short, the whole form in the fountain of life, by which every part of the corporeal frame is supported and influenced, which can be so affected ... [they] cannot sustain life, and yet it could not be done without them. They are the directors.

Andrew Wilson, *Medical Researches: Being an Enquiry into the Nature and Origins of the Hysterics in the Female Constitution*, London, 1776, p.94

Without nervous disorder there can be no great author.

Proust, *Swann's Way*

Culture Viewed in Geological Time

It may appear odd to begin a chapter on the social history of language with an epigraph culled from an eighteenth-century medical text and, as we shall see, with the view of a twentieth-century physicist whose research has earned him a permanent place in the pantheon of science; perhaps more so, when discussions about contemporary culture focus so pre-eminently on local, regional ideologies versus global knowledge, and on relativism rather than on the immutable laws of nature based on reason and logic. But I hope my direction will soon be evident in relation to this seemingly hermetic opening, as I cannot imagine any adequate discussion of the nerves as linguistic constructs without direct recourse to scientific theory over the last four centuries. The reason is plain: too few among us accord the nerves the elevated role they deserve in both the history of our race and in our ordinary, everyday lives. To say that nervous endowment is personal destiny is no exaggeration. It is the theme I want to explore here.

In his book about women, Andrew Wilson claims that the body is organized around the nerves – 'the fountain of life' – and that nerves alone permit doctors to understand hysteria, the most enigmatic of all medical conditions. No other part, Wilson contends, not the blood, lymph, individual organs, should be privileged in this way. Two centuries later, in *Knowledge and Wonder: The Natural World as Man Knows It*, Professor Victor Weisskopf explains how organisms developed within the history of the race and what the accretion of a particular function meant for the differentiation between the bacterial world and man. My theory of 'a semiotics of the nerve' is encompassed by these two views. It assumes that the best historians are those who take the long, almost geological view: contemplating the race over giant leaps of time.

Let us start with Weisskopf, whose grand theoretical claim about the nerves spans millions of years:

> The nervous system is perhaps the most important innovation in the progression from the bacterium to the higher species. Nerves are long strands of special cells that, like telephone wires, transmit messages from one place to another ... The brain itself is a complicated tangle of an enormous number of nerve cells, as many as ten billion, which are interconnected and arranged in a way we do not yet understand. But this tremendous unit of nerve cells is able to react to the stimuli coming from the outside. It can think and feel.[1]

Having established that the human nervous capability is what literally differentiates humanity from all other living forms and creatures on the earth, Weisskopf describes what this nervous apparatus has meant for human destiny viewed over geological time:

> The greatest step forward in this trend for better coping with the environment was the development of the nervous system. This is a special combination of interlocking cells capable of transmitting

stimuli from one part of the unit to the other. Thus, coordination became possible between the functions of different parts. The most important innovations made possible by the development of the nervous system were the sense organs. They are special cell accumulations that are sensitive to messages from the external environment such as light, sound, pressure, smell, etc. The messages received are transmitted through connecting nerve cells to other parts of the unit so that the unit is able to coordinate locomotion and other reactions to the outside conditions.[2]

Then, Weisskopf demonstrates the utility of this coordination capability in prehistoric times:

As a result, the units could react to changes in the environment in many ways that were most useful for the protection of the individual and for the acquisition of food. The structure could move toward light; it could recognize food by its smell or its shape; it could avoid danger by moving away or by protecting itself when a large object approached. Our unit acquired what we call a 'behaviour'.[3]

If nervous coordination permitted humans to communicate with the outside world and escape the prison of their solipsistic selves, as well as acquire the first versions of a behaviour, the further organization of this unit allowed for a brain of a particular type with retrieval capabilities previously unknown in geo-chemical history. The transition was so consequential that it is worth quoting Weisskopf's lucid description at length, especially for a non-scientific readership possibly unfamiliar with this segment of the primitive history of our race:

The development of a nervous system was so useful and effective that any mutation or sexual combination leading to a larger or more intricate nervous system gave rise to increasingly successful units. Thus a continuous evolution toward an increase in nerve cells began, and led to the formation of a brain. This organ is an accumulation of a large number [i.e. over ten billion] of interconnected nerve cells capable of storing the effects of the stimuli that the unit has received. The storage was the beginning of what we call memory. An action that previously has had good results with respect to food intake or avoidance of pain is kept in memory and repeated readily if similar circumstances recur. Obviously the ability to 'remember' such situations was an enormous asset for our units and helped their struggle for survival under difficult conditions. It supplied the ability to learn from experience.[4]

Here then is a primitive person – the first experiential organism learning exclusively by remembering:

At the beginning, such memory and learning mechanisms were not very complicated. With modern electronic equipment one can easily construct a device with a 'nervous system' that remembers past situations and determines its actions on that basis. A machine controlled by a modern computer may serve as an example.[5]

Yet Weisskopf's example now captures the essence of the unit's organization, as our physicist soars to his main point:

A system of interlocking nerve cells is in many ways equivalent to a system of interconnected electronic vacuum tubes or transistors. A device with a few thousand transistors can perform most impressive acts of remembering situations and avoiding them later on. But in fact, the brain of even an insect is a more complicated device. It contains ten to a hundred thousand nerve cells. The human brain has as many as ten billion; it is infinitely more complex than any man-made computer.[6]

This summary of the development of life depends upon this event of brain formation. Although it may seem astounding that a mere insect has a more highly developed brain than Weisskopf's system of interconnected electronic vacuum tubes, and that the human brain is 'infinitely more complex than any man-made computer', it is a truth as wise as any discovered by poets and philosophers. The implication of this theory is the boundary – itself an almost ineffable demarcation – before and after the so-called 'nervous event', that is, before and after the nervous organization of living creatures. Our contemporary imagination, pondering this time before and after, searches for analogues that will permeate the wisdom with concrete meaning. What, we wonder, can it mean that the brain of an insect is a more complicated device than a system of a few thousand transistors?

Further along this line but now gazing more directly into the linguistic realm, let us reflect, as did W.H. Auden in 'Venus Will Now Say a Few Words', that

> Romans had a language in their day
> And ordered roads with it, but it had to die.

So let us imagine an historical time when all reactions to the external stimuli were completely and entirely determined by chemical structure without the advantages of memory and learning. Diachronically and somewhat more contemporarily viewed, let us think that when Vladimir Horowitz moves us to tears he achieves all this solely – or almost solely – by the use of nerves and brain; that he is not feeling or interpreting Scarlatti or Schumann in some unique musical way, not achieving his success at an intellectual level occasioned by a deeper understanding of the composer and his score, but better coordinating his own anatomy, better summoning the synapses of his own nervous apparatus. This disparity between intellection and anatomy – mind and body, construed on another level – is the aspect so consequential, it seems to me, for the cultural history of the Enlightenment, remote as the nerves and synapses may appear at first glance to readers expecting a cultural history of language principally based on socio-political institutions and on the ideas of power and authority that shaped them. As shall become obvious, nerves (body) exercised their own power and authority then. Our pluralistic culture assumes them today as well, but with this difference: we are less prone to articulate our assumptions on this matter (certainly in public) because they are often socially sensitive and politically explosive. The modern discourses of the nerve – they are plural, as we shall see – are imbued with sex, race, and class. The older discourses were already moving in that direction early in the Enlightenment.

The Nerves as Sign and Construct in Early Modern European Culture

Like Addison, when he gazed at the infinity of the universe and described his star-struck wonder in the late *Spectator* papers, the contemporary will feel a similar sense of awe at Weisskopf's analysis of life over millions of years. But Weisskopf reveals nothing about recent history: the last few thousand years, even the last few centuries. He views them as inconsequential in a geological sense. He takes the long view and demonstrates, instead, to what degree this nervous organization rested entirely on 'combinations'. His very language explains that, and language grows increasingly important in this discussion: connections, interlocking communications, transmissions, coordination, function, efficiency. It is clear from his metaphors that the more nervously complex the organism became, the better 'combined', and therefore more efficient, its processes of organization; and it is evident from his language that everything modern humanity has been able to celebrate is in some way the direct consequence of this nervous capability.

Nervous capability – to echo Keats – was therefore meta-regional and meta-national: it transcended regions and countries, affecting the whole rather than a part of the species. Anything indigenous to the nations – the English, French, Dutch, or Germans – would be insignificant in comparison to it; and the facts that England was an island, France more peninsular, and

Germany more landlocked, all pale when compared to the development of nervous capability. The matter that bewilders is not merely that *everything* cognitive and functional is neurophysiological, but that literally everything we think and do is ultimately nervous, and therefore, that the analysis of inchoate subjects like high and low culture in the Enlightenment must be neurophysiological. This recognition does not come easily to those (like most of us writing in this volume) who have momentarily forgotten that if the stomach was the magical human organ of the seventeenth century, the nerves were its equivalent in the eighteenth, and those of us are used to thinking of national and epochal categories. And yet, if we are to acknowledge the point about nervous development, or what might more dramatically be called nervous determinism, we must begin with the distant view rather than, more immediately, with the middle of the Enlightenment. The scientists among us always want to pause, of course, on the plateaus of nervous development and ponder life at the next altitude, so to speak: the historians on its peaks of cultural history. But what is the cultural dimension of nervous development? From Mesopotamia to Munich, Babylonia to Berlin, Latium to London, nerves and brains have barely been interpreted in their socio-cultural contexts, and they cannot be without consulting their sociolinguistic status.

In this capacity Weisskopf and his fellow physicists offer only limited inspiration. The Greeks had a sophisticated theory of nerves and brain based on spirits no one had seen but which all were certain existed.[7] But – and it is a crucial adversative – the Greeks never connected brain with soul, the brain then not lodging in the head. This view endured more or less unchanged throughout the ancient and medieval world, with every philosopher commenting on the subject. Few topics could compete with the brain–soul link, it being the primary proof of God's existence in an anthropocentric universe in which God had to prove to man why he had created him different from other living creatures. Motion and matter, soul and body, therefore existed in particular relationships. Mechanical philosophy changed all this, as it created a dualistic order of mind and body, brain and soul, and then – through its mechanistic anatomists – relocated the brain in the head. In 1766, the *Annual Register* devoted columns to the nervous theories of an obscure French physiologist, M. Bertin, offering him as much journalistic space as news of war and peace received. The *Register* wanted its readers to know that Galen had understood nerves as well as any modern:

> This great man, says M. Bertin, saw very well, upwards of 1600 years ago, that a fluid ought to produce all the wonderful effects which we observe in the exercise of our motions and sensations; and he derived its source from the brain, from whence it diffused itself thro' the rest of the body. If he [Galen] could not see what modern anatomy has discovered, he could still less see those spirits, that subtil fluid.[8]

Notwithstanding his limitation, Galen was credited with the discovery. The philosophical analogy was thus continuous: from the acclaimed Galen and the forgotten Bertin to our twentieth-century Ramon y Cajals and other neurophysiologists, all certain of the vital 'subtle fluid', whether it be mystical substance or electrophysical wave particles. Yet with this difference: among the historical periods – as it were – the first to cling to nervous physiology with a vengeance was the eighteenth century, and in some qualified senses it is historically valid to claim that the whole of this eighteenth-century Enlightenment was one magisterial footnote on nervous physiology, a remarkable attempt to secularize cognition and perception through the brain and its vassal nerves. Other eras demonstrated interest, of course, but nothing remotely approaching the eighteenth century's, which – among other activities – naturalized, theologized, demonized, mechanized, medical-ized, internalized, metaphorized, and analogized the nerves.

Before Dr Thomas Willis and the seventeenth-century revolution in brain anatomy, the ventricles were considered to be the seat of the nerves. These hollow cavities dispersed throughout the body, rather than the brain, were the sites of nervous activity. They had been conceptualized as empty reservoirs dotting the landscape of the spinal cord, and were further imaged as unfilled ponds – vacant cavities – awaiting matter. This was a different picture from the one raised by Willisian anatomy, with its emphasis on the brain as the commander of an army of nerves whose ranks consisted of the solids, animal spirits, and fibres. The earlier, pre-secularized view permitted a plethora of theological symbolism, in the representational sense that the flesh and blood had borne for centuries. For a long time Christian symbolism and local custom had combined to extol the flesh and blood – Christ's blood, Christ's flesh – re-entering the body of every believer in rites of birth and death. But the ventricles played no such symbolic role. After their secularization in the seventeenth century and their intense mechaniza-tion during the Willisian revolution, they stood apart from, indeed in majestic contrast to, the rest of human anatomy, especially the flesh and blood which continued to be construed symbolically, especially in Catholic countries, well into the early eighteenth century.

This is the *carne impassible* about which Piero Camporesi has written so poetically in *The Incorruptible Flesh* and *Bread of Dreams*. But the seculariza-tion of the nerves during the early Enlightenment and in the period of the scientific revolution raised questions not anticipated by believers. For example, the blood – it was thought in the Renaissance – had needed food; was literally fed; the ventricles had none, were often conceptualized as if starved of food. By analogy, what was the food of the nerves? Did the nerves even need food? Perhaps these questions merely represent linguistic traps. Also, the nerves may have been uniquely secular in relation to, and patently different from, their kindred cousins, the ventricles and the blood, precisely because they did not require food. In any case it is clear as we gaze back upon this maze of intricate Renaissance anatomy that the ventricles and their Enlightenment successors, the nerves, have another history and imagery and, as such, a different succession of metaphors that will attach to them. These vocabularies of the nerves and the social codes they employ constitute much of my story.

The eighteenth-century's energy in developing answers to questions about the nerves and in metaphorizing the terms in which these answers were couched was extraordinary. Generally speaking, the entire corpus of English medical writing then was extraordinarily metaphorical, to a greater degree than the authors ever realized and certainly more emphatically than has been recognized by historians of science in our century. More specifically, and within this rampant cornucopia of metaphor often running wild, the language dealing with the nerves was even more metaphorical. This much acknowledged, it is equally crucial to recognize to what degree the period naturalized them, so to speak, as it made the brain and nerves the basis of a vast number of research programmes in secular natural philosophy.[9]

The period philosophized them into a dualism of mind and body from which Western civilization has yet to recover, always attributing this mind–body split to Descartes, it being, more accurately, the proof of a late Renaissance nerve craze that set everyone looking for the key to these vital spirits.[10] It theologized them in both the conservative and radical theology of the day, as nerves were said (by the conservatives) to be a beneficent God's physiological gift to a wicked people who needed them for reformation, as well as (in radical versions such as the Boyle Lectures) revelation of God's goodness in endowing his creatures with the unit of organization they most needed.[11] It demonized them, as empiricists and spiritualists continued to endow them with magical and alchemical powers no one had ever seen.[12] It mechanized and vitalized them in countless anatomical and physiological debates then raging all over Europe.[13] It taxonomized them as well into stronger and weaker nerves, greater and lesser, major and minor, pigmented and non-pigmented, white and black, red and yellow, as Linnaeus and Cullen and many others purported to do in their nosological schemes.[14] It Darwinized them, too, when Erasmus Darwin suggested that the nervous system had been evolving all along (developing in insects as well as more intelligent animals) and would eventually evolve into something much grander than it was by the end of the eighteenth century.[15] It pathologized them into normal and abnormal states – the state of affairs, so to speak, of the nerves that coloured all human health and determined longevity.[16] And it biologized them in the embryological discussions about reproduction, preformation, and epigenesis.[17] In all these activities it was conceded, with remarkably little opposition, and as Hume and other Scots philosophers scrupulously argued, that whatever memory was, the brain and its vassals the nerves could never be far removed. If learning and attention require memory more than anything else, we instantly see what an extraordinary homage to the nerves this is. So crucial were these nerves to the complex human machine (a beast machine of a much more composite and interconnected type) that the eighteenth century – if one may be metonymic about its diverse efforts in this area – almost worshipped at its temple.

This vast theoretical labyrinth had its counterpart in the socialization (and as we shall see in the lingualization) of the nerves; in the ordinary daily life of the time as well. The nerves were medicalized, academized, globalized, climatized, electrified, genderized, and sexualized. Concomitantly, the nerves were engraved in the social history of the day: at spas and resorts, among doctors and patients, among the flourishing cults of sensibility that served – first and foremost – to differentiate the social classes in an era when aristocratic title in itself was insufficient, and when antagonisms between the social classes took more hostile forms than mutual derogation. The nerves were academized at virtually every European medical school, regardless of its reigning beliefs, as students were assigned dissertations on this subject: at Leiden, Harderwyk, Reims, Paris, Montpellier, Marburg, Halle, Wurzberg, Giessen, Göttingen, Leipzig, Erfurt, Jena, Helmstedt, Dresden, Basel, Padua, Rome.[18] Indeed, I have found no medical schools where dissertations on the nerves were *not* written.

The nerves were literally electrified by Wesley, Franklin, and Mesmer, each in his own way aiming to regenerate one social class or another, high and low. The nerves were globalized, nationalized, regionalized, and internationalized, as different countries, climates, and regions were held accountable for particular conditions of the nerves and their ensuing diseases. For the first time, one could talk of 'French' nerves, 'Dutch' nerves, or 'Italian' nerves, perhaps even 'Oriental' nerves, while paradoxically being cautioned that whatever local, indigenous conditions prevailed, the nerves themselves were universal, common to all people all over the earth. Horace Walpole, the prime minister's son who was the most prolific letter-writer of the Enlightenment, spent entire years trying to decide if his health was marred by gout or 'bad nerves'. Eventually his constant correspondent and closest friend Horace Mann, the British envoy in Florence, made a case for 'nerves' and claimed to speak from authority as he too had been afflicted, but by the Italian variety of nerves rather than the English. 'I have suffered horridly this winter', Mann wrote to Walpole on 26 February 1763, 'in my head; not common headaches, but a pulling in my nerves, known here [in Florence] by the name of *stiramenti dei nervi*.' Mann assured Walpole that these 'Italian nerves' caused by a different climate and style of life were another species than the British sort under which Walpole laboured.

And the nerves were genderized and sexualized, as crucial differences between men and women (such as hypochondriasis and hysteria), Caucasian and black, oriental and Mohammedan, heterosexual and hermaphrodite, were attributed to this or that nervous strength or defect. The postulations of the anatomists and physiologists extended beyond this point. The essential differentiation – the 'otherness' – of women was now newly attributed to a defect – discursively represented as an inherent weakness, a lingering form of exhaustion, a fundamental lack of tonic vigour – in female nerves and fibres. On this anatomical disparity between men and women the male scientists of the day spun their new mythology about inherent male vigor and defective female frailty, all lodged in the nerves: a web of representational 'otherness' newly wedged between the sexes and claimed to be absolute, unchanging, eternal now that it had been discovered. When quizzed why their forebears had not fathomed it, the 'doctors' replied as they did about much earlier medicine and science: that each era gazed more profoundly into Nature's secrets than the previous one had.

In *Madness and Civilization* Foucault has described the effect of this new hypothecation of women's 'inferior internal spaces' and its effect on their gender-based maladies of melancholy and hysteria during the age of Sydenham and Willis. Foucault never localized the defect specifically in the nerves and fibres, but this is the anatomic zone to which his argument inexorably leads. His leap was significant in both representational and discursive domains, for in the Enlightenment's radical genderization of the nerves and fibres 'female otherness' (and its effective debility and otherness) was legitimized and demonstrated, it was said, according to the best laws of mechanics. What had been theologically and dogmatically shaped for centuries was now carved, so to speak, in the granite of empirical science. This new view – the view adumbrated by the great Enlightenment anatomists of all European countries and recently captured so intuitively by Foucault – endured throughout the Romantic and Victorian periods. Indeed, it has persisted into the twentieth century and reigned unchallenged until feminist scholars began to interrogate the underpinnings of patriarchal science in the history of Western culture at large. Nevertheless, the Enlightenment doctors (anatomists, physicians, physiologists) did not conceptualize gender in such an equitable mode that *male* and *female* nerves – then said to be the sole source and spring of all higher life in the creation – could be structurally construed as identical entities. Persuaded, as their forebears had been, that women were (anatomically speaking) inferior men from time immemorial, the eighteenth-century anatomists legitimated their separatist views with concrete proof drawn in copious anatomical illustrations and described in prolific (and often prolix) physiological narratives. Everywhere difference between male and female *nerves* was construed as the realistic source of the disparity between the genders, and it was represented in narratives that read more like literary romances than matter-of-fact, anatomical commentaries. But most empiricists then worked as if representation and realism were identical. For example Spallanzani and Le Cat maintained the problem could be traced to the nerve tips in the dermis of the skin, which extended to the cerebrum and cerebellum of the brain. Others claimed that hypochondriasis and hysteria were traceable to the female nervous system. For the first time in medical history, conditions as different as jaundice and low intelligence were attributed to nervous causes. This stage represented a complete departure from the explanations of previous generations, and demonstrates how cultural history can retrieve discourses and cross boundary lines left undiscovered by more traditional disciplines.

The nerves were also internalized and 'mentalized' into the most imaginative processes of which language and art were then capable. In psychology and art criticism throughout Europe, the nerves occupied centre stage, whether in discussions of aesthetic sublimity (such as Edmund Burke's *Enquiry into the Sublime*, 1757) or in more technical debates about the geometry of the painter's hand as he held the brush and stroked the palette, and of the harpsichordist's fingers – a geometry Mozart's world knew well – in stroking the keyboard (as we will see in the primary sources cited in the notes). The nerves were also visually represented in a broad repertoire ranging from anatomy textbooks to satirical cartoons, and in a spate of books about physiology and the all-important physiognomy. The nerves had been versified as a major topos in all countries, perhaps nowhere more extensively than in England, allegedly the home of lunacy, in, for example, Dr Malcolm Flemyng's long epic poem in six cantos called *Neuropathia*, published in 1740:[19] hundreds of lines of Latin hexameter verse celebrating – as Victor Weisskopf has more recently celebrated in a very different context, discussed at the opening of this chapter – the utility of the nervous pathways.

Most intriguingly for students of language and literature, the nerves were also metaphorized and analogized, as a whole new vocabulary developed consisting of words (metaphors, images, neologisms) we hardly recognize today. These metaphors were based on flaccidity and tension, acridity and tone, fermentation and putridity, and – in words that are no longer in any modern dictionaries – 'hippohiatrical' functions and 'levigations' of the nerves; on biliousness, chyle, spasmodic colics and unnatural ferments, affections and cachexies, censoriums and climacterics, contextures and exquisite particles, ferments and fibres of the brain, fluxes and effluvia, tubes and perforations. The trend produced a maze of neologisms whose meanings we no longer readily understand. These include terms such as 'black humour' (whose first use is not by a playwright such as Beckett but in a *medical* text of the 1720s),[20] deobstruents, dimoculations, empyrheumatics, and a repertoire of slang terms and abbreviations whose meanings have long been lost: hypp, hyppos, hyppocons, markambles, moonpalls, strong fiacs, hockogrogles.[21] And – most intriguing to me – this development generated a vocabulary about 'neurospasts', as John Evelyn called these puppets on strings: a concept that fascinated the period, especially in the form of electrified neurospasts.[22]

Even literary criticism and social commentary were culture-bound by this degree of specificity. Critics Joseph Warton and Samuel Johnson, among many others sought to define the gradually evolving 'nervous style', which they construed as a particularly masculine type of muscular and sinewy English prose, best described as 'nervous'. Warton invoked the concept of 'nervous prose' in the *Essay on the Genius and Writings of Alexander Pope* (1762), providing examples culled from the writing of his own generation; Johnson sought to use it whenever possible in his periodical journalism, especially in the *Rambler* and *Idler* papers. This developing nervous style, they believed, was deemed to be superior to all others; some of its positive features profited from the spirit of optimism and belief in progress which prevailed during the period. Within this linguistic activity, generated in an era when language theory itself was rapidly changing, the nerve became the sign of a semiotics of analogy.

To invoke the nerves then, whether in medical, philosophical, or literary discourse – as, for example, Mandeville did in the *Treatise of the Hypochondriack and Hysterick Passions* and Cheyne in *The English Malady* – was usually to indulge in radical analogizing. No linguistic trope was then so important for philosophical and scientific analogy as that of the nerves. The nerves also presided over the seats of pleasure and pain. To claim then, as Dubois instructs Juliet in the Marquis de Sade's *Les 120 Journees (The 120 Days of Sodom)*, that all pain is in the nerve, was to reiterate a paradigm too well known to require further amplification. Similarly the seat of insanity and madness, according to Dr William Battie (from whose name the English word for lunatic derives and who is sometimes called the father of modern psychiatry, predating Pinel and Esquirol), resided in the nerves regardless of the patient's gender. Diseased spirits, diseased nerves, diseased imagination; this was the sequence of the mind's malady – the surest sign in recognizing lunatics, its linguistic counterparts were found everywhere in the prose and poetry of the period: in Johnson's famous apologue *Rasselas* (1759), in which Imlac keeps returning to the concept of diseased imagination, as well as in some of Collins's and Blake's poetry. Furthermore even the erotic lunacy that springs from love-sickness (a state of mind Breuer and Freud were later to call hysteria) was neuralized, as the English poet Anthony Selden wittily purported in a minor poem called 'To Rack the Nerve' in 1749:

> While Grief and Shame her Face o'erspread,
> Upon her Knee she lean'd his Head.
> Then points the Dart, and with her Hands
> The crystal-rooted Film expands.

But, O! the rack was so immense,
So twing'd the Nerve, and shock'd the Sense,
He begg'd her, yelling with Despair,
The fruitless Torture to forbear.
Confounded with the horrid Pain,
He storm'd, and rav'd, and rag'd in vain.

By mid-century the rhetoric of the nerves had invaded all the realms of English prose and poetry; perhaps more evident in certain genres and authors than in others, to be sure, but nowhere entirely absent or obscured. This development could not have occurred two or three centuries earlier and was tied as much to the social history of the upper classes, and to their need to reassert their difference from other social strata, as to the scientific theories that had explained the significance of the nerves for human economy and material production.

Rank and Class: The Fashionability of Nerves

Given this intensity of mythologization, it was predictable, if not inevitable, that nerves would become fashionable. The notion that they had also been democratically bestowed or acquired – in the sense that nerves had been created equally in all persons – depending upon one's model of biology then, was not within the scope of this neuralizing of culture high and low. That the nerves became fashionable even when viewed solely from the perspective of the political and ideological tropes in written texts and spoken interchanges testifies to their vigour and degree of infiltration. But the history of nerves and the metaphors that attached to them had been more complex than this. For centuries, and certainly since the discussions of Guicciardini and Machiavelli, the 'body politic' had been a commonplace to describe the mysteries of government, yoking together politics with the body – or corpus – of civic polity.[23] In the eighteenth century these tropes altered to 'nervous government', as James Lowde, an early follower of Malebranche and Locke, noted in his tract, which viewed humanity within man's anatomic and political dimension.[24] Yet just as the political state was nervous, so was the individual human being – microcosm reflected macrocosm; and the analogies between the nervous one and the nervous many, the small and the large, the private and public, increased proportionally to this new degree of nervous mythology.

Nor were social distinctions omitted. If anything obtained here, what I am calling nervous mythology segregated the social rank and file anew, and provided all the classes with an important new model of aristocratic life. Nerves also provided a model by which human behaviour could be predicted, and made possible an acceptable code of social behaviour at a time when it seemed there might soon be none. The new social and geographical mobility of the eighteenth century obscured worth and station, which now had to be asserted – even reasserted over and again. The easiest methods were external: publicly through architecture and domain, privately through fashion (clothes) and illness (disease). In our post-Romantic age we tend to construe disease in terms of pain and suffering; previously, when pain was the norm of life, illness had other significations. These exterior signs, then, became the new tropes of rank and class. If the lower classes emulate the upper in all centuries and live vicariously through them, they certainly did so in the eighteenth century, as seamstresses and charwomen, pickpockets and prostitutes like Moll Flanders and Fanny Hill, fantasized that they too could be as 'nervous' as their 'gentlewomen' mistresses. 'My nerves are all unstrung', a corpulent and robust servant exclaims, emulating her mistress, in a minor novel of 1751.[25] The resonance of the remark requires precise interpretation. But it would be wrong to believe that its utterance depends upon a mythology of nervous culture that required an *antecedent scientific theory*. Just the reverse is true. The theories of nervous sensibility of Haller (the famous physiologist) do not validate the principles of nervous government or nervous aristocratic life; the reverse is the case. His physiological hypotheses profoundly reflect, and then manifest, his *own* nervous culture – in Switzerland, Germany, wherever he lived in northern Europe – no less than did Freud's in *fin-de-siècle* Vienna. For science, then as now, is culture bound, partaking of the varying degrees of empiricism and positivism, relativism and ideology, that permeate every age.[26]

So too, for imaginative literature, so far as this osmosis of nervous mythology into cultural sensibility is concerned. The assimilation is as evident in the language of political theory as in fictional narratives. *Tristram Shandy* is permeated with the same metaphors derived from the animal spirits and nervous fibres that will become analogized in Scottish treatises on the law and other areas of government. For writers of discourses as diverse as Haller and Sterne one assumption is shared; the nervous myth is already widely disseminated by the time they encode their fictions – whether of physiology or solipsistic autobiographical revelation – into narrative forms. Yet since the nerves produced no mortal disease, as, doctors agreed, did consumption and cancer, they were not morbidly feared, and no reason existed to demystify or demythologize them to the same degree.

The anatomical principle underlying this tangled web of science and language was actually less complex than it now appears at such a remove of time. It was palpably this: the more mysterious the vital fluid (the unseen life spirit within the hollow tube) – so the inner voice of the upper classes might have described the concept of the nerves in physiology if it had been conscious of these processes – the better for all those now reasserting their class rank in a milieu where grave doubts existed about the stability of this social hierarchy. This, in a nutshell, was the myth. Did the process represent calculated collusion between those who generated (formulated and articulated) physiological theory and those (political figures, business people, professionals) who led the masses? Surely not. Yet all the groups involved bought into the new mythology of the nerves, and it is therefore historically important to note to what degree this semiotic of the nerve was class bound and – of course – gender bound.

At the same time gentility and delicacy were reinvigorated and rearmed with new tropes. For snobs, parvenus, and social climbers, all of whom relied heavily on language to attain and sustain their social status, the way to rise socially was through the nerves: be hyppish, nervous, bilious, and rich. For those who already possessed status and demonstrated that they were naturally nervous, the social consequence was plain – could even be feigned with the assistance of English pounds. Moreover, if consumption was then the disease of poverty and deprivation, nervous malady (similar to the nervous breakdowns of the early twentieth century) was the precondition of high standing. How convenient then that this cultural shift should occur just at the historical moment when the sign of upper-class status was based on image rather than power, and when, as the historians of sex and the family have shown us, the genders were growing further apart. If it was fashionable to blush and weep and faint, it was more glamorous to present oneself with nervous symptoms. If it was politic to associate with those who were also nervous, it was better still to be in a constant correspondence – as so many fine ladies then were – with equally nervous others. The style of intimate letters and the language of private correspondence then (especially among women such as Elizabeth Carter and Catherine Talbot) reflected a rich vocabulary drawn from this recently invigorated 'nervous' myth. The psychology underlying this gentrification of nervous behaviour had deep sociological as well as linguistic implications: to be nervous was to be romantic; to be romantic, divinely to be wished for among those middle-class newcomers who until recently thought they could never be either rich or upper class. Even suicide was deemed to be nervously delectable and endowed with new status: and suicide then was widely held to be an act, as Hume and other philosophers claimed, which issued directly from diseased nerves – the *sine qua non*, the very anatomical precondition for social status – of deranged imagination and certifiable lunacy.[27]

So the nexus of science, society, and language was composed in this complex web of attitudes and behaviours, and it would be difficult to disentangle them adequately into cause and effect. Indeed, in the interplay of social differentiation and the constant need to reassert it lay a perception that the upper classes were writing themselves out, as it were, of chronic nerves. But the very opposite was true. Nervous language did not exhaust or consume itself, in Stanley Fish's sense of literary style in *Self-Consuming Artifacts* (1972), but proliferated – was transformed into new protean shapes: in the novel as well as in the English poetry of sensibility in the second half of the eighteenth century, one strain of which culminated in Blake's vision of the body that required anatomical nerves for its existence. Furthermore, in this line of social and literary linkage, what is Sterne's *Tristram Shandy* (see the opening paragraph of the novel) but a set of variations on the theme of disordered nerves, fibres, and animal spirits? Language and body fused differently in the imagination of other writers; there, 'to read' the book necessitated 'the reading' of the 'body'. Thus, the reader's penetration *into* Richardson's *Clarissa* coincides – literally as well as conceptually – with penetration into the protagonist's own body (i.e. the rape); and the more Clarissa writes, the more nervous she becomes; taken literally, the progression must, as it does, end in death.[28] This version of the outline of Richardson's tragic story represents a much too simple model; nevertheless, the state of the heroine's nerves cannot be overlooked, as literary critics have begun to recognize. And, finally, the politics of nerves must not be omitted. Here the lines of reason are complicated and cannot be developed at any length, but they permitted Adam Smith, for one, to believe that sympathy, as well as trade imbalances among nations, cemented civil societies. And what is sympathy if not a predisposition of the nerves associated into higher states of feeling and ideation?[29]

The social ramifications of this newly nervous culture were not to be minimized, as whole professions and classes, if not an entire gender (women), realigned and reasserted themselves under the weight of a new nervous mythology. If the rich felt themselves under the gun to prove their separateness, what better way to assert superiority than by fashioning themselves differently and frequenting different places for rest and rejuvenation. The best-known resorts in eighteenth-century Britain were Bath and Tunbridge, Harrogate, Scarborough, and Llandrindod, comparable to Monaco, Palm Beach, and Scottsdale today. Elsewhere, the Belgian water resorts (especially Spa), the French Aix-les-Bains, and the various 'Mariabads' (Maria baths) of central Europe were then coming into their own, as were the attendant professions of doctors, physicians, apothecaries, nurses, midwives, quacks, mountebanks, empirics, who now catered to the whims and caprices of the newly neurasthenic rich. 'He was the greatest of the *nerve doctors*', the Edinburgh Dr John Makittrick Adair was to concede of his conspicuous rival of the previous generation, the popular and much sought after Dr George Cheyne[30] – a bewildering concession in view of the universal jealousy of doctors and in view of Cheyne's well-known exorbitant fees. The professions flocked to the resorts, as the places (the Spas and Harrogates) met the needs of the wealthy neurasthenics who became their devotees. These developments partook, of course, of the larger economic consumption and wealth that permitted the leisured classes to be more pampered than ever. Indeed, the entire period was permeated with an ever-growing degree of economic consumption, not merely in the transfer of property of all types but in the uses of spare time and the acquisition of a new repertoire of goods. For all these reasons – economic, social, medical, scientific, linguistic – it makes sense to invoke a newly constituted category called 'nervous discourse' without worrying excessively about charges of generating unitary labels. The signification becomes all the more persuasive if we define this term ('nervous discourse') as a network of often disparate and even contradictory narratives. But first we must explain what precisely is meant by the semiotics of the nerve.[31]

In brief, we are searching for a broad understanding of this sign – the nerve – rather than trying to trace its disciplinary or diachronic history as if we were cultural archaeologists. We also hope to bestow upon it Clifford Geertz's 'thick description', delineated in *The Interpretation of Cultures*; that is, we want to retrieve its signification; want to fathom how it can be that a particular sign becomes suffused with meaning in a particular culture and under what specific conditions. But we will not be satisfied with its logocentric legacy – those traces left in words only – or view it narrowly, glossed over in thin description. We want a more holistic picture; an archaeology of nerves that excavates words and things, diachronic and synchronic arrangements, especially the role played by social history in the development of language; providing a picture that disentangles discourses rather than separates disciplines (history, language, science, medicine); one able to dissect the nerve in the light of the whole picture of civilization then, not merely one of its manifest components. This will be a much larger canvas than merely the verbal one, even when considered within the contexts of the social history of language.

The nerve, then, becomes the repository of the whole culture. Given the structures of authority and the fluidity of the social classes that obtained in the long eighteenth century, it was predictable that the upper class should have contrived these mechanisms of separation with virtually no opposition from the medical profession, which anyway had considered itself an intrinsic part of this stratum of society for centuries. Medicine and ideology beg to be conjoined here. Yet the only ideology most doctors knew then was the politics of the pound; they were thus the least likely collective group to oppose the new nervousness on logical or empirical grounds. Of course they quarrelled among themselves, as the dozens – even hundreds – of extant pamphlet attacks demonstrate; battled just as doctors do today, especially when their egos and, sometimes, ideologies come into conflict. Some of the so-called 'nerve doctors' had their scruples, their principles, upon occasion their philosophies. But viewed from without, outside their own local world and from this distance of time, after the lapse of two centuries, they appear almost to be in league with the rich, as mi'lady 'this' had her private doctor 'that', who – so common in the diaries and private letters of the era – 'was called to her side for nerves every day this week'.[32]

Mi'lady's imprecations often invoked the metaphor of mercy: of literally being *at the mercy of* her nerves, as if she had no choice or say whatever in the matter. She presented herself as soulless and psycheless when in the face of the oncoming wave of nerves. The extraordinary aspect of this usage of 'being at the mercy of' is the way it invited mechanical explanations. So long as those ministering to mi'lady – her doctors, her apothecaries – explained this tug of nerves, this pull, in mechanical terms, she knew exactly what had happened to her and what to expect. She was suspicious of explanations centring on her so-called passions of the mind, a catch-all often used by medical doctors in consulting as well as writing. No matter what her notion of womanhood, mi'lady had little sense of a dark psyche compelling her will or depressing her nerves – this the female letters and diaries of the time make abundantly clear, as does the drama. Indeed, her psyche was off limits: a sign of difference she very much wanted to avoid in view of what the nerves affirmed socially. Mi'lady inquired, of course, into the conditions surrounding her latest bout of nerves and the way they overcame her; and she understood a much-watered-down lay version of mechanical explanations; but she could not cope with what we call psychological explanations (nor were they offered!) resorting to dark psyches and demonic forces. The protracted correspondence of Ladies Mary Wortley Montagu and Mar are plain in this regard, as we will see below. Eventually these metaphors became institutionalized codes clustered around buzz words and rhetorics understood by all the parties involved. This language is most revealing to us for the way it uncovers class filiations that have become obscured over two centuries. Even more so, this dynamic *sorting out* – this renewed separation of the rich and powerful from their inferiors – precipitated a reinvigorated emulation of the higher strata by the lower classes. By mid-century it was not unusual to see those persons ascend to higher position who could invoke 'the language of the nerves' while circulating in society. One needed more, of course, than mere vocabulary to rise; but language was essential to the process. These sociolinguistic developments lie at the heart of the cults of nervous sensibility and the nervous mythologies they engendered.

Just as the upper classes sought new ways to strengthen the social distinctions between them and the rest of society as those lines became more tenuous, so too did those demarcations extend to their physical selves. The focus was the state of the body's anatomic nerves; the cure was for their 'tonic strengthening', a phrase that means little to cultural historians today unless it is decoded and glossed.[33] The concept and methods of 'tonic strengthening' baffle us even when anatomic and physiological equivalencies are taken into account. To strengthen the nerves would seem – linguistically

– to be a metonymy for toughening the character or (as North Americans might say in the vernacular) getting one's act together. In our quasi-macho, Westernized, twentieth-century culture, the nerves remain genderized and imbued with a sense of femininity. For eighteenth-century women and men, nerves were palpably real, although often metaphorized for excessive effects. To be sure, there were some who utterly condemned this fragility and its attendant nervous physiology, who claimed that nerves were not all-important; and it would be an interesting exercise in literary history, for example, to tease out the patterns of similarity among great writers (Defoe, Swift, Fielding, John Gay) who were seemingly unaffected. Yet as the century progressed, the number of untouched writers waned as the most fashionable persons, including some of the smartest readers, hastened to the consultation rooms of the great nerve doctors of the day.[34] To reiterate, there was no conspiracy or collusion in this nervous tidal wave: it swept through culture as so many other waves of the past have. To distance it and see it for what it was – this is the hardest task for the cultural historian. No wonder then that Henry Mackenzie, for example, who understood men and women of feeling as well as anyone, and who fictionalized his beliefs about the new creatures of sentiment he saw as heroic, stated in a letter to a friend very plainly: 'this is an Age of Sensibility'. So it is not surprising that Jane Austen believed she was responding to the aesthetic of an era when she endorsed it under her own imprint as a culture of 'sense and sensibility'. To think that it would *not* take its toll on the imaginative literature of the day: this remains the foible of our internalist literary historians who read at the level of the individual texts only.[35] But what is sensibility but emotion, memory, and imagination, all of which depend upon the nerves for their being? Not until Blake and the symbolists will this tide turn.

The cults of the nerve reverberated in other domains as well. Town development and urban planning were affected as much as anything else. History documents the Baths and Tunbridges, the Harrogates and Scarboroughs, all operating under ruthless schemes for gain and profit. Here, lurking everywhere, were not merely doctors and apothecaries, patients with their undiagnosed conditions, but mounds of food and drink (one cannot help noticing in this medical context to what degree this set was literally eating itself into the grave). Here, also, were pump rooms and elegant assembly halls, booksellers and musicians, architects and landscape gardeners, charities, drums, and routs: all commanding amounts of wealth. Not to have weak nerves and a delicate constitution was to be out of place in this milieu, a social misfit. Lady Luxborough (an addict of Bath, who was Bolingbroke's sister) assured her constant correspondent, the poet William Shenstone: 'my disorder . . . turned to a fever of a slow kind, chiefly nervous, attended with pains in my bowels, which, added to want of rest, have weakened me so much, that I have not yet crossed my room.'[36] Shenstone replied: 'as your Complaints are *entirely nervous*, [you] must have an undoubted tendency to further it!' His advice intended to console her for a somatic disorder. But mi'lady confessed to him on another occasion that black melancholy – an unspeakable sense of emptiness caused by vacancy and solitary, pensive thoughts – threw her into these nervous fits: 'None but the friendly Robin Red-breast soothes my ear after those sounds [of solitary pensive thoughts]: but in the *melancholy month of November, in which the English hang themselves*, I expect more pleasure than from the Robin.' The exchanges of Mrs Ralph Allen and Mrs Beau Nash – not to mention their lesser female epigoni – were similar, written in what seems a kind of code language to us now.[37] Selina, the wealthy Countess of Huntingdon, another exclusive Cheyne patient, was not much better off, sunk, as she almost always was, in nervous depressions of religious origin, even after the completion of her Methodist chapel.[38] Fiction was much the same in this as epistolary writing. In Fanny Burney's *Evelina*, the aloof young Lady Louisa Larpent despairs when her lover leaves her; Lovel (her lover) comforts her: 'Your Ladyship's constitution ... is infinitely delicate.' '"Indeed it is", cried she, in a low voice, "I am *nerve* all over!"'[39] The sign is evident even in the most ephemeral gibberish of the time. At the same time Smollett and Christopher Anstey were still at Bath in the 1760s, the silly farrago that called itself a *Register of Folly ... written by an Invalid* trivialized these ailments by personifying them in absurd couplets:

> Tho' I own I am sorry such trifles still flurry
> My Ogilby-nerves, to produce such a hurry.[40]

Other 'valetudinarian guides' then cranking out a million-pound industry provided their own versions of nervous mythology. The astonishing aspect of this 'nervous trade' was its variety, especially the different therapies claimed to have been developed for its sake. Just for the treatment of lunatics there had developed by the late part of the eighteenth century a wide and expensive repertoire, including 'bladder-filling', and the implanting of the nerves with gas; as well as 'tying down', which required the whole body to be distended and then blown up with gas. Throughout the century, however, on many levels there was opposition to such therapies as these, as well as more philosophical objections to what I am calling the mythology of nerves. Nervous mythology was criticized as merely a hoax to induce the consumption of pills and potions, doctors and diets, resorts and retreats, in a culture that was already consuming extraordinary amounts of material goods – but no substantial objections altered history's path. An anecdote, whose veracity has never been corroborated, makes the point: near the end of his life Samuel Johnson described the sense of diseased or weakened nerves as 'medical cant',[41] but the objection had no impact, as others eventually realized when later they inveighed against the trade in drugs for the nerves.

Actually, a repertoire of nervous therapies has yet to be compiled. One is needed for not merely the quack nostrums but the dozens of panaceas, ranging from what we would call health food diets (Cheyne's regimen of 'lettuce, seed, milk, and wine') and balneological treatments (whether of waters cold or hot, mineralized or sulphuric) to James Graham's celestial beds and aphrodisiac cures for the nervously sterile and barren (Sterne never took his Tristram to Bath as Austen did Lydia as a consequence of poor Tristram's flaws); and also included Mesmer's electric shocks and animal magnetisms which were calculated to stimulate even the most withered nerves of any affected person, but especially those who were rich.[42] The following are only some of the nervous nostrums that filled actual pharmacopoeias: analeptic and asafoetida pills; Anderson's drops, William Tickell's aetherial spirit and Ward's aether pills; Raleigh's confection, Bishop Berkeley's tar water, Dover's drops, Pierre Pomme's recipes, John Hill's wild valerian roots, Mrs Stephens's juleps, Backer's cure of dropsy; the more generic class of pearl and closet cordials, plain Nantz, quicksilver, calyx of zinc, acid of lemon rind, rhubarb and magnesia, not to mention hyppish medicines like extract of saturn, the most exotic of the lot (prescribed in John Goulard's 1777 *Treatise on the Effects of . . . Lead*), and tartars of mercury (discussed a few decades earlier by Malcolm Flemyng, the physician–writer already mentioned as the author of *Neuropathia*).[43]

The Social Milieu of the Nerves

It was in this cultural atmosphere and social ambiance that the literature of 'sensibility' (as men and women in the eighteenth and nineteenth centuries *themselves* called it) flowered, and if one is to understand the social history of language it is essential to be alert to its nomenclature. For the decoding of the sign is as much an analysis of the *word* as anything else. Semiological interpretation requires close linguistic interpretation viewed within the contexts of the culture: its anthropology, linguistics, sociology, history, etc. What then was this *literature of sensibility*? Whether viewed in its Smollettian version in such novels as *Ferdinand Count Fathom* (1753) or *Humphry Clinker* (1771), whose openings are set in spa locales, or in many other prose and poetic forms during the second half of the eighteenth century, the literature of sensibility broke off from its earlier forms of a hundred years earlier (in England written by Milton and Dryden, in France by Marivaux and Crebillon), and became highly medicalized. Smollett's irritable hero Matt Bramble attributes his misanthropy to 'the nerves of an invalid, surprised by premature old age, and shattered with long suffering'. His nephew Jery Melford discounts his uncle's nervous explanation and substitutes another nervous one: 'tender as a man without skin, who cannot bear the slightest touch without flinching'.[44] Bared nerves indeed! – we might say today. But if the nerves, as our contemporary physicist Victor Weisskopf has shown us while taking a very different perspective, endowed humankind with the most sophisticated communication system imaginable, they nevertheless mandated these reasserted social stratifications when the upper classes came under pressure to prove who they were. It was predictable that novelists like Smollett (a practising physician, medically trained and thoroughly conversant with the scientific debates about the nerve) would respond directly to these transformations.[45] Sterne also did in his inimitable way, as did dozens of minor novelists no longer read today.

The economic dimension of nerves and its linguistic attachments have received less attention than they deserve, considering that the pound cost of sensibility, in whatever version, was significant. The tribes of quacks who hung about the spas were countless, and even the tribe of certified doctors and apothecaries in Bath (not to mention the fashionable continental watering holes) was large and continually proliferating. These were no ordinary doctors but self-appointed and almost always untrained and unqualified shamans of the rich. When the Duchess of Northumberland returned to Sion House, having visited her cousin the Duchess of Newcastle, at Bath, she expressed surprise at 'the wigs and golden canes everywhere about the parades and crescents'.[46] Never before had she seen such an assortment of the medical tribe. For centuries, of course, there had been rich patients for doctors to treat; what differed now was the doctors' manner of diagnosing. The point is not – as some medical historians have alleged – that medical practice suddenly altered under the weight of new scientific evidence or medical theory, but that a cultural myth engulfed medical theory *itself*, privileging the nerves and exalting them as never before.

In contrast to these hordes of quacks was a flourishing tribe of the medical elite who brought status and consolation to their patients. Here the physicians' status was as important as the patients'. Bath was, to be sure, a unique resort, a singular city for the restoration of health, adorned as much by parades and squares as by crowds of patients and their pills, but even there in 1740, for example, all but three of the physicians had Oxbridge degrees, the exceptions being two from Leiden, and one – actually, Dr Cheyne himself – from Edinburgh.[47] The Bath Corporation and the hospital it regulated placed some controls on the undergrowth of quackery, but fees and therapies, and what we would call the quality of the care given, remained almost exclusively in the physicians' hands. The doctors quarrelled among themselves, and entered into paper wars calculated to raise their socio-professional status and increase their number of patients, allegedly because 'nervous diseases' were on the rise. Even the prime minister, Robert Walpole, had come to Bath to be treated 'for nerves' by the famous doctor, then president of the Royal Society, Richard Mead.[48]

The mythology of the nerves flourished and had a remarkably heightened impact in England and Scotland during the eighteenth century. Its linguistic counterpart created a vocabulary of neologisms coined in English, with the development of a new language using expressions such as tonic health, taut or flaccid nerves, fibres and animal spirits. New metaphors were loosely drawn from nerves and applied to realms far removed from medicine. A popular vernacular sprang up based on these nerves. In medical and other writing there were discourses of the nerve and the formulation of an aesthetic of nervous English prose style.

Even so, this development of 'nerves' was not an exclusively British phenomenon, emphasized as it was in this unique island culture. In Europe, nerves also flourished. For example, S.A. Tissot, the Swiss Protestant physician whose renown was due in part to his anti-masturbatory campaign, had been as explicit about the role of nerves in human life and culture as any Bath nerve doctor. His *Essai sur les maladies des gens du monde* and *Traité des nerfs et de leurs maladies* called attention to the nervous revolution, blaming on the nerves many social ills: excessive masturbation, sodomy, nymphomania, hysteria, even suicide.[49] Tissot's approach to the nerves was anthropological: he began by classifying medical conditions by nations and regions. But the symptomology he uncovered and the agenda which he set for himself was similar to that of his British medical brethren. While his works were being translated into English in the 1760s (works such as his *Essay on Diseases Incident to Literary and Sedentary Persons* [1769]), Robert Whytt, the Scottish physician and professor of medicine at Britain's most progressive university, Edinburgh, was lecturing to medical students about the crucial importance of nerves, as well as training a generation of physicians who would invade London and Edinburgh, as well as Bath and other valetudinarian haunts, in the aftermath of Cheyne. By the time the American colonies revolted in 1776, Tissot's works had been widely disseminated throughout Britain in English translation, and Whytt's name, especially as the 'nerve doctor', had become a household phrase. Tissot's account of peoples and their maladies was thought to be the authoritative medical explanation of how national types grew ill and under what anthropological conditions. His subtext was otherwise: a progression, like Adair's (about whom we shall hear more in a moment), and constituting further proof that this was not merely a Scottish phenomenon: be nervous, be fashionable, be courted, be rich. The paradigm was prescriptive – a recipe for success based on the equation of social station and anatomic destiny. *Au fond* Tissot's rhetoric had its intended effect of directing any aspiring social climber, or one already there, into 'nerves'.

Early medical anthropologist though he was, Tissot had not explained the *sociology* of the phenomenon: how nerves conceived as an ethic, or even ideology, had caught on. This was left to James Makittrick Adair, who became Cheyne's successor in Bath by the end of the century.[50] Adair was an odd mixture of erudition, experience and self-puffery. An ardent admirer of Oliver Goldsmith (whom he frequently cited and of whose Edinburgh medical education he was well aware), Adair made a reputation by writing out his hobbyhorses. These described the miseries of the natives involved in the African slave trade; the deleterious effects of crowded rooms and polluted spaces (here he was entirely original, and ought to engage the attention of modern students of cultural history much more than he has); the adverse effects of putrid air on health (of great interest to our ecologists today); and the extraordinary proliferation of female doctors and female quacks during his generation. These theories somewhat resembled the traditions of ecological learning found in 'Smelfungus' Smollett's *Humphry Clinker*. This knowledge, Adair claimed, was partly derived from his experiences in the Leeward Islands and on the island of Antigua, where he obtained high posts in medicine as well as the law. His books were not as popular as Dr Cheyne's best-selling *English Malady*, but they continued to be reprinted, as did his very popular *Essay on Fashionable Diseases*, which he brought out in 1786 and continued to reissue in altered versions until 1790. The *Essay*, discussed below, is a 260-page prose *Dunciad* of the medical world containing a mock-dedication to Philip Thicknesse, 'the Censor-General of Great Britain, Professor of Empiricism and Nostrum, Rape, and Murder-Monger to the St. James Chronicle'; a boast of having discovered the secret of Dr James's fever powders; dramatic dialogues on air pollution; castigations on Mrs Hardcastle (Goldsmith's comic mother and female quack who dowses her 'lumpkin son' in *She Stoops to Conquer*); and a mock-epic finale devoted to attacking Anton Mesmer of animal-magnetism fame.

Adair added to his mystique by launching a public attack on Phillip Thicknesse while both men were in Bath. Thicknesse was well known there and had promoted himself in ways, as well as written guides to health, to which Adair was vigorously opposed. Adair, still in Bath in the 1770s, churned out books on nervous conditions and their treatment, always emphasizing his own regimens for recovery. In actuality these were self-advertisements calculated to make him appear the discoverer – and healer – of a new province of medicine. Whether he was or not (and there is some validity to his claim that he had genuine expertise in the field), Adair stood to profit. He justified his literary productions on the partly original grounds that medicine itself was a social institution requiring new forms of analysis: 'Should any of my fashionable readers express their surprise at meeting with a dissertation on fashion in a medical essay, my reply is ready; that as medicine, as well as some other arts, is become subject to the empire of fashion, there can be no impropriety in considering by what means this has been effected.'[51]

Impropriety there was none, as historians have begun to show, but plenty of distortion. Modestly claiming that he hoped to chronicle the rise of fashionable diseases in the eighteenth century, Adair gave us descriptions that are as revelatory for our semiotic purposes in decoding the sign of the nerves as anything his forebear Dr Cheyne wrote. Always acknowledging his teacher's famous essay on nervous diseases of 1764 (Whytt's *Observations on the Nature, Causes, and Cure of those Disorders which have been commonly called Nervous, Hypochondriac, or Hysteric, to which are prefixed some Remarks on the Sympathy of the Nerves*), Adair, like Cheyne, delivered up to his readers the explanations they wanted to hear. He gave them nothing less than a recent history of the nerves in linguistic and cultural history:

Upwards of thirty years ago, a treatise on nervous diseases was published by my quondam learned and ingenious preceptor DR. WHYTT, professor of physick, at Edinburgh. Before the publication of this book, people of fashion had not the least idea that they had nerves; but a fashionable apothecary of my acquaintance, having cast his eye over the book, and having been often puzzled by the enquiries of his patients concerning the nature and causes of their complaints, derived from thence a hint, by which he readily cut the gordian knot – *'Madam, you are nervous'*; the solution was quite satisfactory, the term [nervous] became quite fashionable, and spleen, vapours, and hyp were forgotten.[52]

According to Adair, a single word – the term 'nervous' – had this potent and transformative power. Adair attributed this magic to *language* rather than to science or medicine. The 'solution' he proposed was linguistic, not medical, and in his view the *word* (in the abstract) became 'fashionable' in advance of the concept or its medical condition. But Adair also recognized the dangers of such a loaded term as 'nerves' when transformed to designate everything fashionable. The word could be abused by physicians, as well as confused by patients. Adair himself announced the degree to which he privileged the *linguistic* portion of his campaign as a 'fashionable nerve doctor'. He comments in the *Treatise on Fashionable Diseases*:

Names or terms, when improperly employed in matters of science, necessarily create confusion and error; but had this fashionable term [i.e., nerves] been productive of no untoward *practical* consequences, I should have considered any attempt to combat the idea, as unnecessary and absurd. But I have observed so many injurious effects from the adoption of this idea [i.e., of nerves], that I think it my duty to be at some pains to point out the danger of it.

This he did, while refining its taxonomies. For example, he worked out schemes of 'depraved sensibility' and 'deficient sensibility', and descriptions of the nerves in every physiological state: tonic, taut, defective, flaccid, and so forth. Moreover, his memory about the previous generation was corroborated by the linguistic history of the interim period 1760–90, in which one has to search far and wide for discussions of spleen, vapours, and hyp. Now – as he indicates – on the eve of the French Revolution all was 'nervous'. Still, the transition was not as abrupt as Adair intimates in this passage. Although spleen and vapours were forgotten among the denizens of Lady Luxborough's circle, for example, the cultural historian with his or her broader vision can see the similarities among a number of works all of which empower the nerves: Sydenham's hysteria (1690s), Mandeville's hypochondriasis (1710s), Robinson's vapours and spleen (1720s), Cheyne's 'English malady' (1730s), David Hartley's nerves vibrating according to the laws of Newtonian science (1740s), Haller's 'sensibility' and 'irritability' (1750s), Robert Whytt's 'hypochondriacal and hysteric disorders' (1760s), Andrew Wilson's medical research on the nervous origin of hysterics (1770s), and then – in the 1780s – Thomas Coe's 'bilious conditions', which he had popularized in the 1750s, and on which Adair claimed to build his own theory of fashionable nervous diseases in the 1780s.[53] But neither medical symptomology nor a glossary of linguistic transformations (from the language of the spleen and the hyp to the byzantine neologisms of 'bilious concretions' and 'bilious solids', which require whole glossaries with definitions to become intelligible to us today) makes the crucial point as much as does the concept of *fashionable disease*. For all these conditions, their names are as important to social rank as any pain suffered. A person as well known as the 'immortal Doctor Cheyne', in Pope's memorable phrase, had justified the cult and popularity of nerves to the growing progress of expanding civilizations: 'We have more nervous diseases', Cheyne wrote in the *English Malady*, 'since the present Age has made Efforts to go beyond former Times, in all the Arts of Ingenuity, Invention, Study, Learning, and all the Contemplative and Sedentary Professions.'[54]

By the 1780s, Adair had abandoned medical therapies for what he considered to be a new approach to medicine. This he plainly called 'fashion'. For him, disease was romantic, glamorous, idealized – the ultimate proof of social difference. Yet he also believed that the interpretation of disease could not remain static because taste would change, as did the geography one inhabited in an era of unprecedented social mobility. What Adair recounted about the taxonomic transformations of nervous conditions from melancholy, spleen, and hysteria to biliousness and now nerves, Dr Thomas Dover – the so-called 'quicksilver doctor', for his advocacy of the compound – had also retailed in an extraordinary passage of 1732 (a half-century earlier) about its geographical spread:

At first, the *Spleen* was said to be the entire Property of the Court
Ladies; here and there indeed a fine Gentleman was pleas'd to catch it,
purely in Complaisance to them. Soon after, Dr. *Ratcliffe* [sic] out of
his well-known Picque to the Court Physicians, persuaded an Iron-
monger's Wife of the City into it, and prescribed to her the Crying
Remedy of carrying Brick-dust; the City Physicians took the Hint; and
the Country Doctors remov'd it into the Hundreds of *Essex*, whence a
learned Academick brought it with him to *Cambridge*: Soon after it was
heard of in the Fenns of *Lincolnshire*, and it crossed the *Humber* in
1720. The Contagion [of spleen] has at last extended itself into
Northumberland.[55]

On one level Dover's delightful bagatelle amounts to little more than an
eighteenth-century version of modern communication theory, i.e. how
information spreads, even through the shires and back roads of eighteenth-
century England. On another, its infectious wit is too silly even to be
discredited and revels in the same fictive play of mind apparent in Pope's
Dunciad, as the goddess's roll-calls echo round the town. Yet this social
genealogy of spleen appears in a purportedly serious medical work, Dr
Dover's *Treatise on Hypochondriacal and Hysterical Diseases*, which aims to
explain why disease is so fundamentally genderized; the specific reasons why
men develop hypochondria and women hysteria; all in a book every bit as
didactic as Cheyne's *English Malady* or Adair's *Fashionable Diseases*. But like
theirs, Dover's book also assumes the force of the unwritten assumption
operative here: the notion that although both men and women have nerves,
female nerves are the more delicate, the more sensitive, the more in need of
tonic strengthening.

We see this unwritten paradigm about the nerves more clearly if we look
ahead to the nineteenth century, to Charcot, Breuer, and Freud. By that
time, men will be said to be as prone to hysteria as are women, not so much
out of any innate anatomic difference that translates into unavoidable
physiological process, but rather because men labour to conceal their
feelings in a different way from women. Female suppression was thought to
be different: usually of sexual desire – it will be said – and thrusting them
into a state of unavoidable hysteria. In the eighteenth century the pathologi-
cally normal body was said to allow the expression of the passions (i.e.
feelings). Cheyne's and Adair's patients are not nervous because they have
suppressed their emotions; on the contrary, all their hysteria arises out of their
bodily conditions, especially the loosening and tightening (flaccidity and
tautness of the solids and fluids) in the nervous system.[56] So the point in
both centuries is not so much that male nerves are less sensitive and fragile
than those of the female; rather that there is a fixed state of mind in each
gender from which hypochondria and hysteria arise. It is not unexpected

then that the most elusive states of mind – imagination, creativity, genius, even memory – would be medicalized under the weight of such emphasis on gender and body.

Furthermore, when many persons in the late eighteenth century were, it seems, aping the fashions of the wealthy and powerful under the need to assert class distinction, why should disease be omitted from the repertoire of methods? The phenomenon of emulating aristocracy *to this extreme degree* is itself unparalleled before the eighteenth century. Therefore, the splenetic fits of Queen Anne or the Duchess of Marlborough were duly noted, and, as we have seen, in virtually every middle-class novel of the period from Defoe to Fanny Burney, most lower-class females made it a point to observe the mannerisms of 'gentlewomen' and then emulate or pretentiously copy them, as the case might be.

What needs decoding and dismantling, then, is not merely the tone of Dr Dover's astonishing and detailed passage about the invasion of nerves into England's fens and marshes, but the embedded, unwritten assumptions that inform it. This is the genuine work of a semiology (language and culture) that hopes to retrieve the significance of particular signs within lost cultures and bestow upon them, as we have indicated, thick description. Yet the activated 'systems' of all these fashionable 'nerve' doctors – from Willis to Cheyne, from Sydenham to Mandeville, from Garth to Mead, from Haller to Tissot, from Hartley to Cullen – can never be dismantled until we can identify why these thinkers could uniformly claim, as Adair did here, that 'no part of the physiology has engaged the attention more or reaped greater consequences in our time, than the nerves.'[57] No one today wants to revert to Hazlittian 'spirits of the age' that characterized epochs often by the most simplistic of labels (an 'Age of Reason', an 'Age of Passion'), or regress to Basil Willey's 'world views' and 'world pictures'. Certainly no one should contend that this was an 'Age of Nerves', as if upper-case 'Ages' were discreet entities whose boundaries could be charted, as previous cultural historians have argued for 'Ages of Reason' and 'Ages of Passion'. But for the upper classes, much social differentiation *did* lie in the nerves, just as nervous philosophy and sympathetic reasoning resonated with meaning as a discriminating mechanism for the Adam Smiths, the Humes, and the Scottish Moralists. This same resonance caused imagination theory to become highly medicalized in the eighteenth century,[58] and, alternatively, prompted an anonymous writer in 1744 – could he have been a grub-street hack? – to think there could be a readership for a prose work he dared to title *The Anatomy of a Nervous Woman's Tongue: A Medicine, A Poison, A Serpent, A Fire and Thunder*.[59] We will soon see who this developing readership was.

The fantasies inspired by this nervous mythology also require decoding. They are as intriguing as the projects of Fellows of the Royal Society, who in an attempt to discover the essence of this vital nervous fluid tried to dissect and reproduce nerves artificially. Yet if the constellation of illnesses passing under the rubric of consumption was then thought to be the *fatal* English malady – the disease from which people actually *died* – nervous sensibility assumed a prominence because it reflected the *life force*: the vital *je ne sais quois* of the upper class; the spring of vitality and creativity that set class apart from the *hoi polloi* or rank and file, but at a price that was sometimes high: psychological misery in the form of depression, accidie, indolence, as in Thomson's mythic castle, or lassitude in the shape of the noonday demon, the waste of sloth.[60]

This version of semiological analysis brings passages to life that would otherwise remain unexamined. Mounds of writing formerly consigned to the closets of obscurity or the shades of hermeticism suddenly gather meaning. A brilliant example, though hardly obscure in this case, is the correspondence of Richardson and his female confidantes. Mrs Donnellan consoled her friend, the novelist, in words that could be another epigraph to this chapter:

> Misfortune is, those who are fit to write delicately, must think so; those who can form a distress must be able to feel it; and as the mind and body are so united as to influence one another, the delicacy is communicated, and one too often finds softness and tenderness of mind in a body equally remarkable for those qualities. Tom Jones could get drunk, and do all sorts of bad things, in the height of his joy for his uncle's recovery. I dare say Fielding is a robust, strong man.[61]

Robust, that is, unlike Richardson! This is no mere 'attempt to console Richardson for his perpetual ill-health', as Ian Watt long ago suggested,[62] or if consolation, certainly not merely a mindless comfort, but the clearest indication – the semiotic I have been attempting to identify and isolate for scrutiny – of a veritable revolution in social thinking. Mrs Donnellan's *unstated* premises are the mythologies of the age. They can be schematized and epitomized as follows:

1 The soul is limited to the brain.

2 The brain performs all its work through the nerves.

3 The more exquisite and delicate one's nerves – morphologically speaking – the greater the ensuing degree of sensibility and imagination.

4 Upper-class people are born with more exquisite nervous anatomies; the tone and texture of their nervous systems are more delicate than those of the lower classes.

5 Greater nervous sensibility makes for greater writing, greater art, greater genius.

It may be an odd sequence, alien to the pluralistic habits of mind so firmly ingrained in our late twentieth-century culture. Yet its logic was clear to the generations of men and women in England at the time of the Georges and even – in some cases – in Paris and Rome. The term which I have used, 'nerves' as a shorthand throughout this essay, was in some ways an *English* myth whose national dimension also requires much identification and analysis. If difference, in the Derridean sense, is the chief signpost of cultural semiotics, then, we may suggest, *not* to read these differences, as stated in the above sequence, may entail loss over the power of explanation. For example, the poet Pope used these self-delusive, ironic words at his death: 'I was never hyppish in my whole life.'[63] Earlier in his life, in his mature poetry, when Pope lamented 'this long disease, my life', and complained in his letters about 'this crazy constitution', his complaint indicated difference. Chronic nerves were living, anatomic emblems of gentility and delicacy: the more chronic, the greater the living evidence. There was no advantage to avoiding them, no virtue in doctors' concealing nerves from their patients or pretending they were inconsequential, as was done in the case of cancer or consumption. Philander Misaurus, an alias for a grub-street hack writing for 'females of parts' in 1720, advised them, in the already excessively metaphorical jargon of the day, that 'when sharp, fermenting Juices (not easily miscible) shall meet, and by their furious Contest, cause cruel Twitchings of your nervous Fibres; comfort your Heart, and be extreamly pleas'd.'[64] *The Honour of the Gout* is one of the wittiest satires of physicians and their ineffective remedies of the century. It abounds with ridicule and insight into medical remedies. But its language, apart from its wit, is also noteworthy, containing hundreds of technical-sounding words, many of them invented to lambast the doctors who were coining such terms as a means of keeping their unknowing patients in the dark. The language of satires like this one would repay further study, especially where the tone of certain phrases (e.g. 'vicious humours', 'pernicious spirits', 'delectable nerves') carries a loaded message to the patient. John Midriff, another fashionable nerve doctor like Dover and Adair, wrote a long book in 1720 for those 'who have been miserably afflicted with these Melancholy Disorders since the Fall of the South-Sea, and other public Stocks'.[65] But his language was more modest. Forty-eight years later, long after the emotional turbulence caused by personal economic loss in the Bubble subsided, Daniel Smith, a surgeon with deist leanings, who was also well read in Newtonian philosophy, expounded the same ideas in a medico-theological idiom: *A Dissertation upon the Nervous System to show its Influence upon the Soul.*[66] Nervous mythology was not a credo for one generation only. Its great positivistic energy was such that it has persisted through the late twentieth century, as our neurophysiological activities make evident.

To return to our Enlightenment, the physicians of the fashionable were quick to isolate 'nerves' as the cause of many disturbances in their patients, almost as if they had identified the crucial gene of ailment and distress. Indeed, the discovery of nerves was cause for celebration, as in the case of Boswell, who advertised his melancholy at home and abroad.[67] Nerves were neither the signs nor symptoms of ephemeral ilness but an inherited condition that, if undetected, would eventually surface. Inherited like wealth or milk-white skin, nerves and their fibres were unique among the organic structures: ingrained, they could neither be bought nor stolen, copied nor caught. That was why Elizabeth Carter, the brilliant letter-writer already mentioned, ministered to her ailing correspondent Catherine Talbot with the evangelism of a prophetess: 'The low spiritedness ... of which you complain, assures me you cannot be well, nor ever will be, while you have the strange imagination that a weak system of nerves is a moral defect, and to be cured by reason and argument.'[68] As we saw in the communication of Mrs Donnellan and Richardson, the sequence here is also crystalline: weak nerves are never the signs of moral defect, as Elizabeth Carter stresses, but the proof of acute discrimination and delicacy. The patient should therefore never use reason to rid herself of them, as Miss Talbot seems eager to do. Mrs Carter even psychologizes the nerves here with a corollary about concentrated activity or what her contemporaries called 'attention': 'I must enjoin you for two months to amuse yourself, and wile away the time, and be as trifling and insignificant ... and never during that time to apply to anything that requires close attention'.[69] Shades of Lady Conway and her fierce headaches in a previous generation, and the Renaissance tradition (Bacon, Sir William Temple, Addison et al.) urging sufferers not to engage in difficult mental activity requiring spans of attention if they wished to heal themselves! *Far niente*, an Italianate 'do nothing': this was the best cure for a condition whose mortal consequence was trivial. But the villain, the perfidious culprit, was attention and concentration; the same steady, close attention that invaded the nerves of literary and sedentary persons, as Tissot had shown, and caused them to become neurasthenically depressed. For those prone to the dictates of the imagination, such as scholars, writers, religious types, and romantic women, a life of focused attention was as dangerous as the worst fistula or cancerous ulceration. So the mythology went; but the reality was otherwise: Richardson did not die of focused attention any more than Carter and Talbot (or Horace Walpole for that matter) expired from the fatigue of letter writing.

Ponder the nerves though one may have in the eighteenth century, they would never *consume* the body, as did other medical conditions. Exempt from contagion, no pollution could be caught from them. 'I am genuinely relieved', exclaimed Lady Mary Wortley Montagu to her sister Lady Mar (melancholic and depressed in 1727), 'to learn that the *worst* is delicate nerves; this I can manage; the excrescences of a diseased liver, stomach, or bowels would be so much worse.'[70] In mi'lady's world 'delicate nerves' were always preferable to decaying vital organs, though organs and nerves thrived on each other. Nervous sensibility was thus a dissemination rather than a disease; an outreach whose extension was the *sine qua non* of fashion. Nerves could be excruciating, but the pain was said to be mentally lodged and never posed the threat of death to the body. Even the poets were amazed at the proximity of pain and pleasure in the nerve. Samuel Garth, the poet of *The Dispensary* and a leading physician at the turn of the eighteenth century, remarked with surprise: 'How the same Nerves are fashion'd to sustain / The greatest Pleasure, and the greatest Pain!'[71] Within this context of pain the nerves were an anti-gout; often accompanying the real gout, but much more discriminating in its victims. And the proof – in the collective fantasy – that nerves were the supreme life force of the fashionable was that nerves would never lead to death, only to the *fear* of death: *timor mortis*. These were always subtle but essential discriminations. From our vantage we wonder to what degree they were articulated, and in what ways, throughout the long eighteenth century.

An apocryphal story about Samuel Johnson's last days survives from the early nineteenth century, prominently spread out over the pages of the *European Magazine*.[72] Its veracity counts for less (it was almost certainly fabricated) than the fact that it continued to be repeated in the next century, in part because Johnson's final depression and melancholy – primarily thought to be nervous, or located in the nerves – had become so legendary by then. It relates that just a few months before his death, Johnson consulted Nan Kivel, a fashionable London physician. Johnson provided his full case history, only omitting *timor mortis*, the fear of death. Kivel seized upon the omission, to which Johnson replied: 'Alas, it is so, it is so.' To this Dr Kivel rejoined: 'I only wanted that symptom [the fear of death] to make your's a complete case of hypochondriasis, which will only require a little exertion on my part, and rather more on your's, to *entirely cure*.' Johnson soon died, not from intercostal involvement, then thought to lie in the seat of the hypochondrium, but from a combination of old age, stroke, and depression. The noteworthy aspect is Kivel's confidence in an 'entire cure' despite the diagnosis of male hypochondriasis, and the fact that Regency and Victorian readers wanted to hear the story of Johnson's last days mythologized in this way. Kivel's 'cure' assumes the complete benignity of nerves – nerves may lead to fear of death, never to death itself. The distinction was then crucial.

Other onlookers who could pierce through the mythologies of these (often crude) discourses of the nerve objected – even screamed. Sometimes they did so in an altogether different mode, as in Austen's refined assault in *Sense and Sensibility*, where the hypocrisies of the ethic of moral sensibility are exposed through the characters of the group hanging around the Dashwood women; sometimes trivially, as when a 1732 caricaturist claimed, facetiously, in an engraving 'Of the Hypp: The pleasures of melancholy and madness', that 'there are Pleasures in Madness, which the Splenetick, of all sufferers of the nerve, are least acquainted with.'[73] To those who were neither parvenus nor social climbers, nor anxious about their niche in polite society, the octopus that nervous mythology became by the late eighteenth century seemed a remote social phenomenon too difficult to be self-reflective about, let alone a scientific hypothesis to be evaluated: a cluster of concepts or ideas that neither could, nor would, impinge on them. They never grasped what the debate about nerves entailed. For the others, especially the social climbers and those who were already in high places, nerves had become a way of life, to be taken for granted, as was the language that attached to it, touching on everything important: sex, love, sanity, insanity, and – most crucially – one's social standing.

As the eighteenth century wore on, the myth intensified, as the languages and vocabularies of the literature of the latter decades reveals. Accreted to the myth eventually was a sense that the reckless and the lecherous, sometimes elided into the sensuous and the erotic, behaved as they did out of an innate propensity lodged in the nerves rather than because their nerves had grown diseased in any way. The eighteenth-century medical view was that even strong and healthy nerves were weakened and rendered 'morbidly flaccid' by lechery and late nights. Congenitally 'weak nerves' (defective from the time of birth) were weakened even more. As the body's ultimate state of health depended upon the tonic condition of the nerves above all, it followed that the high living was injurious to the body and therefore to human well-being. Historically, the fact is that conspicuous consumption of every type was also taking its toll. The upper classes in the worlds of Hogarth and Rowlandson were eating themselves into the grave; indulging their senses in lechery, and wrecking their health by late nights. The discourses of the nerve that constitute the main fabric of the mythologies I have been discussing coped with this reality of excess in a diversity of ways. They especially did so by emphasizing that 'nerves' signified no disease of passion – as nineteenth-century TB would – but were the sign of *passion itself*. Nerves and sex were thus intimately connected, as they would be in the oeuvre of the Marquis de Sade;[74] direct and concrete proof that all along one had been capable of understanding passion's kingdom. Those who were not nervous could never respond adequately to sexual desire, let alone to its unspoken substratum, conceptualized at the level of '*toujours la chose genitale*'.

This concretion of the body is what unites all the discourses of the nerve among those who pronounce upon it: Mandeville, Robinson, Cheyne, Tissot, Bienville – the entire company. The doctors' explanations reveal why: nervous persons could contract diseases with devastating somatic effects; in the myth, though, *all* their troubles were nervous, whether they were diagnosed as hyppish, splenetic, vapourish, or hysterical women in the older nomenclature, or bilious and nervous in the newer, or whether pronounced to be hypochondriacal or melancholic men. Conventional medical wisdom was that the nerves of white males were superior to those of others. White females or black and yellow males – to specify what is at stake in the generic examples – possessed nerves clearly inferior to those of white males no matter how perfect their state of health; and the fact that neither the nerves nor, obviously, the degree of their tonic strength could be seen with the naked eye counted for nothing. Physiognomy was then considered the truest universal science, precisely because it established links between the unseen and the seen, based as it was on a semiotics of the invisible. Thus the nerves of a Chinese male warrior or African Hottentot – to consult only the physical expressions of their degree of health – might ultimately take the form, respectively, of terrific physical prowess and edenic sexual fecundity; even so, their nerves were deemed to be defective in comparison to those of northern white men. The white class was thought to possess the highest potential for complete health, especially in the poised equilibrium of taut and flaccid states, and (as important) in the sheer degree of physiological sensibility within the animal spirits and fibres. The hierarchy of social class and rank within class also played a part, whether owing to aspects of racial degeneracy, or to the climate and broad geographical conditions of life. Again and again, gender, class and race determined the shape of the sign: nerves *in relation to these factors of sex, social station, and colour*. If we continued in this anatomical vein through the nineteenth and twentieth centuries, we would trace the line that extends from the Scots Enlightenment doctors – the Cullens, Whytts, and Adairs – to the Aryan supremacists in Germany: Nietzsche, Wagner, Stefan Georg, eventually the Nazis. The doctrine that anatomy is destiny takes this form among its various courses.

These ramifications about racism must be developed elsewhere. Here I have merely been attempting to demonstrate that as the middle classes at mid-century continued to demand liberty and the rabble the franchise – in suburban Middlesex and other boroughs – the upper classes increasingly aimed to set themselves apart. The social mechanisms of this separation remain to be explained by sociologists. My point is merely that nerves provided them with a convenient myth about their origins: an aristocratic model of life they could follow, one as simple as the notion that anatomy is destiny. Late in the twentieth century many of us ascribe to that notion without comprehending its origins. It was alive, of course, in the medieval and Renaissance world, but was not nationalized and systematized until the Enlightenment.

The Formation of the Nervous Personality in Cultural History

By these diverse cultural means, embodying different social practices formed in a variety of social institutions, the nervous personality of the eighteenth and nineteenth centuries gelled into a type we continue to recognize today: the idealized consumptive type; the romantic type poet or artist wasting away and eventually decaying; the neurotic genius who comes almost directly from William Cullen's lecture notes; in women, the creative Crazy Janes (as in Blake's poem) and compulsive anorexics (as in the notorious fasting woman in Tutbury, Staffordshire) who will haunt the nineteenth-century imagination. The language of the nerves also altered as these types hardened into the stereotypes.

The difficult aspect of the coagulation and the stereotype, so to speak, is not its various strands or internal contradictions, but the process of organic formation itself. It was a slow, dynamic growth extending over many decades, eventually lending credence to the belief that those who were nervous partook of a type of vitality nowhere else to be seen, even if the vitality – for example, in Bergsonian creative evolution or in the Shavian life force – itself could only be anatomically surmised. This 'principle of vitality' had been not merely medically and scientifically validated (i.e. the Enlightenment doctrines of vitalism), but also culturally grounded. Eventually the notion proved imperialistic over time so far as the domain of the nerves was concerned, extending its vast sway in the eighteenth century from the already mentioned Drs William Battie (who held that madness itself actually resided in the nerves) and Cullen (whose 'neuroses' of 1768 were the first set of classifications of nervous types),[75] to early nineteenth-century accounts claiming that overly sensitive nerves were the *sine qua non* of genius. Seen whole, this movement was a cultural wave extending from the nebulous borderlines of sanity and insanity in the Restoration (as Dryden had said in 1681, 'Great wits are sure to madness near allied'),[76] to the medicalization of the creative act under the strain of genius, and eventually to the nervous agony of creative writers like Richardson the fragile valetudinarian, Cowper the religious melancholic, and Chatterton the nervous suicide, who in their very *different* ways were inmates of an all-too-familiar prisonhouse of language: i.e. the mechanistic-materialist one dictating that nervous anatomy is destiny.

'When I was young', Théophile Gautier wrote, 'I could not have accepted as a lyrical poet anyone weighing more than ninety-nine pounds.'[77] Over a hundred years earlier, Mrs Donnellan, as we have seen, ventured to apply this angle of vision to hypochondriacal novelists like Samuel Richardson. In brief, what had been reserved for Bath's fashionable parades and England's newly developing seaside resorts, frequented by wealthy sets, became commonplace in its towns and cities by the mid-nineteenth century. For decades London had been smart in this way but not other cities. All this was now changing. Yet it would be wrong to think of the 'nervous type' as a *nineteenth*-century formation. It developed much earlier. The neurasthenic woman suffering from a myriad of female maladies – anorexia, hysteria, even dementia, among other types – certainly flowered in the nineteenth century; she was not, so to speak, born then, and the difference of her body from the male form, especially the gender differences of her nervous system, had already been fully adumbrated by the learned doctors. Somewhat paradox-ically, then, the neurasthenic woman's malady was also believed by many to be a source of her strength: what permitted her to have rhapsodic, almost magical and quasi-sexual, friendships unavailable to women with ordinary nerves. A bit later Hegel hypostatised these female 'nervous friendships' (*nervenschwachen Freundinnen*), claiming that they partook of animal magnet-ism and other magnetic phenomena. Clearly he had in mind the earlier tradition of belief about the nerves we have been recreating here: anatomical, physiological, electrical, mesmeric – traditions defined earlier than in Hegel's German academic milieu at the turn of the nineteenth century. The early nineteenth century, granted, was important in the transmission of these now hardened traditions about nerves and animal magnetism, but it did not invent them. For that, we must look to an earlier period, to its diverse discourses and iconographies. In the latter sense, if Crazy Jane and her demented sisters infused the visual imagination of Byron's and Walter Scott's society, they nevertheless appeared throughout the annals of late eighteenth-century discursive (literary as well as medical) literature.

As the nineteenth century evolved, nervous mythology altered; it was not eradicated but transformed, as it gradually became apparent that a newly constituted English aristocracy need not distance itself in these same ways any longer. Disease remained the reward, however ironically, for sin – as it was to be for Emma Bovary – not for mere neurosis or self-indulgence, and it has remained so up to our own time. Disease has been internalized and personalized in our century as all sorts of groups (not merely Christian fundamentalists) continue to claim that AIDS is the reward for promiscuity, cancer for emotional repression, heart disease for the extremes of decadence (the terror of high living once again) and lethargy (especially lack of exercise), and so forth for the major killers. Cultural historians of varied persuasions have interpreted the symbolism of disease in the last two centuries as if it existed apart from its moral dimensions, but just the opposite has more likely been the case. And it is, once again, the eighteenth-century formation of these real and imaginary maladies that remains the genuine product of the semiotics of the nerves: a domain of modern myth-making extending beyond any isomorphic system of signs and their significations, as in defective nerves signifying the want of refinement and politeness in persons thus constituted, or organic symptoms correlated to their medical taxonomies, as in the charts of eighteenth-century medical texts which relate pathological states and specific maladies. For these reasons, among others, hysteria and hypochondria became the nervous ailments *par excellence* in the Enlightenment, but imbued with equivocation and ambiguity about the relation of the seen to the unseen; and gout – hysteria's opposite and the most visible of bodily conditions – the least nervous within the broad medical panoply.

Further along these lines, hypochondria, especially among men, remained something different from the imaginary illnesses with which we automatically associate it today, something constructed socially in different ways to those in which we are prone to think of real and imagined sickness. Perhaps this is why the correspondence of Georg Christoph Lichtenberg (the distinguished professor of physics at Göttingen University who was also a prolific commentator on Hogarth's satires) and J.F. Blumenbach (the academic physiologist so crucial to the Romantic vitalist movement) seems so remote to us today. A dwarfish hunchback, somewhat resembling the poet Pope, Lichtenberg's deformity repelled more women than it attracted, and he was forever complaining to Blumenbach about a sexually induced chronic hypochondria. But the matter is not that Lichtenberg's medical condition was unusual, but that hypochondria was something other than we think. As nervous disease became more localized and specialized than it had been in the eighteenth century, upper-class 'male hypochondria' practically vanished as a topic of investigation – this under the new nineteenth-century obsession with sexuality as a regulating force, and in the belief that females, rather than males, were incarnations of the senses. The new idea was that males were subject to stress in the workplace that made them prone to a type of melancholy unknown to women, as in Charles Lamb's bizarre 'tailor's melancholy'.[78] Coupled to this male ailment were a whole series of female nervous maladies predicated on a developing science of female hysteria that would culminate in the discourses of Gilles de la Tourette, Breuer and Freud.

As TB and cholera competed with nervous ailments for attention and government subsidy, there was less spotlight on exclusively nervous conditions and hence on the older competing discourses of the nerve. Lunacy, though still essentially somatogenic, came to be seen as the higher sensitivity, especially after the reforms of Pinel, Esquirol, and Charcot; it too was partly unmoored from its former, monolithic, neurologic base. The intimate bond that had existed between the upper classes and their inherited nervous apparatus was punctured but not torn away, replaced by a new moralizing and psychologizing of illness that made disease the symbol of human character, as it remains in our time with AIDS. In the case of fatal disease – which *nervous* diseases had never been – it was a *hamartia* (fatal flaw) over which no one, high born or low, could triumph. Not even in the neurasthenic versions associated with late nineteenth-century French decadence was our nervous condition said to be morbid.[79] Proust, like Wilde and other decadents in their Franco-English milieu, linked his neurasthenia to creativity; not to be nervous and ill, he came to believe, was not to write. His long seance in bed was not so different from Wilde's compulsive retreats to the seaside, where Wilde wrote in what he perceived to be exquisite solitude, almost always ill, or at least reputedly suffering, often in bed or undressed. And Schumann's reputation we must not forget, *rose* after he threw himself into the Rhine. Neither version was so very far removed from Richardson's neurasthenic creativity, although we have constructed a mental notion that the 'rational' eighteenth century was somehow immune from these developments. But Richardson's creative condition also flourished under the distress of a nervous ailment which his physician, Dr Cheyne, could never precisely define to his inquisitive patient. The emplotments into rhetoric and utterance of these sufferings form a crucial aspect of the social history of language. And what are all these versions if not derivative from a mythology linking nerves to neuroses, anatomy to creativity, the body to social and artistic destiny?

The remainder of my story in the nineteenth and twentieth centuries has yet to be recounted. The sheer bulk of extant material offers an *embarras de richesse* for the cultural historian. Indeed, I can only suggest the shadows of its discourses here: the literally hundreds of scientific and para-scientific books written about the nerves, in relation to man and woman generically viewed, range from Thomas Trotter's *Nervous Temperament* (1807) and John Cooke's *Treatise on Nervous Diseases* (1822) in England, to Broussais's books in France in the 1820s, especially his *Traité de l'nervosité et de la folie*, a type of early nineteenth-century Foucaldian approach that stresses the discourses of nervous physiology and links the clinical nerve to its social manifestation.[80] In the nineteenth century there developed a theory of character, already evident in Jane Austen, but which also flowers in De Quincey's *English Opium Eater*, the Brontes, Melville's *Ambiguities*, and Carlyle, and which showed moral fibre to be lodged in the nerves. Already in *Mansfield Park*, when an extraordinary revelation is about to be made, Austen shrewdly narrates: 'It was not in Miss Crawford's power to talk Fanny into any real forgetfulness of what had passed. – When the evening was over, she [Fanny] went to bed full of it, her nerves still agitated by the shock of such an attack by her cousin Tom, so public and so persevered in.'[81] To the end of *Mansfield Park*, nerves hold a key to character, as they do in others of Jane Austen's novels, especially when Sir Thomas is about to pass judgement on Fanny; 'he knew her to be very timid, and exceedingly nervous.' These are no extravagant metaphoric representatives of universal anatomy but attempts to capture the thing itself – the literal nerves that have consequences for life and will hurl Austen's heroines into some of their most poignant moods.

The culture of Europe at approximately 1800 is imbued with this unspoken paradigm: from the literary representations of nerves in novels and poems to the correspondences we have already traversed; from Blake's 'Auricular Nerves of Human Life' in *The Four Zoas* to the pre-eminent role of the nerves in such disparate terrains as the relatively new discourses of lunacy (mental illness) and the science of physiognomy. The topics embraced are far-ranging, extending from the aesthetics of sympathy and empathy, from Burke in his *Sublime*, through various transformations in Novalis, Keats ('negative capability'), Jean Paul, and eventually to 'art for art's sake' and to the *Einfühlung* (i.e. empathy) that will form the basis of *fin-de-siècle* psychological aesthetics. They also include the nineteenth-century cults of blushing and tears – not merely the old sorrows of Werther, but now the new sorrows of Charlotte too (as in Charlotte Smith),[82] and the pervasive malaise and ennui such moral tears inevitably induce – a malaise and decay extending at least to the French existentialists of our century. And then there are the nineteenth-century theories of the optic nerve in relation to the painter's gaze, evident not only in Turner and the English School but in other painters as well; and the same century's aesthetics of the imagination, which follow almost predictably from the eighteenth's and which claim that Mozart's music made a more lasting impression on its listeners than all others because 'it assaulted the nerves more'; down to Coleridge's paean to the nerves as the truest sources of growth and organic form: 'They [the nerves] and they alone can acquire the philosophic imagination, the sacred power of self-intuition, who within themselves can interpret and understand the symbol, that the wings of the air-stylop are forming within the skin of the caterpillar.'[83]

These are only some of the discourses of the nerve requiring retrieval. Among the types of material that need to be culled and interpreted are nineteenth-century medical 'theories' of the affluent classes – as in Thomas Beddoes's *Hygeia: Or . . . the Personal State of our Affluent Classes* (1802–3) – which continue to promote the significance of the nerves, as well as Moritz Heinrich Romberg's famous *Nervous Diseases of Man* (1853, English translation) composed at the peak of Victorian civilization, George Miller Beard's description of neurasthenia in his now famous 1880 *Practical Treatise on Nervous Exhaustion* as the new disease of American civilization, and twentieth-century works including Abraham Myerson's *The Nervous Housewife* (1920), and the more eccentric Daniel Schreber (Freud's patient)'s *Memoirs of My Nervous Illness*. This development reaches a peak during the heyday of Bloomsbury, when Virginia Woolf claims in her diaries of the 1920s 'writing calls upon every nerve in my body to hold itself taut';[84] and Sylvia Plath revealed to Anthony Alvarez just before her death in 1962 that her suicide will be no swoon, no attempt 'to cease upon the midnight with no pain', but something both excruciating and orgiastic 'to be felt in the nerve ends and fought against' at the level of the nerve tips.[85] Some soldiers and politicians also experienced the harrowing pain at that level. Long before Woolf and Plath commented on these matters. Edward Gibbon, the historian of Rome, speculated about damaged nerves. He wrote to Lord Sheffield, as the *ancien régime* was crumbling, that 'a Tour to the Continent would be the best medicine for the shattered nerves of a soldier and politician.' Furthermore, everyone knows, and moreover many quote, the old saw that the nineteenth century witnessed the growth and flowering of psychology. It is much less often said that it was also a century *par excellence* of neurophysiology, in which the discourses of the nerve reached their fullest maturity under research programmes as diverse as laboratory experiment and rational positivism. If, however, one divides the century into waves of growth and development in this regard, a good case awaits mounting that a second wave, so to speak, developed when Charles Darwin and other zoologists elevated these same nerves in their phylogenetic studies of the emotions of animals, thereby returning us to our physicist Victor Weisskopf, who views the nervous system with a geochemical gaze and who sees its aesthetic impulse and influence spread over geological time.

There is, of course, an opposition to each of these cultural movements – a counter-culture, as it were, which has not been explored here for reasons of space, extending from Mary Wollstonecraft, who denounces nervous women in *The Rights of Woman* as useless creatures who accomplish nothing, to all sorts of moralists, like Carlyle and Emerson, who see, in these nineteenth-century nervous mythologies and nervous discourses running wild, no hope for the progress of culture. But the movement is there none the less: pervasive, encoded in both verbal and iconographic discourses, ultimately indelible. Eventually it will have to be studied, if for no other reason than that neurophysiology, now in such a positivistic and imperialistic phase, continues to claim to have made such strides in our own time.[86]

Conclusion

The sketch provided in this chapter needs to be charted in much greater detail, with more attention paid to context and to the linguistic manifestations of these developments. But let me conclude on a note about significance: the significance of this story, the significance of these different discourses of the nerve, and the crucial matter of explaining why I have privileged these discourses over others. The contradictions of the nerve story are obvious: no inner logics, no agreement among themselves, only obeisance to the mythologies of social class, a type of social determinism of cultural practices and arrangements. Equally significant are the discursive practices of these narratives. Previously, we have viewed these discursivities in isolation: as the narratives of literature, the narratives of science, the narratives of history, and so forth, without viewing them comparatively.[87] And however distinct these discursive narratives, we have usually viewed them from *within* rather than without: that is, as insiders rather than outsiders; as practitioners or critics of the distinct narratives of literature, of science, of history, and so forth, with the consequence that we have lost the outsider's gaze, whose perspective can be the more acute by reason of distance, balance, objectivity, sturdiness. So that those who are most familiar with the discursive practices of literature, for example, might actually see deeply into the narratives we have called science, and historians into the narratives commonly reserved for the literary critic's eye. Nor have we comparatively studied allusions and tropes common to all these narratives, to establish, as it were, a grammar of allusions, common to all the various discursive narratives.

But another essay, perhaps several others, would be required to interpret the social processes I have been discussing, especially the dynamics of class formation, and the antagonisms of the upper and lower classes, just as another chapter would be needed to evaluate the theoretical models best suited to this material. But most of all, the discourses of the nerve are significant for embedding the deepest so-called scientific and metaphysical questions of the last hundred years: what is the universe, what is human life, what are mental processes? Can mental processes operate without a body? What is a computer? What is the body of a computer? Can a computer think for itself, feel, make love, use its imagination, grieve? What is artificial intelligence? What is sexual desire, sexual attraction, sexual orientation? All these questions have been asked in our century within the context of biology. But more recently, and as the new biology, psychology, and sociobiology have shown themselves to rely on an even more fundamental neurophysiology, the deepest of these questions would all seem to have neurophysiological underpinnings. These developments demonstrate why the action, so to speak, and heat in science today (especially the trends in funding) lie at the juncture of neurophysiology and computer science, the points of reference where one can explore questions about mental processes operating without a body. And perhaps this is why the human body itself, and its various discourses, have been so predominantly privileged in the last few decades. Indeed, no set of discourses has been more emphasized than those of the body: isolating their tropes and metaphors as well as their cultural referents and comparative allusions.

Neurophysiology did not spring full-blown, as if from Athena's head, in the twentieth century. It has an older legacy, especially in the seventeenth and eighteenth centuries. In the face of this ancient but nevertheless somewhat contradictory discourse of the nerve, my own sense of awe takes over. I find myself bewildered at the idea of our contemporary neurophysiologists that for us humans there is only nerve and brain, and nothing *but* nerve and brain; a notion with which the eighteenth century would not have found itself entirely uncomfortable. Let us see why. To think that in the most abstract and non-referential discourse of all – classical music – that even there, and especially in its performance and interpretation, there should be brain and nerve primarily: this is what confounds. Some would say brain and nerve *only* – just. Can we really believe that the late Vladimir Horowitz performing classical music – Scarlatti, Schumann, Chopin, Rachmaninoff – is nothing but an extraordinary nerve machine? This is the question. Perhaps in the end the newly positivistic neurophysiologists and research physicists have a point: 'nerves' have perhaps been the greatest gift of all. It may be so, but it remains an odd position when viewed outside Weisskopf's geological time. More locally, viewed within the frame of a few generations, I find myself rebelling against this position and constantly arguing that there must be more. I have been claiming here that our counterparts in the Enlightenment were as baffled as we are today, even if their own positions appear to be more solidly positivistic. As Andrew Wilson had said: 'nerves are in short, the whole form in the fountain of life'.

NOTES

This essay was originally delivered in a much shorter version at the Aberdeen Conference on Cultural History in July 1987 under rigid constraints of time, and the reader will soon see that my style abounds in ellipticisms (where possible two words instead of ten). I have allowed this version to stand rather than reconstruct the essay along new lines. Each style – the oral and the written – obviously has its advantages, and I trust that readers expecting a more formal and discursive version than this somewhat oral one will forgive whatever infelicities have crept in to this version. The relation of orality (especially oral theory) to the nervous physiology developed here is interesting in itself.

1   Victor Weisskopf, *Knowledge and Wonder: The Natural World as Man Knows It* (Cambridge, Mass.: MIT, 1979), p. 220.
2   Ibid., p. 264.
3   Ibid.
4   Ibid., p. 265.
5   Ibid.
6   Ibid.
7   For nerves and the ancients see: Friedrich Solmsen, 'Greek Philosophy and the Discovery of the Nerves', *Museum Helveticum*, 18 (1961): 150–67; Walther Riese, *A History of Neurology* (New York: MD Publications, 1959).

8 *Annual Register*, III (1766): 234. For the anatomical revolution created by Willis see Robert G. Frank, *Harvey and the Oxford Physiologists* (Berkeley, Cal., and Los Angeles: University of California Press, 1980) and the same author's chapter on Willis in G.S. Rousseau (ed.), *The Languages of Psyche: Mind and Body in Enlightenment Thought* (Berkeley, Cal., and Los Angeles: University of California Press, 1990). P. Camporesi, *The Incorruptible Flesh: Bodily Mutation and Mortification in Religion and Folklore* (Cambridge: Cambridge University Press, 1988) and *Bread of Dreams: Food and Fantasy in Early Modern Europe* (Chicago: University of Chicago Press, 1989).

9 An extended note on the historiography of nerves provides a much-needed perspective here. As the seventeenth and eighteenth centuries evolved, nerves played an increasingly prominent role in all sorts of research agendas, including those of the laboratory as well as in more logocentric projects, as I tried to demonstrate over a decade ago in 'Nerves, Spirits and Fibres: Toward the Origins of Sensibility', in R.F. Brissenden (ed.), *Studies in the Eighteenth Century* (Canberra: The Australian National University Press, 1975), pp. 137–57. My point, then and now, has been that there was a progression from nerves to the cults of sentiment and sensibility, and that European Romanticism could not have occurred without this sequence. It is, to be sure, a diachronic theory, and nowhere have I ever maintained that nerves and sensibility were *the* (superlative) cause of Romanticism. In this essay, I attempt to show more fully than previously the roles of the nerves in cultural history. But see also, for a medical historian's view of the subject, George Rosen, 'Emotion and Sensibility in Ages of Anxiety: A Comparative Historical Review', *American Journal of Psychiatry*, 124, 6 (1967): 771–84.

Sensibility has had, of course, its own historiography, although it has been a scanty one, carved up by specialist disciplines, never gazed at sturdily or synoptically; see, in reverse chronological order: John Mullan, *Sentiment and Sensibility* (Oxford: Clarendon Press, 1989), an erudite book filled with interesting ideas about the language of feelings but fatally marred by a tenacious and inexplicable refusal to recognize the importance of medicine and physiology in the formation of sentimental vocabulary; L.I. Bredvold, *The Natural History of Sensibility* (Detroit: Wayne State University Press, 1962); Caroline Thompson, 'Sensibility', *Psyche*, xv (1935): 46–161; and, for lexical critiques of the word, E. Erämetsä, *A Study of the Word 'Sentimental' and of other Linguistic Characteristics of Eighteenth-Century Sentimentalism in England* (Helsinki: Suomalaisen Tiedeakatemian toimituksia, 1951), and Raymond Williams, *Keywords: A Vocabulary of Culture and Society* (London: Fontana 1976), pp. 235–8. There has not even been a bibliographical survey of *primary* works, such as Joanna Heywood's *Excessive Sensibility* – a tradition enduring into the nineteenth century that included such famous novels as Austen's *Sense and Sensibility*.

These traditions would actually require a book to adumbrate properly, especially in relation to the scientific movement, and more specifically to the rise and dissemination of mechanism then, but some important primary foci include: the works of Thomas Willis during the Restoration; later on, *c*1705–20, the Boyle Lectures; in the 1750s, see Richard Barton, *Lectures in*

Natural Philosophy, Designed to be a Foundation (1751); Albrecht von Haller, 'Elementa Physiologiae Corporis Humanae', in Shirley A. Roe (ed.), *The Natural Philosophy of Albrecht von Haller* (New York: Arno Press, 1981). Important secondary work includes: Edwin Clarke, 'The Doctrine of the Hollow Nerve in the Seventeenth and Eighteenth Centuries', in Lloyd G. Stevenson and Robert P. Multhauf (eds), *Medicine, Science, and Culture: Historical Essays in Honor of Owsei Temkin* (Baltimore: Johns Hopkins University Press, 1968), pp. 123–41; Theodore M. Brown, 'From Mechanism to Vitalism in Eighteenth-Century English Physiology', *Journal of the History of Biology*, 7 (1974): 179–216; F.W.P. Dougherty, 'Nervenmorphologie und -physiologie in den actziger Jahren des 18. Jahrhunderts', *Göttinger Beitrag zur Forschung und Theorie der Neurologie in der vorgalvanischen Ara; Gehirn-Nerven-Seele, Anatomie und Physiologie im Umfeld Soemmerrings* (Soemmerring-Forschungen III, Stuttgart: Gustav Fischer, 1987), pp. 286–312; Jacob Bronowski, 'A Sense of the Future: Essays in Natural Philosophy', in Rita Bronowski and Piero E. Ariotti (eds), *The Visionary Eye; Essays in the Arts, Literature and Science* (Cambridge, Mass.: MIT Press, 1978); and – in relation to the sciences of man – S. Moravia, 'From *Homme Machine* to *Homme Sensible*: Changing Eighteenth-Century Models of Man's Image', *Journal of the History of Ideas*, 39 (1978): 45–60, and the same author's *Filosofia e scienze umane nell 'eta dei lumi* (Florence: Sansoni, 1982). Even the Swiss professor of philosophy and philology at the University of Basel during this period, Samuel Werenfels, whose writings were influential for rhetoric and style in England, develops a programme that includes 'nervous science' in discussions of the rhetoric of sublimity; see, for example, his *Discourse of Logomachys, or Contraversys [sic] about Words* ... (1711).

But the agenda was not limited to natural science; it was also evident in the arts (as in Daniel Webb's *An Inquiry into the Beauties of Painting* [London: 1760], where the nervous system is discussed in relation to art, pp. 9ff.), and in music (as in Richard Browne's *Medicina Musica: Or a Mechanical Essay on the Effects of Singing, Musick, and Dancing, on Human Bodies* [1729]). Guichard Duverney, a late seventeenth-century French anatomist who made the ear his area of expertise, believed the organ of hearing among humans to be the most divine and for this reason the most capable of receiving music therapy; he also believed the nerves in the ear to have been constructed more subtly by the diety, thus prompting 'Men and Birds to excite one another to sing'; see *A Treatise of the Organ of Hearing* (1737; originally pub. 1683), pp. 88. This agenda was also evident in theories of acting and dancing (as in John Hill's *The Actor* [1750]), as well as in theories about the branches of government and political economy (as evident in Adam Smith's discourses). For nerves and theories of acting, see George Taylor, '"The Just Delineation of the Passions": Theories of Acting in the Age of Garrick', in Lloyd G. Stevenson and Robert G. Multhauf (eds), *Essays on the Eighteenth Century English Stage* (London: Johns Hopkins University Press, 1972). This widely disseminated agenda was a cultural development of the Enlightenment whose ideology and influence we have yet to take stock of. A sense of its breadth is found discussed – most perceptively and intuitively – in Christopher Lawrence, 'The Nervous System and Society in the Scottish Enlightenment', in Barry Barnes and Steven Shapin (eds), *Natural Order: Historical Studies of Scientific Enlightenment* (Beverly Hills: Sage Publications, 1979), pp. 19–40. Even so, Lawrence merely scratches the surface; much more remains to be done outside the local confines of eighteenth-century Edinburgh.

Even the novice reading through these diverse discourses of the nerve soon realizes that the nerves were genderized throughout this period, especially as discourses about the nature of women's bodies developed; see, for example, Edward Shorter, *A History of Women's Bodies* (Harmondsworth: Penguin, 1983). The means by which nerves became genderized – male nerves taking one set of attributes, female ones another, more delicate, if hysterical version – also would require another essay, if not a book in itself. Suffice it to comment here that as theories developed separating the genders further and further, and accounted for all types of hermaphrodites and monsters, as well as sexual deviants (in our anachronistic language homosexuals and lesbians), the nerves were thoroughly implicated, and it is equally inconceivable to imagine Enlightenment discourses of these anatomical types without discussion of the nerves. By mid-century a physician such as J. Raulin could maintain in his *Traité des affections vaporeuses du sexe* (Paris: 1758) that nervous disorders were limited entirely to the female sex; over a century later, Albert Moll, a German doctor, claimed in his treatise, *Berühmte Homosexuelle: Grenzfragen des Nerven- und Seelenlebens* (Wiesbaden: Bergmann, 1910), p. 11, no. 75, that the etiology of homosexuality in both genders was caused by defective, degenerating nerves entirely. The nerves, then, were anything but delimited in their perceived ability to account for the generation of physiological and psychological types.

The recent neurophysiological critique of nerves is more idealistic and positivistic; i.e. claiming that neurophysiology explains everything, and thoroughly confident in the view that no other set of explanations, either mental nor physical, can compete with it. See, for example: John Eccles, *The Neurophysiological Basis of Mind* (Oxford: Clarendon Press, 1953); E. Graham Howe, *Invisible Anatomy: A Study of Nerves, Hysteria and Sex* (London: Faber and Faber, 1955); Walther Riese, *A History of Neurology* (New York: MD Publications, 1959); I.H. Burn, *The Automatic Nervous System* (Oxford: Blackwell, 1963); J. Spillane, *The Doctrine of the Nerves* (Oxford and New York: Oxford University Press, 1981); *Historical Aspects of the Neurosciences: A Festschrift for Macdonald Critchley* (New York: Raven Press, 1982); E. Clarke and L.S. Jacyna, *Nineteenth-Century Origins of Neuroscientific Concepts* (Los Angeles: University of California Press, 1987).

10   Mind–body dualism was still in its post-Cartesian flowering: being massively attacked on all sides, but still far from overthrown. The most bewildering physical and metaphysical question debated then was whether the nerves were inherently a part of mind (soul) or body, or some substance in between, and there was no agreement about the proper method of asking and answering this question. There was also (*c*1700–80) a vast, developing discourse of the nerves in relation to mental faculties, passions, and insanity, and to the specific role the nerves played in pathological states. For the dualism of mind and body, see L.J. Rather, *Mind and Body in Eighteenth-Century Medicine* (Berkeley, Cal., Los

258   G. S. ROUSSEAU

Angeles and London: University of California Press, 1965) and M.D. Wilson, 'Body and Mind from the Cartesian Point of View', in R.W. Rieber (ed.), *Body and Mind: Past, Present and Future* (New York: Academic Press, 1980). The most thorough treatment is found in G.S. Rousseau (ed.), *The Languages of Psyche: Mind and Body in Enlightenment Thought* (Berkeley, Cal., and Los Angeles: University of California Press, 1990), whose bibliography of primary and secondary works should be consulted for nerves as well. For 'vital spirits' and vitalism, see particularly: Jacques Roger, *Les Sciences de la Vie* (Paris: NRF, 1963); A.A. Cournot, *Materialisme, Vitalisme, Rationalisme,* ed. Claire Salomon-Bayet (Paris: Librairie Philosophique J. Vrin, 1979); Richmond Wheeler, *Vitalism – Its History and Validity* (London: H.F. and G. Witherby Ltd, 1939); John W. Yolton, *Thinking Matter: Materialism in Eighteenth-Century Britain* (Minneapolis: University of Minnesota Press, 1983). For the body in relation to this dualism see: Jonathan Benthall, *The Body Electric: Patterns of Western Industrial Culture* (London: Thames and Hudson, 1976); Francis Barker, *The Tremulous Private Body: Essays on Subjection* (New York: Methuen, 1984); Bryan Turner, *The Body and Society* (Oxford: Basil Blackwell, 1984).

11   The argument from nature, more locally from anatomy and physiology, was made many times, with reference to both genders and under virtually every type of ideological banner, conservative and radical, and in practically every political shade then available. A conventional example is found in William Derham's *Creation of the World* (1712), one of the Boyle Lectures, and in the next generation in the physician-philosopher David Hartley's influential *Observations on Man, his frame . . .* (1749), containing 'pt. 1: Observations on the frame of the human body and mind, and on their mutual connexions and influences'; but there were others. In general, the clergy were especially quick to claim that defective nerves, often arising from a diseased religious melancholy, would lead to morbid hypochondria and hysteria, about which more will be said later. As late as the 1760s R.J. Boscovich, the philosopher of science, was inquiring about the role played by nerves within the human organism's functioning (see his *Theory of Natural Philosophy* [Venice: 1763]), and in the 1780s the Catholic apologist Laurent François Boursier was still explaining how those who had fallen from grace through sin also fell into convulsions through the explicit deterioration of their nerves; see his *Mémoire théologique sur ce qu'on appelle les secours violens dans les convulsions* (Paris: 1788).

12   For the generalized view, see Herbert Thursten, *The Physical Phenomenon of Mysticism* (1950). There remains no study of what I label 'the tradition of counter-nerve', embodied in the critiques – especially through the trope of analogy (*analogia*) – of the mechanistic approaches to the nerves developed by Paracelsus and van Helmont through Swedenborg, Blake, Ebenezer Sibley (in *A Key to Physic, and the Occult Sciences: Opening to Mental View, the System and Order of the Interior and Exterior Heavens; The Analogy betwixt Angels, and Spirits of Men* [1794]) and eventually Carlyle; a post-Rabelaisian world of jumbled discourses rather than social structures, culled from competing disciplines – some anti-scientific, others not – which Bakhtin would have well understood if he had stumbled upon the discourses. This 'tradition of counter-nerve' encouraged the hysteria induced by incubi and succubi, that dark, spectral,

night-time world of ghouls and ghosts that threw the anatomical nerves into fits and convulsive paroxysms; for a detailed tour through this terrifying domain see John Bond, *An Essay on the Incubus, or Night-Mare* (London: Wilson and Durham, 1753).

For some sense of this tradition of counter-nerve before the seventeenth century, see Brian Vickers, *Scientific and Occult Mentalities in the Renaissance* (Cambridge: Cambridge University Press, 1984). It is a tradition that flowered throughout Europe, as rich and diverse (if not empirically predictive) as that of the nerves. For example, De Valmont, a French speculator, produced a long *Dissertation sur les Maléfices et les Sorciers selon les principes de la théologie et de la physique, où l'on examine eu particulier l'etat de la fille de Tourcoing* (Tourcoing: 1752), dealing with witchcraft in relation to nervous physiology, and there were others throughout the period who continued to believe that the nerves could be manipulated in supernatural ways: alchemically, zodiacally, nutritionally, demonically. Throughout the long nineteenth century, there were attempts to retrieve this critique, as in Richard Robert Madden (the author of a best-selling Victorian book about nightmares, Gothic illusions, dreamlike monsters, male *couvade* – the entire spectral night-time world)'s 'Nervous States-Inspired Religious Vision', in his *Phantasmata or Illusions and Fanaticisms of Protean Forms*, 2 vols (1857), 2: 517, and in Walter Cooper Dendy (the Sussex surgeon who also wrote poetry and travel literature)'s 'Fantasy from Sympathy with the Brain', in his *Psyche: A Discourse on the Birth and Pilgrimage of Thought* (1845), pp. 115–16. The most serious attempt to retrieve counter-nerve was made at the turn of this century by a French physician, Lucien Nass, who ransacked the closet of history to discover what extreme convulsive states had done to figures of the past; see his *Les Névroses de l'histoire* (Paris: 1908), a book as mystical as it is scientific.

13   Looking at its empirical dimensions we can now see, in hindsight, that this was nothing less than the history of the anatomy and physiology of the eighteenth century, as Jacques Roger showed long ago in *Les Sciences de la Vie*.

14   Cullen, *Vitalism* (1750); see also n. 75. The role played by the nerves in the Enlightenment debates over racism was considerable and should not be minimized by scholars interested in the eighteenth-century discourses of sex, race, and gender. For one development, see G.S. Rousseau, 'Le Cat and the Physiology of Negroes', in Harold Pagliaro (ed.), *Racism in the Eighteenth Century* (Cleveland: The Case Western University Press, 1973), pp. 369–87. The nerves were especially crucial in these debates; for example, R.C. Dallas, writing a *History of the Maroons*, 2 vols (1803), adjudged that Negroes could never be integrated into 'cold climes' because their nerves and fibres could not withstand 'the pinching of frost' (I: 200–1).

15   See Maureen McNeil, *Under the Banner of Science: Erasmus Darwin and his Age* (Manchester: Manchester University Press, 1986), and Peter Morton, *The Vital Science: Biology and The Literary Imagination 1860–1900* (London: Allen and Unwin, 1984) for discussion of the nerves in Darwin's works.

16   Such prolific commentators on nerves in relation to health as Nicholas Robinson, George Cheyne, and Robert Whytt had much to say on this subject. For Robinson, see: *A New System of the Spleen, Vapours, and Hypochondriack*

Melancholy; Wherein all the Decays of the Nerves, and Lownesses of the Spirits are Mechanically Accounted for. To which is Subjoined, a Discourse upon the Nature, Cause, and Cure of Melancholy, Madness, and Lunacy (1729), and *A New Theory of Physick and Diseases, Founded on the Principles of the Newtonian Philosophy* (1729). John Purcell's *Treatise of Vapours, or, Hysterick Fits* (London: J. Johnson, 1707) and Sir Richard Blackmore's *Treatise of the Spleen and Vapours: or Hypochondriacal and Hysterical Affections, with Three Discourses in the Nature and Cure of the Cholic, Melancholy,a nd Palsies. Never before Published* (London: J. Pemberton, 1725) were among the first to coin a repertoire of neologisms based on the nerves. Study of this newly emerging vocabulary in the first quarter of the eighteenth century would repay the effort. A sense of its dense metaphoricity is found in Donald Davie, *Science and Literature 1700–1740* (London: Sheed and Ward, 1964). The classic study of melancholy remains R. Klibansky, Erwin Panofsky and Fritz Saxl, *Saturn and Melancholy* (London: Nelson, 1964).

17   Some idea of the range of this application in biology is found in Brian Easlea, *Witch Hunting, Magic and the New Philosophy* (Hemel Hempstead: Harvester Wheatsheaf, 1980), esp. ch. 4; Shirley A. Roe, *Matter, Life and Generation: Eighteenth-Century Embryology and the Haller-Wolff Debate* (Cambridge: Cambridge University Press, 1981), and the same author's 'John Turberville Needham and the Generation of Living Organisms', *Isis* 74 (1983): 159–84; C.U.M. Smith, *The Problem of Life: An Essay in the Origins of Biological Thought* (New York: Wiley, 1976).

18   England and Scotland did not practise a tradition requiring medical students to produce a Latin medical dissertation as did the continental universities, but many medical treatises dealing with the nerves were, nevertheless, written in English; as, for example, David Bayne's *New Essay On the Nerves* (1738), or a generation later John Hill's (he was the notorious Renaissance man of mid-Georgian England sometimes publicly known as the 'Inspector' or the quack Dr Hill) *Construction of the Nerves* (1768). In Germany, a spectacular medical treatise about the nerves, not originally written as a university medical dissertation, was J.F. Isenflamm's *Versuch einiger praktischen Anmerkungen über die Nerven zur Erläuterung verschiedener Krankheiten derselben, vornehmlich hypochondrischer und hysterischer* (Autälle: 1774). The Dutch, who produced the largest number of medical dissertations after the Germans, poured forth thesis upon thesis dealing with the bile in relation to nervous disorders, as in T.W. Gartzwyler's *De bile atra, ejusque effectibus* (Leyden: 1742). In Italy, many medical works on the nerves also appeared, such as Giovanni Giacinto Vogli's *Fluidi nervei historia* (Padua: Julii Borzaghi, 1720).

19   See Malcolm Flemyng, *Neuropathia: sive de morbis hypochondriacis et hystericis* (1740). Flemyng, who was obsessed with mechanistic and vitalistic questions about the nerves, had also written 'A New Critical Exam of an Important Passage in Locke's *Essay on Human Understanding* to which is added, an extract from the fifth book of anti-Lucretius, concerning the same subject . . .' (1751), John Armstrong, another physician who (like Flemyng) also wrote poetry, produced *The Art of Preserving Health* (1744), a long didactic poem teaming with images of nerves, spirits, and fibres.

20   See Samuel Beckett's tropes of nervous laughter in his plays.

21   In James Makittrick Adair's *Medical Cautions for the Consideration of Invalids . . . Containing Essays on Fashionable Diseases* (Bath: R. Cruttwell, 1786). Adair, M.D., was a member of the Royal Medical Society, as well as Fellow of the College of Physicians in Edinburgh. The *Medical Cautions* also continued to be reissued by Dodsley in London, as it was a bestseller.

22   See John Evelyn, *The History of Religion*, 2 vols (London: H. Colburn, 1850), 2: 281. The 'nervous style' in English prose is discussed below in n. 41. Suffice it to say here that it had roots in Port Royal Grammar and in Ben Jonson's 'full-blooded style', whose rhetorical components were correlated to the anatomical organs; but in Jonson style is skittish and fickle and can meander any sexual way – male or female – whereas the aesthetics of nervous prose during the Enlightenment always mandated its masculinity.

23   For the body politic as a phrase and concept in English, see David Armstrong, *Political Anatomy of the Body* (Cambridge: Cambridge University Press, 1983); Martha Banta, 'Medical Therapies and the Body Politic', in Jack Salzman (ed.), *Prospects, An Annual of American Cultural Studies* (Cambridge: Cambridge University Press, 1985); John O'Neill, *Five Bodies: The Human Shape of Modern Society* (Ithaca, NY: Cornell University Press, 1985); and John Blacking, 'The Anthropology of the Body', in John Blacking (ed.), *ASA Monographs* (London and New York: Academic Press, 1977), Monograph 15: 19–21.

24   See John Lowde, *A Discourse concerning the Nature of Man . . . both in his Natural and Political Capacity* (London: 1694).

25   John Hill, *The History of a Woman of Quality; or, the Adventures of Lady Frail* (London, 1751), p. 76. A vocabulary of words originating as technical terms in anatomy, which later lost their technical usage and became common household terms, begs for study. These include: tension, corruption, excitation, delicacy, irritation, sensibility. Indeed, much of the vocabulary of the School of Taste, in the period from Reynolds to Wordsworth, appropriated this technical anatomical language for its own aesthetic purposes.

26   This idea has been revolutionary in our time and cannot be discussed in detail here; but see Bruno Latour, *Science in Action: How to Follow Scientists and Engineers through Society* (Cambridge, Mass.: Harvard University Press, 1987); and Pierre Bourdieu, *Distinction: A Social Critique of the Judgement of Taste* (London: Routledge and Kegan Paul, 1984).

27   The close tie between suicide and nerves was constantly then noticed, especially as applicable to the situation of persons in high rank and class. Later on, in the 1770s, as sentimental cults were more dispersed, and as increasingly more persons aped the habits of the great, suicide grew more common, its etiology and dynamic changing as well. In France, J.P. Falret called suicide a class malaise in *De l'hypochondrie et du suicide. Considérations sur les causes, sur le siége et la traitement de ces maladies, sur les moyens d'en arreter les progrés et d'en prévenir le dévelopement* (Paris, 1822). The social history of suicide in the Enlightenment remains to be written.

28   For whatever complex reasons, the feminists have not explored this aspect of Richardson's masterpiece, although they have understood so much else about it. A broad approach is found in Catherine Gallagher and Thomas Lacqueur (eds), *The Making of the Modern Body* (Berkeley, Cal., and Los Angeles:

University of California Press, 1986); see also Ann van Sant's forthcoming study of sensibility and the novel (Cambridge: Cambridge University Press, 1991) and n. 9 above.

29   See Adam Smith, *Theory of Moral Sentiments* (Edinburgh: 1759).

30   James Makittrick Adair, *Essays on Fashionable Diseases* (1786). Adair thought he had discovered the principle underlying the sociology of medicine in his time when he wrote (p. 3) that 'medicine is become subject to the empire of fashion', and on p. 4 that '*Fashion* has long influenced the great and opulent in the choice of their physicians, surgeons, apothecaries, and midwives; but it is not so obvious how it has influenced them also in their *choice* of their *diseases*.' The point is crucial and forms a theme of this chapter. For Cheyne see ns 47, 50; for his diets see Hillel Schwartz, *Never Satisfied: A Cultural History of Diets, Fantasies, and Fat* (New York: Free Press, 1986), p. 350; for his rhetoric, prophecy, and millenarianism, G. S. Rousseau, 'Medicine and Millenarianism: Immortal Doctor Cheyne",' in Ingrid Merkel and Allen Debus (eds), *Hermeticism in the Renaissance: A Festschrift for Dame Frances Yates* (Washington, DC: Folger Shakespeare Library, 1985), pp. 192–230.

31   In the theoretical sense that semiotics provides the deepest clue to the concept of the 'fibre' (here one wants to say 'nerve-centre', except for the obvious inaccuracy) of a culture; see Tzvetan Todorov, *The Conquest of America* (New York: Harper and Row, 1985). Good work in this semiotic vein that is also particularly germane to the cultural history of the Enlightenment is found in Sylvain Auroux, *La Semiotique des encyclopedistes: Essai d'epistemologie historique des sciences du langage* (Paris: Payot, 1979).

32   Henrietta Knight [Lady Luxborough], *Letters of Lady Luxborough . . . to the poet William Shenstone* (London: J. Dodsley, 1775).

33   'Tonic strength' then denoted the degree of essential health of the nerves, its opposite being a state of morbid weakness, but there were many synonyms, common usages, and metaphoric abbreviations (for example, exquisite delicacy) applied linguistically as well. By the 1730s a dense metaphoric jungle of words describing this constellation – both healthy and diseased – had arisen. in his dialogical *Treatise of the Hypochondriack and Hysterick Diseases* (1711) Mandeville often inquires about the meaning of the 'tonic strength' of the nerves; see pp. 160, 172; later on John Armstrong versified some of the same ideas of tonic strength in his long didactic poem, *The Art of Preserving Health* (1744). More recently, the late Raymond Williams has teased out some of the extended metaphors of sensibility in *Keywords*, pp. 235–8, but without referring to the great nervous underbelly – anatomically and metaphorically – of the development. If he had, he would have discovered a rich untapped vocabulary of phrases such as tonic strength, essential tension, exquisite tautness, and many others, which were originally medical, but which by mid-century had passed into common parlance as part of the diverse cults of sensibility, about which more is said below. Moreover, tonic strength of the nerves was believed by many of the so-called 'nerve doctors' to be seasonal, producing the most 'tonic period' in the spring and summer, when nerves could enjoy the benefits of the six non-naturals (exercise, diet, good air, sleep, regular evacuation, the passions); their worst as the leaves were falling, under cold, grey, dank skies;

see the medical exposition of this theory in Andrew Wilson, MD, *Short Remarks on Autumnal Disorders of the Bowels* (Newcastle upon Tyne: J. White and T. Saint, 1765).

34   The great nerve doctors of the day, including such well-known authors, in England, as Thomas Willis, perhaps the first physician to recognize that the nerves merited more attention than they had ever been given; Thomas Sydenham, important for his theory of hysteria, as well as his generally empirical approach to nervous disorders; Bernard Mandeville; George Cheyne, whose treatise *The English Malady* (1733) was one of the century's best-selling books; Robert Whytt, the so-called philosophical doctor, whose *Observations on the Nature, Causes, and Cure of those Disorders which have been commonly called Nervous, Hypochondriac, or Hysteric* (Edinburgh: T. Becket and P. Du Hondt, 1765) became the classic statement of his generation; Thomas Coe, Francis Adair, and many others (see n. 53 below). Their lives and practices beg for a proper narrative. Even John Fothergill, the great anatomist William Hunter's friend, whose medical practice did not specialize in the nerves, wrote *An Account of a Painful Affliction of the Nerves of the Face, Commonly Called Tic Douloureux* (1804).

35   New historicism would suggest that these doctors were bound to exert power and sway in a society as stratified and hierarchical as that between 1660 and 1820 in England, the so-called long eighteenth century; see D. Veeser, *The New Historicism* (New York: Columbia University Press, 1989).

36   Knight [Lady Luxborough], *Letters of Lady Luxborough . . . to the poet William Shenstone*, pp. 67–9, 79, 214, 304–16, 329–31, 360, 481. The passage about 'the friendly Robin Red-breast' is found on p. 395.

37   Mrs Ralph Allen, an educated woman whose great parlour and reception rooms in Bath could be considered the English equivalent of a salon, would have known more than most mothers of the period about the intimacy between the fevers of their children and the inflammation of the nerves; it had been spelled out by many of the nerve doctors she herself had heard pronounce on these matters in the privacy of her own home; to complement her view see Thomas Kirkland, MD, *A Treatise on Child-Bed Fevers . . . to which are prefixed Two Dissertations, the one on the Brain and Nerves; the Other on the Sympathy of the Nerves, and on Different Kinds of Irritability* (1774), esp. pp. 168–72.

38   See C.F. Mullett (ed.), *The Letters of Dr. George Cheyne to the Countess of Huntingdon* (San Marino, Cal.: The Huntington Library, 1940). Richardson's prose is permeated with the language of the nerves, which forms an intrinsic part of his version of sensibility; for his view of nerves see Anna L. Barbauld (ed.), *The Correspondence of Samuel Richardson*, 6 vols (London: R. Phillips, 1804), 4: 30, 282–4, and Raymond Stephanson, 'Richardson's "Nerves": The Physiology of Sensibility in *Clarissa*', *Journal of the History of Ideas*, 49 (1988): 267–85. At this time nervous mythology was intrinsically tied to myths about the English nation and their developing nationalism as the most melancholic people on earth: depressed by their perpetually foul weather, dispirited by new stresses of high living, even unusually suicidal; as the poet Thomas Gray would say in a letter dated 27 May 1742, a nation epidemically stricken by 'White Melancholy' or 'Leucocholy'. Elsewhere I consider nervous mythology in its

national contexts exclusively, demonstrating that in every country it was grounded in national history and current politics, but that even these paled in comparison to the 'consumer consumption of nerves'; that is, the new relation between high living and leisure time on the one hand, and physical stress and bodily transformation on the other.

39   Frances Burney, *Evelina*, ed. Edward A. Bloom (London and New York: Oxford University Press, 1968), p. 286 (vol. 3, letter III). A systematic survey of English novels of the late eighteenth century would produce literally dozens of examples of this type.

40   This was the printer-cum-potion entrepreneur Francis Newbery's best-selling spa book, *The Register of Folly: Or, Characters and Incidents at Bath and the Hot-Wells, in a Series of Poetical Epistles, by an Invalid* (1773). For Anstey's similar books see Peter Wagner (ed.), *Christopher Anstey: The New Bath Guide* (Hildesheim: George Olms Verlag, 1989).

41   Johnson's 'nervous prose' has received some attention as 'masculine' and 'energetic'; see Cecil S. Emden, 'Rhythmical Features in Dr Johnson's Prose', *RES*, 25 (1949): 38–54; John Arthos, *The Language of Natural Description in Eighteenth-Century Poetry* (Ann Arbor: University of Michigan Press, 1949); W.V. Reynolds, 'Johnson's Opinions on Prose Style', *Review of English Studies*, 9 (1933): 433–46; W. Kenney, 'Addison, Johnson, and the "energetic style"', *Studia Neophilologica*, 33 (1961): 103–14; and the classic study by W.K. Wimsatt, *Philosophic Words* (New Haven: Yale University Press, 1948). But the development of an Enlightenment 'nervous style' at large, crossing national boundaries and different cultures, has not been viewed within the contexts of the semiotic of the nerves or considered for the literature of the period at large. One need only think of the prominence given to nervous vocabulary in such didactic treatises as Burke's youthful *Enquiry into the Sublime* (1757) and, alternatively, to the manuals for actors then, to comprehend what a mine there is to quarry.

Viewed synoptically and linguistically, nervous style was an elision for all things masculine in language: tough, strong, assertive, taut, concise – anything but feminine and soft, loose and spacious, weak and flaccid. It was a much admired, if also phallocratic, style in the mid-eighteenth century, whose cultural production and influence has not yet been explored. For example, David Garrick's language in his dramatic criticism is permeated with the language of the nerves, as when he wrote of the French actress Clairon, so prominent on the Paris stage, that: 'her heart has none of those instantaneous feelings, that life blood, that keen sensibility that bursts at once from genius and like electric fire, shoots through the nerves, marrow bones and all over every spectator' (quoted by Earl R. Wasserman in 'The Sympathetic Imagination in Eighteenth-Century Theories of Acting', *Journal of English and Germanic Philology*, 46 [1947]: 268). Johnson, Fielding, Smollett, Goldsmith – all were all commended and decorated, so to speak, at one time or another, by some *male* critic or commentator, as their critical heritages show, for displaying this nervous *je ne sais quoi* in their prose, and none more so than Johnson, the literary lion of the age. In *The History of . . . Tom Jones* (ch. 9, introduction) Fielding wrote about 'those fine and nervous descriptions which great authors themselves have taken from life'. Charles Churchill, the decadent satirist of the 1760s, commented in *The Apology* (l. 164) on Smollett's 'nervous weakness', his ironic inversion merely underscoring the opposite: i.e. that an irritable temperament in real life had produced such a 'nervous style' in art. And William Cowper, the melancholy poet, wrote to his constant correspondent the Very Rev. Unwin, that epitaphs should be as pointed as epigrams: 'there is a closeness of thought and expression, necessary in the conclusion of all these little things, that they may leave an agreeable flavour upon the palate. *What ever is short should be nervous, masculine, and compact*' (see James King and Charles Ryskamp (eds), *The Letters and Prose Writings of William Cowper*, 5 vols [Oxford: Clarendon Press, 1979–86], I, p. 359, Cowper to Unwin, 2 July 1780: also discussed in n. 72 below). Elsewhere, Dr James Drake, a medical doctor whose tropes are ridiculed and whose metaphors satirized in the pages of Sterne's *Tristram Shandy*, and a man who had written the most popular textbook of antaomy in a generation until Cheselden's replaced it in the 1730s, summed up 'nervous style' succinctly when he wrote of a colleague's that 'it [his prose style], both *Latin*, and *English*, was Manly yet Easie; Concise, yet Clear and Expressive'; see James Drake, *Anthropologia Novum* (1707), p. ix. Even the anonymous hack author of *A Letter of Congratulation, and Advice from the Devil to the Inhabitants of London ... on their Conduct before ... the Late Earthquakes* (London: Printed by a Fool, n. p.) comments, while capitalizing on the terror of the mob after the prognosticated earthquakes of 1750, that the devil communicates to his constituency by 'nervous arguments'.

42 Much has been written about Mesmer, in many languages and countries, but often without clear sight of the direct role he played in nerve therapy. But what was animal magnetism if not the strongest stimulus the nerves could receive from an artificial, external source? Mesmerism was not, of course, the only (if somewhat radical) form of nerve therapy; music and dance therapy, especially singing, legitimated themselves throughout the period on the grounds that they exercised the nerves and restored them to a tonic state; see, for example, Richard Browne, *Medicina Musica: Or a Mechanical Essay on the Effects of Singing, Musick, and Dancing, on Human Bodies* (London: 1729).

43 The effect of these preparations on the royal office and their implication for profit and gain is important. The late eighteenth century was, of course, the era *par excellence* of developmental patent medicine, the first patent medicines having been brought out in the 1770s after the patent office had opened in England; it is not surprising that a flurry of these quack therapies and remedies rushed to the public before they could be scrutinized by the officers of the patent office. See J.H. Young, *The Toadstool Millionaires* (Princeton, NJ: Princeton University Press, 1961).

44 Lewis Knapp (ed.), *The Adventures of Humphry Clinker* (Oxford: Oxford University Press, 1966), p. 34.

45 The gouty Matthew Bramble, Smollett's last hero, serves as a perfect example of his maker's (Smollett's) intuition. Bramble has spent much of his life trying to understand his imperfect 'nerves', only to discover that their essence continues to elude him.

46 Sion House MSS.

47   Dr William Derry of Bath compiled a still unpublished manuscript archive of
     the eighteenth-century Bath doctors, now in the Bath Public Library. As early
     as 1699 the soothing effects of these spa waters specifically on the nerves had
     been commented upon (Benjamin Allen, *The Natural History of the Chalybeat
     and Purging Waters of England* [1699]). A generation later, Dr Thomas Guidott
     claimed that the restoration of the nerves to health was the principal value of a
     visit to the pump rooms (Thomas Guidott, *An Apology for the Bath* [1724],
     indicating in a period of developing urban sprawl how well understood was the
     factor of stress. But British Enlightenment theory did not merely generate
     abstract discussion of societal stress; it explicitly located that stress in a
     particular part of the anatomy in an attempt to discover how the nerves could be
     repaired and strengthened after depletion through wear and tear. For nerves in
     relation to social rank and class in Bath society, see R.S. Neale, *Bath: A Social
     History 1680–1850 or a Valley of Pleasure, yet a Sink of Iniquity* (London:
     Routledge and Kegan Paul, 1981) and Georges Lamoine, 'La vie litteraire de
     Bath et de Bristol 1750–1800', University of Paris III doctoral dissertation,
     1978. Comments on Bath doctors and their patients, sorted out by class and
     wealth, are mentioned in an anonymous tract in the British Library: *Two Letters
     from a Physician in London, to A Gentleman at Bath . . . with some Observations on
     the Present . . .* (1744). Useful work on Dr George Cheyne at Bath is also being
     conducted at present by Dr Anita Guerrini. On the crucial subject of quackery
     see Roy Porter, *Health for Sale* (Manchester: Manchester University Press,
     1989). Most of all, though, it is necessary to demonstrate how this semiotics
     and mythology of nerves reflected views then held regarding gender, class, and
     race.

48   Dr Richard Mead, thought by some to be the nation's leading physician, and a
     former president of the Royal Society, also wrote about the nerves, especially
     within the terms of Newtonian aether; for nervous juices and fluids see his
     Mechanical Account of Poisons (1702), pp. 9–21, reprinted in his *Collected Works*
     (1762), pp. 455–61.

49   A useful study of Tissot's theory of nerves in relation to his medical practice
     and therapy is found in Heini W. Bucher, *'Tissot und seine Traité des Nerfs: Ein
     Beitrag zur Medizingeschichte der schweizerichen Aufklärung'*, Zürcher medizinges-
     chichliche, Neue Reihe, no. 1 (Zurich: Juris-Verlag, 1958).

50   If cultural history crosses the lines of traditional disciplines and teaches us how
     to view these boundaries and borders with scepticism, it also allows us to
     retrieve lost discourses such as those of the crucial nerve, as Weisskopf in our
     opening section would say; and within this specific domain it demonstrates that
     Adair merits a full-length biography, as do Dr George Cheyne and the Bath
     eccentric and prolific medical commentator Phillip Thicknesse. See Thicknes-
     se's *New Prose Bath Guide for the Year 1778* (Bath: 1778), his *The Valetudina-
     rian's Bath Guide; Or the Means of Obtaining Long Life and Health* (Bath: 1780),
     and his *Letters to Dr. Falconer of Bath* (Bath: 1782). Useful information about
     Cheyne's career as the doyen of 'nerve doctors' is found in William Falconer,
     Remarks on Dr. Cheyne's Essay on Health and Long Life (Bath: Leake [1745]).

51   James Makittrick Adair, 'Medical Cautions for the Consideration of Invalids',
     in his *Essays on Fashionable Diseases*, p. 3. The factions in Bath were these: Adair

looked to Cheyne as his mentor; Cheyne had taught Coe to join among the ranks of the 'nerve doctors'; Adair approved of Coe's work; Falconer and Adair were allies against Thicknesse; the greatest animosity was between Adair and the querulous Thicknesse, for which see Phillip Thicknesse, *A Letter to Dr. James Makittrick Adair* (Bath: 1787) and Adair's brutal reply: *Curious Facts and Anecdotes Not Contained in the Remarks of Phillip Thicknesse, Esq . . . dedicated to that Gentleman, by Benjamin Goosequill and Peter Paragrape* (London: J. Ridgway, 1790).

52 Adair, 'Medical Cautions', p. 6. The subsequent passages are found on pp. 4–9; Adair's taxonomies of nervous states are found throughout the book. Here it is important to recognize to what degree a diagnosis of 'nervous' was gender neutral, whereas a verdict of 'hysteric' (for example) was laden with feminine connotations. When, at the end of the eighteenth century, the great physician Edward Jenner discovered he had the symptoms of an hysteric he noted: 'in a female I should call it Hysterical – but in myself I know not what to call it, but by the old sweeping term nervous'; see G. Miller (ed.), *Letters of Edward Jenner* (Baltimore: Johns Hopkins University Press, 1983), p. 109. By Jenner's time, hysteria had long since been diagnosed in men under the name hypochondriasis (Willis, Sydenham, Purcell, etc.), but for another century – indeed up to Freud – it was the female malady *par excellence*, although plenty of male hysterics had been observed and diagnosed. For the terminology of nervous diseases, see also the work of A. Wilson quoted in the epigraph of the chapter: *Medical Researches*, p. 176.

53 Adair discusses Dr Coe in the *Essay on Fashionable Diseases*, p. 6; see also Thomas Coe, *A Treatise on Biliary Concretions* (London: 1757). Coe, like other popular English physicians (Cadogan, Hill, Robinson, Cheyne), claimed that gout could be an entirely 'nervous affliction' whose first sign was the debilitation of the nerves, fibres, and animal spirits. Adair's relation to Coe remains problematic: the two are not known to have met, and it is unclear why Adair modelled his theory on Coe's system rather than the better-known one of Cheyne; furthermore, there were others than Coe who claimed that biliary processes determined nervous pathology. See, for example, T.W. Gartzwyler, *De bile atra, ejusque effectibus* (Leiden: 1742).

54 George Cheyne, *The English Malady: Or a Treatise of Nervous Diseases of All Kinds* (Bath and London: 1773), p. 41.

55 See Thomas Dover, *The Ancient Physician's Legacy to his Country* (1733), which was attacked upon publication, went through several editions in only a few years, and was translated into French within twelve months as *Leys d'un ancien médecin a sa Patrie* (The Hague: 1734). Dover discusses nervous diseases on pp. 22, 57–62, 129–33, 183. His book is permeated with discussion of fashionable female nervous maladies such as 'The Tympany, Tympanites', which he calls 'another Species of Dropsy, to which the Fair Sex are only liable . . . as they are of a much finer Texture of Body than Men, they are more subject to the Passions of Mind, which have often been the Cause of this Distemper' (p. 22).

56 This direct link between nerves and hysteria requires full treatment and is being discussed by Sander Gilman, Helen King, Roy Porter, G.S. Rousseau

and Elaine Showalter in *Hysteria in Western Civilization*, now in press at the University of California Press. Briefly, the theory of the eighteenth century (in so far as one can reduce its diversity and generalize about it) was that all mental and emotional states depend on this elasticity or tightness of the nerves. Mechanists and vitalists alike, indeed most others too, shared in the belief, especially in the notion of tension as the key element. Through this doctrine the looser cultural concept of 'tension' between persons, and even more internally between one part of the psyche and another, arose, and was eventually metaphorized into popular culture at large as a psychological state. The precise mechanisms by which the nerves interacted with fluids in different degrees of tension, often causing melancholy and even the more extreme hypochondriasis (in men) and hysteria (in women), was the subject of many medical dissertations in Europe.

57   Adair, *Essays on Fashionable Diseases*, p. 25. In medical theory Adair had been influenced by the Swiss medical writer François Boissier de Sauvages, a derivative Stahlian vitalist who believed that the soul (and possibly the brain too) activated the nervous mechanisms of the body, and whose *Nosologia Methodica* (1768) represents an extreme Linnaean application to taxonomize all disease. For these figures and their relation to Stahlian nervous physiology, see L.J. Rather, 'G.E. Stahl's Psychological Physiology', *Bulletin for the History of Medicine*, 35 (1961): 37–49, and the same author's *Mind and Body in Eighteenth-Century Medicine* (London: Wellcome Historical Medical Library, 1965).

58   The imagination was becoming medicalized under the influence of the seventeenth-century mechanists, and became increasingly so in the eighteenth century; for this development see G.S. Rousseau, 'Science and the Discovery of the Imagination in Enlightened England', *Eighteenth-Century Studies*, III (1969): 108–35; for the Aristotelian tradition, see Michael V. Wedlin, *Mind and the Imagination in Aristotle* (New Haven: Yale University Press, 1989). Some of this work, as found in C.G. Gross, *De morbis imaginariis hypochondriacorum* (1755), specifically addressed the imagination in relation to somatic diseases generated in the locale of the hypochondrium. In 1691 Timothy Rogers, a sedentary MA from Oxford, published a confessional treatise, *A Discourse concerning Trouble of Mind, and the Disease of Melancholy, linking Mind and Melancholy through the Medium of the Nerves*. Others, such as the German physician J.F. Mossdorff, writing *De valetudinariis imaginariis, von Menschen, die aus Einbildung kranck werden* (1721), were more concerned with illnesses that had no detectable somatic manifestations (i.e. what we would call psychological conditions). In Italy, Lodovico Antonio Muratori, the empirical philosopher-poet whose book on imagination and dreams (1747) was widely discussed, suggested that the imagination played a central role in the formation of illness. In England, J. Richardson (of Newent), who was not even a medical man, wrote *Thoughts upon Thinking, or, a New Theory of the Human Mind; wherein a Physical Rationale of the Formation of our Ideas, the Passions, Dreaming, and Every Faculty of the Soul is Attempted upon Principles Entirely New* (1755), and suggested that the nerves meditate between ideas and illness. In all these discussions, and others, the nerves played a central role.

59   I have found only one copy of this obscure work, in the British Library.

60   Richard Kuhn has surveyed the long tradition in *The Demon of Noontide: Ennui in Western Literature* (Princeton, NJ: Princeton University Press, 1976), but is rather inadequate on the Enlightenment, leaving out such obvious candidates as the melancholic Boswell – perhaps the greatest sufferer of the century, as his Dutch journals show – who titled his most sustained work of periodical journalism *The Hypochondriack*; see the edition by Margery Bailey called *Boswell's Column* (London: W. Kimber, 1951).

61   See Barbauld, *The Correspondence of Samuel Richardson*, 5 vols, 4: 30.

62   Ian Watt, *The Rise of the Novel* (Berkeley, Cal., and Los Angeles: University of California Press, 1957), p. 184.

63   George Sherburn (ed.), *The Correspondence of Alexander Pope* (Oxford: Clarendon Press, 1956), IV: 526. In his *Essay on the Genius and Writings of Pope* (1762), Joseph Warton attempts to show that Pope's genius resulted from a delicate sensibility founded on a nervous personality. Warton also considered 'nervous' composition to be one of 'three different species' which he adumbrates in the *Essay*, I: 170. Adam Smith commented in his *Theory of Moral Sentiments* on the stylistic (i.e. couplet) 'nervous precision of Mr. Pope'.

64   Philander Misaurus, *The Honour of the Gout* (London: J. Roberts, 1720), pp. 18–19.

65   The full title deserves a place in the history of stress-related illnesses associated with global economic depression, such as the worldwide crash of 1929, and for its jumble of medical-economic metaphors; see John Midriff, *Observations on the Spleen and Vapours: Containing Remarkable Cases of Persons of both Sexes, and all Ranks, from the aspiring Directors to the Humble Bubbler, who have been miserably afflicted with these Melancholy Disorders since the Fall of the South-Sea, and other publick Stocks; with the proper Method for their Recovery, according to the new and uncommon Circumstances of each Case* (1721).

66   William Smith, *A Dissertation upon the Nervous System to show its Influence upon the Soul* (1768). In France, Le Camus, a physician, also constructed a *Medicine de l'Esprit* (1769), showing the link between the nerves and the soul.

67   Boswell's melancholy has been studied by Alan Ingram in *Boswell's Creative Gloom* (London: Macmillan 1984), but without attention to the scientific, medical, or cultural semiotics of the matter.

68   See Elizabeth Carter, *A Series of Letters between Mrs. Elizabeth Carter and Miss Catherine Talbot from the year 1741 to 1770*, 4 vols (London: J. Rivington, 1809), 2: 156. More generally, the passions, reason, morality, and insanity were linked together specifically by the nervous apparatus, as suggested here and in dozens of other similar passages in different kinds of writing by both sexes. Two generations after Elizabeth Carter wrote, the prolific (if also prolix) Rev. Trusler, the moralizer of Hogarth who made his fortune by combining alleged medical expertise with clerical eccentricity, claimed to have penetrated to the truth about cowardice – in his view the most feminine of all moral defects, implying just the kind of genderized nerves we have seen gradually developing throughout the century. Trusler wrote in his Memoirs (Bath: John Browne, 1806): 'What then is cowardice? – It is the effect of weak nerves. – Who would not be brave if he could? *Acquired* courage may be the result of strong

reasoning, refined courage, and a sense of duty, as in the simple case of the officer: *mechanical* courage, is often the effect of example, as in the soldier: – one man keeps the line, because another does, they consider themselves merely as parts of a great machine; but *natural* courage is the effect of strong nerves, which every man is not blessed with [compare Mrs Donnellan's advice to Samuel Richardson and my synoptic paradigm above]. I might pity a coward, but I would not condemn him, for want of resolution, more than I would condemn a weak man for want of strength. They are, like *nerves*, gifts of Providence bestowed on particular men' (p. 46).

69   Carter, *A Series of Letters*, 2: 156. More work needs to be done on the social and linguistic history of 'attention' in relation to 'diversion' and 'melancholy'. For Lady Conway's nervous headaches see M.H. Nicolson, *Conway Letters* (Oxford: Oxford University Press, 1930), pp. 421–2. For the Renaissance tradition see Francis Bacon, 'Of Regiment of Health, Essay 30', *Essays of Sir Francis Bacon.* ed. W.A. Wright (London: Oxford University Press, 1892), pp. 132ff.; Addison's *Spectator* 411 is worth citing: 'the Pleasure[s] of Fancy are more conducive to Health than those of the Understanding, which are worked out by Dint of Thinking, and attended with too violent a Labour of the Brain. Delightful Scenes, whether in Nature, Painting, or Poetry, have a kindly Influence on the Body, as well as the Mind, and not only serve to clear and brighten the Imagination, but are able to disperse Grief and Melancholly [sic], and to set the Animal Spirits in pleasing and agreeable Motions'; see D. Bond (ed.), The *Spectator*, 5 vols (Oxford: Oxford University Press, 1965), IV: 539.

70   Robert Halsband (ed.), *The Complete Letters of Lady Mary Wortley Montagu*, 3 vols (Oxford: Clarendon Press, 1965–76), II: 63. Lady Mar suffered from acute melancholy and nervous depression in 1727 and became so mentally deranged by the spring of 1728 that a battle over her custody ensued. Lady Mary's pronouncements on nerves and their afflictions are worthy of study in themselves; see *Letters*, III. 96, 171; for sensibility III: 245; for mind and body, II: 397.

71   See Frank H. Ellis (ed.), *Poems on Affairs of State: Augustan Satirical Verse, 1660–1714, Vol. VI: 1697–1704* (New Haven, Conn.: Yale University Press, 1970), 6: 64, 35–6.

72   *European Magazine* (1812). William Cowper, the poet, almost blindly subscribed to a genderized version of nerves, but the myth was so broadly disseminated throughout his culture that one can hardly fault him for being less vigilant than he was to its sexual resonances. See his letter, already mentioned in n. 41, to the Rev. Unwin for 2 July 1780: 'I like your Epitaph, except that I doubt the propriety of the word *immaturus*; which, I think, is rather applicable to fruits than flowers, and except the last pentameter, the assertion it contains being rather too obvious a thought to finish with; not that I think an epitaph should be pointed, like an epigram. But still there is a closeness of thought and expression, necessary in the conclusion of all these little things, that they may leave an agreeable flavour upon the palate. What ever is short should be nervous, masculine, and compact. Little men are so; and little poems should be so; because, where the work is short the author has no right to the plea of weariness; and laziness is never admitted as an available excuse in anything.'

The insanity of these poets – including Collins, Cowper, Smart, and others – is discussed by William B. Ober, *Bottoms Up!: A Pathologist's Essay on Medicine and the Humanities* (Carbondale: Southern Illinois University Press, 1989), but without reference to these nervous mythologies.

73 'Of the Hypp', was originally published in the *Universal Spectator* (18 November 1732): 214, n. p., and was reprinted in the *Gentleman's Magazine*, 2 (1732): 1062–3; the anonymous author claims 'to have dabbled in the art of medicine'.

74 See Pierre Fedida, 'Les exercices de l'imagination et la commotion sur la masse des nerfs: un érotisme de tête', in *Oeuvres completes de Marquis de Sade*, 16 vols (Paris: Au cercle du livre precieux, 1967), 9: 613–25. Perceptive discussion of the nerves in Sade's prose is found in David Morris, 'The Marquis de Sade and the Discourses of Pain: Literature and Medicine at the Revolution', in G.S. Rousseau (ed.), *The Languages of Psyche: Mind and Body in Enlightenment Thought* (Berkeley, Cal., and Los Angeles: University of California Press, 1990), 291–330. The notion that anatomy is destiny, and that the eroticized body amounts to an excess of nervous concentration, abounds in Sade's ethics of the erotic; see Marcel Henaff, *Sade: l'invention du corps libertin* (Paris: Presses Universitaires de France, 1978). While Sade was generating his fictional version of moral and revolutionary hedonism, Cabanis – amongst the most philosophical of doctors of the post-revolutionary period – correlated the nerves to specific stages of human perfection in an almost Lamarckean and pre-Darwinian sense; see Pierre-Jean-Georges Cabanis, *On the Relations Between the Physical and Moral Aspects of Man* (ed.), George Mora, 2 vols (Baltimore: Johns Hopkins University Press, 1981). Nervous mythology declined somewhat in the early nineteenth century, as the schools of vitalism (Bichat, Barthez, Blumenbach, Novalis, the German romanticist philosophers, the French School) gained ascendancy and replaced it with a series of metaphors for the romantic body energized, sexualized, politicized, which was less mechanistic and materialist, but nerves nevertheless did not die out; they were merely transformed and then again metaphorically recharged. And nervous mythology has endured well into the twentieth century, as any systematic study of its varieties would show; see, for example, the mythologies that underlie such diverse books, both written by physicians, as Joseph Collins's *The Way with Nerves; Letters to a Neurologist on Various Modern Nervous Ailments, Real and Fancied, with Replies thereto Telling of Their Nature and Treatment* (New York and London: G.P. Putnam's sons, 1911), and Bernard Hollander's *Nervous Disorders of Women: The Modern Psychological Conceptions* (London: Kegan Paul, 1916). The imaginary nervous ailments here are as germane as the so-called 'real' ones.

75 See William Cullen, *Nosologia*; translated as *Nosology; or, a Systematic arrangement of diseases* (Edinburgh: 1768; 2nd edn 1800), p. 238. J.M. Lopez Pinero has traced the tradition from Willis and Cullen down to current time in his *Historical Origins of the Concept of Neurosis* (Cambridge: Cambridge University Press, 1983). For Enlightenment vitalism see Roger, *Les Sciences de la vie*; G.S. Rousseau, 'Bakhtin and Enlightenment: An Essay on Vitalism for our Times', in F. Burwick and Paul Douglass (eds), *The Crisis of Modernism* (Cambridge: Cambridge University Press, 1991).

76   'Absalom and Achitophel', in *The Works of John Dryden, The California Dryden*, eds Edward Niles Hooker and H.T. Swedenberg, 20 vols (Berkeley, Cal., and Los Angeles: University of California Press, 1956), 2: 10, l. 163.

77   In the same Paris milieu in which Gautier and his fellow decadents flourished, Pierre Jules Descot, a physician, published *Dissertation sur les affections locales des nerfs* (Paris: 1882), showing how all pleasure and pain were situated in the nerves at the tip of the genitals, and why these erotogenic zones were consequently the most crucial part of human anatomy, for pleasure as well as reproduction. Hegel's discussion of 'magical relationships' and 'nervous friendships' is found in Hermann Gockner (ed.), *Samtliche Werke*, 26 vols (Stuttgart: Fromann, 1927–40), 2: 223, section 405. A valuable discussion of mesmerism in German medicine and natural philosophy is found in D. von Engelhardt, 'Mesmer in der Naturforschung and Medizin in der Romantik', in Heinz Schott (ed.), *Franz Anton Mesmer und die Geschichte des Mesmerismus* (Stuttgart: Franz Steiner, 1985), pp. 88–107.

78   See *The Works of Charles Lamb*, ed. E.V. Lucas, 7 vols (London: Methuen, 1903–5), I: 175. As across the English Channel, the literary-medical milieu in England was also interwoven with figures having an impact in each realm, artistic and medical. In Lamb's world the physician-poet Thomas Trotter could publish a significant study of *A View of the Nervous Temperament* (1807), which correlated personality types according to their anatomical-physiological constitutions, as well as a volume called *Sea Weeds: Poems written on Various Occasions, chiefly during a Naval Life* (Newcastle and London: 1829). For male hysteria, different to the melancholy discussed here, see Mark Micale, 'Diagnostic Discriminations: Charcot and the Nineteenth-Century Idea of Masculine Hysterical Neurosis', Yale University doctoral dissertation, 1987, and the same author's 'Hysteria and its Hysteriography: The Future Perspective', *History of Psychiatry*, I (March 1990): 33–124.

79   Taking her cue from Dr Cheyne's bestselling book *The English Malady* of 1733 (see n. 34 above), Elaine Showalter has studied the conditions under which the nerves were invoked in analyses of female somatic and psychogenic disorders in the nineteenth century; see *The Female Malady: Women, Madness and English Culture, 1830–1980* (London: Virago, 1987). During the peak of high Victorianism, numerous doctors wrote about the nerves; in Germany, discourses of the nerve were as important as they were in England, and treatises such as the German physician M.H. Romberg's *Nervous Diseases of Man* (1853) were quickly translated into English.

80   This link remains the one to be explored among various discourses, and it is a glaring shortcoming of this essay that I do not undertake it here. My excuse (such as it is) is that I do not have the space, which will perhaps not stand up, but I nevertheless wish to acknowledge how crucial it seems to me to establish these networks of connection.

81   The extraordinary matter to be grasped here is not that Jane Austen should allow common parlance about nerves to invade her highly eclectic prose vocabulary, but rather that she permits it without more irony, as any systematic lexical study of her use of nervous language would show (I have collected over two dozen of these passages but do not include them here for reasons of space).

Whole ranges of scientific vocabularies and their metaphors are rigorously denied entry into her fictive discourse; but the nerves enter with little if any resistance. The question is why. Perhaps Austen knew more about nervous medicine than has been credited to her, and a study of her reading in, and knowledge of, current physiology might repay the effort. As she was composing her novels of sentiment and delicacy (of which *Mansfield Park*, incidentally, has the largest number of uses of nervous vocabulary, and which is infused with the female sensibility of Richardson and Frances Burney), English doctors in her own geographical locale, were writing works like Dr M. Hall's *On the Mimoses [sic]: Or, A Descriptive, Diagnostic and Practical Essay on the Affections usually denominated Dyspeptic, Hypochondriac, Bilious, Nervous, Chlorotic, Hysteric* (1818).

82 For this tradition, see n. 9 above and Robert Brissenden, *Virtue in Distress: Studies in the Novel of Sentiment from Richardson to Sade* (London: Macmillan, 1974). The Apollonian–Dionysian dichotomy has also played a role within this tradition, especially as the justification for art for art's sake. Denise Levertov, the contemporary poet, discovers herself on the side of the nerves and sensibility within the rational–emotional split, and has written that: '*Art as process* is undertaken by artists . . . for its own sake, from an instinctive desire to *make*, to form things in a particular medium; and they have towards that medium . . . a marked preference not of the intending will but of the sensibility, indeed I would say of the nervous system, which makes them more sensitive not morally or emotionally, but *aesthetically* . . . than others'; quoted in Joanne Trautmann (ed.), *Healing Arts in Dialogue: Medicine and Literature* (Carbondale, Ill.: Southern Illinois University Press, 1981), p. 150.

83 Coleridge's anatomy and medicine have not received the attention they deserve, despite Trevor H. Levere's excellent study of his science (*Poetry Realized in Nature: Samuel Taylor Coleridge and Early Nineteenth-Century Science* [New York: Cambridge University Press, 1981]); without understanding these two realms one cannot comprehend Coleridge's contribution to the discourse of the nerves. One would have thought that his philosophical lineage as a Hartleyan and his aesthetics of immediacy would automatically privilege the nerves; see Wallace Jackson, *Immediacy: The Development of a Critical Concept from Addison to Coleridge* (Amsterdam: Rodopi, NV, 1973); but although Coleridge writes abundantly about immediacy there is less material about nerves in his prose than one would have imagined; nevertheless see his pronouncements 'On Sensibility', in *Collected Works*, 16 vols (Princeton, NJ: Bollingen, 1962–). At the same time that Coleridge was writing, such scientific associates of his as Drs Thomas Young (the prolific naturalist who wrote about colour theory) and John Cooke (the president of the Medico-Chirurgical Society) were also discussing the nerves: Young especially in a *Treatise on Phthisis* (1822) and Cooke in a two-volume *Treatise on Nervous Diseases* (1823; Boston edn 1824).

84 See Leonard Woolf (ed.), *The Diary of Virginia Woolf*, 3 vols (London: Hogarth, 1980), II: 123. Virginia Woolf's relation to this neurophysical tradition deserves much more attention than it has received, not least because she herself was among the most 'nervous' of writers and connected the creative act to the state of the nerves during the processes of imagination. Like the eighteenth-century

274 G. S. ROUSSEAU

poet William Cowper, whose manic states were emplotted in a series of confessional genres, and like Mary Shelley's deranged scientist Frankenstein, whose 'nervous agony' was renewed at the mere sight of a 'chemical instrument' ever after the appearance of his vision, Woolf often composed under the siege of mania and in nervous agitation. Throughout her life she remained interested in the dawn of creativity as an unexplored zone between specific nervous states and leaps of imagination; and one unusual aspect of Woolf's insight is that she tried to give language to this procrustean no man's land. The passage in *To the Lighthouse* in which Lily is struggling with her painting captures this essential belief about the relation of physiology, desire, and artistic creation: 'Phrases came. Visions came. Beautiful pictures. Beautiful phrases. But what she wished to get hold of was that very jar on the nerves – the thing itself before it has been made anything.' This nervous moment, this 'jar on the nerves ... before it has been made anything', makes plain that Woolf's aesthetic bears a neuroscientific component worthy of study, especially for its linguistic representations. Furthermore, Sterne was Woolf's favourite prose writer of the eighteenth century, though she also read and delighted in the witty prose of Addison and Steele (as one would know from reading *Orlando*); yet it is inconceivable that in her constant reading of, and writing about, Sterne she had overlooked his own fascination with nervous prose (n. 41 above) and the various ways in which Sterne and his contemporaries had transformed the discourse of animal spirits, nerves, and fibres – literally from the first paragraph of *Tristram Shandy* – turning it upside down and metaphorizing and satirizing medical dissertations about nerves of just the type discussed in this essay. For further discussion of Sterne in this sense, see G.S. Rousseau, 'Smollett and Sterne: A Revaluation', *Archiv für das Studium der neueren Sprachen und Literaturen*, 207 (1972): 286–97. Yet Woolf should be viewed in a wider and more medical context than this. She grew up in a late Victorian England that had heard (for example) medically trained lecturers like Andrew Wilson speaking on *The Origin of Nerves. A Lecture Delivered Before the Sunday Lecture Society on 24 December 1878* (London: 1879). And she herself was profoundly interested in theories of nervous disorder and neurosis, in part as a result of her own mental states when she composed, but also in view of her oblique sexuality. Her diaries continually exude wrenching remarks about the effort her writing had cost her: 'it [the act of giving language to states of mind] calls upon every nerve to hold itself taut.' Later on, in her mature years during the 1920s, there was talk everywhere – from Havelock Ellis, Edward Carpenter, D.H. Lawrence, Walt Whitman, Otto Weininger, even within the Bloomsbury circle – about the relation of nervous mechanism and physiology to sex and love. For these diverse reasons, neuroscience could not elude her. In passing, one suspects that Woolf might have sympathized with Schreber's analysis of his own nervous condition; see I. Macalpine and R. Hunter (eds), *Daniel Paul Schreber: Memoirs of My Nervous Illness* (London: Dawson, 1955). For Cowper's mania see W.B. Ober, 'Madness and Poetry: A Note on Collins, Cowper, and Smart', *Bulletin of the New York Academy of Medicine*, 46, no. 4 (1970), and the same author's *Bottoms Up!*

85   A. Alvarez, *The Savage God: A Study of Suicide* (New York: Random House,

1970), p. 19. See also J. Babinski and J. Froment, *Hysteria or Pithiatism and Reflex Nervous Disorders in the Neurology of War* (London, 1918), p. 311. For Gibbon see J.E. Norton (ed.), *The Letters of Edward Gibbon*, 3 vols (New York: The Macmillan Company, 1956), 3: 34.

86   By the turn of this century a school of thought had developed around the belief that nervous ailments could be treated successfully by moral therapies; see Arnold Stocker, *Le traitement moral des nerveux* (Geneva: Rhone, 1945). Most have been discredited by now.

87   But now, in our post-disciplinary age, the discourse of postmodernism, as Habermas has suggested, brings them together; see Jürgen Habermas, *The Philosophical Discourse of Modernity* (Cambridge, Mass.: MIT Press, 1987).

8

'Expressing Yourself Ill': The Language of Sickness in Georgian England

ROY PORTER

Medical terminology affords a good instance of the multiple functions which language has to fulfil. It is a technical, esoteric jargon, yet it must also serve to communicate (or, sometimes, 'discommunicate') between doctor and patient, and enable the latter to make sense of sickness.[1] It is a neutral, objective expression of scientific knowledge, while at the same time also entangled in socio-commercial transactions and therapeutic aspirations. This essay aims to tease out some of these complexities by examining discussions of the puzzles and pitfalls of medical language mounted by certain eighteenth-century physicians.

Sickness inevitably puts language under strain. We have a pain: we grope for the right word to convey the nature and intensity of the feeling, and to clarify just where under the skin it is located. This is a difficult business, for our pain language is neither well differentiated nor objective. Often we then need to go on to identify the pain as a symptom of some more comprehensive entity: a malfunction, disability, disturbance, disease – and much obviously hinges upon which of these categories it is felt applies. After all, endowing the trouble with a label will, it is hoped, defuse the anxiety of ignorance.

Disease-naming involves classification, promotes prognosis, and indicates therapy. As the old saying puts it, a disease named is a disease half cured.[2]

But the relations between medical realities and medical names are obviously highly complex, certainly involving more than a straightforward business of identification, of 'pointing and naming', as it were. After all, many disease terms are unwelcome to the ear. It is one thing to have a fever; to be told it is meningitis is far more disturbing: here the disease label generates apprehension. When a tumour is in question, everything may turn upon the key words 'benign' or 'malignant'.

Nomen est omen. The ominousness of words of course reflects the banal fact that some diseases are authentically more painful or life-threatening than others. More, however, is at stake. Different disease terms convey radically distinct metaphorical and moral messages (the same is true for the names for body zones and functions). Insanity, syphilis, and, today, AIDS are, as Susan Sontag has shown, high-stigma disorders, whereas tuberculosis, though once no less lethal, could be relatively eligible as a disease from which to be declining. For long, cancer was the 'dread disease' that could hardly be named.[3]

Partly because of the incrustations of meaning gathering on medical terms, the very language of disorders undergoes continual modification. Some words become taboo, others slip into hopeless vagueness. Technical medico-scientific advances also play their part in wordshifts, as does intra-professional medical in-fighting. Thus divergent meanings will be attached to a category such as 'hysteria' or 'schizophrenia', depending upon the school to which the practitioner belongs: is his or her viewpoint essentially physicalist or psychological? Or is he or she by training a gynaecologist, a neurophysiologist, or a psychiatrist? Indeed, at one extreme of the psychiatric spectrum, Thomas Szasz and his supporters argue that the very concepts of 'hysteria' or 'schizophrenia' are themselves fictions, spectral ideological constructs, terms without anchorage in authentic organic lesions.[4]

And the instability of medical terms is exacerbated by the multiplicity of illness lingos in circulation. We could start by noting a crude division between lay terms and professional jargon (the patient's 'heart attack' is the doctor's 'myocardial infarction'). But within professional medicine, as Dirckx has shown, doctors themselves speak with various degrees of solemnity; and British, French, German, and American physicians do not use identical illness vocabularies (French doctors traditionally make heavy use of diagnostic terms indicating liver-related complaints, Germans have a penchant for disease-notions relating to the heart, the British emphasize the stomach and bowels).[5] There are also many lay languages, differentiated by age (baby talk, etc.), dialect, class, gender, and occasion.

When a sufferer takes his or her 'complaint' before the doctor, translation difficulties often arise between the idiom of the patient and the technical argot of the profession.[6] Semantic skirmishing may follow. One source of ultimate authority resides with the sick person (the disorder is, after all, *that person's*, and he or she alone can render his or her 'complaint' into words); another with the doctor (he or she knows all the authorized disease specifications in the book). Negotiation often ensues, to determine precisely what the trouble will be called, with doctor and patient angling for their own preferred label (the patient might find personal reassurance in thinking of his or her pain as just a 'chill', but has to persuade the doctor to put 'gastro-enteritis' on the sick-note to impress his or her employer).

Not least, medical language has never been divested of a certain magic or psychological potency. Rather as the witch, or witch-doctor, can induce sickness with a curse, the physician can heal with an appropriate diagnosis and a soothing bedside word, perhaps washed down with some placebo medicine. Breuer's patient, 'Anna O', gave the name of the 'talking cure' to what was to become the technique of psychoanalysis.[7] For their part, hypochondriacal patients can talk themselves sick with words; or, more complexly, can conjure up nameless disorders.[8] This is not, of course, automatically to accept Groddeck's contention that all disease is wholly in the mind,[9] or rather the unconscious; but words sometimes possess uncanny powers of focusing, defining, and informing our reactions to pain and disorders. Suggestivity is never to be underestimated.

The foregoing remarks may be applied broadly to medical problems, past, present, and future. Here I shall treat them as background for an examination of certain tension-points in medical language in eighteenth-century Britain. Antedating the rise of the modern teaching hospital and of scientific medicine, the Georgian doctor deployed a lexicon fairly close to common speech, one more readily accessible to, and usable by, his patients than would be the case nowadays.[10] The traditional physician had no option.

For, unlike the doctors of today, he had no battery of diagnostic technology at his disposal,[11] and so was forced to rely pre-eminently upon the sickness story his patient told (what was known as 'taking the patient's history'). In any case, lacking, unlike the modern professional, the supporting authority of an institutional hierarchy and career ladder, the pre-modern doctor depended for advancement very largely upon his capacity to please private patients. He necessarily had to speak their language, even defer to it. Otherwise, they would transfer their custom, perhaps patronizing quacks, grand masters of the gift of the gab and ingratiating manners.[12]

Finding the right linguistic currency to be exchanged between practitioner and patient required great tact. As fashionable Georgian physicians such as George Cheyne and Sir Richard Blackmore complained, it could be devilish hard to frame diagnostic formulae at which polite society patients would not take offence.[13] Yet, amongst such circles, the eloquent physician could impress, relieve by suggestion, and go far:

A Physician that has his Tongue well hung [opined the Italian physician, Giorgio Baglivi] and is Master of the Art of Persuading, fastens, by the mere force of Words, such a Vertue upon his Remedies, and raises the Faith and Hopes of the Patient to that Pitch, that sometimes he masters difficult Diseases with the silliest Remedies; which Physicians of greater Learning could not do with nobler Remedies, merely because they talk'd faintly, and with a soft dead Air.[14]

Of course, satirists and critics made merry with revelations of this kind, implying none too politely that medicine was *vox praeterea nihil*, a hot-air hoax, and that regulars were themselves charlatans (*'ciarlatani'*: literally 'chatterers'), every bit as much as the quacks.[15] Be that as it may, a serious point was involved. Georgian England was an increasingly commercialized society. Its socio-economic activity focused upon transactions in the marketplace.[16] Before the exclusive, state-regulated professional control which developed in the mid-Victorian era, medicine – despite the genteel pretensions of its upper echelons – was essentially determined by market forces. It was a commodity with negotiable exchange values. And, I shall suggest by examining a number of commentaries by contemporary doctors upon the state of their art, language – both oral and written – constituted the prime medium of exchange in what a contemporary physician dubbed the 'sick trade'.[17]

Words were diseases, and they were contagious, insinuated Bernard Mandeville, best known today for his provocatively paradoxical social, economic, and moral views, expressed above all in the *Fable of the Bees*, but by profession a physician and a lively medical writer.[18] In his *Treatise of the Hypochondriack and Hysterick Diseases* (1730),[19] Mandeville examined the twin psychopathological and psychotherapeutic powers of language through a fictitious dialogue conducted between a physician, Philopirio, a gentleman patient, Misomedon, and his wife, Polytheca (their names immediately reveal their natures). The dialogue significantly opens with the ailing Misomedon, who 'is very talkative'[20] and 'seems to take Pleasure in talking of his Ailments, and relating the History of his Distemper',[21] requesting a 'long' consultation with Philopirio; these days, the patient complains, physicians dash off, to create the impression, or illusion, of being ever in demand.[22] The itch to converse *ad nauseam* about his illness (Mandeville hints to the reader) is part of his complaint.

Misomedon relates his history. In better days, he had been a comfortably off, raffish, well-bred gentleman scholar, who got into the habit of ruining his constitution by 'good living'. Succumbing to stomach disorders and exhaustion, he consulted a succession of learned physicians, discussing his condition with them as an equal, desiring 'as the Prerogative of a Man of Letters, that I might be acquainted with the Cause of my Distemper'; for, as Mandeville glosses, 'it is Pride in the Patient, that makes him in love with the Reasoning Physician, to have an Opportunity of shewing the Depth of his own Penetration.'[23]

None of their treatments worked – indeed their drug cocktails greatly worsened his condition; but the consequence of such endless verbal commerce with these physicians was to reduce Misomedon into a 'Hypochondriacus Confirmatus . . . a Crazy Valetudinarian',[24] captivated by the suggestive powers of medical discourse.[25] Convinced he was sinking from every sickness known to scholarship, he developed 'a mind to study Physick' himself[26] – but his studies merely made bad worse. Not least, he convinced himself that he had been infected with venereal disease – 'when I grew better, I found that all this had been occasion'd by reading of the *Lues*, when I began to be ill; which has made me resolve since, never to look in any Book of Physick again, but when my head is in very good order.'[27]

Sympathizing with Misomedon in the course of a series of protracted conversational consultations, Philopirio deplores the perversion of modern medicine by linguistic quackery. For one thing, the sciences of anatomy and physiology had become dominated by theorists – notably the neurological pioneer, Thomas Willis – who advanced grandiose speculations about the workings of the internal organs (e.g. the stomach, represented as a furnace or a still), all of which amounted to nothing but verbal flights of imagination, entirely bereft of empirical basis.[28] 'These Similes, I confess', states Philopirio – here as elsewhere presumably Mandeville's mouthpiece – 'are very diverting for People that have nothing else to do . . . what Pity it is they won't cure sick People.'[29]

For another, clinicians themselves mistreat the language, bandying around for effect 'hard Names', 'Technick Words', and 'cramp Terms',[30] and prizing polite bedside chit-chat above authentic diagnostic acumen. Such a fellow, judges Philopirio, 'in his Talk cures all Diseases by Hypothesis and frightens away the Gout with a fine Simile.'[31] And the sick further encourage this deception by giving their plaudits to the silver-tongued operator. The consequence is that, because in our 'sprightly talkative Age . . . the silent Experience of Pains-taking Practitioners is ridicul'd',[32] the aspirant physician must 'converse with and learn the Language of the Beau Monde',[33] and must 'make his court chiefly to the Favourites of the Ladies, keep company with Men of superficial Knowledge, and all the great Talkers about Town'.[34] There is, Philopirio claims, profound wisdom in the botanist's maxim: '*non verbis sed herbis*';[35] regrettably that is not the highroad to success these days, when 'if you can Chat, and be a good companion, you may drink yourself into Practice' – notoriously what Dr George Cheyne did in the London taverns when first trying to set up in practice.[36]

Above all, Mandeville complains, ventriloquizing through Philopirio, treatment has become dominated by the fetish of the prescription. In the good old days, physic was largely an art of regimen, offering recommendations as to healthy diet, exercise, and temperance. No longer: the virtue of the modern physician has become concentrated in, and transmitted through, his drugs. And now, as Philopirio acerbically remarks, that 'all the Skill is wrapt up in the Prescription',[37] the doctor's prime action is the palaver of writing words, inscribing himself in his pharmacological hieroglyphics.

Mandeville's dialogue bubbles with paradox. He shows Misomedon finally curing himself – of his self-inflicted hypochondria – merely by pouring out his tale of woe to the sagely quiet Philopirio. Thus one could talk oneself *into* sickness by trading words with doctors, but the process could apparently also work in reverse. Hence a tract that *prima facie* presented itself as a warning against the infectious nature of words ends triumphantly by insinuating that, at least with a sagacious physician, words can truly be therapeutic (a notion which might be called the distant ancestor of Freudian free association). Neat irony: a book, written for the succour of the sick, whose message is that books written for the sick are themselves hazards to health. It would not take a hardened cynic to suggest that Mandeville's work, crammed with denunciations of the subtle tricks turned by physicians to drum up custom, was itself a brazen instance of the pot calling the kettle black (did it, one wonders, prove effective in drumming up custom for the canny doctor?).[38]

What is beyond dispute is that Mandeville had his ears pricked for the play of language. Worries about words were typical of his times. Enlightenment epistemology was preoccupied with the need for words (verba) soberly to match things (res): otherwise reality was occluded by fiction, fantasy, or metaphysics. Such was the message handed down by philosophers from Bacon and Hobbes, through the Royal Society and Locke, to the linguistic reformism of Condillac and Horne Tooke.[39]

Yet the practice of such nominalistic semantic hygiene was surely easier in the laboratory than by the bedside. Many eighteenth-century physicians were profoundly aware of the difficulties, for patients and doctors alike, of finding the right words for maladies. Reflecting sympathetically upon the hypochondriac's plight, Thomas Beddoes, the prominent Bristol physician active around the close of the eighteenth century, noted that 'the hypochondria sufferer always finds language fails him, when he gives vent to his complaints.'[40] Despite the sufferer's efforts to find the words to say it, they all sounded inadequate or anti-climatic: 'He tells you he has heart-burn, dreadful flatulence', and so forth, but these are at best distant approximations to his actual feelings. And so, 'after vain and unsatisfactory efforts, his conclusion generally is, "In short you see before you, the most miserable wretch upon the face of the earth".'[41]

Beddoes, himself a prolific writer ever alert to the seductions of language, believed this situation was in various ways revealing. At one level, it exemplified the human 'tragi-comedy': it was, doubtless, endemically difficult to vocalize one's pains or verbalize one's body. Above all, with sporadic, sudden, and unpredictable conditions such as fits or twinges, accurate inner descriptors were particularly lacking:

> language has not yet been adjusted with any degree of exactness, to our inward feelings. Hence medical reports, where these feelings come in question, stand a double chance of inaccuracy. The invalid, with whom the representation must originate, may express himself ill [sic!]; and the physician may misconceive him if he takes him simply at his word, or by trying to help him out, may substitute his own ideas. How little then can we depend upon generalisation of such obscure data![42]

Such a situation, Beddoes believed, was particularly characteristic of hypochondria, the prime-time disorder of the day. In this instance, being lost for the right words was actually symptomatic of the condition; for, with the hypochondriac,

> the intellect itself is subject to fits of intermission. There is a frequent incapability of mustering the ideas, or of finding words for the thoughts. The memory, at such moments, is extinguished; the fountains of the imagination are dried up, and on a hundred little occasions in life, which demand an expedient or present a choice of difficulties, invention and judgment are both totally at fault. 'The head is a desert', as one who speaks from experience, expresses it.[43]

As these acute observations reveal, Beddoes was amongst the earliest to discern in speech defects symptoms of neurological disease.[44]

Beddoes moreover considered the shortcomings of medical language were ineradicable. For one thing, symptoms had no rigid boundaries, and diseases themselves no fixed, permanent manifestations. How easy the diagnostic art would have been had it been possible to frame disease nosologies rather as Linnaeus had pencilled in the classification of plants. Certain authors had indeed 'laboured, so much in vain, to give *definitions* of diseases, similar to those which occur in books of botanical nomenclature': the labour, however, was abortive.[45] Dismissing the taxonomic nomenclature of his erstwhile mentor, the great Edinburgh professor William Cullen, Beddoes concluded that his 'definitions of diseases have perhaps more authority than value'.[46]

Such difficulties, however, did not lead Beddoes to conclude that medical terminology could never escape the mire of arbitrariness. For, despite the claims of Brunonianism that disease was unitary in its nature, distinct disease complexes truly existed, which required to be distinguished by individual terms.[47]

Faced with the task of fixing such a nomenclature, however, Beddoes saw little cause for optimism. It might have been expected that, with time, experience, and the march of science, and especially as the medico-scientific community strove to refine its definitions, medical language itself would grow more exact and stable. Not so, however; for those very forces of change actually produced the opposite effect. The 'progress of knowledge', Beddoes confessed, 'renders stability of language impossible. Hence, in treating of a new science, licence of expression is allowed.'[48] Here Beddoes reflected upon his own experience in England as a champion of the new Lavoisierian chemistry, with its expressly revolutionary vocabulary: 'Whether I have abused this privilege by disoxygenated and other terms of "learned length", persons, skilled alike in the philosophy of things and words, may decide.'[49] Scientific innovation always required new coinings. Ideally, being fresh minted, and not yet clipped or defaced, these should possess the virtue of exactitude; the reality was that nobody could agree upon their precise cash value.

If the prospects for a pellucid, unambiguous, scientific language of medicine were thus dim, everyday speech was no more satisfactory. For in the end, even words in common currency could not escape the galling growth of private and in-group meanings. 'There are a number of terms in language', reflected Beddoes, 'which every man, at least till he is cross-examined, can define to his own satisfaction, but no one to the satisfaction of others ... Mad is one of those words, which mean almost every thing and nothing.'[50]

Not content with merely identifying the polysemic quality of that signifier, Beddoes endeavoured (in a manner which we will see was highly characteristic of him) to explain the historico-social reasons why 'mad' had spawned a multitude of meanings. 'At first it was, I imagine, applied to transports of rage', he surmised, gesturing towards a speculative history of human progress from emotional rudeness to refinement; 'and when men were civilized enough to be capable of insanity, their insanity, I presume, must have been of the frantic sort, because, in the untutored, intense feelings seem regularly to carry a boisterous expression.'[51] (And here, alongside Beddoes's intriguing fragment of conjectural history, it could be added that the multiplying of meanings for the word 'mad' might be taken as a symptom of the spread of madness itself; for, in Georgian opinion, sanity was marked by the reign of stable, regular meaning, whereas madness frolicked in a Babel-world of abused words and rampant nonsense.)[52]

Common-or-garden terms do not merely bear a plurality of subjective meanings. Simply by virtue of being *common*, Beddoes argues, they carry accretions of associations which are positively misleading and even harmful. He ventured an instance: 'In a variety of cases, mankind act upon associations formed by sounds, without further enquiry. What more natural therefore, than that he who has contracted a disorder called a *cold*, should expect to remove it by heat.'[53] This, however, was a 'delusion'. Hence, when writing popular health-care works for the public at large, Beddoes announced his decision to abandon the common 'cold' as an illness term, and, having weighed up but rejected 'rheum', on the grounds that it was obsolete, decided to 'risk the imputation of pedantry in using catarrh instead'.[54]

Comparable confusion attended the term 'light'. Those suffering from gastric disorders were often advised to follow a 'light' diet, i.e., properly understood, one readily digested. But, 'seduced by the treachery of sound', such patients eat things 'specifically light as mealy potatoes, and very porous bread, not things easily digestible, especially by them'. The mischief did not stop there. 'The same idea of lightness frequently misleads the dyspeptic to give an imprudent preference to liquids over solids, and sometimes to a liquor so very ascesent as water-gruel.'[55]

Beddoes, in short, wrestled with, and finally resigned himself to, the irremediable instability of medical terminology. What irked him was that it was being rendered unnecessarily looser and less perspicacious, thanks to the perverting power of fashion. In various theatres of life, Georgian commentators deplored the focus subverting the direct and honest representation of reality: fashion, the masquerade, the mask, hypocrisy, advertising, puffery, and so forth, all of which involved an insidious divorce of signifier from signified.[56] Sartorial sophistication above all hid reality behind appearance, and fashionable linguistic usage produced parallel effects, clouding the content of utterances in a stream of gibberish. Modish hyperbole devalued the currency, while euphemism created destabilizing obscurity. Fashion sanctioned the incantatory use of buzz-words such as 'genteel', 'polite', and 'liberal'; inflation devalued them, and overuse emptied them of meaning. Beddoes feared such a fate was overtaking illness language in polite society. A sort of private jargon was gaining ground, opaque to anyone outside the charmed circles, and strictly speaking medically meaningless.

The acceleration of terminological turnover worsened the problem: nobody could afford to be seen dead in yesterday's diseases. Such a dizzying semantic whirligig was satirized by the Bath physician and *belles lettrist*, James Makittrick Adair. In his *Essays on Fashionable Disorders* (1790), Adair deplored that fact that medicine had been sucked into the vortex of fashion, which 'like its companion Luxury, may be considered as one of those excrescences which are attached to national improvement'.[57] The Janus-face of fashion was, doubtless, the key to the civilizing process. 'As societies advance in civilization, the active mind of man, not contented with the means of satisfying our natural wants, is anxiously employed in creating artificial wants, and inventing the means of their gratification.' The consequence was the 'empire of fashion'.[58] This had 'now become universal; it is not confined to the decorations of our persons, or the embellishment of our houses and equipages; but extends to our politics, morals, religion, and even in some degree to our sciences. Men and women of fashion are supereminently distinguished from those of no fashion, or whom, no-body knows.'[59] Naturally the workings of the mode were communicated through the medium of smart-set parlance.

Even medicine, regretted Adair, 'is become subject to the empire of fashion'.[60] By this, he emphasized, he was not simply regurgitating the hoary banality that 'fashion has long influenced the great and opulent in the choice of their physicians, surgeons, apothecaries, and midwives'. The present age, he claimed, showed something shockingly new: for fashion was nowadays directing the *beau monde* 'also in the choice of their diseases'.[61]

How so? It was thanks to the loadedness of language. Physicians had to affix names to every disorder ('which may, or may not', Adair adds with a barb, 'be expressive of the nature of the disease').[62] Hence, 'if both patient and doctor are people of fashion, this circumstance is alone sufficient to render the term fashionable', for the elite are adept at spreading the contagion of their own terms. 'As people of fashion claim an exclusive privilege of having always some thing to complain of', he observed, 'so the mutual communication of their ailments is often the topic of conversation; the imagination frequently suggests a similarity of disease, though none such really exists; and thus the term becomes soon completely fashionable.'[63]

Adair ventured a historical narrative of successive disease-name epidemics. 'In the latter end of the last and beginning of this century, spleen, vapours or hyp was the fashionable disease.' For this, royalty could take dubious credit.

The Princess, afterwards Queen Anne, often chagrined and insulted in her former station, and perplexed and harrassed in the latter, was frequently subject to depression of spirits; for which, after the courtly physicians had given it a name, they proceeded to prescribe Rawleigh's confection and pearl cordial. This circumstance was sufficient to transfer both the disease and the remedy to all who had the least pretensions to rank with persons of fashion. In process of time, however, these fashionable and palatable shop drams became by repetition too weak; and many of the patients, tired of the expence and inefficacy of the remedy, found a more ready and more powerful substitute in closet cordials and plain Nantz [i.e. brandy].[64]

In other words, labels such as the 'vapours' ran their fashionable course, became *demodé*, and slithered down the social scale. No matter: others crowded to replace them:

Upwards of thirty years ago, a treatise on nervous diseases was published by my quondam learned and ingenious preceptor Dr Whytt, professor of physic, at Edinburgh. Before the publication of this book, people of fashion had not the least idea that they had nerves; but a fashionable apothecary of my acquaintance, having cast his eye over the book, and having been often puzzled by the enquiries of his patients concerning the nature and causes of their complaints, derived from thence a hint – 'Madam, you are nervous!' The solution was quite satisfactory, the term because fashionable, and spleen, vapours and hyp were forgotten.[65]

After some half a century of hard wear, however, even 'nerves' had had their day, being eclipsed by more brilliant terminological novelties:

Some years after this, Dr Coe wrote a treatise on biliary concretions, which turned the tide of fashion: nerves and nervous diseases were kicked out of doors, and bilious became the fashionable term. How long it will stand its ground cannot be determined.[66]

Biliousness still seems to have been *à la mode* a decade later, in Beddoes's time.[67] Discussing that appellation, the Bristol doctor commented, 'delicate women are peculiarly liable ... They style themselves bilious in consequence. Indeed, the term *bilious* threatens to become synonymous with *lady*, as Hamlet declares, "*Frailty*, thy name is woman".'[68]

None of this would matter, Adair concluded, if it were not positively destructive of health. Alas, 'names or terms, when improperly employed in matters of science, necessarily create confusion and error.' For the connotations of biliousness led to compulsive self-dosing with purgatives, ruinous to the stomach. The crowning irony was thus that when patients filed along to the physician, complaining 'Doctor, I am bilious', the wound was generally self-inflicted, the consequence of consuming gallons of self-prescribed anti-bilious draughts.[69]

Beddoes confirmed Adair's diagnosis. 'There is no error more common or more mischievous among dyspeptic, hypochondriacal and hysterical invalids than to suppose themselves *bilious. The bile! the bile!* is the general watchword among them; and they think they can never sufficiently work it off with aloes, magnesia or salts.'[70] This tiny term, and the train of perilous auto-medication it set in motion, was destroying the nation's fibre. 'I once heard', gossiped Beddoes, 'the maid of the lady, whom a brisk course of this kind, determined by the dread of bile, had brought very near to death's door, observe that "it was no wonder – for her mistress was never easy, but when she was on the *chaise percée*!"'[71]

What was the solution? One might, insinuated Adair in Mandevillian fashion, try to cure word-induced diseases through words themselves – an echo of the homoeopathic doctrine of similars? In particular, a little familiarity with etymologies might come to the rescue. In Greek the term for bile ('choler') also denoted anger. It was worth reminding patients of this fact, for:

Were the British Fair, especially the Fashionable, whose polished education has a manifest tendency to regulate, if not almost totally annihilate, all the tumultuous passions, apprized of this circumstance, they could not possibly conceive that any of their bodily or mental evils originated from or were connected with, an excess of gall or bile; and instead of continuing to adopt it as a fashionable disease, they would resign it to the nymphs of St Giles and Billingsgate.[72]

In surveying the circulation of faddish illness vocabulary, Adair and Beddoes spied a further process at work, a 'trickle-down effect', whereby valuable technical terms deployed *bona fide* within the medical profession unfortunately passed into common currency, becoming devalued in the process, and misconstrued by the masses.[73] Particularly deplorable, in this respect, was the epidemic of popular 'Teach yourself medicine' books, bestowing upon the educated laity a smattering of ill-digested medical parlance. Self-styled 'lady and gentlemen doctors' – that term is Adair's;[74] Beddoes says such fine folks call themselves 'private practitioners' –[75] were spending their time poring over 'dispensatories and practical compilations with great avidity'. Not just that, but they acted upon what they read, dosing up their friends as well ('numbers circulate scraps of paper, marked with medical hieroglyphics, just as they circulate scandal, for want of other employment') –[76] a practice reflected perhaps in Tony Lumpkin's accusation against his mother, that 'you have been dosing me ever since I was born. I have gone through every receipt in the Family Physician ten times over; and you have thoughts of coursing me through Quincy next spring.'[77] Beddoes hated to see 'people who have never been in the way of medical information take up the terms in which medical opinion has been delivered, and use them as battledores to strike nonsense backwards and forwards like a shuttlecork [sic]!'[78]

Both Adair and Beddoes disapproved on principle of all such 'Be your own physician' primers. What made matters worse was the failure of communication they typically involved. The authors of such manuals were little 'capable of divesting [themselves] of technical or professional views' – [79] no popular author (Beddoes judged) had succeeded 'in measuring our information according to the wants of the common reader'.[80] The result was that purchasers acquired an indigestible *olla podrida* of medical jargon, which they then ignorantly misapplied. Precisely this had happened with 'biliousness'.[81] 'Bilious' had once possessed an exact medical meaning before being vulgarized:

> For general languor, nausea, foulness of the tongue, want of appetite and indigestion, accompany or follow the excessive action of the liver, and therefore even by medical writers these complaints are said to be produced by too large a quantity of bile in the first passages. This opinion having been spread by the publications and conversation of physicians, those who feel languor, squeamishness and all the other symptoms, only not those of real jaundice, ascribe them without scruple to bile upon the stomach.[82]

In short, medicine had its own professional jargon; but the workings of what Beddoes called the 'sick trade' – the kind of process exposed by Mandeville in his saga of Misomedon's experiences – resulted in a variant of Gresham's law, whereby good terms were driven out by bad. How lamentable that physicians themselves were party to such devaluations, for 'such shallow nonsense from a regular physician to common readers gains credit for quacks, whose advertisements usually run in the same strain.'[83]

Beddoes, who decried the toadying of the scions of his profession to Quality clients,[84] believed their word-games – sins both of commission and omission – were deeply pernicious, a prostitution of the Aesculapian art. For instance, doctors all too often entered into unhealthy collusion with the families of tuberculosis sufferers. It would be tacitly agreed that the ominous term 'consumption' would never be mentioned, especially in front of the sick person's face – some euphemism such as 'delicacy' would be made to stand service:

> A young person in consumption feels herself low, and is hysterical in various ways; she is therefore persuaded that the cough is *nervous*: that is, she and her friends persuade themselves there is no danger, or that a treatment very different from that likely to answer is requisite.[85]

By consequence of this semantic smokescreen, opportunities for early treatment were scandalously squandered, and mortality needlessly increased. Rather, plain speaking was needed. Beddoes's annoyance at this mystification was shared by at least some patients, unable to pierce the murky euphemisms of the physicians.[86]

Would that Beddoes himself had practised what he preached! His own *Hygeia* (1802–3), a massive, three-volume guide to healthy living, targeted at the educated middle classes, detailed those chronic disorders which he considered the bane of modern civilization – indeed, as diseases of civilization itself.[87] Beddoes viewed nervous ailments as epidemic: when mild, they took the form of hypochondria; when more serious, they manifested themselves as epilepsy and mental disorders stretching all the way up to madness proper. A major cause of this catastrophe, he believed, was masturbation. This habit, commonly begun at boarding school, was subsequently (according to Beddoes) encouraged by the sedentary habits of high society teenagers, who were allowed to loll on sofas reading lubricious romances: 'novels render the sensibility still more diseased', he accused, 'they increase indolence, the imaginary world indisposing those, who inhabit it in thought, to go abroad into the real.'[88] Their imaginations being thus inflamed, the results were dire, for self-abuse led to debility and disease. Onanism was thus another disorder caused, or exacerbated, by the suggestive, seductive power of language. Not least, Beddoes believed, masturbation had been the cause of Jonathan Swift's premature senility, with its 'loss of associative power' and attendant 'nervous complaint', culminating in the 'madness of misanthropy'.[89]

How many readers of *Hygeia*, however, actually picked all this up from Beddoe's text? How many gathered the meaning of what he regarded as his most crucial warning? For the fact is that nowhere, throughout the numerous pages devoted to the subject, did Beddoes use any term whatsoever – be it 'onanism', 'self-abuse', or 'masturbation' itself – which directly and explicitly denoted the practice. His entire discussion was cloaked in windy circumlocutions and emotive generalities. Indeed, throughout his popular advice works, on many occasions when he felt obliged to address sexual matters, Beddoes routinely took refuge in the decent obscurity of a foreign or a learned tongue. At one point, discussing female libido, he printed a passage about *'fureur érotique'* entirely in French;[90] and elsewhere he broke into Latin to broach the topic of seminal emissions, stating that a particular patient had had a 'debilitating' night, and adding, in a footnote, *'hoc nomine designatur pollutio nocturna.'*[91] Elsewhere he surveyed giddiness as a symptom of sexual irregularity in a page of Latin 'to avoid giving offence'.[92] He further states that he will desist from mentioning one of the causes of hypochondria by name, wishing to 'avoid scandalizing the overdelicate among my readers'.[93]

Regarding Swift's complaint – Beddoes clearly believed that Swift had induced senile dementia by his own hand – Beddoes beat about the bush by saying that his mental condition 'scarcely admits of any but a physical solution', and contending that literary critics, 'not being professional men,

[had] failed to develope the mystery fully'.[94] In other words, even in a work explicitly committed to breaking the magical, and pathological, power of misleading pseudo-medical terms, Beddoes found the pressures too powerful to permit straight talk.

As G.S. Rousseau shows in the preceding essay in this volume, 'nerves' formed the most ambivalent diagnostic category in Georgian popular medicine. Critics crowed over the confusion. What finally makes Beddoes a constructive critic is that he went beyond scoring points and striking poses, recognizing the need to investigate what might be called the 'life histories' and 'social personalities' of medical terms. In dissecting the term 'nervous', Adair was flippant; Beddoes by contrast went to the heart of the problem.[95]

Verbal ambiguity in such matters, Beddoes suggested, stemmed from the inescapable problem of deciding what was truly to be diagnosed a nervous complaint.[96] It would not be helpful, he decided, to specify in advance an inventory of symptoms deemed both necessary and sufficient conditions for the use of the term 'nervous'. Herein lay, Beddoes contended, not a weakness, but a strength, of the concept; for 'nervous' was a useful catch-all for such authentic complaints as failed to present a single fixed set of symptoms, but had a broader, more protean repertoire. Hysteria was a further disease entity where flexibility in relating name to symptoms was not vagueness but a reflection of reality:

> The same hysterical person shall tremble at one moment, and become blind or deaf, or lose the use of a limb, at another. Then a sneezing or retching of the most excessive violence shall supervene. Not only so, but the paralytic limb shall be restored, in the twinking of an eye, to its full powers, upon the commencement of sneezing or retching; upon a fit of laughing or crying, or the rising of a ball in the throat, or upon the occurrence of any other of the symptoms, which shew themselves in this infinitely diversified complaint.[97]

Of course, he notes the risk that meaning might thereby be diluted: 'By extending the term *nervous* upon the strength of one or two circumstances of resemblance, we are in danger of losing all meaning, and reducing the most heterogeneous affections to one head.'[98] The problem was real. 'It will, therefore, if we would keep clear of embarrassment in language, be necessary to have a word entirely new, or some addition to that which we have hitherto retained, in some cases where nervous symptoms occur.'[99] If one accepted that a truly nervous disease involved involuntary motion, disturbance of perception, and intellectual impairment, it was plain that, though convulsions were generally symptomatic of nervous disease, under some circumstances – e.g. in smallpox – convulsions should not be taken as indices of nervous disorder at all. Hence a clear distinction had to be retained between what was a 'proper nervous disease' and what, by contrast, was merely 'inflammatory'.[100]

Experience and analysis would help. By carefully attending to a range of cases, it would be possible 'to call only certain complaints nervous', which in turn 'may enable the writer to be more concise, without being less perspicuous, which is the proper use of general terms'.[101] Herein lay a lesson for readers at large. 'In common life, there would be much less confusion and somewhat fewer mistakes, if the term *nervous* were not indiscriminately employed, both where there exist or have existed symptoms of a different and peculiar nature, and where there do not.'[102]

So what would constitute an adequate medical conceptualization of nervous complaints? 'They are disorders in which the limbs move irregularly, or without the direction of the will, in which the organs of perception suffer, and the intellectual functions are disturbed; and this, in most instances, without any preceding or concomitant systems of a different nature, either general or partial.'[103] Even so, having tried to escape from the terminological maze, Beddoes candidly admits that problems remain: 'It is not easy, and perhaps not possible, to invent a term, which shall point out any one set of disorders to the exclusion of others.'[104]

Yet if 'nervous' were liable to abuse, it also had its uses. In any case, it should not be expected that the naming of diseases could be treated as a once-and-for-all matter; classification had to evolve over time, according to needs. 'In medicine it will, I fear, for a long time, be equally easy to object to a general term and difficult to replace it by another, free from just objections.'[105]

Perhaps it was of paramount importance, therefore, not to attempt to fix ideal, timeless, meanings, in the manner of the French Academy, but to accept that words had their own evolutionary patterns, whose pathways, if not immutable, were themselves *intelligible*, especially when socially and historically contextualized. Back to 'nervous': 'We familiarly speak of a nervous style, and of a *nervous* person. But in those instances one feel the sense to be totally different.'[106] In the first case, we imply strength. In the latter, as when we refer to 'certain peculiarities of feeling, and as it would seem also of movement', a weakness is in mind. So how was this migration of meaning to be explained? History once again pointed to the answer:

> The tendons or sinews that attach the muscles to the parts which they move, were anciently comprehended under the term *nerve*; and the strong were marked by superior size of muscle and tendon. Hence Junius might be indifferently called a nervous, a sinewy or a strong writer. But when we hear of a *nervous* man or woman, we never think of any thing in the shape of Hercules.[107]

In other words, it was the development of more exact and specialized anatomical knowledge which facilitated the semantic shift in question.[108] Beddoes identified a similar mutation of meanings with the term 'relaxed', where common custom had 'vulgarly'[109] sanctioned a meaning related to the 'secretions which keep the membranes moist': when 'in excess, this in common language is called relaxation; and females in incredible number suffer from a relaxation of a particular kind.'[110]

Beddoes's point was that language could not be frozen for ever, by committee or dictionary; usage must keep in step with science, but scientific usage should not run ahead of understanding: 'In all departments of knowledge, the nomenclature must be as the information. Where one is deficient, the other will be vague.'[111]

For, at bottom, the public would hear only what it wanted to hear. One of the worst pseudo-medical disorders of the day was wilful, selective deafness. People employed language to shield them from unwelcome truths. Take gourmandizing. Dinner party chit-chat often contained exchanges rather as follows: ' " – do let me send you some more of this mock turtle" – "another pâte" – "Sir, some of the trifle" – "a few slices of cucumber" – "I SHALL INSIST upon your trying this nice melon".'[112] Instead of these irrefusable politenesses, the 'language of hospitality' might more candidly 'run in this strain':

> 'shall I send you a fit of the cholic' – 'do let me help you to a little bilious vomiting and purging' – 'Ma'am, you cannot refuse a touch of inflammation in the bowels – It may come to a tight race between your intestines and your physician. But I hope it will stop before it gets quite to the undertaker and the sexton.'[113]

If this example carried a facetious air born of hopelessness, Beddoes offered other demystifications of language in good earnest. Thus he warned about the insidious and pretentious language of sensibility. It was an abuse of words – and of people – to assume that only the feeble, languid, and idle possessed 'finer feeling'. Strip the verbal veneer and its patina of associations, and you would discover that, in reality, 'Healthy children appear as quick in feeling as the majority of persons easily fluttered; but healthy children also derive incessant, or to be very precise, greatly preponderating enjoyment, from being exquisitely alive all over.'[114] And parallel to 'sensibility' was 'delicacy', with all its arch and euphemistic overtones:

> Alas! for the abuse of terms. Do we not hear the diseased perpetually styled *delicate*? Heaven knows how many this one *catachresis*, for that is the name of the said figure of speech, may have led to become candidates for disease, or at the least seduced into self-neglect. Could

they but have been well aprized of the indelicacies of many a delicate constitution – indelicacies which I surely do not mean to disclose![115]

People should be ashamed of all the humbug about the 'advantages of a feeble constitution'.[116]

Given all these language traps, 'how are we', demands Beddoes, 'to set about to practise for improvement in health?'[117] Perhaps, he concludes, teasingly, fatalistically, the answer was to issue 'a little dictionary of medical nonsense'. This 'may indeed be of use to the practitioners as well as to the patients. For as they cannot have any ideas, it is so much the more urgent to insure them a plentiful supply of words, relative to the art of the physic.'[118]

NOTES

1   H. Brody, *Stories of Sickness* (New Haven, Conn.: Yale University Press, 1987); A. Kleinman, *The Illness Narratives: Suffering, Healing and the Human Condition* (New York: Basic Books, 1988); Roy Porter and Dorothy Porter, *In Sickness and in Health: The British Experience 1650–1850* (London: Fourth Estate, 1988); Dorothy Porter and Roy Porter, *Patient's Progress: Doctors and Doctoring in Eighteenth-century England* (Stanford, Cal.: Stanford University Press and Polity Press, 1989).

2   K. Keele, *Anatomies of Pain* (Oxford: Blackwell Scientific Publications, 1957); D. De Moulin, 'A Historical-Phenomenological Study of Bodily Pain in Western Medicine', *Bulletin of the History of Medicine*, 48 (1974), 540–70. On medical language see J.H. Dirckx, *The Language of Medicine. Its Evolution, Structure, and Dynamics* (New York: Praeger, 1983); Roy Porter, 'The Language of Quackery in England, 1660–1800', in P. Burke and R. Porter (eds), *The Social History of Language* (Cambridge: Cambridge University Press, 1987), 73–103; Roy Porter, 'The Doctor and the Word', *Medical Sociology News*, 9 (1983), 21–8.

3   S. Sontag, *Illness as Metaphor* (New York: Farrar, Straus and Giroux, 1978; London, Allen Lane, 1979); S. Sontag, *AIDS as Metaphor* (Harmondsworth: Allen Lane, 1989); J.T. Patterson, *The Dread Disease. Cancer and Modern American Culture* (Cambridge, Mass.: Harvard University Press, 1987); S. Gilman, *Difference and Pathology* (Ithaca, NY: Cornell University Press, 1985); S. Gilman, *Disease and Representation: Images of Illness from Madness to AIDS* (Ithaca, NY: Cornell University Press, 1988).

4   T.S. Szasz, *Schizophrenia. The Sacred Symbol of Psychiatry* (Syracuse, NY: Syracuse University Press, 1988); T.S. Szasz, *The Myth of Mental Illness* (New York: Paladin, 1961); T.S. Szasz, *The Manufacture of Madness* (New York: Dell, 1970). For discussion see Mark S. Micale, 'Hysteria and its Historiography: A Review of Past and Present Writings', *History of Science*, xxvii (1989), 223–61, 319–51.

294   ROY PORTER

5   Dirckx, *The Language of Medicine*; on national differences today, see Lynn Payer, *Medicine and Culture. Notions of Health and Sickness in Britain, the U.S., France and Western Germany* (London: Gollancz, 1989).

6   Good accounts of these processes are to be found in A. Kleinman, *Patients and Healers in the Context of Culture: An Exploration of the Borderline between Anthropology, Medicine, and Psychiatry* (Berkeley, Cal.: University of California Press, 1980); A. Kleinman, *Social Origins of Distress and Disease. Depression, Neurasthenia, and Pain in Modern China* (New Haven, Conn.: Yale University Press, 1986); A. Kleinman, *The Illness Narratives*; A. Kleinman and B. Good (eds), *Culture and Depression. Studies in the Anthropology and Cross-Cultural Psychiatry of Affect and Disorder* (Berkeley, Cal.: University of California Press, 1985); E.J. Cassel, *Talking to Patients* (Cambridge, Mass.: MIT Press, 1985); Brody, *Stories of Sickness*.

7   C. MacCabe (ed.), *The Talking Cure. Essays in Psychoanalysis and Language* (London: Macmillan, 1981).

8   S. Baur, *Hypochondria: Woeful Imaginings* (Princeton, NJ: Princeton University Press, 1988).

9   G. Groddeck, *The Meaning of Illness*, trans. G. Mander (London: Hogarth Press, 1977).

10   N. Jewson, 'Medical Knowledge and the Patronage System in Eighteenth Century England', *Sociology*, 8 (1974), 369–85; N. Jewson, 'The Disappearance of the Sick Man from Medical Cosmology, 1770–1870', *Sociology*, 10 (1976), 225–44; Porter and Porter, *Patient's Progress*.

11   S.J. Reiser, *Medicine and the Reign of Technology* (Cambridge: Cambridge University Press, 1978). See also W.F. Bynum and Roy Porter (eds), *Medicine and the Five Senses* (Cambridge: Cambridge University Press, 1992).

12   Roy Porter, *Health for Sale. Quackery in England, 1650–1850* (Manchester: Manchester University Press, 1989).

13   Cheyne specialized in what we might call cases of neurotic disturbance. He felt he had to be particularly careful to avoid diagnostic terms hinting at mental disorder, because lunacy and insanity carried such appalling stigmas. It taxed diplomacy, he stressed, to find the right softening phrases when handling conditions of that type, for 'nervous *Distempers especially, are under some Kind* of Disgrace *and* Imputation, *in the Opinion of the* Vulgar *and* Unlearned; *they pass among the Multitude, for a lower Degree of* Lunacy, *and the first Step towards a* distemper'd Brain; *and the best Construction is* Whim, Ill-Humour, Peevishness *or* Particularity; *and in the* Sex, Daintiness, Fantasticalness, *or* Coquetry.' The tensions which such diagnostic ambivalences created challenged bedside tact to the limits, for 'Often when I have been consulted in a Case, before I was acquainted with the Character and Temper of the Patient, and found it to be what is commonly call'd Nervous, I have been in the utmost Difficulty, when desir'd to define or name the Distemper, for fear of affronting them or fixing a Reproach on a Family or person' (George Cheyne, *The English Malady; or, A Treatise of Nervous Diseases* [London: G. Strahan, 1733], 260).

14   Quoted in Porter and Porter, *Patient's Progress*, 142.

15   Gregory Glyster [pseud.], *A Dose for the Doctors; or the Aesculapian Labyrinth*

Explored (London: Kearsley, 1789). See, more broadly, Porter, *Health for Sale*, ch. 7.

16   N. McKendrick, John Brewer, and J.H. Plumb, *The Birth of a Consumer Society: The Commercialization of Eighteenth-Century England* (London: Europa, 1982); John Brewer and Roy Porter (eds), *Consumption and the World of Goods* (London: Routledge, 1992).

17   T. Beddoes, *A Letter to the Right Honourable Sir Joseph Banks ... on the causes and removal of the prevailing discontents, imperfections, and abuses, in medicine* (London: Richard Phillips, 1808). For the market orientation of eighteenth-century medicine see I.S.L. Loudon, 'The Origin of the General Practitioner' (The James Mackenzie Lecture of the Royal College of General Practitioners for 1982), *Journal of the Royal College of General Practice*, 33 (1983), 13–18; I.S.L. Loudon, 'The Nature of Provincial Medical Practice in Eighteenth-Century England', *Medical History*, 29 (1985), 1–32; I.S.L. Loudon, *Medical Care and the General Practitioner 1750–1850* (Oxford: Clarendon Press, 1986); J. Lane, 'The Medical Practitioners of Provincial England in 1783', *Medical History*, 28 (1984), 353–71; I. Waddington, 'General Practitioners and Consultants in Early Nineteenth Century England: The Sociology of an Intra-Professional Conflict', in J. Woodward and D. Richards (eds), *Health Care and Popular Medicine in Nineteenth Century England: Essays in the Social History of Medicine* (London: Croom Helm, 1977), 164–88; I. Waddington, *The Medical Profession in the Industrial Revolution* (Dublin: Gill and Macmillan, 1984); M.J. Peterson, *The Medical Profession in Mid-Victorian London* (Berkeley, Cal.: University of California Press, 1978); Porter and Porter, *Patient's Progress*; Porter and Porter, *In Sickness and in Health*.

18   For the latest research on Mandeville, see Francis McKee, 'The Earlier Works of Bernard Mandeville, 1685–1715' (Ph.D. thesis, Univerity of Glasgow, 1991).

19   B. Mandeville, *A Treatise of the Hypochondriack and Hysterick Diseases* (2nd edn, London: Tonson, 1730; reprinted Hildesheim: George Olms Verlag, 1981).

20   Ibid., xii.

21   Ibid., xiii.

22   Ibid., xii, xiii.

23   Ibid., 8, iv.

24   Ibid., 21.

25   Cf. Thomas Beddoes, *Manual of Health: or, the Invalid Conducted Safely Through the Seasons* (London: Johnson, 1806), 40, where he states that he knows a woman who is an avid reader of '*guides to health*': 'She has lately taken to books of *veterinary* medicine; and one of her nearest friends begins to fear in earnest that she will make a regular progress through the diseases of animals next.'

26   Mandeville, *Treatise*, 21.

27   Ibid., 49.

28   On Willis see Robert G. Frank, jr, 'Thomas Willis and his Circle: Brain and Mind in Seventeenth Century Medicine', in G.S. Rousseau (ed.), *Languages of Psyche: Mind and Body in Enlightenment Thought* (Berkeley, Cal.: and Los Angeles: University of California Press, 1990), 107–46; K. Dewhurst, *Willis's Oxford Casebook (1650–52)* (Oxford: Sandford Publications, 1981); see also

K. Dewhurst, *Thomas Willis as a Physician* (Los Angeles: University of California Press, 1964); Hansruedi Isler, *Thomas Willis, 1621–1685, Doctor and Scientist* (New York: Hafner, 1968); J. Spillane, *The Doctrine of the Nerves* (London: Oxford University Press, 1981).

29　Mandeville, *Treatise*, 98.

30　Ibid., 202.

31　Ibid., 36.

32　Ibid., v.

33　Ibid., 205.

34　Ibid., 205.

35　Ibid., 36. Literally: 'not by words but by herbs [will a cure be effected].'

36　Ibid., 205. Cheyne's autobiographical account is contained in Cheyne, *The English Malady*.

37　Mandeville, *Treatise*, 203.

38　Many works trade upon precisely these ambiguities: words being simultaneously pathogenic and therapeutic. See Roy Porter, 'Against the Spleen', in V.G. Meyer (ed.), *Laurence Sterne: Riddles and Mysteries* (London and New York: Vision Press, 1984), 84–99.

39　See S. Tucker, *Protean Shape* (London: Athlone Press, 1967); W.R. Wimsatt, *Philosophical Words* (New Haven: Yale University Press, 1948); L.J. Jordanova (ed.), *Languages of Nature* (London: Free Association, 1986); Hans Aarsleff, *From Locke to Saussure: Essays on the Study of Language and Intellectual History* (Minneapolis: University of Minnesota Press, 1982); Hans Aarsleff, *The Study of Language in England, 1780–1860* (Minneapolis: University of Minnesota Press, 1983); and, for Horne Tooke, the essay by Dan Rosenberg in the present volume.

40　T. Beddoes, *Hygeia*, 3 vols (Bristol: Phillips, 1802–3), vol. 2, Essay viii, p. 78 (henceforth references to this will appear thus: 2 viii 78). For Beddoes's life, see J.E. Stock, *Memoirs of the Life of Thomas Beddoes MD* (London: J. Murray, 1811); D.A. Stansfield, *Thomas Beddoes M.D. 1760–1808, Chemist, Physician, Democrat* (Dordrecht: Reidel, 1984).

41　Beddoes, *Hygeia*, 2 viii 78.

42　Ibid., 3 ix 40.

43　Ibid., 2 viii 78.

44　His friend, Erasmus Darwin, himself victim of a severe stammer, was also deeply interested in speech disorders; see his *A Plan for the Conduct of Female Education in Boarding Schools* (London: 1797), 86. See also D. Rockley, *Speech Disorder in Nineteenth Century Britain* (London: Croom Helm, 1980).

45　Beddoes, *Hygeia*, 2 vi 13.

46　Ibid., 3 ix 21.

47　W.F. Bynum and Roy Porter (eds), *Brunonianism in Britain and Europe* (*Medical History*, Supplement No. 8, 1988). Beddoes himself was attracted to John Brown's system of medicine while a student at Edinburgh, and dabbled with Brunonian ideas.

48　Beddoes, *Manual of Health*, 47.

49　Ibid., 47.

50　Beddoes, *Hygeia*, 3 x 39.

51   Ibid., 3 x 40.
52   For a discussion of meanings of 'madness' at this time, see Roy Porter. *Mind Forg'd Manacles: Madness in England from the Restoration to the Regency* (London: Athlone, 1987), ch. 1.
53   Beddoes, *Hygeia*, 2 v 72.
54   Ibid., 2 v 72.
55   Ibid., 2 viii 70.
56   For Beddoes's denunciations of fashion, see Roy Porter, 'Reforming the Patient. Thomas Beddoes and Medical Practice', in Roger French and Andrew Wear (eds), *Medicine in the Age of Reform* (London: Routledge, 1991); and more generally Roy Porter, 'Making Faces: Physiognomy and Fashion in Eighteenth-Century England', *Etudes Anglaises*, 38 (1985), 385–96; M. Shortland, 'The Body in Question; Some Perceptions, Problems and Perspectives of the Body in relation to Character, 1750–1850', Ph.D. thesis, University of Leeds, 1985; M. Shortland, 'Skin Deep: Barthes, Lavater and the Visible Body', *Economy and Society*, 14 (1985), 273–312; M. Shortland, 'The Figure of the Hypocrite: Some Contours of an Historical Problem', *Studies in the History of Psychology and the Social Sciences*, 4 (1987), 256–74.
57   J. Makittrick Adair, *Essays on Fashionable Disorders* (London: Bateman, 1970), 1.
58   Ibid., 2.
59   Ibid., 3.
60   Ibid., 3.
61   Ibid., 4.
62   Ibid., 4.
63   Ibid., 5.
64   Ibid., 5.
65   Ibid., 6.
66   Ibid., 6. G.S. Rousseau, in 'Towards a Semiotics of the Nerve' in this volume, suggests that nerves continued fashionable for much longer.
67   Beddoes, *Manual of Health*, 301.
68   Ibid., 301.
69   Adair, *Essays on Fashionable Disorders*, 8, 25.
70   Beddoes, *Hygeia*, 2 viii 102.
71   Ibid., 2 viii 102. Beddoes means a close stool.
72   Adair, *Essays on Fashionable Disorders*, 25. For the subversive use of etymology at this time, see the essay by Dan Rosenberg in the present volume.
73   For 'trickle-down effects' see D. Miller, *Material Culture and Mass Consumption* (Oxford: Basil Blackwell, 1987).
74   Adair, *Essays on Fashionable Disorders*, 73. For such advice literature see Ginnie Smith, 'Prescribing the Rules of Health: Self-Help and Advice in the Late Eighteenth-Century England', in Roy Porter (ed.), *Patients and Practitioners: Lay Perceptions of Medicine in Pre-industrial Society* (Cambridge and New York: Cambridge University Press, 1985), 249–82; Ginnie Smith, 'Cleanliness: the Development of an Idea and Practice in Britain 1770–1850', University of London, Ph.D. Thesis, 1985; C. Lawrence, 'William Buchan: Medicine Laid Open', *Medical History*, 19 (1975), 20–35; C. Rosenberg,

298 ROY PORTER

'Medical Text and Medical Context; Explaining William Buchan's *Domestic Medicine*', *Bulletin of the History of Medicine*, 57 (1983), 22–4; Roy Porter, 'Commerce and Disease in Eighteenth Century England', in S. Hallini (ed.), *Commerces* (Paris: Publications de la Sorbonne, 1991), 55–73.

75 Beddoes, *Hygeia*, 1 ii 28.

76 Ibid., 1 ii 29.

77 Quoted in Adair, *Essays on Fashionable Disorders*, 48. Quincy was a popular medical writer, author of *Pharmacopoeia Officinalis and Extemporanea; or, A Compleat English Dispensatory* (2nd edn, London: A. Bell, 1719).

78 Beddoes, *Manual*, 26.

79 Ibid., 39.

80 Ibid., 1 i 46.

81 Ibid., 2 viii 112.

82 Ibid., 2 viii 112.

83 Ibid., 2 viii 112.

84 For Beddoes's condemnation of his colleagues, see Roy Porter, 'Plutus or Hygeia? Thomas Beddoes and Medical Ethics', in Robert Baker, Dorothy Porter, and Roy Porter (eds), *The Codification of Medical Morality in the Eighteenth and Nineteenth Centuries*, vol. i (Dordrecht: Kluwer, 1992); Porter, 'Reforming the Patient'.

85 Beddoes, *Hygeia*, 3 ix 11.

86 For Beddoes on tuberculosis see Roy Porter, 'Consumption: Disease of the Consumer Society?', in Brewer and Porter, *Consumption and the World of Goods*. For a patient faced with the verbal equivocations of the doctors, see Porter and Porter, *In Sickness and in Health*, 134–5.

87 On the eighteenth-century notion of a disease of civilization see Porter, 'Reforming the Patient'; Roy Porter, 'The Enlightenment as Medicine', in J. Black and J. Gregory (eds), *Culture, Politics and Society in Britain, 1660–1800* (Manchester: Manchester University Press, 1991), 154–83.

88 Beddoes, *Hygeia*, 1 iii 77. On masturbation see P.-G. Boucé, 'Les Jeux Interdits de l'Imaginaire: Onanism et Culpabilisation Sexuelle au XVIIIe Siècle', in J. Céard (ed.), *La Folie et le Corps* (Paris: Presses de l'Ecole Normale Supérieure, 1985), 223–43; E.H. Hare, 'Masturbatory Insanity: the History of an Idea', *Journal of Mental Science*, 108 (1962), 1–25; R.H. MacDonald, 'The Frightful Consequences of Onanism', *Journal of the History of Ideas*, 28 (1967), 423–41; J. Stengers and A. Van Neck, *Histoire d'une Grande Peur: La Masturbation* (Brussels: University of Brussels Press, 1984); L.J. Jordanova, 'The Popularisation of Medicine: Tissot on Onanism', *Textual Practice*, 1 (1987), 68–80.

89 Beddoes, *Hygeia*, 3 ix 184–90. Far the most illuminating discussion of Swift and masturbation is Hugh Ormsby-Lennon, 'Swift's Spirit Reconjured: Das Dong-An-Sich', *Swift Studies*, 3 (1988), 9–78.

90 Beddoes, *Manual*, 79.

91 Beddoes, *Hygeia*, 3 ix 41. One wonders whom it is that Beddoes is trying to protect: is it women? Or is it children? For the continuing uses of Latin, see the essay by Peter Burke in this volume.

92 Beddoes, *Hygeia*, 3 ix 157.

93   Ibid., 2 viii 89.
94   Ibid., 3 ix 194. This seems a splendid instance of the pot calling the kettle black.
95   Ibid., 3 ix 6.
96   For general discussion on eighteenth-century 'nervousness', see Jeffrey M.N. Boss, 'The Seventeenth Century Transformation of the Hysteric Affection', *Psychological Medicine*, 9 (1979), 221–34; G.S. Rousseau, 'Science and the Discovery of the Imagination in Enlightenment England', *Eighteenth-Century Studies*, 3 (1969–70), 108–35; G.S. Rousseau, 'Nerves, Spirits and Fibres: Towards Defining the Origins of Sensibility; With a Postscript', *The Blue Guitar*, 2 (1976), 125–53; G.S. Rousseau, 'Psychology', in G.S. Rousseau and Roy Porter (eds), *The Ferment of Knowledge* (Cambridge: Cambridge University Press, 1980), 143–210; John Mullan, 'Hypochondria and Hysteria: Sensibility and the Physicians', *The Eighteenth Century: Theory and Interpretation*, 25 (1984), 141–77; John Mullan, 'Psychology', in Rousseau and Porter, *The Ferment of Knowledge*, 143–210; Roy Porter, 'The Rage of Party: Madness in Eighteenth Century England', *Medical History*, 27 (1983), 35–50. See also, of course, the essay by Rousseau in the present volume.
97   Beddoes, *Hygeia*, 3 ix 7.
98   Ibid., 3 ix 8.
99   Ibid., 3 ix 8.
100 Ibid., 3 ix 9.
101 Ibid., 3 ix 9.
102 Ibid., 3 ix 9.
103 Ibid., 3 ix 10.
104 Ibid., 3 ix 10.
105 Ibid., 3 ix 12.
106 Beddoes, *Manual*, 85.
107 Ibid., 85.
108 Ibid., 86.
109 Ibid., 182.
110 Ibid., 98: more euphemisms.
111 Beddoes, *Hygeia*, 3 ix 12.
112 Beddoes, *Manual*, 307.
113 Ibid., 307.
114 Ibid., 68.
115 Ibid., 17.
116 Ibid., 3.
117 Ibid., 21.
118 Ibid., 319.

'A New Sort of Logick and Critick': Etymological Interpretation in Horne Tooke's *The Diversions of Purley*[1]

DANIEL ROSENBERG

Hermes, you know, put out the eyes of Argus: and I suspect that he has likewise blinded philosophy: and if I had not imagined so, I should never have cast away a thought upon this subject. If therefore Philosophy herself has been misled the Language, how shall she teach us to detect his tricks?'

John Horne Tooke, *The Diversions of Purley*, vol. 1, p.8

In an essay published in 1810, the Scottish philosopher Dugald Stewart warns against 'deceit' and 'dazzlement', against 'cabalistical mysteries' and 'presumptuous fictions of human folly', all of these the dangers of *etymology*.[2] Stewart's essay was occasioned by ΕΠΕΑ ΠΤΕΡΟΕΝΤΑ *or the Diversions of Purley* (two volumes, 1786 and 1805),[3] the influential work on language by the English radical John Horne Tooke (1736–1812).[4] Stewart's concern was that with Horne Tooke, etymology had been cast loose from its moorings in history and had drifted into the realm of philosophy. Practised as *history*, Stewart observes, etymology 'may often furnish important data' especially in areas of research in which 'we have no historical records'.[5] But, as the quotation from Horne Tooke above indicates, practising 'history' was not at all what Horne Tooke set out to do.

Stewart worried that in the work of Horne Tooke and his many partisans (Stewart gives the example of Erasmus Darwin's *Zoonomia*), philology and philosophy were becoming confused.[6] He argues, 'when the speculations of the mere scholar, or glossarist, presume to usurp, as they have too often done of late, the honours of Philosophy', these speculations become sophistry and frivolity.[7] Stewart's attack on etymology takes part in a larger defence of disciplinary boundaries. His claim is not that etymology is necessarily presumptuous or deceitful; it is only when etymology unsettles disciplinary lines that frivolity results.

Stewart must be credited with understanding the basic aims of Horne Tooke's project. Horne Tooke was precisely after 'a new sort of Logick and Critick', which he thought could only be fashioned by taking down the artificial walls between philosophy and language study.[8] Making a philosophy of language without first properly understanding the language of philosophy is folly, Horne Tooke argues. But if the general principles laid down in Horne Tooke's etymologies 'were admitted as sound', Stewart claims, they 'would completely undermine the foundations both of logic and of ethics'.[9] Horne Tooke could not have agreed more.

Although John Horne Tooke is less remembered today for his work on language than for his politics,[10] he exerted a powerful influence on language study. As Hans Aarsleff has demonstrated in *The Study of Language in England, 1780–1860*, until the 1830s in England, a full twenty years after Horne Tooke's death, his shadow loomed large. Aarsleff quotes an astonished reviewer of the 1840 edition of *The Diversions of Purley*: 'It is with a mixture of mirth and amazement that we look back to the position [*The Diversions*] used to occupy; when even those who felt it to be wrong and ridiculous, could only qualify themselves to appear as its opponents by first paying homage to its ingenuity and learning.'[11] According to Aarsleff, it was only in the 1830s, with the arrival from Germany of 'the new philology' of Grimm, Schlegel, and Bopp (deriving, ironically, from the work of Horne Tooke's contemporary Sir William Jones), that Horne Tooke's influence collapsed. Before that time, he served as an intellectual model for figures as diverse as Samuel Coleridge, William Cobbett, and Erasmus Darwin.[12]

Since the development of 'modern linguistics' in the nineteenth century, Horne Tooke's theories have appeared to most linguists as a last vestige of the pre-modern or pre-scientific. Suffering a fate common to most etymology, Horne Tooke's work has been discredited as linguistic theory and research. The basic line of argument against etymology in general and Horne Tooke in particular is that both ignore the properly historical issues of language change by asserting the *identity* of modern words and their ancient roots.[13]

But the dichotomy of history and etymology has obscured the complexity of Horne Tooke's project. So much so, in fact, that Horne Tooke's modern partisans have found it necessary to defend him by turning him into a precursor of nineteenth-century historicism.[14] It is true that Horne Tooke shares some concerns with the comparative and historical linguists whose work displaced his in the nineteenth century. In particular, Horne Tooke adamantly defended the Anglo-Saxon and Gothic roots of English words against classical etymologists who sought English roots only in Greek, Latin, and Hebrew.[15] But what is interesting and useful in Horne Tooke's etymology is lost in either approach: Horne Tooke's primary concern was neither *history* nor *origin*.

As Olivia Smith has shown well in her recent book *The Politics of Language, 1791–1819*, Horne Tooke used his etymological work to intervene in a debate about language and society which was charged with immediately political issues. In late eighteenth-century England, Smith argues,

> the political and social effectiveness of ideas about language derived from the presupposition that language revealed the mind. To speak vulgar language demonstrated that one belonged to the vulgar class; that is, that one was morally and intellectually unfit to participate in the culture. Only the refined language was capable of expressing intellectual ideas and worthy sentiments, while the vulgar language was limited to the expression of the sensations and the passions.... 'The vulgar and the refined', 'the particular and the general', 'the corrupt and the pure', 'the barbaric and the civilized', 'the primitive and the arbitrary' were socially pervasive terms that divided sensibility and culture according to linguistic categories.[16]

These binaries formed the establishment against which radical language theorists struggled.

Horne Tooke's particular assault against the edifice of language theory was two pronged. On the one hand, he attacked the elitist rationalism of universal grammar in the works of James Harris (*Hermes; or, a Philosophical Inquiry Concerning Language and Universal Grammar* [1751]) and James Burnett, Lord Monboddo (*Of the Origin and Progress of Language*, [1774–92]); on the other, the conservative tendency of codifications of the language such as Samuel Johnson's *Dictionary* (1755). In their influential treatises on philosophical grammar, Monboddo and Harris had both argued that abstraction is the measure of the refinement of language. That is, the farther a language is from simple concrete reference (the more terms it employs of strictly structural value), the more intellectually capable it is. Against this, Horne Tooke argues that abstraction in language is the product only of the *abbreviation* of concrete terms and not of their supersession. As Smith shows,

Horne Tooke's defence of concrete language has a political pay-off. She writes, 'By disrupting the ideological construct of language's relation to the mind and 'civilization', Tooke refuted the major philosophical justification of class division in the last half of the century, and the myriad ideas which depended on it.'[17] Horne Tooke's opposition to Johnson has similarly immediate political implications. As Horne Tooke reads Johnson, the principle of definition in his *Dictionary* is usage. While there is a superficial populism in this method, Horne Tooke argues that the real effect is only to reinforce currently dominant understandings regardless of their veracity. To Horne Tooke it is fully apparent that Johnson's lexicographic method leads to being 'very clear concerning Ghosts and Witches, all the mysteries of the divinity, and the sacred, indefeasible, inherent, hereditary RIGHTS of Monarchy', but not acknowledging the 'RIGHTS of the people' at all.[18]

Even wider political implications of Horne Tooke's opposition to definition by usage are illuminated by John Barrell's treatment of 'custom' and 'usage' in his *English Literature in History, 1730–80*. There, Barrell shows how the libertarian ring of 'custom' in language and in law was appropriated in late eighteenth-century England for essentially conservative ends. Barrell writes,

> The defence of the authority of common usage over rational analogy was modelled at the start of the century on arguments endorsing the resistance of the English to the absolutist designs of the Stuart monarchy, at the end, on those by which the customary practices and arrangements in the law and the constitution were defended against the suggested improvements of enlightened reformers. Most important, for our purposes, though all men were understood to be governed by the laws of the language – which, like the laws of the land, were claimed to have been established by 'the public free Consent' – some members of the language community were enfranchised, and could use their voice in making the laws which bound them, and some were not.[19]

The argument for common usage against the rational analogy of a Monboddo or a Harris implied a defence of Englishness against foreignness, but it did not imply either a defence of the plebeian against the elite or a defence of enlightened reform. The argument for usage was rather an argument for 'submission to the custom of the polite . . . as a confirmation and not as a loss of freedom'.[20] Horne Tooke is adamant in his arguments against elitism, authority, and classical learning. Identifying both the appeal to rational analogy and the appeal to usage as fundamentally compromised, Horne Tooke seeks to free the potential of language through etymology, to show, by appeal to the etymological meaning of words, the 'imposture' of both rationalism and definition by usage.

The notion that etymology might serve well as a form for political and social commentary is hardly surprising. Stories of word origins have long served political and social roles. Howard Bloch, for example, has shown brilliantly how the strategy of appeal to origins in medieval etymology provides a structural analogue for historical, theological, and genealogical arguments.[21] Nancy Struever has argued more generally, in her article 'Fables of Power',[22] that etymology can take advantage of a very straightforward narrative assumption. No matter how 'raffish' or jumbled the particular instance, etymology can always imply a common-sensical narrative continuity. Because of the public character of language, this continuity, she argues, is concomitant with a historical perspective on society. She writes, 'All [aspects of etymological narrative] – derivation, constraint, use – have a 'historical' dimension; power, resonance, social cohesion are essentially time-bound. The biography of the word which is the etymology is a major symbolic form expressing this linearity, and its use in argument is to advocate a linear social cohesion.'[23] The generic power of etymology derives from these formal qualities.

But, as Struever is well aware, etymology is not *always* written to take advantage of narrative continuity. In fact, in modernist literature and in post-structuralist criticism, it may be argued that etymology is used precisely because it cuts across time *without* invoking the burdensome narrative apparatus of history. Struever aims an extended polemic against 'modernist' etymology (including post-structuralism) for squandering the formal benefits of the 'linear fundamentalism' of classical etymology. The anti-narratives of post-structuralism become apolitical on account of their denial of 'narrative realism'. She writes,

> A history of etymological practice reveals a very sharp and suggestive antinomy: analysis of the discourse of 'classical' etymologizing uncovers a layer of egregious narrative realism: a policy which asserts the quintessentially 'historical' nature of linguistic force, and the quintessentially 'linear' nature of social identity. But modernist etymologizing finds this narrative disturbing and rejects it. I maintain that the modernist subversion of narrative fundamentalism constitutes a cession of a domain of proper investigative interest, and is a subversion, or abdication, of intellectual range and disciplinary power.[24]

Horne Tooke's politics are a mystery to Streuver. Strangely, to her, he appears to be a proponent of a kind of psychologistic universal grammar.[25] In part this must be accounted to Horne Tooke's aberrance in the terms of Struever's typology, classical/modernist. Locked into a narrative-realist formula for political commentary, she is unable to acknowledge the politics of an interpretive practice which takes neither history nor origin as its object.

Horne Tooke's politics began in realms foreign to the study of language.[26] Born the son of a Westminster poulterer in 1736, graduated from Cambridge in 1756, ordained priest in 1760, he was then swept up in the political excitement of the moment. In 1765, he wrote a pamphlet defending the radical John Wilkes. Introduced to Wilkes in France later that year, Horne Tooke became a prominent supporter. Among other visible activities, he involved himself in parliamentary politics, agitated for the prosecution of a soldier who had killed a bystander during the St George's Fields riots, and participated in the establishment of the influential reformist Constitutional Society.

Known for an incisive written style, Horne Tooke penned various pamphlets and engaged in several published debates, such as that with Wilkes in 1770–1 when Horne Tooke accused Wilkes of corruption, and that with Junius, the anonymous radical pamphleteer who some had suspected was Horne Tooke himself. Horne Tooke made several unsuccessful bids for parliamentary seats straight through to the 1790s. In 1801, his successful election in the rotten borough of Old Sarum was nullified owing to his ordainment. After this last attempt at Parliament and until his death in 1812, Horne Tooke's connection with public affairs occurred mainly through his renowned weekly dinners. Over the years, guests included Thomas Paine, William Godwin, Thomas Boswell, Samuel Coleridge, and many other important political and intellectual figures. Horne Tooke was known on these occasions to pick arguments with his guests. Godwin was a constant butt of Horne Tooke's jokes; on one occasion, Coleridge, with perhaps a bruised ego, reported having at least fared better than Godwin.[27]

But probably Horne Tooke's greatest notoriety derives from his two trials, the first in 1777 for seditious libel and the second in 1794 for treason. In the first trial, Horne Tooke was convicted for having published an advertisement under the aegis of the Constitutional Society in order to raise money for American victims of the Lexington skirmish two years earlier. In the second trial, like Thomas Hardy and John Thelwall, Horne Tooke was unsuccessfully accused of fomenting revolution through the London Corresponding Society.

Importantly, it was on the occasion of the 1777 trial that Horne Tooke first saw the social implications of some philological speculations which he had long before abandoned. Believing the charges against him to be constructed in such a crude and imprecise manner that in effect he was charged with nothing at all, Horne Tooke took up his own defence on grammatical grounds.[28] His argument failed, however, and he was sentenced to a year in King's Bench Prison. During this year, he wrote the famous

'Letter to John Dunning, Esq.' (1778) which was soon published as a pamphlet. The 'Letter' elaborated a theory of etymology which Horne Tooke thought would clarify the grammatical points he had tried to make in court. As Horne Tooke later wrote, 'I undertook [the 'Letter to John Dunning'] because it afforded a very striking instance of the importance of the meaning of words; not only (as has been too lightly supposed) to Metaphysicians and School-men, but to the rights and happiness of mankind in their dearest concerns – the decisions of Courts of Justice.'[29] These first etymologies were political in the very immediate sense that they challenged the propriety of Horne Tooke's conviction. But, as early as the 'Letter', the systematic political implications of Horne Tooke's etymology were becoming clear. Horne Tooke saw language as the key problem in philosophy and politics. Reflecting on the 'Letter', Horne Tooke writes, 'I very early found it ... impossible to make many steps in the search after *truth* and the nature of the *human understanding*, of *good* and *evil*, of *right* and *wrong*, without well considering the nature of language, which appeared to me to be inseparably connected with them.'[30] The etymologies in *The Diversions of Purley* would reveal the abuses of language practised by the authorities (of whatever kind, political, linguistic, philosophical) against the interests of the 'generality'.

The *Diversions* is a strange text, apt to digress into politics, ethics, or literary criticism in the midst of an otherwise dull etymological proof. The title of the work is emblematic of this generic indeterminacy. Over the years, many readers have picked the book up by its title only to be disappointed at the relative dryness of the contents.[31] On the other hand, many readers have found the text not puritanical enough, diverted constantly from the straight path of linguistic investigation by political harangues, jokes, and asides. The title suggests further the possibility that the practice of etymology was in part a shelter for more dangerous kinds of commentary, a diversion in the military sense.

The form of the text is a dialogue. In the first volume, Horne Tooke has two interlocutors, Dr Beadon (B), master of Jesus College, Cambridge, and William Tooke (T), friend and benefactor. In the second volume, the interlocutor is the radical parliamentarian Sir Francis Burdett (F), whom many considered to be a disciple or even a puppet of Horne Tooke.[32] The importance of the identities of these characters to the work is debatable, but their function in the text is both to permit Horne Tooke to converse on diverse subjects easily and to allow for ambiguity, where the 'Letter' was of needs more direct.[33]

The *Diversions* is a strikingly self-conscious text, so it is not at all surprising that in volume II, Horne Tooke poses explicitly the etymological question of etymology itself; that is, what is truth? In the 'classical' formula, etymology is the study of truth or of true speech. As it is put by the eighteenth-century French etymologist Charles de Brosses, '*La vérité des mots, ainsi que celle des idées, consiste dans leur conformité avec les choses: aussi l'art de dériver les mots a-t-il été nommé* etymologie, *c'est-a-dire* discours véritable; etumos, verus; logos, sermo[34].' While the 'mechanism' of de Brosses's method is quite specific, his observation about the word '*étymologie*' and its implications are standard fare during and before the eighteenth century. The Italian philosopher Giambattista Vico's explanation of 'etymology' is almost identical to that of de Brosses. He says, 'We ... have the definition of the word "etymology" itself as meaning *veriloquium*.'[35] The etymology of the word 'etymology', in both cases, reveals etymology itself as the revelation of truth.[36] For both de Brosses and Vico, the etymological project, once tautologically grounded, can proceed to speak the essential, root meanings of the words it treats. Proper derivation will yield a definition of a word unadulterated by historical degeneration: a true picture of the thing itself.

Horne Tooke contests the notion of etymology as *veriloquium* not because etymology is somehow false, but because the simple translation of 'etymology' offered by de Brosses and others fails to explain the problem of 'truth', which subtends it. Horne Tooke parodies the wilful deafness of his etymological predecessors to the question of truth. 'What is TRUTH?',[37] Horne Tooke's interlocutor Sir Francis Burdett (F) asks. This is the reflexive question which the translation of 'etymology' into 'true speech' fails to pose. Sir Francis continues,

> You know, when Pilate had asked the same question, he went out, and would not stay for the answer. And from that time to this, no answer has been given. And from that time to this, mankind have been wrangling and tearing each other to pieces for the TRUTH, without once considering the meaning of the word.[38]

The traditional belief in the truth of etymology relies upon a crucial elision, that of the meaning of 'truth' itself.

Ironically, the meaning of truth which Pilate scorned or feared would not have scared him if he had heard it. Horne Tooke shows this by quoting from an alternative version of the Pilate story in the Gospel of Nichodemus in which Pilate *does* stay for Christ's answer: 'Our Lorde sayd to Pylate, Understande TROUTH how that it is judged in earth of them that dwell therein.' – *Nychodemus Gospell*, ch. 2.'[39] By Horne Tooke's reckoning, Christ's answer to Pilate does not change Pilate's position. Truth is what men judge it to be. For Pilate this truth was already self-evident, for he had posed to the Jews the very proposition of who should be released and who should be crucified. Thus Horne Tooke says: '[T]he story is better told by John: for the answer was not worth staying for.'[40] Truth is relative and individual, but in a system of abused authority, truth is no more or less than that abuse. In this way, the answer was not worth staying for and was none the less *true*: '[T]here is something in it perhaps'.[41] Horne Tooke writes. Unlike his etymological forerunners,[42] Horne Tooke derives 'truth': 'this word will give us no trouble.'[43] He writes, 'TRUE, as we now write it; or TREW, as it was formerly written; means simply and merely – That which is TROWED. And, instead of its being a rare commodity upon earth; except only in words, there is nothing but TRUTH in the world.'[44] Only in the confusion created by philosophy's misappropriation of language is truth obscured. 'From the time of Edward the third to Edward the sixth',[45] 'trew' was the written form of the past participle of the verb 'to trow', which meant to think or to believe. Thus truth means what is thought or firmly believed. This is precisely consistent with the Nichodemachean definition, and with Horne Tooke's ethical and epistemological programme. First the ethics:

> That every man, in his communication with others, should speak that which he TROWETH, is of so great importance to mankind; that it ought not to surprize us, if we find the most extravagant and exaggerated praises bestowed upon TRUTH. But TRUTH supposes mankind; *for whom* and *by whom* alone the word is formed, and *to whom* only it is applicable. If no man, no TRUTH. There is therefore no such things as eternal, immutable, everlasting TRUTH; unless mankind, *such as they are at present*, be also eternal, immutable, and everlasting. Two persons may contradict each other, and yet both speak TRUTH: for the TRUTH of one person may be opposite to the TRUTH of another. To speak TRUTH may be a vice as well as a virtue: for there are many occasions where it ought not to be spoken.[46]

This kind of relativizing ethics produces the dilemma of the Pilate story: any sustained discourse on the meaning of truth which has as its assumptions a positivist framework will bring itself down. The ethical problem posed by the Pilate story can only be successfully resolved by posing the question of truth without an authoritarian framework supporting it. As long as Pilate's question is posed in the Biblical context, that is with the assumption that the determination of truth is itself an absolutist decision about life and death, the question of the true meaning of truth can never productively be posed.[47]

The epistemological question about truth, of course, cannot be solved without the further etymology of the verb 'to think'. 'To think' in Latin is '*réor*'. Horne Tooke goes on, '*Res*, a thing, gives us *Reor*, i.e. I am *Thing-ed*: *Ve-reor*, I am strongly *Thinged*.... And *Verum*, i.e. strongly impressed upon the mind, is the contracted participle of *Vereor*.'[48] To think is to be thinged. In response to this further reduction, Francis Burdett (F) asks incredulously, 'Who ever used such language before?'[49] The answer to this, Horne Tooke gives in his footnotes: Epicurus, who said that the senses are never deceived.[50] The doctrine which Horne Tooke refers to somewhat obliquely here is his etymological doctrine, adapted from Locke, that all abstractions can be traced back to concrete words, nouns or verbs.[51]

The invocation of Epicurus, the observation that 'truth' is the past participle of 'to think' and that 'to think' is only 'to be thinged', raises the question of a materialist or a sensationist foundationalism quite clearly. For here, truth might be taken to be the thing or the perception at the root of abstraction. Horne Tooke is quite clear that it is not. He writes,

> Truth, in my opinion, has been improperly imagined at the bottom of a well: it lies much nearer to the surface: though buried indeed at present under mountains of learned rubbish; in which there is nothing to admire but the amazing strength of those vast giants of literature who have been able thus to heap Pelion upon Ossa.[52]

Horne Tooke questions depth metaphors for etymology. Truth is not root-like, but is rather a surface phenomenon, its obscurity lying in the confusion and obstructions thrown before it, not in its own depth.[53] Truth, furthermore, is a relative phenomenon; it is culturally and individually variable.

The central problem with philosophy is two-fold, according to Horne Tooke: it complicates simple things needlessly and then pretends that the complication is learning. It puts on false appearances to empower itself.[54] Philosophical grammar provides a striking example of this process. In the time of Aristotle, Horne Tooke explains, grammarians attempted to categorize all words according to the types of thing in the world, centrally *res quae permanent* and *res quae fluunt*, which correspond with nouns and verbs. But since so many words proved 'so stubborn, that no sophistry nor violence could by any means reduce them'[55] to the codified categories of *things*, grammarians reversed the process and attempted to categorize things according to the different kinds of word. This method proved still more unfortunate as grammarians churned out category after category and it was supposed that for each of these mistaken distinctions a group of things in the world could be found.[56]

If the great error of antique philosophical grammar was ontological, Horne Tooke suggests, the great modern error is epistemological. The moderns, Harris and Monboddo in particular, no longer consider words the signs of things: 'Modern grammarians acknowledge them to be . . . the signs of *ideas*.'[57] This method introduces all sorts of misconceptions about the nature of mind. Horne Tooke writes, 'The different operations of the mind are to account now for what the different things were to account before: and when they are not found sufficiently numerous for the purpose, it is only supposing an imaginary operation or two, and the difficulties are for the time shuffled over.'[58] If the product of this kind of reasoning were merely error, Horne Tooke would object less strenuously, but it is precisely the mastery of these false distinctions which governs the whole system of learning to which Horne Tooke objects.[59]

One of the claims common to Monboddo and Harris which Horne Tooke blasts is that some words (some conjunctions and prepositions, for example) have *no meaning* at all, that they function merely to hold the language together, and further that these words by their very abstraction distinguish refined from vulgar language. Harris defines the preposition as 'a part of speech, devoid itself of signification; but so formed as to unite two words that are significant, and that refuses to coalesce or unite of themselves.'[60] Horne Tooke counters that *all* words have meanings. He shows this through etymology. As he says of prepositions, they 'are the names of *real objects*. And these *petits mots* happen . . . to be so, merely from their repeated corruption, owing to their frequent, long-continued, and perpetual use.'[61] For example, etymologically 'from' means 'beginning', 'beneath' means 'bottom', and 'down' means 'deep'.[62] This position affords him not only a critical razor for slicing apart the claims of the philosophical grammarians about refined and vulgar language, but also an instrument for debunking the transcendence of metaphysical and religious ideas. In a passage which deserves longer quotation, Horne Tooke writes,

> These words, these Participles and Adjectives, not understood as such, have caused a metaphysical jargon and a false morality, which can only be dissipated by etymology. And, when they come to be examined, you will find that the ridicule . . . justly bestowed upon the Papists for their absurd coinage of Saints, is equally applicable to ourselves and to all other metaphysicians; whose moral dieties, moral causes, and moral qualities are not less ridiculously coined and imposed upon their followers.

Fate	Providence	Spirit
Destiny	Prudence	True
Luck	Innocence	False
Chance	Substance	Desert
Accident	Fiend	Merit
Heaven	Angel	Fault
Hell	Angel	&c. &c.
	Apostle	
	Saint	

as well as JUST, RIGHT and WRONG, are all merely Participles poetically embodied, and substantiated by those who use them.[63]

Against various sorts of metaphysics, Horne Tooke contends that there is no such thing as an abstract or a complex *idea*. Appropriating the Lockean notion of a 'simple idea' with its origin in sensation, Horne Tooke claims that all ideas are simple. He writes, 'The business of the mind, as far as it concerns Language, appears to me to be very simple. It extends no further than to receive impressions, that is, to have Sensations or Feelings. What are called its operations, are merely the operations of Language.'[64] Anticipating his readers' perplexity at this reduction, Horne Tooke makes Dr Beadon (B) say,

> By what you have advanced [the matter of the parts of speech] seems ten times more unsettled than it was before: for you have discarded the differences of *Things*, and the differences of *Ideas*, and the different *operations* of the *Mind*, as guides to a division of Language. Now I cannot for my life imagine any other principle that you have left to conduct us to the *Parts* of Speech.[65]

The principle which Horne Tooke proposes is abbreviation, and the method for understanding it is etymology.

According to Horne Tooke, language, from its beginnings, has had two goals. 'The first aim of Language was to *communicate* our thoughts; the second, to do it with *despatch*.'[66] It is the goal of brevity in communication which is most overlooked in theories of language. As the flux of thought is much faster than any language could possibly be, when language develops, it tends to combine and to shorten. This principle accounts for the combinations of terms which Locke explained as 'complex ideas'. This being the case, etymology is not only an historical concern: it also governs the possible combinations of ideas in discourse and thought. Horne Tooke writes, 'Every purpose for which the composition of Ideas was imagined [is] more easily and naturally answered by the composition of Terms: whilst at the same time it does likewise clear up many difficulties in which the supposed composition of Ideas necessarily involves us.'[67] Beyond the functions of the simple idea, he claims that all of the ideational processes which Locke enumerates are strictly linguistic. Locke's explanations are reclaimed under the mantle of 'abbreviations': complex ideas are really only phrases condensed into terms. And thus Horne Tooke contends that Locke's entire *Essay on Human Understanding* would be better understood if the reader filled in 'terms' wherever the word 'ideas' appears.[68]

Horne Tooke goes so far as to speculate that Locke himself had begun to reconsider his exile of language to the functions of representation and communication merely. In particular, some of Locke's hesitations in Book 3 ('Of Words') suggest to Horne Tooke an indecision concerning the relationship of language to the larger system elaborated in the first two books of the *Essay*.[69] Horne Tooke speculates, 'The perfections of Language, not properly understood, have been one of the chief causes of the imperfections of our philosophy. And indeed from numberless passages throughout his Essay, Mr. Locke seems to me to have suspected something of this sort.'[70] Similar observations about Locke's implicit and explicit considerations of language introduce Paul de Man's essay 'The Epistemology of Metaphor' (1978). De Man writes, 'At times it seems as if Locke would have liked nothing better than to be allowed to forget about language altogether. . . . But, scrupulous and superb writer that he is, by the time he reaches book 3 of his treatise, he can no longer ignore the question.'[71] There is an uncanny echo of Horne Tooke in de Man's discovery of language as the unspoken principle of Locke's essay.

A comparison of Horne Tooke and de Man on the subject of language in Locke clarifies what is at stake in Horne Tooke's revision. Like Horne Tooke, de Man refuses to accept 'simple ideas' as the building blocks of understanding in Locke's philosophy. For Horne Tooke, 'the *whole* of Mr. Locke's Essay' is a philosophical account of 'abbreviations in terms',[72] and thus Locke's treatment of simple ideas is only ancillary to the achievement of the *Essay* overall. De Man treats Locke's simple ideas almost identically. He writes, 'Simple ideas are . . . in Locke's system, simpleminded: they are not the objects of understanding. The implication is clear but comes as something of a shock, for what would be more important to understand than single ideas, the cornerstones of our experience?'[73] For the cornerstones of experience in Locke, de Man shows that we must look to language, to rhetoric in particular.

According to de Man, Locke's simple ideas are simple-minded precisely because they are so epistemologically and semantically trouble free. The absolute correspondence of word and entity, property and essence, in effect takes these ideas out of the realm of definition altogether. Definition of simple ideas can, by definition, only be tautological. And Locke says as much: '"The *names of simple* ideas *are not capable of any definitions.*"'[74] There is no differential play possible in this realm, and thus, in our post-Saussurian age, no meaning, unless of course differential play enters in some other way.

This pure correspondence is immediately threatened by the approximate and potentially deceitful operations of metaphor. De Man shows quite beautifully the way in which Locke's self-defence against the threat of metaphor in simple ideas emerges: in order to show the difficulty of defining simple ideas, Locke considers the term 'motion'. Motion, Locke writes, has been defined by some as 'passage from one place to another'.[75] But what is 'passage' itself other than 'motion from one place to another'? Passage can only be a tautological definition for motion. 'This is to translate and not to define',[76] Locke concludes. De Man notes that Locke's critique of translation above is already a critique of metaphor:

Locke's own 'passage' is bound to continue this perpetual motion that never moves beyond tautology: motion is a passage and passage is a translation; translation, once again, means motion, piles motion upon motion. It is no mere play of words that 'translate' is translated in German as *'ubersetzen'* which itself translates the Greek *'meta phorein'* or metaphor. Metaphor gives itself the totality which it then claims to define, but it is in fact the tautology of its own position. The discourse of simple ideas is figural discourse or translation and, as such, creates the fallacious illusion of definition.[77]

De Man shows that, repeatedly, where Locke would like to find the certainty of analytic definition (complex ideas and mixed modes present similar problems) he encounters the troubling presence of metaphor or trope. In order to demonstrate that the simple idea 'motion' cannot be defined by the word 'passage', Locke is forced to resort to using yet another equivalent of the same, 'translation'. The moral of this story, for de Man, is that even the discourse of simple ideas, that in which 'there can . . . be no room for play or ambivalence between word and entity', is itself a figural discourse.

This notion is in apparent contradiction to Horne Tooke's reading of Locke. For Horne Tooke, there seems to be a level of the simple, both in the strict Lockean sense (which is relatively unimportant) and in a related sense by which all words maintain concrete significations. This is the point at which de Man's critique of Locke would seem to bear most heavily upon Horne Tooke. Where for de Man, that 'passage' and 'translation' are etymologically identical demonstrates tautologically that 'translation' or 'metaphor' is fundamental even to the definition of translation itself, for Horne Tooke it seems that etymology produces a concrete referent. In fact, it should be clear that de Man's argument implies Horne Tooke's but not the other way around. For de Man does not in fact respect the fully tautological status of his 'translations': he refers them to metaphor, which he does not, finally, retranslate.

De Man makes a similar move with Locke's discussion of the simple idea 'light'. Since the *idea* 'light' is distinct from the sensation of light, he writes,

> To understand light as idea is to understand light properly. But the word 'idea' (*eide*), of course, itself means light, and to say that to understand light is to perceive the idea of light is to say that understanding is to see the light of light and is therefore itself light. The sentence: to understand the idea of light would then have to be translated as to light the light of light (*das Licht des Lichtes lichten*), and if this begins to sound like Heidegger's translations from the Pre-Socratics, it is not by chance. Etymons have a tendency to turn into the repetitive stutter of tautology.[78]

The passage of the etymon into the 'stutter of tautology' does not occur in Horne Tooke. His etymologies use the mechanism of concrete reference to *shift* the ground of meaning. Like de Man, Horne Tooke understands the problem in Locke to do with linguistic substitution. For Horne Tooke, however, the discovery of metaphor at the root of what Locke considered an analysis of ideas is insufficient. As if using Locke's criticism of translation to defend Locke against de Man, Horne Tooke suggests that positing translation or metaphor as the goal of etymology fails to exploit etymology's transvaluing potential. He writes,

> [My Critics] seem to think that *translation* is *explanation*. Nor have they ever yet ventured to ask themselves what they mean, when they say that any word *comes* from, is *derived* from, *produced* from, *originates* from, or *gives birth* to, any other word. Their ignorance and idleness make them contented with this vague and misapplied metaphorical language: and if we should beg them to consider that words have no *locomotive* faculty, that they do not *flow* like rivers, nor *vegetate* like plants, nor *spicuate* like salts, nor are *generated* like animals; they would say, we quibbled with them; and might perhaps in their fury be tempted to exert against us 'a *vigour beyond the law*'. And yet, untill they can get rid of these metaphors from their *minds*, they will not themselves be fit for etymology, nor furnish any etymology fit for reasonable men.[79]

For Horne Tooke, recognizing identities and then employing the common etymological metaphors of generation in order to make one term flow from another fails at the crucial task of etymology.

In Horne Tooke's etymology, there is always a sensible word as etymon. So where de Man finds in etymology only tautology, Horne Tooke arrives at substance: 'Remember, where we now say *I Think*, the antient expression was – *Me Thinketh*, i.e. *Me Thingeth*, *It Thingeth me*.'[80] By finding in etymology a means to take the stutter out of philosophy, Horne Tooke defies the metaphorizing movement which de Man would like to insinuate into Locke. Understanding, which falls under the aegis of thought, betrays itself not as the thought of thought, but as the process of being thinged.[81]

These transitions in Horne Tooke rely on an analysis of abbreviation as *substitution*. Contrary to the impression given by some analyses of the *Diversions*, the process is far from straightforwardly degenerative. Horne Tooke writes,

> H. – ... I am inclined to allow [the] rank [of parts of speech] only to the *necessary* words: and to include all the others (which are not necessary to speech, but merely *substitutes* of the first sort) under the title of *Abbreviations*.

B. – Merely Substitutes! You do not mean that you can discourse as well without as with them?

H. – Not as well. A sledge cannot be drawn along as smoothly, and easily, and swiftly as a carriage with wheels; but it may be dragged.[82]

Beadon's objection, 'Merely Substitutes!', is a figure for the mistake of all philosophy: the degeneration of corruption itself as linguistic process and the *substitution* of jerry-rigged linguistic structures for the process of corruption and *substitution* is the mistake which leads philosophy to pile terms upon terms and to lose itself in clutter.

The notion of substitution is a radically polyvalent one in Horne Tooke. As he makes clear to Beadon, abbreviations and substitutes are the wheels of language, but they are also its ruin: 'Abbreviations open a door for doubt; and by the use of them, what we gain in time we lose in precision and certainty.'[83] Furthermore, he says, 'Abbreviations and substitutes undoubtedly cannot safely be trusted in legal instruments. But it is an unnecessary prolixity and great absurdity which at present prevails, to retain the substitute in these writings at the same time with the principal, for which alone the substitute is ever inserted, and for which it is merely a proxy.'[84] The development of language (which is also its synchronic principle) is an ambivalent process.[85]

In stark contrast to heroic etymological narrative,[86] Horne Tooke's story of language is one of illegitimate filiation and compromised origins. The contrast between Vico and Horne Tooke is telling. Vico derives the important term 'interpretation' from the term 'father', and thereby inscribes a linear relation between the Word and the word, one of authority and patriarchal filiation (etymology is implicit in Vico's 'interpretation').[87] Of the critical term 'substitute', Horne Tooke says, 'Substitute is in England the natural offspring of prostitute.'[88] As is the case throughout the *Diversions*, Horne Tooke refuses to ground his etymology in *authority*. Horne Tooke's etymology is relentlessly illegitimate. Linear genetic metaphors are misleading, Horne Tooke asserts. Patriarchal descent is not guaranteed. The etymon does not function as logos.

The complex economy of 'substitution' in the *Diversions* facilitates the text's movement from one domain of criticism to another. Horne Tooke writes,

Substitute is in England the natural offspring of *Prostitute*. In consequence of virtual being *substitute* for real representation; we have innumerable commissioners of different descriptions *substitute* for our antient Juries; Paper *substitute* for money: Martial Law *substitute* for the antient law of the land: *Substitutes* for the Militia, for an army of Reserve, for Quota-men. But the worst of all these Substitutes (and I fear its speedy recurrence) is a *Substitute* for BREAD; the harbinger of wide-spreading putrefaction, disease, and cruel death.[89]

The polyvalence of the term is clear here. By maintaining the meaning of 'substitute' while employing it variously, Horne Tooke crafts a critical tool. This process mimics that of his etymology generally. By asserting the *unity* of a word's meaning regardless of its semantic context, he is able to contest usage, and in so doing, the political, ethical, or philosophical status quo. To use John Barrell's phrase, he asserts the freedom of the user against the hypostatized freedom of use.[90] Paradoxically, then, Horne Tooke's unities are always disseminating. Horne Tooke's word play (in particular, the play on 'offspring') in another context brings this point humorously home:

> *'Well! 'tis e'en so! I have got the London disease they call Love. I am sick OF my husband, and FOR my gallant.'* ...
> This poor lady had a complication of distempers; she had two disorders: a sickness OF Loathing – and a sickness OF Desire. She was sick FOR Disgust, and sick FOR Love.
> *Sick* of *disgust* FOR *her husband.*
> *Sick* of *love* FOR *her gallant.*
> *Sick* of *disgust* OF *her husband.*
> *Sick* of *love* OF *her gallant.*
> Her disgust was the OFFSPRING of her husband, *proceeded from* her husband, was *begotten* upon her *by* her husband. Her gallant was the *cause* of her love.[91]

Whatever this is, patriarchal filiation it is not.

Substitution, like prostitution and like offspring, is an ambivalent figure for linguistic and social generation. Unlike Vico's patriarchal allegory, Horne Tooke's allegory of etymology (which is no less ideological or gendered) does not suppose an identity between origin and derivation.[92] Horne Tooke's etymologies work on principles of identity, but they are not linear identities. Prostitution and substitution, for example, exist in a mutually conditioning relation. The derivation of substitute from prostitute clarifies Horne Tooke's objection to 'translation'. Translation is redundant and reactionary. Etymology properly practised is transvaluation. It is political and social critique.

If Horne Tooke's etymology of the word 'truth' is the epistemological moment of transvaluation in the *Diversions*, his etymology of the word 'rights' is its ethical equivalent. The dialogue between Sir Francis Burdett (F) and Horne Tooke which begins volume II of the *Diversions* raises the issue of 'the Rights of man'. In this complicated dialogue of pronouns without antecedents, Horne Tooke and Burdett set up on apparently opposite sides of the question of political rights. Burdett criticizes reactionary opposition to the notion of rights; Horne Tooke, paradoxically, seems both to oppose such reaction and to oppose the rights in question. He says of reactionary 'regular' governments who condemn the rights of man that they,

> do not see that a claim of RIGHTS by their people, so far from treason or sedition, is the strongest avowal they can make of their subjection: and that nothing can more evidently shew the natural disposition of mankind to rational obedience, than their perpetual application of it to all which they desire, and to everything which they deem excellent.[93]

For Burdett, opposition to rights is wicked, but to Horne Tooke it is not only wickedness but folly. Not understanding Horne Tooke's position, Burdett responds, 'certainly if men can claim no RIGHTS, they cannot *justly* complain of any WRONGS.'[94] To which Horne Tooke replies with a still more perplexing inversion,

> H. – Most assuredly. But your last is almost an identical proposition; and you are not accustomed to make such. What do you mean by the words RIGHT and WRONG?
> F. – What do I mean by those words? What every other person means by them.
> H. – And what is that?
> F. – Nay, you know that as well as I do.
> H. – Yes. But not better: and therefore not at all.[95]

Horne Tooke prods Burnett to provide him with a consistent definition of the word 'right', to which Burdett responds with a number of different uses and the hypothesis that 'right' must be an 'abstract idea'. To assuage Horne Tooke's scepticism about abstract ideas (Horne Tooke considers that dodging the issue altogether), Burdett turns to Samuel Johnson's *Dictionary*. He finds, however, that although many definitions of 'right' appear, there is only one explanation given, an unsatisfactory definition of the phrase 'right hand'. According to Johnson, 'RIGHT hand means – "not the Left."' And 'left hand', Johnson says, means '"sinistrous, Not right."'[96]

The problem with Johnson's definition is, as expected, that instead of performing an etymological reduction of the word, he attempts to understand it on the basis of its usage. This is 'fraud, cant, and folly'.[97] Further, it is mischievous because it puts on sham appearances of 'labour, learning and piety'.[98] The ethical importance of Horne Tooke's position here is that it refuses to find essential social definitions in established social practice. Barrell writes of Johnson,

The unity of the language community is represented . . . as something already there, and at the same time . . . the existence of a hierarchy . . . and of social divisions within that community, is asserted also. The strategy is familiar to us by now: to represent the community as at once naturally unified, and naturally stratified.[99]

The practice of lexicography which takes usage for definition is intimately bound up with the political practice which takes the status quo for granted. This is why Horne Tooke says to Burdett that knowing the common use of a word is as good as knowing nothing at all.

But in order to understand the importance of the transvaluations which Horne Tooke suggests, it remains to follow the lead of his own etymology. 'RIGHT', he says, 'is no other than the RECT-*um* (*Regitum*), the past participle of the Latin verb *Regere*.'[100] Hence the Italian '*ritto*' and '*dritto*' and the French '*droit*'. 'Right' is a past participle of the verb 'to order'. Similarly 'law' is the past participle of the verb 'to lay down'. Horne Tooke says,

> Thus, When a man demands his RIGHT; he asks only that which it is *Ordered* he shall have.
>
> A RIGHT conduct is, that which is *Ordered*.
>
> A RIGHT reckoning is, that which is *Ordered*.
>
> A RIGHT line is, that which is *Ordered* or *directed* – (not a random extension, but) the shortest between two points.
>
> The RIGHT road is, that *Ordered* or *directed* to be pursued (for the object you have in view).
>
> To do RIGHT, to do that which is *Ordered* to be done.
>
> To be in the RIGHT, to be in such situation or circumstances as are *Ordered*.
>
> To have RIGHT or LAW on one's side, to have in one's favour that which is *Ordered* or *Laid down*.
>
> A RIGHT and JUST action is, such a one as is *Ordered* and *commanded*.
>
> A JUST man is, such as he is *commanded* to be – qui *Leges Juraque* servat – who observes and obeys the things *Laid down* and *commanded*.[101]

Here, then, is an ideal example of Horne Tooke's etymological method. Where Johnson had 'between thirty and forty'[102] definitions of the word 'right', Horne Tooke suffices with one. But it should also be clear that Horne Tooke's reductions do not discipline language: the fact that an identical word can be used in all of these different ways immediately demands the intervention of some kind of interpretation. Further developing his relativism, Horne Tooke writes,

[H. –] The RIGHT hand is, that which Custom and those who have brought us up have *Ordered* or *directed* us to use in preference, when one hand only is employed: and the LEFT hand is, that which is *Leaved, Leav'd, Left*; or, which we are taught to *Leave* out of use on such an occasion. So that LEFT, you see, is also a past participle.

F. – But if the laws or education or custom of any country should *order* or *direct* its inhabitants to use the LEFT hand in preference; how would your explanation of RIGHT hand apply to them? And I remember to have read in a voyage of De Gama's to Kalekut, (the first made by the Portuguese round Africa,) that the people of Melinda, a polished and flourishing people, are all *Left-handed*.

H. – With reference to the European custom, the author describes them truly. But the people of Melinda are as *Right-Handed* as the Portuguese: for they use that hand in preference which is *Ordered* by their custom, and *Leave* out of employ the other; which is therefore their LEFT hand.[103]

Horne Tooke's cultural relativism does not put him beyond making ethical judgements. Consistent with his critique of usage, Horne Tooke rejects *essential* value in cultural norms. But this relativism does not stop at the level of culture: 'A thing may be RIGHT and WRONG, as well as RIGHT and LEFT. It may be *commanded* to be done, and *commanded* not to be done. The LAW ... i.e. That which is *Laid down*, may be different by different authorities.'[104] What is at issue once again, rather than contradiction or translation, is transvaluation, a reversal of assumptions which does not merely replace the one with the other but questions the systematic separation of the two. In reference to his own relation to the law, Horne Tooke says appropriately, 'I have always been most obedient when most taxed with disobedience.'[105] Thus, Horne Tooke subverts his own references to political, philosophical, and religious authority. This is not to say that Horne Tooke is beyond 'using half an argument from a great name',[106] but the contexts and ironies of any reference to authority must be carefully observed.

In her article 'Fables of Power', Nancy Struever underlines 'the nature of the classical role of the etymologizer as a public trust; his duty is to demonstrate specific social constraints on the individual's (reader's) use of language; he is engaged in a kind of linguistic jurisprudence'.[107] Horne Tooke undoubtedly would have agreed. But his etymologies are specifically intended to question the authority of classical learning and the established juridical system. Rather than demonstrate social constraints as guides, Horne Tooke attempts to reveal them as legitimizing myths.

For Struever, rhetorical 'power' is necessarily bound up with the question of social cohesion. Etymology has access to power through its character as social narrative. Struever writes,

> Etymological narratives operate within an intricate system of force and time.... The root represents a social convention, or choice, which is beyond the domain of individual choice; ... Each narrative would define one particular social constraint which would, in a situation of good faith, serve as guide to both narrator and reader.[108]

It is as if Struever's etymology were conceived precisely to refuse the ethical and epistemological questions which Horne Tooke poses: what kinds of intellectual, social, and libidinal investments do we make such that normalizing discourses have a claim on us? How is it that rights come to be rigorously separated from wrongs? That truth gets separated from belief? That legitimacy inscribes itself in all of our metaphors for generation? How does language inexorably produce all of these conditions?

This is not to suggest that there are no narrative or historical aspects to Horne Tooke's investigations; it is only to shift the ground, as he does, away from the static terrain of established disciplines. The narratives which Horne Tooke invokes do not run from origin to derivation along the well-worn paths of etymological plot. When Horne Tooke fables, he does so in order to introduce a way of reading across texts for meanings which usage occults. In a Tookean moment, Derrida writes,

> The primitive meaning, the original, and always sensory and material, figure ... is not exactly a metaphor. It is a kind of transparent figure, equivalent to a literal meaning (*sens propre*). It becomes a metaphor when philosophical discourse puts it into circulation. Simultaneously the first meaning and the first displacement are then forgotten. The metaphor is no longer noticed, and it is taken for the proper meaning. A double effacement. Philosophy would be this process of metaphorization which gets carried away in and of itself. Constitutionally, philosophical culture will always have been an obliterating one.[109]

For Struever, the Derridean etymological move which treats erasure and accumulation as aspects of the same (economic) process represents a loss of 'linearity as a productive category of inquiry'[110] and a fixation on the notion of *loss* and *scar*.[111] But Horne Tooke's anti-linear approach to philosophy's putting into play of metaphor, far from fixating on inert signs, engages in a highly contentious political discourse. In fact, neither Derrida's 'modernist' nor Horne Tooke's (perhaps ventriloquized modernist) words bear out Struever's anxiety.

Or perhaps they do: Horne Tooke's etymology of the word 'poltroon' occasions his retailing the following story from *The Times*. He says,

> We ... have many POLTROONS in this country; qui sacramenta

militaiae fugiunt; for want of rational motive, not want of courage.

In October 1795, 'One Samuel Caradise, who had been committed to the house of correction in Kendal, and there confined as a vagabond untill put on board a King's ship, agreeable to the *Late Act*, sent for his *Wife*, the evening before his intended departure. He was in a *Cell*, and she spoke to him through the *Iron Door*. After which he put his hand underneathe, and she with a mallet and chissel, concealed for the purpose, struck off a finger and thumb, to render him unfit for his Majesty's service.'

The story continues,

There was some affection between this *able-bodied* vagabond and his wife – (*Able bodied* was the crime which by the operation of a *Late Act*, cast him into this *Cell* with the *Iron Door*.) – To avoid separation they both subjected themselves to very severe treatment. Some lawyers maintained that they were both liable to death, under the Coventry Act. The husband and wife would have thought it merciful.

'To take them both, that it might neither wound.' Such a sentence however, in such a case, has not yet, I believe, been put in execution. For a similar performance now, upon a husband in his Majesty's service – (I submit it to the Attorneys general) – might not a wife, by a still *Later Act*, be condemned to death for this new method of *seduction*? Or will a new Statute be necessary (it would soon be made, and may be expected) *flammis ultricibus comburendum eum – et eam?*[112]

As is Horne Tooke's custom, he uses the stability of lexical meaning to construct his ironies: they are ironies which question the ethical construction of language.[113] To be able-bodied is a crime; to kill two wounds none. Sentences and executions bear haunting double meanings. And, in the first instance, separation is unity.

In addition, there is the question of the temporality of this example. Struever contends correctly that etymology has a special link with memory, but (*contra* Struever) it is not through the mechanism of linearity that this relationship obtains. The connection with memory is with memory as counter-history. In Horne Tooke's text, this excessive moment from *The Times* becomes a crucial interpretive lens. History abates, but 'one Samuel Caradise' persists.

It would be a mistake to take this too literally: Horne Tooke's allegory is not memorial *per se*. But it is counter-historical in a way which suggests that the mechanisms of memory, polymorphous as they are, provide potential ways of recoding diachronicity away from history and origin. What such a possibility demands is the rigorous extension of etymology as a rhetoric of temporality. It demands the reinstatement of the whole question of meaning and usage in historical practice ... this time anticipating Horne Tooke's dialogue:

> F. – What do I mean by those words? What every other person means by them.
> H. – And what is that?
> F. – Nay, you know that as well as I do.
> H. – Yes. But not better: and therefore not at all.

NOTES

1   For careful reading of earlier drafts of this paper, thank you to Steven Knapp, Joe Zizek, Tom Laqueur, Carla Hesse, Richard Ohmann, Nicolai Meador, Edward Kuntz, Beatrice Kuntz, Sarah Ells, John Leedom, Roy Porter, and Randy Starn. For other help, Erika Naginski, Jane Shaw, Brendan Fletcher, Louis Galdieri, Meg Galluci, Kim Friedlander, Lisa Rothrauff, Lisa Cody, and Grace Lee. Remembering Amy Jean Kuntz.

2   D. Stewart, 'On the Tendency of Some Late Philological Speculations', in *Philosophical Essays* (G. Ramsay, London, 1810), pp. 147–204. This essay was written some time earlier, and, as Hans Aarsleff points out, Stewart had lectured on Horne Tooke as early as 1778–9. See H. Aarsleff, *The Study of Language in England, 1780–1860* (University of Minnesota, Minnesota Press, Minneapolis, 1983), p. 103.

3   The first volume of *The Diversions of Purley* appeared in London in 1786 with many sentences visibly deleted by a publisher wary of sedition charges. A second edition of this volume with responses to critics embedded in the text came out twelve years later. In 1805 Horne Tooke published volume 2, which featured even more elaborate etymological arguments about 'truth', 'rights', 'justice', and other highly charged terms. A third volume on the subject of verbs was to be published, but, before his death, Horne Tooke apparently burned the manuscript of this volume along with his papers and correspondence. In 1829, a new edition was published by Richard Taylor with the original deletions reinserted, with some textual emendations made on the basis of Horne Tooke's extant notes, and with the text of the 'Letter to John Dunning, Esq.' appended.

   For uniformity, I have chosen to cite the London 1840 edition throughout. This edition follows Taylor's 1829 version. Although this version is paginated as one volume, I have indicated the original volume number with the citations. I have compared all citations with the 1798 edition of volume 1 and the 1805 edition of volume 2, both London.

   The title *ΕΠΕΑ ΠΤΕΡΟΕΝΤΑ* translates from Greek as 'winged words', a reference to Horne Tooke's theory of abbreviation. He writes, '*Abbreviations* are the *wheels* of language, the *wings* of Mercury' (p. 13). On one occasion, Coleridge referred to the book ironically as 'hasty words'. See H.J. Jackson, 'Coleridge, Etymology and Etymologic', *Journal of the History of Ideas*, 44 (1983), p. 81. The frontispiece of the *Diversions* depicts Mercury removing the wings from his ankles.

4   John Horne Tooke was born John Horne in Westminster in 1736. He added the name Tooke in 1782. His biographers explain this as a show of friendship (and designation as heir) for his then benefactor William Tooke, after whose estate at Purley Horne Tooke's book is named. For simplicity I have used 'Horne Tooke' throughout as that was his name at the time that both volumes of the *Diversions* were composed. See L. Stephen, 'John Horne Tooke', in L. Stephen and S. Lee, eds, *Dictionary of National Biography* (Oxford, London, 1921–2), vol. 19, p. 971; M.C. Yarborough, *John Horne Tooke* (Columbia, New York, 1926), p. 108; A. Stephens, *Memoirs of John Horne Tooke interspersed with Original Documents* (J. Johnson, London, 1813), vol. 2, p. 44. Most biographical information has been drawn from these sources.

5   Stewart, 'On the Tendency of Some Late Philological Speculations', p. 188.

6   Ibid., p. 185.

7   Ibid., p. 188.

8   Horne Tooke, *Diversions*, I, p. 19; II, p. 644. Horne Tooke is citing Locke here.

9   Stewart, 'On the Tendency of Some Late Philological Speculations', pp. 168–9.

10 On Horne Tooke's politics, see J. Brewer, *Party Ideology and Popular Politics at the Accession of George III* (Cambridge University Press, Cambridge, 1976); J. Brewer, 'The Wilkites and the Law, 1763–74: A Study of Radical Notions of Governance', in J. Brewer and J. Styles, eds, *An Ungovernable People: The English and their Law in the Seventeenth and Eighteenth Centuries* (Rutgers, New Brunswick, 1980), pp. 128–71; E.P. Thompson, *The Making of the English Working Class* (Vintage, New York, 1966).

11 *Blackwood's Edinburgh Magazine*, 'Review of *The Diversions of Purley*', 47 (1840), p. 496; cited in Aarsleff, *The Study of Language in England*, p. 113. This review too accuses the *Diversions* of frivolity.

12 For Erasmus Darwin's tribute to Horne Tooke, see Aarsleff, *The Study of Language in England*, p. 48; in general see ibid., pp. 73–113, 'Horne Tooke's Influence and Reputation'. On Coleridge and Cobbett, see O. Smith, 'Winged Words: Language and Liberty in John Horne Tooke's *Diversions of Purley*', and 'Variations of the Languages of Men: Rustics, Peasants, and Plough-boys', in Smith, *The Politics of Language, 1791–1819* (Clarendon, Oxford, 1989), pp. 111–53, 202–51. On Coleridge, see Jackson, 'Coleridge, Etymology and Etymologic'; J.C. McKusick, 'Coleridge and Horne Tooke', *Studies in Romanticism*, 24 (1985), pp. 85–111; and A.C. Goodson, 'Coleridge on Language', *Philological Quarterly*, 62 (1983), pp. 45–68.

13 For example, in his book on Saussure, Jonathan Culler writes, 'A root was a rudimentary name, a basic representation, and later developments could be thought of as metaphorical extensions or accretions, if not distortions of these

basic signs. The derivations in Horne Tooke's *The Diversions of Purley* are only the most amusing examples of a mode of thought extremely common in England and France in the eighteenth century' (J. Culler, *Ferdinand de Saussure* [Cornell, Ithaca, NY, 1986], pp. 68–9; cited also in O. Smith, *Politics of Language*). On the general fate of etymology in modern linguistics, see Aarsleff, *Study of Language in England*, esp. chs 4–6; Y. Malkiel, 'Etymology and Modern Linguistics', *Lingua*, 36 (1975), pp. 101–20; and D. Attridge, 'Language as History/History as Language: Saussure and the Romance of Etymology', in D. Attridge, G. Bennington, and R. Young, eds, *Poststructuralism and the Question of History* (Cambridge University Press, Cambridge, 1987), pp. 183–211.

14   See Stephen, 'John Horne Tooke', p. 973; L. Stephen, *The English Utilitarians* (Duckworth, London, 1900), vol. 1, p. 138; and, in a different way, M. Cohen, *Sensible Words: Linguistic Practice in England, 1640–1785* (Johns Hopkins, Baltimore, 1977), pp. 129–36.

15   The *Diversions* even includes a chart of Anglo-Saxon and Gothic characters in order to increase their familiarity to his readers. Horne Tooke, *Diversions*, I, pp. 50–1.

16   Smith, *Politics of Language*, pp. 2–3.

17   Ibid., p. 130.

18   Horne Tooke, *Diversions*, II, p. 303.

19   J. Barrell, *English Literature in History, 1730–80: An Equal, Wide Survey* (St Martins, New York, 1983), pp. 112–13.

20   Ibid., p. 138.

21   H. Bloch, *Etymologies and Genealogies: A Literary Anthropology of the French Middle Ages* (University of Chicago Press, Chicago, 1983), esp. pp. 30–63.

22   N. Struever, 'Fables of Power', *Representations*, 4 (1983), pp. 108–27.

23   Ibid., pp. 111–12.

24   Ibid., p. 108.

25   Struever writes, 'Tooke's etymologies produce evidence of the inner workings of Leibnitzian monads, and attempt to define the psychological and even neurophysiological functions of individual minds' ('Fables of Power', p. 117).

26   Biographical information from Stephen, 'John Horne Tooke'; Yarborough, *John Horne Tooke*; and Stephens, *Memoirs of John Horne Tooke*.

27   See Yarborough, *John Horne Tooke*, pp. 205, 221.

28   See Smith, *Politics of Language*, pp. 113–14. The issue was the meaning and function of the word 'that'.

29   Horne Tooke, *Diversions*, I, p. 40.

30   Ibid., p. 7.

31   One reviewer writes, 'We remember perfectly our boyish disappointment in first making acquaintance with the well-known work of Horne Tooke. From the attractions of its title and frontispiece, we had selected it as a sure source of entertainment for a Christmas week; and dire was our dismay when we found that *Diversions of Purley* consisted in discussions upon prepositions, pronouns, and past participles, even duller and drier than those to which our school studies condemned us' (*Blackwood's Edinburgh Magazine*, 'Review of the Diversions', p. 484; cited also in Yarborough, *John Horne Tooke*, p. 109).

32 An 1807 caricature has a small Burdett atop a pole grasped by Horne Tooke bearing the inscription 'The Diversions of Purley'. In the drawing, Horne Tooke says, 'The finest puppet in the world. Gentlemen – entirely of my own formation, I have only to say the word, and he'll do anything.' Burdett says, 'Huzza – Liberty and Independence!!!' Mary Dorothy George, *Catalogue of the Prints and Drawings in the British Museum, Division I: Personal and Political Satires* (British Museum, London, 1947), vol. 8, pp. 535–6, plate 10733.

33 Compare, for example, p. 694 in the 'Letter' with p. 62 in the *Diversions*. In the 'Letter', Horne Tooke disposes of possible objections relatively summarily. For example, 'They will probably say I still carry with me my old humour in politics though my subject is now different; and that according to the hackneyed accusation, I am against authority, only because authority is against me.' By contrast, in the *Diversions*, the accusation is not at all 'hackneyed'. Instead, it emerges through the voice of Horne Tooke's friend Beadon. Beadon is made to say, 'I am afraid, my good friend, you still carry with you your old humour in politics, though your subject is now different. You speak too sharply for philosophy. Come, confess the truth. Are you not against *Authority* because Authority is against you?' To which Horne Tooke responds in his own voice, 'I hope you know my disposition better.' The later formulation leaves room for a somewhat ironic reading of Horne Tooke's position, especially given his generally oppositional posture.

34 De Brosses's etymological treatise, *Traité de la formation mechanique des langues* (1765), is quoted in G. Genette, *Mimologiques: Voyage en Cratylie* (Seuil, Paris, 1976), p. 85.

35 G. Vico, *The New Science* (1744; English translation, Cornell, Ithaca, NY, 1976), p. 129.

36 Andrea Bertolini offers a useful reading of Vico on this issue, in which he stresses the connection between etymological derivation and patriarchal filiation. A. Bertolini, 'Vico on Etymology: Toward a Rhetorical Critique of Historical Genealogies', *Yale Italian Studies*, 1 (1977), pp. 93–106.

37 Horne Tooke, *Diversions*, II, p. 604.

38 Ibid., p. 605.

39 Ibid., pp. 605–6. Horne Tooke notes that 'Nicodemus was the Patron Apostle of our ancestors the Anglo-Saxons.'

40 Ibid., p. 606.

41 Ibid.

42 '[I]t is not my fault if I am forced to carry instead of following the lantern; but at all events it is better than walking in total darkness' (Horne Tooke, 'Letter', p. 694).

43 Horne Tooke, *Diversions*, II, p. 606.

44 Ibid., p. 607.

45 Ibid.

46 Ibid.

47 There is a clear implicit reference to Horne Tooke's own experiences with the courts here.

48 Horne Tooke, *Diversions*, II, p. 608. Like most of his etymologies, Horne Tooke's etymology of the word 'truth' has received sharp philological

criticism. But it is interesting to note how commonly an ethical disagreement is coupled with the philological critique. For example, in the middle of a philological discussion, an 1835 article in the *Quarterly Review* blurts out the following: 'In all inquiries after *truth* the question is, not what people, who may or may not be competent to form an opinion, *think* or *believe*, but what *grounds* they have for believing it' (*Quarterly Review*, 'English Lexicography', 54 (1835), p. 320).

49 Horne Tooke, *Diversions*, II, p. 608.

50 Ibid., p. 605n. Horne Tooke quotes the *Encyclopaedia Britannica*: '*The Stress of Epicurus' Canonica consists in his doctrine of the criteria of truth....* The great canon or principal or Epicurus' logic is, that *the senses are never deceived*; and therefore *that every sensation or perception of an appearance is true.*'

51 See, for example, McKusick, 'Coleridge and Horne Tooke', p. 92: 'Tooke more boldly defends the extreme materialist position, and is, consequently, much more consistent in his account of language than any of his predecessors.' By contrast, Struever considers Horne Tooke an exponent of psychologism: '[*The Diversions of Purley*] rejects Vico's definition of etymological science as social science; its strategy represents, in contrast to Vico's, a total retreat into a psychologistic domain' ('Fables of Power', p. 117).

52 Horne Tooke, *Diversions*, I, p. 6. The giants tried to attack the gods by placing Mount Pelion upon Mount Olympus and Mount Ossa upon Pelion in order to attain sufficient height.

53 For example, see ibid., p. 101: 'Mr. Locke missed the explanation: for he dug too deep'; ibid., p. 163: 'Succeeding ingenuity and heaps of misplaced learning increase the difficulty, and make the error more obstinate'; ibid., p. 297: 'The garden of science is overrun with weeds.'

54 Horne Tooke once said (in a non-linguistic context), 'If you wish to be powerful, pretend to be powerful' (Yarborough, *John Horne Tooke*, p. xiv). This insight clearly marks his philosophical and linguistic analysis as well.

55 Horne Tooke, *Diversions*, I, p. 11.

56 For example, 'Conjunctive, Adjunctive, Disjunctive, Subdisjunctive, Copulative, Negative copulative, Continuative, Subcontinuative, Positive, Suppositive, Casual, Collective, Effective, Approbative, Discretive, Ablative, Presumptive, Abnegative, Completive, Augmentative, Alternative, Hypothetical, Extensive, Periodical, Motival, Conclusive, Explicative, Transitive, Interrogative, Comparative, Diminutive, Preventive, Adequate Preventive, Adversative, Conditional, Suspensive, Illative, Conductive, Declarative, &c. &c. &c., which explain nothing; and (as most other technical terms are abused) serve only to throw a veil over the ignorance of those who employ them' (Horne Tooke, *Diversions*, I, p. 56).

57 Ibid., p. 12.

58 Ibid.

59 Horne Tooke writes, 'a little more reflection and a great deal less reading, a little more attention to common sense, and less blind prejudice for his Greek commentators, would have made Mr. Harris a much better Grammarian, if not perhaps a Philosopher' (*Diversions*, p. 151).

60 Quoted in Horne Tooke, *Diversions*, I, p. 155. In another instance, Horne

Tooke rails against those who have treated conjunctions not as 'parts of language, but only such *accessaries* as *salt* is to meat, or *water* to bread; or that they are the mere *edging* or *sauce* of language; or that they are like the *handles* to cups, or *plumes* to helmets, or *binding* to books, or *harness* for horses; or that they are *pegs* and *nails* and *nerves* and *joints*, and *ligaments* and *glue*, and *pitch* and *lime*, and *mortar*, and so forth' (ibid., p. 75).

61   Ibid., p. 171.
62   Ibid., pp. 184–9, 220–1, 244–6.
63   Ibid., II, pp. 313–14.
64   Ibid., p. 25.
65   Ibid., p. 23.
66   Ibid., p. 14.
67   Ibid., p. 20.
68   Ibid., p. 19.
69   Ibid., p. 22–3.
70   Ibid., p. 19.
71   P. de Man, 'The Epistemology of Metaphor', *Critical Inquiry*, 5 (1978), p. 14.
72   Horne Tooke, *Diversions*, I, p. 15.
73   De Man, 'Epistemology of Metaphor', p. 17.
74   Locke, *Essay on Human Understanding*, Book 3, ch. 4, quoted by de Man, 'Epistemology of Metaphor', p. 17.
75   De Man, 'Epistemology of Metaphor', p. 17.
76   Ibid.
77   Ibid.
78   Ibid., p. 17–18.
79   Horne Tooke, *Diversions*, I, p. 139–40.
80   Ibid., II, p. 609.
81   A better modern analogue for this Tookean practice might be Jacques Derrida's demonstration of the mutual implication of value and signification. Without engaging Derrida's argument here, let me suggest that a comparison his employment of such a fraught word as 'usure', which bends away from linguistic 'usage' towards the economic (though antithetical) notions of usury (an excessive accumulation) and effacement (loss), and Horne Tooke's use of such a term as 'substitution' could further highlight the connections between the critical practice of language in the late eighteenth century and the present. See, especially, J. Derrida, 'White Mythology', in *Margins of Philosophy* (University of Chicago Press, Chicago, 1982) where he uses 'usure'. See also, for example, his discussion of the 'disposability' of the sign in Derrida, *Archaeology of the Frivolous: Reading Condillac* (Nebraska, Lincoln, 1980), e.g. pp. 118–19: 'The sign is *disposability*: if through the imperception and the absence of the thing (time) the sign assures our ideal mastery, puts . . . 'at our disposal', the sign – fragile and empty, frail and futile – can also, immediately, lose the idea get lost far from the idea, this time, and not only from the thing, from sense and not only from the referent. Consequently, the sign remains for nothing, an overabundance exchanged without saying anything, like a token, the excessive relief of a defect: neither merchandise nor money. This frivolity does not accidentally befall the sign. Frivolity is its congenital breach: its

entame, *arche*, beginning, commandment, its putting in motion and in order – if
at least, deviating from itself, frivolity, the sign's disposability, can ever be or
present *itself*. Since its structure of deviation prohibits frivolity from being or
having an origin, frivolity defies all archaeology, condemns it, we could say, 'to
frivolity.'

82   Horne Tooke, *Diversions*, I, p. 24.
83   Ibid., p. 124.
84   Ibid., p. 125n.
85   On the ambivalent quality of the 'progress' of language from savage to
      civilized, see ibid., p. 217.
86   On etymology in a heroic mode, see Struever, 'Fables of Power', p. 113: 'If
      etymology is a species of biography, the etymon as hero may be Promethean,
      but also may be picaresque – travelling hard, and shaped by close encounters.'
      See also Attridge, 'Words as History', esp. pp. 189–90.
87   For an interesting account of the relationship between etymology and
      patriarchal filiation in Vico, see Bertolini, 'Vico on Etymology'. Compare with
      Bloch, *Etymologies and Genealogies*, in the broader metaphorical question of
      lineage.
88   Horne Tooke, *Diversions*, II, p. 335n.
89   Ibid.
90   Barrell, *English Literature in History*, p. 143.
91   Horne Tooke, *Diversions*, I, p. 198.
92   There is an interesting discussion of grammatical gender on Horne Tooke,
      Diversions, I, pp. 26–9. For general considerations on gender and etymology,
      see ch. 1 of D. Baron, *Grammar and Gender* (Yale, New Haven, 1986), entitled
      'Etymologizing Man and Woman'.
93   Horne Tooke, *Diversions*, II, p. 302.
94   Ibid.
95   Ibid.
96   Ibid., p. 303. Horne Tooke's note reads, 'Johnson is as bold and profuse in
      assertion, as he is shy and sparing in explanation. He says that RIGHT means
      – *"True."* Again, that it means – *"passing true judgement"*, and – *"passing a
      judgement according to the truth of things"*. Again, that it means – *"Happy"*. And
      again, that it means – *"Perpendicular"*. And again, that it means – *"In a great
      degree"*. All false, absurd, and impossible.'
97   Ibid.
98   Ibid., p. 304.
99   Barrell, *English Literature in History*, p. 156.
100   Horne Tooke, *Diversions*, II, p. 304.
101   Ibid., p. 306.
102   Ibid., p. 302.
103   Ibid., pp. 307–8.
104   Ibid., p. 310. Horne Tooke's footnote reads: 'In an action for damages the
      Counsel pleaded, – "My client was travelling from Wimbledon to London: he
      kept the LEFT side of the road, and that was RIGHT. The plaintiff was
      travelling from London to Wimbledon: he kept the RIGHT side of the road,
      and that was WRONG".

"The rule of the road is a paradox quite.
  In driving your carriage along,
If you keep to the LEFT, you are sure to go RIGHT;
  If you keep to the RIGHT, you go WRONG."'

105   Ibid., p. 311.
106   Horne Tooke, 'Letter', p. 694.
107   Struever, 'Fables of Power', p. 111.
108   Ibid., pp. 111–12.
109   Derrida, 'White Mythology', p. 211.
110   Struever, 'Fables of Power', p. 121.
111   Ibid., p. 115.
112   Horne Tooke, *Diversions*, II, p. 320.
113   See also ibid., pp. 676–7.

Afterword

DELL HYMES

It is a pleasure to read these essays and to comment on them. Let me say something about the standpoint from which I do so. It is as a linguist working in anthropology, and it is in the hope that social history will more and more be a partner in building up a general understanding of language as a part of social life.

A variety of disciplines contribute studies of contemporary life and diverse cultures. History is a resource of cases as well, and a much needed one. The situations it can address are valuable in their own right, and valuable as perspective. Linguists, anthropologists, sociologists, and others may take for granted much that is not true, and marvel at much that is not new, without the contribution social historians can make. That a first book called *The Social History of Language* has here a successor makes one hopeful that the contribution will steadily increase.[1]

If, in the comments that follow, I address not only the essays as such, but their relation to a wider field, there are two reasons. One is inveterate habit. The other is a sense, to adapt the words of a hymn, that, despite the pervasiveness of a 'linguistic turn' in the intellectual world, 'everybody talkin' 'bout language aint a-gettin' there.' Let me sketch why that seems so.

Thirty or forty years ago, linguistics had barely become established as a separate discipline. To those, like myself, who entered it then, it began with the work of people mostly still alive to teach us. Its history seemed short indeed. Or, rather, there were two histories. A longer history had to do with the development of 'comparative' linguistics since the early nineteenth century, of methods for determining language families, most notably Indo-European, reconstructing their earlier stages, and tracing their processes of change. The shorter history had to do with methods for describing the make-up of languages, especially the units and relations of phonology and morphology (the make-up of words). For there had been descriptions of the sounds of languages, and of the patterns of sound in languages, but never before methods and principles for the systematic study of such things in general – applicable to any language, arguable as properties of all language.

For those taking part, it was a dawn some themselves had seen, and for their students, hardly yet noon. All accounts of language were to be reconstructed on new foundations, and, some were quick to notice, there was promise of an approach to human affairs that could be rigorous, but did not need to count or quantify. Between the humanities and natural sciences, a third way beckoned.

A linguist in anthropology, however, could feel faced with a struggle on two fronts. To many anthropologists, linguistics seemed abstract and difficult (too much like algebra), or irrelevant to social life, or both; to many linguists, social life seemed irrelevant to the structures of language, or too multifarious and messy to be dealt with – a circumstance not without precedent. There are indeed two genres, two intermittent traditions of writing, which an historian might someday trace – writing addressed to anthropologists (and other social scientists and scholars), arguing the relevance of language, as analysed linguistically, and writing addressed to linguists, arguing the relevance of social life. The two genres resolved into a pair of questions:

1 You work with what people say and write; they do so by means that have elements and structures, which may condition what is done, what you take as your material; should you not attend to the elements and structures, not take them for granted?
2 You analyse what people say and write; they do so in various contexts, to various purposes, with various abilities, and in various ways, all of which may condition the elements and structures that occur, what you take as your material; should you not attend to persons, contexts, and styles, not take them for granted?

If thirty or forty years ago I had been asked to write in regard to social history, I would have done so in these terms, just as I often did, on the one hand in urging anthropologists, sociologists, and folklorists to attend to linguistic detail, on the other in urging linguists to recognize the social foundations and ingredients of their work.

There may seem no need to urge any longer. Surely 'language' and 'discourse' are recognized as relevant everywhere? Peter Burke's introduction to the preceding volume in this series is an informed and excellent guide. And yet even those linguists who address 'pragmatics', politeness, conversation, may do so with *a priori* and unexamined assumptions, taken, I believe, from their own social background.[2] On the other hand, many of the best and brightest linguists eschew involvement with use and social life. Personal intuitions, or the intuitions of one's spouse and friends, remain a sufficient source of data as to the line between what is 'grammatical' and what is not. The rest (the most absorbing part) is book-keeping – how to square such data with one's model. This in itself can be absorbing and a creative stimulus, interacting with aspects of psychology, philosophy, and 'cognitive science'. Questions of what counts as a language are not of concern. One simply applies a name, 'English', 'French', and the like, to one's results without concern for the relation between part and whole.

The term 'language' of course tends to imply use and social life. Out of honest recognition of that fact, I think, the most famous formal linguist of our time, Noam Chomsky, a few years ago withdrew from calling his work a theory of 'language', taking the view that there could not be a systematic theory of such a thing. One could work on a theory of 'grammar', but not of 'language'.[3]

In sum, if linguists are to be involved in the social history of language, one must choose some kinds of linguist, and not others. To many one would still need to argue the case for what a social history of language includes. To put it crudely, not every department of linguistics would think it needed such a person. But if linguists are to be involved in the social history of language, one must have some kinds of data, and not others. Not everything called 'language' would seem to offer a linguist anything to do.

The range of one word, 'language', is of course a source of the problem. We can speak of 'language' as embracing a way of life, and we can also speak of a few words as the 'language' of this or that. To someone trained in linguistic ways of thinking, both can seem to fail to offer a purchase. For those who balk at 'way of life', one can offer examples of analysing social life, not as an infinite confusion, but as ordered in ways continuous with the ordering of language. For those who balk at calling a few words a 'language', one can call attention to cases in which such terms have been analysed, if not as a 'language', then as a semantic set or as diagnostic of a style. In both cases, of course, what the linguist will need to see is relevant data, data that links verbal elements to patterns and contexts of use, and does so in ways that permit the identification of elements and relations.

For whatever else linguists may do, they analyse elements and relations. Put in general terms, they start from sets of elements, defined as a set by contrast, that is, by the possibility of one element substituting for another, and thereby making a difference relevant to whatever form or activity of which the set is part. Analysis begins with determining, or knowing, what can count as an element in that regard; what are the features in terms of which the elements contrast; what are the dimensions in terms of which the features are defined; and in what contexts the set can occur.

To illustrate briefly, if we consider a set of terms which might answer the question of what kinds of relative you have, the terms would include 'mother', 'father', 'aunt', 'uncle', 'daughter', 'son', etc. To change the term would change the relative. Some pairs of terms contrast solely in terms of gender (e.g. mother: father, etc.). Some pairs contrast in terms of generation (e.g. mother: daughter). Some contrast in terms of lineality (e.g. mother-: aunt). If we consider terms which might answer the question of what you call your relatives, there might well be a variety of terms for the same relative (e.g. 'Mum', 'Mommy', 'Mother'). These would point to other dimensions, dimensions of social meaning, involving attitude and situation. This second aspect would involve the fact that naming, reference, identifying someone as someone's mother, say, is only one of the things such terms do, and would lead to the question of what, for these people, in fact is the set of things that such terms can be used to do.

Whatever the subject, whether sounds, or words, or constructions, whether dialects, or languages, or modes of discourse, if it is possible to identify a set of elements, the contrasts among the members, and how and when the set is used, someone trained as a linguist could believe he or she had work to do.

Of course there is much about language that escapes this approach. Methods appropriate to language address elements and relations internal to a body of data. So do many methods appropriate to social life, whether extrapolated from language or simply congruent with them. But congruent methods may be strange in practice. The historian may feel ill at ease with phonetic transcriptions and grammatical analyses, even if they are understood in principle. The linguist may recognize congruity of method in an analysis of social life, yet feel out of place for lack of familiarity with the sources of data. Each may find it tiring to look up something the other does not recall learning. And much of what happens in history is not congruent with analysis of internal relations at all, but with contingencies external to the person, community, or language in question. the obsolescence of a language has systematic consequences within the language itself, but the language itself cannot explain the fate of its users: for example, take the epidemics of European disease that so devastated the people of the New World. However much linguists can offer historians in getting language right, and thinking through questions of its use and meaning, the social history of language will ultimately have to be written by historians.

To turn now to the essays: I take them to contribute to a perspective on language which starts, not from a language, but from a community. They point to a notion of a community (or society, or region) as having, not 'a language', but a repertoire, a series or set of communicative means, each with its own appropriateness and social meaning. To say that 'English' is the language of England is to say very little, to the point indeed of misinformation. What in fact are the actual resources? What languages? What varieties and styles? No normal person has only one. In what niches? With what functions? Associated with what attitudes? How distributed among persons, communities, institutions, and places? How contested?

Let me say something about the book as a whole in this regard. Burke, Smith, and Ormsby-Lennon each addresses a language as a changing part of a changing repertoire in the early modern period. The terms of change are largely choice from within. Kiernan surveys a large part of the world in terms of change imposed from without. The reference points are named languages (Latin, Hebrew, English, and, let us add, Edenic or 'pre-Adamic'), although the content of the name cannot be taken as constant. The basis of community is first of all religious in the cases studied by Smith and Ormsby-Lennon, and religion is of major importance in the studies by Burke and Kiernan, although other institutions and locality enter as well (e.g. the 'Quaker Galilee').

Gladstone and Joyce call attention to dialect, one to its study and one to its use. Study and use alike are contested, and the fact of each has a social significance. The principal communities are geographical, local, although modes of production and class relations enter as well.

Rousseau and Porter take up an institutional context, that of medicine and the body. Class and profession are principal factors in defining the relevant groups. Rosenberg also takes up an institutional context, that of the study of language itself, and explores the motives and social consequences of pursuing it in a certain way at a certain time. That what Horne Tooke wrote mattered says something about the place of 'language', the 'English language', and its study in the world view and cultural values of the society of which he was part. Or, more accurately, says something about the audience that gathered as a community by attending to what he wrote. It is not a given that anyone care about etymology.

Let me turn now to each of the contributions individually.

Burke makes clear how mistaken it is to think of Latin in terms of a temporal line, before which Latin, after which 'modern' languages. Before the rise of the 'modern' languages, Latin was contested; since their rise, it has continued to be used. Nor is the proportion true, Latin : vernacular :: Catholic : Protestant. Even less the proportion, Latin : hegemony :: modern language : autonomy.

Continued use of Latin as a language of prestige may be fairly well known. Much less known is continued use of Latin as a lingua franca, for diplomacy, for international currency (as evidenced by translations into Latin from a number of European languages), and, strikingly, in Hungary as a language of liberty as against the imposition of German. (Recall that A. Nebrija's grammar of Castilian, asserting its autonomy as against Latin, also asserted the suppression in the Iberian peninsula of other varieties and languages.) Burke calls attention also to a dialectic of inter-influence, the 'Latinization' of the vocabulary of the modern languages, and the domestication in various respects of Latin itself. These twin processes have analogues in language change in other parts of the world, as in the relation between 'Frenchified' Creole, and creolized French, in Haiti. One wonders what one would see if a trace-element for Latin could be diffused through the United States, colouring the society a bit for each coin with '*E pluribus unum*', each state seal and flag with a motto such as '*Ad astra per aspera*', each crossword puzzle with '*amo*' or '*amas*' or '*amat*' as an answer, each church service and concert with '*Agnus Dei*'.

In demonstrating the diversity of the fate of Latin, indeed, Burke shows that its history is part of a world history, set in motion by the development of modern Europe and its penetration of the rest of the globe. One need not subscribe to the details of Immanuel Wallerstein's 'world system'[4] to recognize that a multitude of kinds of change, studied under different names – standardization of languages, construction of artificial and auxiliary languages, linguistic acculturation, pidginization and creolization, language loss and obsolescence, specialization in function of once autonomous languages – are all facets of a process that has overtaken the world. Burke makes clear that Latin's changing role is a case in point.

The social dynamics touched upon are revealing. Particularly striking is the emergence of *new* ways to use Latin as a boundary marker – the Tridentine decision that vernacular Mass be anathema, in debated response to the Reformation, and before that, the contribution of the Italian humanists who rescued classical Latin, to the decline of Latin as a living language. A sudden discovery of discontinuity with the past was pervasive, of course, as shown by Seznec.[5] As long as pagan gods were depicted dressed in the garb of the day, they were in a sense not dead. Now accuracy of costume had to be vouched for. So also with language; for some it had to be attested in Cicero. Sandys tells of the scholar Muretus laying a trap. In lectures in Rome he introduced words omitted in a lexicon taken as normative.

> Some protested that it was simple torture to listen to such barbarisms; but, when Muretus actually showed them his authority in the pages of Cicero, the words that had just before been deemed harsh and rough, at once became 'smooth and sweet and delightful to the ear'. Similarly, the superlative *illustrissimus* lay under grave suspicion, so long as it was supposed that the earliest authority for its use was Gellius; but, as soon

as it was discovered in Varro, it was no longer necessary to resort to the circumlocution *maxime illustris*.[6]

The further study for which Burke calls will enrich our understanding of verbal repertoires, and underscores that Western scholars cannot take for granted the history of their own.

So also with Smith's account of Hebrew in the English Revolution. It highlights a circumstance too seldom noticed, one in which a language is part of a personal repertoire, not through transmission or imposition, but through being sought out. The account shows how one may miss phenomena that go together if one starts from a particular language. For many the period had a unity, not of language, but of function, the function of access to the Holy Spirit and the intention of God. Some thought no natural language, descendant of Babel, could suffice, and sought a language before Adam (as Ormsby-Lennon discusses). Some believed in the possibility of immediate access to the Holy Spirit, such that any language could be the instrument. For some, presumably, the long and familiar use of Latin in the Church made it inseparable from the Word (although it too had begun its sacred role as a 'vulgar' tongue). For some Greek was wanted for access to the original of the Gospels, for some Hebrew for access to the original of the 'Old Testament'. And, as Smith shows, for some Hebrew became a vehicle itself of vision, and an orthographic key to the interpretation of English.[7]

The role of the autodidact (see also Joyce on nineteenth-century England) has a general implication. In formal linguistics, such as that of Chomsky, there is assumed a natural, Feuerbach-like identity among those who acquire a language.[8] In sociolinguistics and sociology of language, the focus is usually on the characteristics of communities and coherent groups. Those who depart from group norms are likely to be set aside.[9] Only in the study of narratives is one likely to focus on individuals. Seldom does one learn of individuals who seek out, adopt, and adapt new means, especially means of writing, and who, if not a group by residence, kinship, or the like, yet have an existence that reveals something significant.[10] Yet I sense that in a stage of fluent bilingualism and cultural autonomy many American Indians arrived, reflectively and individually, at English equivalents for native words. The evidence is scattered in notebooks and diverse experiences. There is analogy to the stage in the elaboration of modern English when new formations from Latin were freshly coined, many more than have survived in general use.[11]

Ormsby-Lennon has called the English seventeenth century a period of crisis in language, with new aspirations active on every side, from religion to science. Here he shows how striking the Quakers are from the standpoint of verbal repertoire. They share with others a desire for original meaning, and, as Kenneth Burke might say, join in 'perfecting' the quest, rejecting the historical languages of Bible and church ('postlapsarian dust'). Pure language, true names, are on the other side of Adam. Yet with some others they also regard their own English as open to the purity sought (and perhaps able to contain their new names?).

What Ormsby-Lennon brings out, however, is language only in part. Quaker critique of language, and English, as a whole, apparently did not itself define and cost them. What did so was a set of features, non-verbal as well as verbal, that together make up a way of using language, speechways, ways of participating in salient communicative events: hat-honour, the second-person pronouns marked for social respect, general neglect of salutation, refusal to swear oaths (and for a few, bareness of body on occasion as well as bareness of words). From such features, few in proportion to a language as a whole, but highly marked, large consequences were feared.

It is a principle of linguistics that small distinctions can have large consequences. The point is made usually with regard to small physical differences, which, by making one consonant, say, different from another, can make a word or utterance different. Here the principle applies to choice of words. As the social anthropologist Frederic Barth has stressed, quantity of difference is not a guide to boundaries. If groups wish to differentiate themselves, one or a few differences will suffice.[12]

Such differences fall beyond the kind of relations linguists have conventionally analysed. They are not paradigmatic differences, among the members of a set of sounds or morphemes or syntactic relations, by which one contrasts with another. They are not syntagmatic differences, having to do with what can co-occur, follow, or precede, in a sequence or combination. They do not have to do with any one level of linguistic structure, or with the expression of one level in terms of another. The features pointed out by Ormsby-Lennon are a style, a selecting and grouping together of elements from various aspects of speaking and behaviour, elements that a structural analysis would not connect, elements that go together because a group of people have put them together. It is styles, speechways, more generally communicative ways, that are ultimately the true object of analysis in the social study of language, both in history and in the field.[13]

Kiernan's essay came to hand just as I was asked by a colleague if there were any general treatment of language and conquest, and could think of none. It is welcome both for that and for its scope, bringing into attention in considerable detail the importance of the Near East and the histories of Arabic, Persian, and Islam. That said, it should be noted that much of the dispersal and differentiation of language throughout the world need not have involved conquest. When the first human beings entered the New World, and spread throughout its length, there of course was no one already there to conquer. Lapse of time and separation themselves will lead to diversity. Shift of boundaries can come about through intermarriage and bilingualism.

Multilingualism itself can persist in complex ways as a normal part of social structure.[14] And no one with experience of an oral way of life would imply that people do not think, exchange ideas, plan in the absence of writing. If medieval Arabic literature, in the written sense, belonged to the small privileged ruling minority, it does not follow that for the masses, religion had to suffice. A rich body of oral epic has continued to this day.[15] In ancient India abstract analysis of Sanskrit grammar, an accomplishment still admired, was done and initially transmitted orally. Again, to speak of only one alphabet is to overlook the invention of the Korean *hangul*.[16]

It remains that the phenomena to which Kiernan calls attention are important and relatively neglected. Linguistics has penetrated ways of analysing and reconstructing change over time within a language, and language family – the initial stages were one of the major accomplishments of the nineteenth century, to which Darwin himself made appeal. Models for analysis of differentiation and reintegration through contact, due to migration and conquest, are far less advanced. In the last 25 years there has been a growth in the study of pidginization and creolization that amounts to an explosion, and in the last few years a major step in systematic analysis of language contact.[17] We can expect that linguists will be able to bring more and more to the analysis of such situations, but social history – dates, proportions of population, circumstances of communication – is indispensable as well.

The term 'dialect' itself has a social history that deserves study. As Gladstone and Joyce bring out, although in England and the United States 'dialect' is thought of first of all in terms of locality, places where dialect is spoken, it actually involves a complex of social features, including class, mode of production, and evaluation (positive and negative).

To a linguist every variety has integrity, and is to be described in its own terms. To a sociolinguist every variety has social meaning, to be described in terms of choices among varieties, settings of use, attitudes and beliefs. The term 'dialect' has no constant meaning, except that of part to whole in relation to 'language'. Contrary to our European expectation, however, the expression, 'dialects of a language', does not imply that there is a variety which *is* 'the language'. Often there are simply dialects, different enough not to be the same, similar enough not to be mutually unintelligible, together constituting what is called 'language X'. Varieties generally have been like that in the world, related as a matter of series rather than hierarchy, along a river or across a plain. When one variety is superposed, as an expression of institutions dominating others, of course it is usually an object of study and promulgation. Such attention may be taken for granted, but in a hierarchical situation, attention to any variety has a political aspect. As Gladstone and Ray indicate, the history of attention to dialect and use of dialect in England is a political history.

Gladstone's focus on John Ray is striking. A significant book on the history of evolutionary thought begins precisely with Ray, 'one of the great biologists of all time'.[18] Natural history and field linguistics are not activities we readily connect today, but not long ago they were also closely connected in the development of knowledge of American Indian languages. The classification of languages, and peoples, of native North America issued by John Wesley Powell (himself a geologist) became the framework for generations of anthropology; essential to it were the field work and penultimate draft of Henry Henshaw, a Smithsonian ornithologist.[19] The famous naturalist C. Hart Merriam (1855–1942) collected Indian language vocabulary extensively.[20] Striking too is that Ray sought information from local correspondents, as in the nineteenth century Powell would seek vocabularies from people resident among Indians. Ray may be first in a line of scholars whose story over two centuries has yet to be told. What is multidisciplinary today may have been to them only natural (history). The political, religious, and philosophical ingredients of Ray's interest in dialect, considered by Gladstone, may have been accompanied by the view that words are an intrinsic part of the knowledge sought by such a scientist. Loyalty to a dialect of childhood, and a lively sense of relation between place and voice, may have gone together with recognition of local knowledge and its diversity as important to a general effort to describe the world.

It is striking also that Ray linked words to ways of life in presenting both contemporary dialect and classical antiquity. The common approach makes one think of the connections between classical antiquity and contemporary American Indian life that were to be so important in eighteenth- and nineteenth-century ethnology (Lafitau, Lewis Henry Morgan).[21] And it is striking that he sought to present words, not alphabetically, but by a classification in terms of diagnostic features. Here is an early form of major lines of later work with vocabulary, the *Wörter-und-Sachen* approach in European dialectology and the 'ethnoscience' approach to American anthropology.[22]

It is splendid to appreciate the colour of local speech, but sometimes difficult to distinguish between intrinsic colour and surprise. A 'spink', it appears, is a bird named for a perceived sound, but is that more vivid than familiar 'chaffinch', if one recognizes the implied picture? That of 'the species of finch which haunts the barndoor and homestead, where it may be seen picking grains of corn out of the chaff and barn-sweepings' (OED 372).

Joyce begins with an important warning against assuming an inevitable direction of change in favour of a standard or national language. Even when an older form is displaced, it may be succeeded by another variety that is still vernacular, not standard, with localization and value of a similar sort. There is much we need to learn about the world in just this respect. In the United States a fair number of American Indian languages continue to be spoken,

although the disappearance of all of them has been anticipated for generations. Where the Indian language is no longer spoken, there is usually a local
variety of English, usually unstudied. In general, if a type of social
relationship continues, that may go together with a type of linguistic
relationship, but the linguistic means involved may change in nature.[23] As
Joyce brings out, print and standard language may be accepted and used to
serve a still vital oral culture and its non-standard forms.

Conversely, a linguistic means may continue, but undergo a shift in its
role. Joyce highlights the emergence of a significant dialect literature in
tension with a polarization of standard and popular speech. Such a situation
would seem almost certain to involve questions of what counts as dialect, and
of how much of what counts is required for something said or written to
count as being dialect, and Joyce observes that dialect came to be conventionalized in ways that made it accessible to wider audiences. The logic is the
same as that discussed with regard to Quaker communicative style. For a
linguist it may be possible to trace the singling out of certain features as
markers, and perhaps to trace differences in the features, their quantity,
proportion, and kind, required for counting as dialect. Compare what
Gladstone says about Burns and Clare, who, in contextualizing what Ray
inventoried, combined standard sentence structure with dialect words. Such
writers were not continuing dialect so much as creating styles, and even new
varieties. For the sociolinguist, such cases invite comparison with the
growing literature on the formation of 'compromise' forms of speech in the
modern world, pidgins and creoles, and modes of using elements from one
language within another.[24] For a historian the kinds of linguistic relation may
be evidence of kinds of case in social terms, and evidence of the strength of
the social contrast, dialect v. standard. The strength of the contrast may be
found to be not a consequence simply of the persistence of dialect, but a sign
that the contrast is needed and consciously maintained across change in
degree of difference. (Recall what was said about boundaries.)

Joyce is sensitive to shift within communicative repertoire, not in the
presence of elements, but in their ranking relative to each other. He notes a
shift from 'oral-cum-written' to 'written-cum-oral', and later, as between the
first and second half of the nineteenth century, a shift in which the functions
of commentary and reportage in dialect fade with the development of the
popular press, and the function of identity correspondingly increases. He is
sensitive as well to the distribution of elements among genres and scenes of
performance – almanacs, journals, newspapers, holiday annuals, music halls,
broadside ballads, penny pamphlets, penny readings, theatres, cartoons –
and to varieties of language not only as reflection of social identity, but as
generative of it, actual, imaginative, and inter-class.

We are far here from the working assumption of most linguists, in
describing a language, that it is the adequate means of expression of

whatever there is to express. We are engaged with the accurate assumption that languages and varieties of language commonly exist in relation to each other, within and between communities, and that what each is for may be to some extent contested and assigned. Joyce shows that the history of dialect varieties can be a matter of what a dialect is for. A full history would comprise both what counts as dialect and how dialect counts. Such history would provide the adequate context for studies of whatever kind, linguistic, folkloristic, ethnographic. For example, it would show, as does Joyce, that what is called the study of 'language attitudes' in the social sciences falls far short when it asks about attitude, but fails to investigate value.

Rousseau calls attention to a 'nervous discourse' that became increasingly fashionable and important in the eighteenth century. As he remarks in concluding, the story 'needs to be charted in much greater detail, with more attention paid to context and to the linguistic manifestations'. A linguist, indeed, is somewhat at a loss to grasp the phenomenon. One reads variously of a topos, a trope, a rhetoric, a whole new vocabulary (metaphors, images, neologisms), nomenclature, coinages, a popular vernacular, discourses and narratives. One reads of conjoining words and things, of a semiology (language and culture), of a (nervous) mythology, of an ideology. There are methods for studying each of these, in linguistics and other disciplines, but not all at once. Perhaps the whole is too complex to be analysed all at once. Still, parts need to be specified enough to make it possible to begin.

I sense here a general issue. It is associated in my mind with the work of Pocock on 'civic humanism', or 'classical republicanism'.[25] I know that Pocock is an innovative, alert, and responsive scholar, not least from my son, an historian of China, who has benefited from his wisdom.[26] But to a linguist the notion of a vocabulary of civic humanism suggests a kind of inquiry that it evidently does not to an historian. (I base this on having had the opportunity to raise these questions with Pocock at the University of Pennsylvania a few years ago.) If there is a vocabulary of civic humanism, what are the members of the set? How do they contrast with each other? On what dimensions? How does one recognize the presence of the set across texts, across languages? In a nutshell, how could one tell if one had another case? If, in a language elsewhere in the world, there is, or is not, a vocabulary set that is of the same type? Or an inverse type? Or a stage between civic humanism and another type?

In other words, the sociolinguist, the linguistic anthropologist, and others of that kind, see a world with kinds of case in it; a world in which there is a dialectic between analyses and comparative frameworks. One starts necessarily with some framework; arrives, one hopes, at an analysis true to the case in question; and perhaps revises the general framework in the light of it.[27] It is a world in which study of use and history of language depends on such frameworks, which themselves lead to significant questions (are there any recurrent sequences among types? does the presence of certain features of a type indicate the presence of others? does the occurrence of a type covary with something else?).

As with 'civic humanism', so with 'nervous discourse': what kind of a case is it? If it is a question of 'words and things', there are several modes of linguistic work that may be partly helpful – the tradition of ethnographic investigation of dialect known as *Wörter und Sachen*, on the one hand, and the investigation of sets of terms, especially those having to do with the natural world, known as 'ethnoscience'. If trope and metaphor are central, then there is some quite recent work that may be useful. If proliferation of new vocabulary is central, there are studies of English and other European languages since the Renaissance, and of others throughout the world.[28] Finally, if the rise of 'nervous discourse' is like change in language generally, there is no connection between the generic importance of the nervous system to the species and the rise of a 'nervous disease' in the eighteenth century. Languages go along for generations with possibilities that are not realized. Realization requires a historically specific explanation. And if Clarissa's fate in Richardson's novel can be interpreted in terms of nerves, it can also be interpreted in terms of fasting.[29]

While Rousseau brings out class relations as a source of a new mode of discourse about illness, Porter focuses upon institutional transactions themselves. In this respect he makes contact with a growing number of contemporary studies.[30] He does so also in pointing out Beddoes's account of confusion about the understanding of 'light' in regard to diet. Many linguists and anthropologists grew up professionally with an analogous example from the experience of the linguistic anthropologist Benjamin Lee Whorf. Whorf's name has become identified with the thesis that language shapes world-view. He began a famous essay with an experience from work as an insurance claim investigator: A match would have caused an explosion, even though the tank was 'empty' (empty as to gas, but not as to fumes).[31]

Porter's point that terms for disorders undergo continual modification implies a general question. Of what sectors of vocabulary is this true? Are there always some such? Are they always the same, or different in different periods and communities? The anthropologist Charles Wagley once observed that it was impossible to write a book about ethnic relations without offence. Even though one would consult about and check the terms used for groups of people, terms that seemed acceptable might cease to be so. Wagley ascribed this to the unacceptability of the situations in which the terms were used. Continuing inequality and prejudice eventually contaminates terms associated with it. Such cases and some cases of disease may be propelled by negative connotations. Others may change because of acceptance, as when a social elite, or leaders of style, innovate in order to maintain their position relative to others who emulate them. Porter notes that 'Nobody could afford to be seen wearing yesterday's diseases.' There may be yet other types.[32]

Porter points out two other topics of importance. One and the same type of expression or utterance may have a different connotation as between communities. Thus, similar expressions on the part of judges in German and Dutch courts may have different degrees of politeness or force. Translation deceives, if it takes into account only the meaning of the utterance, and not the place of the utterance in a paradigm of alternatives.[33] Again, different national traditions as to productive sources of terminology (liver for French, heart for Germans, stomach and bowels for British) align the professionals of Europe with cultures studied by anthropologists.

Much current research into medical discourse focuses upon the ways in which doctors may misunderstand patients – dialect differences in what terms mean, what terms are used, or simply failure to listen and follow up. That is congenial to anthropologists and linguists and many others. Another side, from those who have investigated medicine itself, is that technical vocabulary and a protocol of questions arise, not to preclude understanding on the part of patients, but to insure accuracy on the part of professionals. Porter indicates that both sides have a history of at least two centuries, and brings out yet another contradiction: speaking the same language may require evasion.

The case of Beddoes and onanism points up again a basic principle. What is to be considered together cannot be recognized from the side of linguistic form, but from the side of function. Here the function is evasion of direct naming, concealment. Beddoes resorts to other languages (French, Latin), on the one hand, and evasive style (circumlocutions, generalities), on the other. (Evidently he did not resort to the third possibility, a new code altogether.)[34]

It is fitting that Rosenberg's essay brings round again a concern for origins. I suspect that loyalty to a local dialect shares with quest for an original language (Hebrew, pre-Adamic) a sense of their having once been a true and transparent connection between name and thing. Horne Tooke's etymology shares such a pursuit with the Germanic philology it for a time withstood as focus of linguistic attention in England. Jakob Grimm was also concerned to establish an original singularity of relation between forms and meanings. The comparative linguistics of which he was a founder ('Grimm's Law') replaced efforts such as that of Tooke, establishing a frame of reference in which etymology was history, not criticism, but abandoned hope of reaching first names, and of more than approximation in what it could reconstruct.[35] But if Tooke's etymology is not acceptable as history, it remains valuable as insight. Kenneth Burke, for example, has made perceptive use of Tooke's concept of abbreviation.[36]

To a linguist and anthropologist, this book as a whole contributes in two important ways. Its essays open up aspects of the history of languages, and parts of a general history of linguistics, that may otherwise escape attention. Linguists study the history of languages mostly as 'internal history', as regards what happens to linguistic elements and relations among them. Social context is brought into view only in connection with internal change. And what counts as the history of linguistics is the history of such research. The 'external history' of languages is often taken as rather obvious – migration, invasion, immigration, conversion, and the like.

A 'general history', if I may use the term, would study more than linguists study. It would be anthropological, sociological, in a word, 'social history'. Its scope would be all that a society over time had taken into account about language. Whatever the features, whoever the concerned, that would be part of the history of attention to language in that society. These essays show how much is still to be learned about such a history, how much is still to be learned about the study of language by people whose names may not be known to linguists, how such scope may shed light on the use and fate of languages themselves.

NOTES

1   Let me mention also the direction of the work of B. Stock, *Listening for the Text* (Baltimore, 1990) and J. Goldberg, *Writing Matter: From the Hands of the English Renaissance* (Stanford, Cal., 1990).

2   I argue this in 'Discourse: Scope without Depth', *International Journal of the Sociology of Language*, 57: 48–59 (1986).

3   See my *Vers la Compétence de Communication* (Paris, 1984).

4   See most recently I. Wallerstein, *The Modern World-System III: The Second Era of Great Expansion of the Capitalist World-Economy, 1730–1840s* (San Diego, 1989).

5   J. Seznec, *The Survival of the Pagan Gods. The Mythological Tradition and its Place in Renaissance Humanism and Art*, (New York, 1953), first published as *La survivance des dieux antiques* (London, 1940).

6   J.E. Sandys, *A History of Classical Scholarship*, vol. II (Cambridge, 1908; New York, 1954), pp. 150–1.

7   On the theoretical point, as to starting from function, see my *Foundations in Sociolinguistics* (London, 1977), pp. 167–8.

8   See discussion, *ibid.* pp. 121–2.

9   See, however, the important work of W. Labov, *Language in the Inner City* (Philadelphia, 1972) on those regarded as 'lame' in a Black English Vernacular-speaking group in New York City (p. 255 *et passim*).

10 A striking American Indian example of individual innovation is described by K. Basso, 'A Western Apache Writing System: The Symbols of Silas John', in his *Western Apache Language and Culture* (Tucson, 1990), pp. 25–52.

11   J. Rée, *Proletarian Philosophers* (Oxford, 1984), calls attention to the importance of autodidacts in a context of recent English social history, not without analogy to the seventeenth century.

12   F. Barth, *Ethnic Boundaries* (London, 1969).

13   I owe the phrase, 'selecting and grouping together', which has come to seem indispensable, to A. Sinclair, *Conditions of Knowing* (London, 1951), a book pointed out to me by K.L. Pike, whose own *Language in Relation to a Unified Theory of Human Behaviour* (Berlin, 1965) opens with a powerful argument for integrated study of verbal and non-verbal behaviour.

14   Some examples are discussed in my article, 'Linguistic Problems in Defining the Concept of "Tribe"', in J. Baugh and J. Sherzer (eds), *Language in Use. Readings in Sociolinguistics* (Englewood Cliffs, NJ, 1984).

15   Cf. Ibn Khaldûn, *The Muqqadimah* (completed 1381), transl. F. Rosenthal (Princeton, NJ, 1967); E. Lane, *An Account of the Manners and Customs of the Modern Egyptians* (London, 1836, and subsequent editions); C.M. Bowra, *Heroic Poetry* (London, 1952), and for a detailed modern study, S. Slyomovics, *The Merchant of Art: An Egyptian Hilali Oral Epic Poet in Performance* (Berkeley, Cal., 1987).

16   See F. Couimas, *Writing Systems of the World* (Oxford, 1989), pp. 118ff.

17   See S.G. Thomason and T. Kaufman, *Language Contact, Creolization, and Genetic Linguistics* (Berkeley, Cal., and Los Angeles, 1988); D. Hymes (ed.), *Pidginization and Creolization of Languages* (Cambridge, 1971); P. Mühlhäusler, *Pidgin and Creole Linguistics* (Oxford, 1986).

18   J.C. Greene, *The Death of Adam. Evolution and its Impact on Western Thought* (Ames, Iowa, 1959; New York, 1961), p. 11.

19   Cf. my 'Kroeber, Powell, and Henshaw', *Anthropological Linguistics*, 3(6): 15–16 (1961).

20   Cf. Merriam, *Indian Names for Plants and Animals among Californian and Other Western North American Tribes*, assembled and annotated by R.F. Heizer (Socorro, N. Mex., 1979), and Merriam, *Studies of California Indians*, ed. the staff of the Department of Anthropology of the University of California (Berkeley, Cal., and Los Angeles, 1962).

21   J.F. Lafitau, *Mouers des sauvages amériquains comparées aux moeurs des premièrs temps* (Paris, 1724); ed. and trans. W.N. Fenton and E.L. Moore (Toronto, 1974); L.H. Morgan, *Of Consanguinity and Affinity of the Human Family* (Washington, DC, 1871).

22   See n. 28 below.

23   See N. Dorian, 'Linguistic Lag as an Ethnic Marker', *Language in Society*, 9: 33–41 (1980), for three stages of this sort in the history of the East Sutherland Gaelic community. For a similar relation involving change from illiterate: literate to poorly literate: highly literate, see my foreword to D. Wagner (ed.), *The Future of Literacy in a Changing World* (Oxford University Press, New York, 1987).

24   See n. 17 above, and M. Heller (ed.), *Codeswitching* (Berlin, 1988).

25   See J.G.A. Pocock, *Virtue, Commerce, and History: Essays on Political Thought and History, Chiefly in the Eighteenth Century* (Cambridge, 1985).

26   Note the prominence given to Pocock's work in P. Anderson, 'A Culture in

Contraflow – II', *New Left Review*, 182: 128ff (1990).

27   This is the logic of Pike's three moments of analysis that have been so influential in anthropology, emic:etic:emic. See Pike, *Language in Relation to a Unified Theory of Human Behaviour*, and discussion in T. Headland (ed.), *Emics and Etics* (Newbury Park, Cal., 1990).

28   Y. Malkiel, 'Words, Objects, Images', *Language*, 32: 54–76 (1957), reprinted in his *Essays on Linguistic Themes* (Berkeley, Ca., and Los Angeles, 1968), ch. 11, examines a recent example of the *Wörter-und-Sachen* approach. M. Mathiot, 'Folk-Definitions as a Tool for the Analysis of Lexical Meaning', in her *Ethnolinguistics: Boas, Sapir and Whorf Revisited* (The Hague, 1979), is a useful guide to the work known as 'ethnoscience' and 'ethnographic semantics'; and E.A. Nida, *Componential Analysis of Meaning* (The Hague, 1975) is a lucid introduction. G. Lakoff and M. Johnson, *Metaphors We Live By* (Chicago, 1980), and Lakoff, *Women, Fire, and Dangerous Things: What Categories Reveal about the Mind* (Chicago, 1987), present stimulating approaches to metaphor. Two readable accounts of lexical innovation centred on semantic analogy are K. Basso, 'Semantic Aspects of Linguistic Acculturation and "Wise Words" of the Western Apache: Metaphor and Semantic Theory', collected in his *Western Apache Language and Culture*.

29   As shown by Maud Ellman, in a lecture 'The Hunger Artists: Self-Starvation and Cultural Change', given at the Commonwealth Centre for Literary and Cultural Change, Charlottesville, in the spring of 1990, and in her forthcoming book, *The Hunger Artists*.

30   Cf. A.V. Cicourel, 'Doctor–Patient Discourse', in T.A. Van Dijk (ed.), *Handbook of Discourse Analysis*, (London and New York, 1985), vol. 4, ch. 11; D. Tannen and C. Wallat, 'Medical Professionals and Parents: A Linguistic Analysis of Communication Across Contexts', *Language in Society*, 15: 295–311 (1986); S.H. Freeman and M.S. Heller (eds), 'Medical Discourse', *Text*, 7(1) (1987).

31   B.L. Whorf, 'The Relation of Habitual Thought and Behavior to Language', in L. Spier, A.I. Hallowell, and S.S. Newman (eds), *Language, Culture, and Personality: Essays in Memory of Edward Sapir* (Menasha, Wisconsin, 1941; reprinted Salt Lake City, 1960). The essay is also in J.B. Carroll (ed.), *Language, Thought, and Reality: Selected Writings of Benjamin Lee Whorf* (Cambridge, Mass., 1956).

32   If innovation due to efforts to imitate an accepted form is 'hyper-correction', then innovation in order to avoid an accepted form might be called 'hypo-correction'. The one seeks to overcome social distance, the other to maintain it.

33   I am sorry not to remember whose work this was. I heard about it in a small conference convened in Philadelphia some years ago by H.D. Lasswell.

34   See discussion of the priority of function, with languages of concealment as example, in my *Foundations of Sociolinguistics* (London, 1977), pp. 167–8.

35   The excellent essay by Malkiel, cited by Rosenberg in his n. 13, is now available also in Y. Malkiel, *From Particular to General Linguistics, Essays 1965–1978* (Amsterdam and Philadelphia, 1983), pp. 497–512. See also three essays in his *Essays on Linguistic Themes*, chs 7, 8, 9.

36   See pp. 7–8 of 'Definition of Man', and the whole of 'What are the Signs of

What? (A Theory of "Enlightenment")' in his *Language as Symbolic Action* (Berkeley, Cal., and Los Angeles, 1966), pp. 359–79. The latter essay is connected with the first chapter of his *The Rhetoric of Religion* (Boston, 1961; Berkeley, Cal., and Los Angeles, 1971).

Notes on Contributors

Peter Burke was educated at St John's and St Antony's Colleges, Oxford. Formerly Lecturer (later Reader) in History (later Intellectual History) in the school of European Studies, University of Sussex, he is now Reader in Cultural History at the University of Cambridge. His publications include *The Renaissance Sense of the Past* (1969), *Culture and Society in Renaissance Italy* (1972), *Venice and Amsterdam* (1974), *Popular Culture in Early Modern Europe* (1978), *Sociology and History* (1980), *Montaigne* (1981), *Vico* (1985), and *The Historical Anthropology of Early Modern Italy* (1987).

Jo Gladstone worked as a television documentarist from 1965 to 1985 in science and humanities programming at the BBC TV Science Features Department (London) and WGBH (Boston, Mass.) Public Television Service. Since the period of her work with Adrian Malone and Dr Jacob Bronowski on *The Ascent of Man* for BBC 2, she has remained committed to a version of social history which attempts to interpret the history of science from an 'externalist' ethnographic perspective. She worked for N.W. Pirie, FRS, in the Biochemistry Department at Rothamsted Experimental Station in Hertfordshire, read Natural Sciences and Social Anthropology at Cambridge, and taught in the History of Science Department at Harvard. She is working on a popular full-length study of Lewis Carroll, John Ruskin, and anti-science in Victorian Oxford.

Dell Hymes is Commonwealth Professor of Anthropology and English at the University of Virginia, Charlottesville. He was educated at Reed College and Indiana University, and has taught at Harvard, Berkeley, and the University of Pennsylvania. He is editor of the journal *Language in Society*, editor with John Gumperz of *Directions in Sociolinguistics* (1972, 1986), and author of *Foundations in Sociolinguistics* (1977), *American Structuralism* (with John Fought) (1981), and *Essays in the History of Linguistic Anthropology* (1983).

Patrick Joyce is Lecturer in History at the University of Manchester. He is the author of *Work, Society and Politics: The Culture of the Factory in Later Nineteenth-century England* (1980) and *Visions of the People: Industrial England and the Question of Class, 1848–1914*, and editor of *The Historical Meanings of Work* (1987).

Victor Kiernan studied at Manchester Grammar School and Trinity College, Cambridge, where he read history. From 1948 until his retirement he was a member of the history Department at the University of Edinburgh. His interest in the history of languages was strengthened by several years in India, where he translated two collections of modern Urdu poetry and became aware of the great importance of linguistic issues in national and regional politics. His publications include *Poems from Iqbal* (1955), *Poems from Faiz* (1971), *The Lords of Human Kind* (1969), and *History, Classes and Nation-States* (ed. H.J. Kaye, 1988).

Hugh Ormsby-Lennon was educated at King's College, Cambridge, and the University of Pennsylvania. He is now Associate Professor of English at Villanova University. Recent publications include: 'Rosicrucian Linguistics: Twilight of a Renaissance Tradition', 'Raising Swift's Spirit: Das Dong-an-sich', and 'Swift and the Quakers'. He is currently completing *New Light on Dark Authors*, a study of the intellectual background to Swift's *Tale of a Tub*.

Roy Porter is Senior Lecturer in the Social History of Medicine at the Wellcome Institute for the History of Medicine. He is currently working on the history of hysteria. Recent books include *Mind Forg'd Manacles: Madness in England from the Restoration to the Regency*; *A Social History of Madness*; *Health for Sale: Quackery in England, 1660–1850*; and with Dorothy Porter, *In Sickness and in Health: The British Experience, 1650–1850*, and *Patient's Progress*.

George Rousseau was educated at Amherst College and Princeton University and has taught at the Universities of Cambridge, Harvard, Leiden, and UCLA, where he is Professor of English Literature and Eighteenth-century Studies. His publications include *This Long Disease My Life: Alexander Pope and the Sciences* (with Marjorie Hope Nicolson); *Goldsmith: The Critical Heritage*; *Tobias Smollett: Essays of Two Decades*; an edition of *The Letters and Private Papers of Sir John Hill*; *The Ferment of Knowledge* (with Roy

Porter); and most recently a trilogy of books dealing with the sexual underbelly of the Enlightenment. At present he is completing a full-scale biography of Sir John Hill, the notorious eighteenth-century English physician and man of letters.

Daniel Rosenberg studied history at Wesleyan University and is currently a graduate student at the University of California at Berkeley. His previous research concerns the history of the concept 'literacy'. He is currently working on problems of language and epistemology in eighteenth-century France and Britain.

Nigel Smith is Fellow and Tutor in English at Keble College, Oxford. He has edited the Ranter pamphlets and is the author of *Perfection Proclaimed: Language and Literature in English Radical Religion, 1640–1660*. He is currently completing a study of the transformation of literature during the English Civil War and Interregnum, and is editing the poetry of Andrew Marvell and the *Journal* of George Fox.

Index